MENZIES OBSERVED

MENZIES
OBSERVED

CAMERON HAZLEHURST

SYDNEY
GEORGE ALLEN & UNWIN
LONDON BOSTON

First published in 1979 by
George Allen & Unwin Australia Pty Ltd
Cnr Bridge Road and Jersey Street
Hornsby NSW 2077

National Library of Australia
Cataloguing-in-Publication entry:

Hazlehurst, Cameron, 1941–.
  Menzies observed.

  Index
  ISBN 0 86861 320 7

  1. Menzies, Sir Robert Gordon, 1894–1978.   2. Prime
  ministers – Australia – Biography.   I. Title.

994′.05′0924

Library of Congress Catalog Card Number: 77-78556

Set in 11 on 12 point Times and 10 on 12 point Plantin
by Asco Trade Typesetting Ltd., Hong Kong
Printed at Griffin Press Limited, Netley, South Australia

CONTENTS

SIR ROBERT MENZIES has fascinated, attracted, and repelled several generations of Australians. He was the dominating Australian political figure of the middle third of the twentieth century. He governed longer than any other Prime Minister; and, even in retirement, he continued to have an impact on the public mind. When he died he was fervently eulogised but little mourned.

As long ago as 1934, Sir Robert himself wrote approvingly of what he called a 'new historical method' which would 'bring the great men and women of earlier days so near to us that, while their heroic proportions may be occasionally diminished, their actual existence becomes credible and significant.' Credibility and significance are touchstones of biographical and historical research. What is credible to the writer and reader depends on how much they know of the variety of human existence. What seems significant is determined by values as well as experience.

It is not necessary to believe that Menzies was a 'great man' in order to think that his life warrants scrutiny. But historians who have wished to study Menzies' life have been daunted by his continuing presence, and the unavailability of many of the public and private records relating to his political career. Most scholars feel comfortable only when their subjects are safely translated beyond the protection of the laws of copyright and defamation. Few will venture into sustained biographical enquiry without guaranteed access to large collections of private papers. But the life of so significant a national leader as Robert Gordon Menzies is too important to be ignored while we await the opening of closely guarded repositories of government and family secrets. My research was done in 1976 and 1977 and the bulk of the text was in proof before Sir Robert's death. Apart from a small number of minor amendments and some brief concluding paragraphs, the work remains as it was when it was completed in early 1978.

This book is biographical but it is not a biography. Nor is it intended as a definitive exploration of any aspect of Sir Robert Menzies' life. Such studies will not be attempted by serious historians until Sir Robert's own papers are available. It does, however, have several respectable scholarly purposes, as well as its primary objective of giving students, citizens, and interested readers in Australia and other countries the first substantial compilation of Sir Robert's own words and contemporary testimony about the role he played in Australian history.

All public personalities—like all human beings—have sentiments, fears, ambitions and other private feelings which are never disclosed. Even the most painstaking and discerning biographers are always kept at some distance from their subjects' innermost selves. But with a major political figure like Menzies, his success or failure is determined by the images that others have of him as much as by his own unarticulated wishes. Thus a study of 'Menzies observed' may go a long way towards revealing the man as a political phenomenon, even when his real motives may remain inaccessible.

Contrary to the assumption that the only things worth knowing about political history are those that someone wants to hide, I have shown how it is possible to discover and understand a very great deal about a man by examining his public record. Events and judgements passed openly at one time may be seen to have greater force or relevance when set in the context of a series of observations stretching over many years. Much that has been written in newspapers, memoirs, biographies, published correspondence and diaries takes on a fresh lustre when it is set against complementary or contradictory statements by other authorities. Similarly, Menzies' own speeches and writings have a multiple resonance when read, not only in their original setting but in a sequence of utterances covering some forty or fifty years.

This book leans heavily on Menzies' own words, and on the works of journalists, politicians, civil servants and others whose lives have at some point intersected with Sir Robert's. In addition to published testimony, however, I have sought to trace previously unused official documents and personal papers of those who knew Menzies, not only in Australia but in Great Britain, Canada, and the United States. And, to the selections from ministerial files and private diaries and letters, I have been fortunate enough to be able to add the recollections of a number of people who have written and talked to me about the Menzies they knew.

In a relatively short study, covering a long life, it is, of course, impossible to do full justice to the subject or to take full advantage of the archival riches and well-stocked memories that can be found. What one can do, however, is to draw attention to the many themes and sources that cry out for historical exploration. Australian historians have neglected the twentieth century. It is time that they began to look closely at the politics of the 1930s, 1940s, 1950s and 1960s, while there are people still living who can remember events that will otherwise be forgotten or misunderstood. If this work does a little to provoke more detailed research in modern Australian political history—whether to confirm or refute some of the speculative perceptions reported and submitted here—it will have achieved one of its major aims.

Inevitably, in a compilation of opinions about a controversial politician, critical comment outweighs praise. This is not simply a matter of editorial bias. It is obvious that a succession of paeans would make tedious reading even for the most committed partisan supporter of Menzies. But, in selecting a number of harsh observations, there has been no intention to denigrate. My intention is to show how a man of Sir Robert's prominence and pugnacity stimulates fierce responses. No one can understand Menzies' career without being aware of the passionate feelings that he aroused. What people said about him, whether in public or in private, has been as much a part of his story as his own hopes, opinions, and plans. People may have been wrong about his motives. They may have been unfair in their assessments.

But, however much they may have misjudged him, his contemporaries have been a part of his history.

For a number of compelling reasons, I have devoted a great deal of attention to the middle period of Menzies' life. Few people now recall, or ever knew, much about the man who was already a major figure in State politics by 1930 and was Australia's Prime Minister by 1939. Yet the story of Menzies' rise to power and his expulsion from office in 1941 is powerful and dramatic. Menzies' first sixteen years in politics hold many of the keys to an understanding of his last sixteen. His character and personality were revealed, his ideas expressed, his methods tested, his strengths and weaknesses uncovered.

Happily, the evidence available for what might be called 'Menzies before the myth' is immeasurably richer than that which is accessible for the 1950s and 1960s. When lips are sealed and files are closed, the prudent historian is also silent. Thus, although I have delineated the achievements and controversies of the post-1949 Coalition Government, it will be obvious that much more remains to be said about the long Menzies' ascendancy.

This book is meant to be enjoyable as well as instructive. It does not attempt to be exhaustive in the use of sources, or to throw light on every aspect of Menzies' life. There are no footnotes. At the end of the book there is a list of sources and acknowledgments (excepting only a handful of people whose identity may not yet be disclosed). And I shall be happy to answer questions and to receive corrections or fresh testimony from those who can also contribute to the record, or the myths.

I am indebted to Humphrey Fisher and Michael Ryan of the Australian Broadcasting Commission who first sponsored my research into Menzies' life; to Patrick Gallagher for encouraging me to continue; to the Australian National University where I have been privileged to work since 1972; and to the Australian War Memorial for financial assistance on a related project that has helped me to a better understanding of the first Menzies Government from 1939 to 1941.

It need hardly be said that, without the aid of Sir Robert Menzies, my task would have been much harder. The Menzies papers in the National Library of Australia are reserved for the use of Sir Robert's official biographer until May 1981. However for his courtesy and cooperation in granting me access to collections of photographs and press cuttings at the National Library, and in giving his permission for me to examine and copy unpublished letters in other collections I am deeply grateful. Although I never met Sir Robert, I once applauded him during an election meeting at Kew Town Hall in November 1963. I do not imagine that Sir Robert would have expected a book of this kind to be completely congenial. But I believe that he would not have wholly disliked it, and that he would, at any rate, have recognised its legitimacy.

In the list of sources I have acknowledged the assistance of many people who have helped with written and oral reminiscences, and those who have allowed me to see private or official papers in their care, to quote from hitherto unpublished documents, or to reprint photographs and extracts from copyright publications.

I wish, however, particularly to acknowledge here the sustained and resourceful assistance of Jan Brazier, the invaluable initial research undertaken by Moira Scollay, and the most able secretarial aid of Pearl Moyseyenko. I am grateful as always to Christine Woodland for research in British archives, and to Professor Robert Bothwell for his help in searching the files of the Canadian Government. My colleagues, Professor Ken Inglis, Dr Allan Martin, and Dr Barry Smith have been good listeners and generous critics, beyond the call of duty.

Cameron Hazlehurst

Canberra
31 January and 31 May 1978

I

FROM BOY
TO MAN
1894–1920

ROBERT GORDON MENZIES was the most famous son of the little Victorian town of Jeparit. He is commemorated in his birthplace by a eighteen-metre steel spire topped by a bronze thistle, erected at the entrance to a park named in his honour. The citizens of Jeparit have long been proud of their association not only with Menzies himself, but also with other talented members of his family—his parents, brothers, and sister. In 1966, a local pharmacist, Mr Fred Raven, produced a small booklet telling *The History of the Menzies Family in Jeparit*. There is no better account of the future Prime Minister's earliest days:

James Menzies (Sir Robert's father) was born in Victoria on 9th August, 1862, after his father migrated from Scotland to Ballarat, in the early 1850's to follow the gold rush in that town, working on mining machinery. James' father died comparatively young, leaving a widow and ten children. James at an early age had to assume a large share of responsibility for the support of the family. He became an apprentice coach painter in Ballarat and finally set up his own coach painting business. Hugh Victor McKay, the inventor of the 'Sunshine' stripper harvester, which started off a revolution in wheat harvesting methods, was manufacturing these harvesters in Ballarat and James Menzies painted his first harvester and many more afterwards. James also became the first selling agent in Jeparit for H.V. McKay.

While in Ballarat, James Menzies met and married Kate Sampson. An interesting sidelight here was that John Sampson (Kate's father), a Cornishman was working as a miner on the Ballarat goldfields and he took an active interest in the conditions under which his fellow miners worked—at one time even leading a miners' strike on the Creswick goldfields for an increase in the wage from 40/- to 42/- a week. He organised a miners' union which was the forerunner of the 'Australian Workers' Union' and he became the first President of the Miners' Federation. . . .

James Menzies' health was not very good and Sydney Sampson (Kate's brother) suggested they move to Jeparit, 250 miles from Melbourne in the North-west of Victoria where perhaps the hot, dry Wimmera climate would suit him better. Sydney Sampson was the proprietor and editor of the Jeparit Newspaper and on his suggestion James Menzies bought a general store on the corner of Roy and Charles Streets, Jeparit. . . .

The year the family arrived at Jeparit was 1893, and the town was in flood from the waters of the Wimmera River. Jeparit must have seemed a pretty bleak place for Mr and Mrs Menzies and their three children—Les, Frank and Isabel, especially when in 1902 a great drought also struck the area.

Soon after the Menzies' arrival in Jeparit, Robert Gordon Menzies was born—on 20th December, 1894. Some time afterwards, James Menzies built a house in which the family lived, near where the 'Jeparit Leader' office now stands. This house was burnt down some years later.

There were really tough pioneering days, as the surrounding land was only just being cleared of virgin scrub for wheat growing and Jeparit consisted of only a few shops and houses, one Hotel and about 200 people. Money was scarce and James had a very difficult time making the business pay. Many a farmer had reason to thank James for giving him food on credit, until their next harvest came in. James used to tour the district with a horse and wagon taking supplies to the outlying farms, while Mrs Menzies served behind the counter.

James Menzies was a man of tremendous energy and he soon became the most prominent person in Jeparit. He was serious in his outlook and, despite his lack of formal education (although he was a great reader), he had a great gift for public speaking but could be quite explosive on occasions when someone did not see 'eye to eye' with him.

Mrs Menzies was more calm and whimsical in her outlook on life, and tempered it with a great sense of humor. She was also a very hard worker and was looked upon by the townspeople with as much respect as her husband. While in Jeparit, the youngest child Sydney was also born—so now the family consisted of Les (the eldest) then Frank, Isabel, Robert and Sydney.

Jeparit: Main Street, looking south, ?1901

The town activities that James Menzies took part in were too numerous to list, but here were some of his interests:

He was one of the first trustees of the Jeparit Methodist Church and laid the foundation stone of the present church in 1925 ... He was a member of the Shire Council and served also as its President for two terms in 1902–3 and 1911–12. He organised drought relief during the 1902 drought by working out a scheme to let stock graze on the bed of the dry Lake Hindmarsh; the construction of the Lorquon railway spur line from Jeparit; the obtaining of land for the Jeparit Showgrounds; grant of land for the Memorial Hall; a new Post Office; formation of the Game Sanctuary on the Wimmera River; Jeparit's first town water storage and many, many more public works. James Menzies' signature appeared also on the 'Petition to declare Jeparit a Town' dated August 16th 1902 and he is listed as a storekeeper along with other citizens of the town such as saddler, blacksmith, surgeon, etc. This historic document is held in the Dimboola Shire offices in Jeparit. He also served as the Liberal Member for Lowan in the Legislative Assembly from 1909–1919. ...

After living in Jeparit for almost 20 years from 1893–1910, James decided to give up the unequal battle of trying to make a living in Jeparit. He had bought a farm of 640 acres for £200 in earlier years and now sold it for £2080 and this money enabled him to move to Melbourne. ... Mr Menzies did not farm the land himself, but let it out on a share basis. ...

James Menzies died at the age of eighty-three in 1945. His wife died a year later, aged eighty. Their children other than Robert—James Leslie ('Les'), Frank Gladstone, Isobel Alice, and Sydney Keith—had varied careers. Les worked in the Commonwealth Trade Commissioner service. Frank became Victorian Crown Solicitor. After a life on the land, Isobel Green went into business after her husband's death, eventually becoming Secretary to the Trustees of the Melbourne Exhibition Building. And the youngest child, Sydney, was a successful businessman. Fred Raven drew on the reminiscences of old Jeparit residents, and also had the assistance of Frank Menzies, in compiling his notes on Robert's earliest years:

> . . . Robert was born at Jeparit on 20th December 1894 in a room at the back of his father's general store on the corner of Charles and Roy Streets, Jeparit. The original building is still standing and is now a furniture shop.
>
> Robert's second Christian name—Gordon—was given to him by his father as an example to live up to, because at that time General Gordon was a famous contemporary figure. This gesture was typical of James Menzies as he had very strict ideas about the bringing up of children and judging by results he must have been on the right track. But of course Mrs Menzies took an equal share in the character building of the children—especially with Robert—as it was generally recognised that she gave Robert his great sense of humour, coupled with much practical common sense.
>
> Robert, or 'Bob' as he was known locally, started at the Jeparit State School in June, 1899, attending school when it was held in the old Mechanics Institute (where the Jeparit Pharmacy now stands in Roy Street) and afterwards where the Jeparit State School now stands . . .
>
> Mr Bert Williams of Albury, N.S.W., a former owner of the 'Jeparit Leader' newspaper, remembers young Bob very well as at that time the 'Leader' office was between the Menzies house and James Menzies' store, and Bob often used to cut through the 'Leader' office on his way to school. Bob often used to deliver the newspapers to the houses in Jeparit, and Mr Williams remembers him as a very inquisitive fellow with a keen brain and a lively mind.

Writing in May 1965 to the principal of the Jeparit State School, Menzies said that he vividly recalled his boyhood years:

> . . . The Head Teacher, irreverently known to us as 'Daddy' Livingston (he wore a beard) had one junior assistant; but he also had a family who have made a great contribution to Jeparit. It could not have been easy to teach several classes at one time. But perhaps this did us no harm. It threw us to some extent upon our own resources, thus producing, in my case, habits of application which have helped me greatly ever since, for, as you of course know so well, one of the functions of

Humffray St State School, Ballarat

the school is not only to use good teachers but to create in the individual student a mental self-reliance and curiosity which will live with him long after he has ceased to be taught by others.

Young Bob's keen brain and lively mind soon exhausted the educational opportunies of the tiny bush town. He was moved to Ballarat to live with his paternal grandmother and attend the Humffray Street State School. Six hours' homework for six nights a week duly brought their reward. Bob was launched into the pages of the metropolitan press on 6 February 1908. In the bottom right-hand corner of page

Robert Menzies, scholarship winner, February 1908

183 of Melbourne *Punch*, together with a small photograph, there appeared this story:

> Master Robert Menzies, son of Mr Jas. Menzies, J.P., Jeparit, succeeded in coming out 'top' of 1400 candidates in the recent State School Scholarship Examinations, scoring 672 marks out of the possible 900, and exceeding the next best scholar by 36 marks. The boy has only just turned 13 years of age, and 'Punch' agrees that he gives promise of a successful scholastic career. For the past two years he has been tutored at Ballarat East School, which has been signally successful in its scholarship examination results for many years past.

Bob's scholarship took him to Ballarat's Grenville College. There he was driven hard by the headmaster, A.A. Buley. He failed in his first attempt at the Senior Public Scholarship examination, but subsequently passed with flying colours. When his father moved to Melbourne, the family was reunited. Bob transferred to the Melbourne Methodist school, Wesley College. He was one of 94 new boys in the Easter term, 1910, being placed in the Pass VI Form, the second highest class. At Wesley he did not shine at sport. He was not a prefect or a form captain. Nor is he listed as having been on the committee of either the Christian Union or the Debating Society. He was, however, a Second Lieutenant in the Cadet Corps, and a member of the Reading Room Committee. He later spoke fondly of the influence of his History and English teachers. The English master, Frank Shann, was also the commanding officer of the Cadet Corps and probably the most influential of Menzies' teachers. In the Christmas 1912 edition of the *Wesley College Chronicle* there appeared a poem, 'adjudged first for Mr C.L. Andrews' prize,' which was strangely prophetic of a personal dilemma that Menzies was to face a few years later:

'ANIMI PATRUM.'

Through the long years the minstrels have been singing
   The praise of martial heroes in their songs,
The clash of battle and the deadliest carnage,
   The rude tempestuous righting of men's wrongs.
The 'thin red line' that fought its way to glory,
   The Light Brigade that rode through shot and shell;
The stubborn squares that beat back every onset:
   'Tis of these heroes that their stories tell!

And well, indeed, that round their noble actions
   The glamour of tradition should be thrown;
Well for the might and glory of our Empire
   That their surpassing deeds should stir our own!
But not alone within the battle's maelstrom
   Have heroes marked their deeds in scrolls of fame,
For peace shrouds acts of sacrificing courage,
   And many a hero dies, without a name!

Long years ago, when o'er our sunny landscape
  The black man held his old nomadic sway,
The bearded pioneers of a new nation
  Set forth into the wilds to find a way.
One was the spirit that impelled the wand'rings
  Of Leichhardt (in some unknown grave he's laid!),
Or that which left brave Burke and Wills to perish
  Beneath the drooping gumtrees' scanty shade.
Our days of searching and of quest are over,
  The horror and the shock of war unknown;
But we may mould our life and thought and action,
  And shape our nationhood, in peace alone!
Ours is the heritage of all that's noble,
  The sacrifice of years that have gone by;
The deeds our fathers did when they were mortal
  Shall guide our steps, like voices from the sky!

But whether in the din of some great combat,
  Or in the milder walks of civil life,
The spirit that our yesterdays bequeath us
  Shall watch our beings in their daily strife.
And may we show, to all the world, the presence
  Of that same courage that enriches men;
Forgetting self, we'd hear the commendation:
  'The heroes of the ages live again!'

R.G. MENZIES.

Menzies always freely admitted that his cricketing prowess was limited. When he played for a Grenville College team as a boy of thirteen, one of his chief functions was to make speeches. This earned him the nickname 'Judkins' after the reformer, W.H. Judkins, renowned for many good deeds but perhaps best known for his denunciations of John Wren's illegal Collingwood 'tote'. Menzies once astonished himself in a match against Queen's College, Maryborough, by holding a catch after being hit in the midriff while fielding in slips instead of his usual position at mid-on. When the scorer called out for the fielder's name, the whole Grenville team replied 'Judkins!' From an early age— perhaps to compensate for his lack of ability—he developed a keen interest in the game. In a school that placed more emphasis on sporting than academic achievements, it is hardly surprising that he should do so, thereby finding some common ground with the popular players. Many years later Menzies told this story:

The symptoms of what some of my earnest friends regard as a weakness of character manifested themselves quite early. When I was a boy in Melbourne, Victoria were playing a touring MCC side at the Melbourne Cricket Ground, not then so massively concreted in as it is today. There were wide spaces between the outer stands. There

were two scoring boards. There were even elm trees to catch the sun
and to twinkle at the breeze. When I arrived at the ground, I found
that I had left my ticket at home, and that I had (as not uncommonly)
insufficient money in my pockets to pay my way in. But this was not
to be allowed to be the end of the matter. I had a packet of sandwiches
in my pocket. By casting around, I found that I could sit under the
shade of a tree in the Yarra Park and see one of the scoring boards
clearly and hear the crack of bat on ball.

If you know what a Melbourne scoring board is like you will appreciate my position. The batsmen out are posted by name with their
scores and 'how out'. The batsmen in are posted by name, their scores
on view. The bowlers are posted by name, their current bowling figures
to mock or encourage them.

And so, that day, it came about that I saw no bowler or batsman or
fieldsman in the flesh, but, what with the sound of the bat and the
rattle of the rollers in the board, I heard the mighty Armstrong make
a century!

The Wesley College headmaster, L.A. Adamson, was sensitive to
the accusation that his school paid too much attention to games. In
his report delivered at the speech night on 11 December 1912, Adamson
pointed out that in 1911 when Wesley were head of the river, equal
premiers in football, premiers in athletics, premiers in rifle-shooting,
and third in cricket, they also had the greatest number of passes in
the Junior and Senior Public examinations that they had ever had.
His address included a ringing denunciation of the Victorian government
for reneging on a pledge and a statutory obligation to increase the
value of secondary school scholarships from £8 to £12 a year. 'We of
the public schools,' he proclaimed in tones that nowadays read like
self-parody:

> believe in playing the game, and I think it would be well if our boys
> looked forward, more perhaps than they do, to taking their share in
> the public life of the country. We might, at any rate, feel assured that
> a Cabinet containing a majority of old public schoolboys would not so
> far forget the lessons learnt in school life as to act in a manner I have
> just described.

One boy, at least, was responsive to this message.

Among those who knew the Menzies family when they first settled in
East Melbourne was Dorothy Blair. She attended the same church,
and later went to Trinity Presbyterian Church at Camberwell where
the Menzies family also worshipped. In letters written sixty years later,
Miss Blair recalled:

> They were a fine looking, well dressed family. I was a friend of
> only daughter Isabel, & of son Frank. Isabel was a beautiful and viva-
> cious young woman, of outstanding ability, but denied the education
> being given to her 4 brothers, & destined for 'domestic duties' at home.

The two older brothers were working & doing law courses at nights & Belle was her Mother's off-sider in the home; perhaps a little surprising, as, by that time 'Young Ladies' were being given the chance of a career, other than marriage—however, it must have been a busy household.

Frank was a good looking, rightminded, & remarkably humourless young man! Bob at that time would have been about 16 years attending Wesley College on a scholarship.

Belle Menzies, my friend, eloped with a suitor, regarded as unsuitable by her family, & the result was some years of uneasy marriage for her.

Bob was always a worry to his Father, who seemed quite incapable of understanding his rough shod methods of overruling everything & everybody. Mr James Menzies was gentle, rightminded, & steady & with, what I call, a pedestrian outlook on life. Mrs Menzies, on the contrary, doted on Bob. He was the centre of her universe & could do no wrong; nobody else really mattered!

An incident, concerning him, which may be of interest . . . took place later in January 1914, at the Menzies home in Fairholm Grove, Camberwell, where I was spending a week end. On the Sunday evening, seated at the long family dining table, 12 of us were assembled for a meal; Mr Menzies, at one end, with me on his right hand, & opposite me, on his left, a man friend. At the other end, Mrs Menzies, & near that end, a group of young people engaged in a lively heated discussion. It sounded like 'Bob Menzies against the Rest!!' & it became so noisy that Mrs Menzies suggested that those who had finished their meal, leave the table & adjourn outside, to finish the argument! This they did, & as they trooped out, Mr Menzies turned to his friend & apologised for his 'bumptious son Bob's precocity'; the man, smiling gently, replied 'Never mind, James, there goes one of our future Prime Ministers.'

The previous day, on Saturday afternoon, some of us had gone to a local tennis party, & Bob's exhibition on the court was deplorable—in fact, in the language of the day, he couldn't play tennis for grapes! He knew the standard of tennis to expect, & should have stayed at home! He tried to 'talk' himself out of the situation & shamed us further!

Bob always had the courage of his convictions in every department! I once attended a concert in the Assembly Hall, Collins St, given by the pupils of Melbourne's leading singing teacher. The audience consisted mostly of a sketchy collection of mothers & aunts & sisters etc, & near the back, sitting alone, was Bob Menzies! Pat Leckie, later his wife, was a pupil performer!

Of his letter in acknowledgement of mine congratulating him on his engagement to Patti . . . in reply to my statement that I always thought of her, when at the Presbyterian Ladies College she was the very charming & popular head girl of the Junior Boarding House, he wrote that she was 'still very charming & popular & now *his* head girl!'

The last time I spoke with Bob was about 20 years ago, on the occasion of a casual meeting at the Windsor Hotel. His gracious courtesy impressed me forcibly, as I thought back to what I always had to expect in the old days [when] he obviously despised me, as he did all those whose intellectual capacity was less than his. He spoke in glowing terms of his sister Belle's outstanding abilities. He said they were such that, had she had the opportunity, she could have outstripped *him*, in many fields.

In 1912, Menzies passed the Senior Public examination in French, Latin, Geography, Algebra and Trigonometry, and was awarded honours in English and History, the subjects that had especially appealed to him at Wesley. He was top of the State in English Language and Literature and won one of the twenty-five Government Exhibitions, worth £40 a year for four years, awarded by the Education Department. He enrolled in Law at the University of Melbourne, and affiliated as a non-resident student at Ormond College, where he had also gained an exhibition. The University archives reveal that he originally planned to sit for the final honours school of History in March 1915, but this intention was abandoned. In December 1916 he graduated as an LL.B., achieving first-class honours and the Bowen Prize for English Essay. Like many able scholars before and since he needed two attempts to pass Latin I; and although he reached honours standard in all his other subjects, he managed only a pass in European History and Political Economy.

Professor Harrison Moore with University of Melbourne Law students, 1914

Menzies was active in student politics and societies, and edited the *Melbourne University Magazine*. An older contemporary with markedly different political views was Guido Baracchi. In a brief memoir prepared half a century later, Baracchi recalled the campus atmosphere and a controversial incident:

In expansive moments (in *vino veritas*) I occasionally brag of being at kindergarten with Casey, at school with Bruce and at university with Menzies, adding that, between them, they made a Bolshevik of me. In 1917, shining in the scholastic firmament with other stars like P.D. Phillips, E.M. Higgins, Clem Lazarus (later public relations man of the Attlee Government), etc., R.G.M. was also prominent in further fields of student endeavour, the Melbourne University Rifles, the *Melbourne University Magazine*, which he edited and to which he contributed verse as well as prose, the University Historical Society, whose discussions constituted the nearest thing to a debating society we had, discussions not infrequently presided over by Prof. Ernest Scott and held in the Biology theatre by the still (though not deep) waters of the University Lake. . . .

By 1917, R.G.M. had retired from editing the *M.U.M.*, for which he wrote in Number 1 (May) an article titled 'Of Politics', only to earn so severe a castigation from Clem Lazarus in Number 2 (August) of that year, in verse based on G.K. Chesterton's famous ode to F.E. Smith, that the new editor, Dorothy Andrews, appended a note to it as follows: 'The subject of our late editor is now closed to discussion' . . .

. . . The much smaller student body of that time was far more bourgeois in its social background than today. A University Labour Club was still unheard of. I remember attending economics lectures delivered by a lawyer called Kelly: he brushed off Marx in a single lecture (or was it two?). Ducky Berry, the belligerent professor of anatomy, never failed to open his course of lectures with the statement: men were born different, therefore socialism was impossible; to remember this was 'of paramount importance' (his favourite phrase). Even a semi-socialist like E.M. Higgins would chide me in the Historical Society if I mentioned 'the class struggle': he regarded this as 'a hopeless way of looking at things' until he went to Oxford and there Andrew Rothstein taught him different. In the same society a semi-Fabian like P.D. Phillips would tut-tùt me if I wanted to abolish 'the wage system': we had to have wages, he opined. For an *encore*, Bob Menzies, very slim and handsome, would reassure us for the twentieth time that he believed in 'the via media', uttered with unction even then. . . .

Baracchi had enflamed conservative opinion with the opening sentence of an article on Guild Socialism in the May 1917 edition of the *Melbourne University Magazine*: 'The war, whatever the jingoes and junkers may tell us, is not primarily our affair' On July 25 after prolonged press controversy and clashes with the university authorities,

The Melbourne University Magazine

| Vol. X., No. 2. | AUGUST, 1916. | Price 6d. |

The Place of the University in the Life of the State.

There is an opinion current to-day, and an opinion so universal and so commonly accepted as to demand our serious attention, that the University has lost touch with the life of the community ; indeed, that it has never influenced the State to any appreciable extent.

We have lively recollections of a member of Parliament, not unknown to fame in these parts, denouncing the University, not perhaps so utterly as to describe it as a "bear-garden of the idle rich," but at the very least as a close preserve for the "sons of gentlemen." Of course, we would fain plead guilty to the charge of being the "sons of gentlemen," did we not realise that, in the mind of the honourable member at any rate, "gentleman" was for the nonce synonymous with riches, and, of necessity, idleness.

Students need no proof of the utter recklessness of such public statements ; twelve hundred sturdy democrats will relieve the editorial staff of *that* task ! But, after that particular misconception has been removed, we still find ourselves confronted by the fact that the University of Melbourne is, to a greater or less (but we fear greater) extent, out of touch with the main currents of the life of the State. Here is an institution, giving instruction to those whom we may surely, and in all humility, describe as some of the ablest men and women of the blossoming generation. A great deal of the higher learning and, at times, genius of the community is here focussed.

Beholding this, we grow satisfied, and devote ourselves (according to the degree of our enthusiasm) to philosophic abstractions in the realms of pure reason and belletristic fancy. Yet the satisfaction will vanish very quickly if we care to take but one step into the world of social problems that lies all about us, and realise, with something of a pang, that in these circles the University man moves all too rarely. The reason is not far to seek. The general democracy distrusts the academic world; it says to it: "You have no part or lot with us; you cannot sympathise with our emotions and our struggles; our paths are diverse."

What are we going to say to this? Are we going to say that King Demos is a foolish fellow, or are we going to be quite honest and admit that King Demos speaks with reason? We do not want to be misunderstood; we do not suggest that the University fails in its duty because it does not go forthwith and join itself to the "freemasonry of the buttygang," as a distinguished contemporary would term it. That is plainly impossible. But there is surely room for much more serious thought on what we are doing for the State; how we are availing ourselves of the chances of leadership, aye, and the responsibilities of leadership, that our superior opportunities must afford us; room for a far more earnest study of mankind.

This does not mean sacrificing the "higher learning"; it does not imply the abating of one jot or tittle of our professional enthusiasm, or idealistic search for truth. It simply means that the theories of life should be woven into the texture of life as it is lived; the abrogation of that time-honoured belief that speculation and execution are mutually exclusive.

Now, all this may seem rather vague; your University man is modest in some things, and he distrusts his capacity to lead. And so he is prepared to stand by

in aloof superiority when popular economics violate every rule in the economic code; to deeply regret the absence of facilities for some sort of advanced and advancing study for those engaged in manual labour, while at the same time doing absolutely nothing to remedy the matter.

The University must realise—we must all realise—that our responsibility to the community is a tremendous one. Having received much, we must give much. It is not childish to have ideals; they are the motive force of all purposeful action; and when we begin to have high ideals of what we can do for the State, when we have learned to look beyond the comparatively narrow bounds of our particular profession to a great world crying for light and leading, then, and not until then, shall the stigma of separateness be removed from us.

Not that we concede all the criticism that has been levelled against us! Cheap sneers in respectable dailies who ought to know better do not convince us that our University is a negligible quantity in the sum total of the body politic—the developments of the last two years have shown the falsity of that! But there is much to do. Organisations like the Workers' Educational Association are pointing us the way to a better utilisation of our ideal energy and our concrete knowledge; they are important, not so much for the actual results they have achieved, as for the indication they give of an awakening consciousness of the "Schoolmen" to their responsibilities.

There have been too many ages when the masters of mind have trodden a lonely path; too many eras when the great idealists have found themselves rigidly shut out from the practical strivings of their fellow-men; too many occasions when men of the supremest intellect and loftiest spiritual insight have found themselves checked at every turn by the stern rebuke: "What should *you* know of us?"

To bridge this gulf and make the expert wisdom of the few the common property of an awakened and vigorous many is a splendid dream. Let us make it something more than that.

Baracchi was due to address a regular Wednesday night meeting of the
Historical Society on 'The Future of Trade Unionism':

> ... I was informed by an acquaintance that there would be a crowd
> of students in the University grounds awaiting my arrival; that they
> would intercept me, grab me and dunk me in the Lake. He advised
> me to give the Society a good reason why I was unable to open the
> discussion and to keep away from the University on the night of July
> 25. I was surprised and appreciative that he should have come to me
> for, socio-politically speaking, he was not of my way of thinking at all.
>
> But, of course, I couldn't follow his advice. I had promised to open
> the discussion on Wednesday night, July 25, and I wouldn't go back
> on my word. Before the meeting others came to warn me, but got the
> same answer. I was going to the Biology School at seven forty-five on
> July 25 to open the discussion in the lecture theatre, as I had under-
> taken, at eight. I wrote out my opening speech in full, so that I could
> read it in case I got rattled. On the night I ate a good dinner, sallied
> forth from the small flat at 70 Collins Street I shared with Dick
> O'Sullivan, a young doctor, walked to Elizabeth Street, caught one
> of those elongated trams that then plied between the city and Bruns-
> wick, alighted at Parkville, crossed Sydney Road and entered the
> University grounds. It was a short walk across the grounds to the
> Biology School. The midwinter night was fine and bitterly cold, if
> not cold enough to freeze the waters of the Lake. As I walked on there
> didn't seem to be a soul about. And then I came on them, about two
> hundred students, as I have said, more or less in a crowd. As I walked
> towards them they were talking in groups, but after sighting me fell
> silent, or nearly so. I walked right up to them, then began to pass
> between the groups at the same rather leisurely pace, nodding or
> saying a word occasionally, without stopping, to someone I knew.
> And so out on the other side of them. I didn't hurry and they didn't
> move. But now I was nearing my destination. If I may butcher *Morte
> d'Arthur*, 'On one side lay the building and on one / Lay a small water
> and the moon was full.' There was a little island in the Lake, too.
> And some grass lawn between the Lake's verge and the narrow roadway
> that ran past the front of the Biology School, along which I was ap-
> proaching, still without increasing my pace.
>
> Faces in the crowd had seemed to me to wear rather an embarrassed
> look when I walked through it. And when I passed on, leisurely,
> sauntering along, my fellow students, as I said, still made no move to
> pursue me. But now, as I began to ascend the few stone steps that led
> up between two great square blocks of stone to the entrance doorway
> of the School, the crowd suddenly realised that its quarry was on the
> point of escaping, sprang into life and, with shouts of mutual encourage-
> ment, set off in hot pursuit. Even then the quarry might have escaped
> the pack if I had raced up the stairway that ran to the sanctuary of
> the lecture theatre, where some of the people who had invited me must
> have been already gathering. But, in fact, I never increased my speed

Melbourne University Grounds

'We will look back, often with tear-dimmed eyes, to the days passed in joyous sunshine and the shadow of the great hall . . . one scene will remain year after year—the vision of sunny lake and lawn . . . '
R.G.M., May 1915

in the slightest degree and the pack caught me on the penultimate step, grabbed me, hauled me down again (but not before I had pitched my small case containing the speech and a couple of books onto the landing) and stood me on one of those two great blocks outside the building, the righthand block as I faced the Lake and 'the long glories of the winter moon' and—the two hundred. I was wearing warm clothes, but the cold struck through.

They gave me some sort of a jumbled trial, I suppose, but I can't recall that I enjoyed much freedom of speech . . . During it a student would come up to me from time to time with an encouraging word; some I knew, others were quite unknown to me. One, a redhead medical student—let us call him Ed.—was specially encouraging. Thank you, Ed., if you are still around.

But the 'trial' didn't last long. It was too cold and they were in haste to execute judgement. I was with them in this. I wanted to get it over with, to go into the lecture theatre and, if it was not too late, to do my stuff there. So judgement was delivered, sentence was passed, I was pulled from the plinth and pushed in zig-zag course towards the Lake. To the very marge of the Lake . . .

But before I take the plunge, I want to get back on my plinth for a moment and make a historical comment. Historical because it concerns a future (now former) Prime Minister of Australia. R.G.M., of course. Long, long after the event, Higgins strongly affirmed to me and, I think, has written somewhere that Menzies was among the throng by the Lake on the night in question. He was very sure of this but, in answer to me, wouldn't say he had seen him there. I looked for him most searchingly and, from the plinth, had a far better chance of spotting him than Hig, than whom I was decidedly more observant, into the bargain. Afterwards, too, I was very positively informed that Menzies was *not* among that crowd outside the Biology School. I accepted this the more unreservedly because someone else assured me Menzies had said he wouldn't have a bar of my views, but thought I should be allowed to express them. Many years later, I had this confirmed to me by a man who had been his friend and fellow-student in 1917. I conclude: if in nothing else, in this and on that occasion Menzies was like Voltaire. 'For', as he has written with truth in his memoir, 'even I had my good moments'. This was one of them.

Baracchi's own account of the incident, written when he was in his eighties, does not tally exactly with the contemporary press version. According to *The Argus* he arrived at about 8.30 p.m. and was rushed straight down to the lake by 'several athletic youths' despite the presence of two policemen who tried to protect him. He was pushed in 'up to his boot tops'—and then tripped forward into the water. The trial followed the punishment. And while some students were still debating whether to push him right in he slipped away to the hall to deliver his paper. Baracchi offered to apologise if he had given offence to any student who had volunteered or returned from the war. But he declined to apologise to those who were fit and eligible for active service yet had not volunteered. Menzies, who fell into this latter category, was absolved by Baracchi who believed that he had not been present. But Menzies was actually billed to speak that night at the same Historical Society meeting. He could not have got into the meeting without being aware of what was afoot. And there are very credible eye-witness accounts of his presence, looking 'benign' and behaving 'as it were presidentially'.

What is, at any rate, beyond dispute is that Menzies was certainly not an absolutely indifferent observer of Baracchi's fate. He had written an article, 'Jingoes and Junkers', which, as part of a deal between the radical and 'patriotic' factions on the editorial board of the *Melbourne University Magazine*, was not printed. A second article by Baracchi on Guilds was also refused publication. After some suave introductory paragraphs, Menzies' unpublished attack on 'that brilliantly epigrammatic nationalist, Mr Guido Baracchi' went on:

I do not pretend to answer the Baracchian Dunciad headed 'Thoughts for the Times', for there is nothing to answer, unless I should take it upon myself to defend some of those attacked, which would be a greater

insult than those they have already been subjected to. But in another
place some sentences catch my eye. 'The war, whatever the jingoes
and junkers may tell us, is not primarily our affair. Essentially it is a
European war, fought by the Allies against Germany to maintain the
balance of European power. ... Nevertheless, through a connection
with the British Empire, on the whole rather tragic, the Commonwealth is deeply involved in the European cataclysm.'

Anybody with the slightest spark of understanding of all that this
war means will see the pitiful shallowness of such a sentence. Anybody
save one who has magnified an imaginary hatred of the capitalist into
a fetish, would know that to write as Mr Baracchi has here written is
really not 'smart'; it is perilously and palpably false. Let us look at
both statements.

1. Is this a local political war? Is it, as several gentlemen of the
Historical Society are never weary of telling us, a capitalists' war?
Some capitalists have made profits out of this war, *ergo* it is a capitalists'
war! The reasoning is easy. The balance of power, coupled with a
superior sneer, and one's reputation as a clever fellow and a keen student of history is for ever established.

Both arguments can be answered together. This is a war for law, for
public right, for the preservation of Europe and the world against the
doctrines of Clausewitz and Treitschke. The balance of power means,
not a piece of political juggling, but that international law and order,
which can alone be maintained by the preservation of the national
lives of Europe. This balance, essential to interstatal matters just as
it is to individual matters, would be threatened by a German hege-
mony, just as it would be by the denationalisation of Germany herself.
Law and order admit no [word omitted in original]; the balance of
power is the outward and visible sign of the democracy of nations.

Belgium, as Mr Baracchi knows perfectly, was trebly guaranteed in
her neutrality by the treaty of 1830, by the Common Law of Nations,
and by The Hague Conference of 1907. Her position was unique, and
Germany knew it. If Mr Baracchi would only look more closely at
the hypocrisy, the callous breaking through of the ties of honour and
law, the cynical Machiavellianism of those first dark days; if he would
then care to follow the progress of events through the long horror
of a land warfare carried on without the faintest regard for the given
word, and a sea warfare as despicable as it was illegal, he would have
less to say about British capitalists, less to say about European politics,
and a far keener appreciation of the national horror and moral loftiness
of the Empire that shelters him!

Self-interest, or, rather, self-preservation? Undoubtedly. No nation
commits suicide, least of all a nation that stands for the world's best
civilisation and the spread of the world's purest religion. We entered
into a treaty in 1839, and when we enter into a treaty we look to our
interests, because we are not a nation of fools. But when we had given
our word, when we had signed our contract, we cast about for no *jus
necessitatis* to justify the breaking of our self-imposed bonds. In 1870

we were prepared to assert the Belgian position by force of arms; consistently in 1914 we honoured our obligations. And in 1914 Germany said to Belgium, 'Go back on your position! Let us through your territory, and we won't molest you.' Thus Germany became an international criminal; she was a burglar; she added to this offence by attempting to induce Belgium to do what no neutral (and much less a country neutral by such solemn guarantees as Belgium) may do, and so the long trial by battle has ensued. What a pity that some of the more weak-minded of the world's jury have begun to babble among themselves of the profits made by the cousin of the prosecutor, and have forgotten to look at the crime-stained felon in the dock.

2. 'A connection with the British Empire, *on the whole rather tragic*'? Can Mr Baracchi be serious when he writes this? I know that he belongs to a school of thought which proceeds on the assumption that everything written by the orthodox historians is hopelessly wrong, and that the true view of the past and the future is found through the columns of the 'New Age'. But let Mr Baracchi for once put the 'New Age' and his pleasant little notions on one side, and let him ask himself the question seriously—'What do we owe to the British Empire?' An antiquated economic system merely? The capitalist merely? The banal *bourgeoisie* merely? Will Mr Baracchi come up from his digging in the miry clay, and stand upon some little eminence, whence we may see a goodly landscape, and breathe the fresh air of God's heaven. What do we see? We see Australia a great and free country, ruling herself under British Institutions of liberty, equality and fraternity, but with no bloodshed of the revolution. We see a people of rich heritage, its archives stored with a magnificent literature, the gift of the British race. We see a justice unbought and uncorrupted, the priceless birthright come down from long centuries of British folk most, and the dashing arms of British freemen. We see a shrill minority waving their arms in the market-place and shrieking their poisoned perjuries to the air—and we see a great people that smiles, and passes on its way. We see a mighty host fighting beneath the banners of truth, and justice, and honour, and all that counts for much in the world's future. Their armour is shining, and their shields are white. Who are they? Listen to the cry that goes fading fast into the derisive silence of eternity—'*These* are the jingoes and the junkers!' Oh, the tragedy of it all!

R.G.M.

Although few people now know of the Baracchi incident, many have heard of Menzies' failure to enlist in the Australian Imperial Force (AIF) in the First World War. Nothing else he did or failed to do in his first thirty years was to have more impact on his future. The imputation of cowardice was to haunt him until the end of his political career. Alternative explanations did not satisfy critics. The suggestion that it was a family decision that kept him at home was credible, if unflattering, in view of the fact that two of his brothers had volunteered

Lieutenant R.G. Menzies

to serve overseas. But other stories circulated. And many people found it easy to believe that the arrogant young man they knew, or had heard of, thought his own life too valuable to the nation to be squandered in the trenches. Understandably, Menzies did not make any elaborate public defence of his conduct. When an explanation was demanded in a virulent parliamentary attack by Earle Page in 1939, Menzies stated that he had served his term as a compulsory military trainee. The decision not to enlist for service abroad was, he said, related to 'intimate, personal and family affairs' which he claimed the right to keep private.

Whatever his reasons may have been, and whether at the time or in retrospect he was entirely satisfied with his own motives, the consequences were serious. He made no secret of his support for the war, and his belief in conscription. He was fit. He was trained, and had advanced by the end of the war to the rank of Lieutenant in the University Rifles. The majority of his brother officers went overseas. Fellow students in the Law School and the Historical Society volunteered, as did friends from the Kew Presbyterian Church. He could not avoid being challenged to justify his conduct. And his fiancée, Phyllis Lewis, saddened by the death of one of her four serving brothers, broke off their engagement in 1918.

From his schooldays at Wesley, where he was known as 'Dag', Menzies had developed a carapace of arrogance. In response to the bewilderment and hostility that he encountered in the war years, it was hardly likely that his protective wit and self-absorption would abate. On the contrary, they were moulded permanently into his character.

The Graduate
'*Your University man is modest in some things, and he distrusts his capacity
to lead . . .*'

R.G.M., August 1916

By 1917, Menzies was a graduate. Nevertheless he continued on campus as a member of the University Rifles, and still he contributed to the *Melbourne University Magazine.* In May 1917, in what was ostensibly a rebuttal of an attack on university students by the Labor MLA, Thomas Tunnecliffe, he produced a manifesto 'Of Politics':

> . . . Students are *not* below the average in ability, and the Law School in particular is not a sort of refuge for the half-witted. Indeed, it is a proposition of a proveable nature that the Law School—but let it pass at that! There is one great mistake that Mr Tunnecliffe made, and one great truth that Mr Tunnecliffe unwittingly stumbled upon, that may not be unworthy of mention.
>
> The great mistake is this. The honourable member was anxious to make his point; speaking, no doubt, to an audience of radical character, he sought to establish the undoubted quality of his own democracy by a cheap sneer at the University. He, and a great number of his fellow-politicians, while professing to be the leaders of political thought and the exponents of an enlightened political faith, are really still involved in the mental mists and superstitions of the Middle Ages. Somebody told them ten, twenty, thirty years ago that the University was a resting place for the sons of the idle rich. They accepted the statement; it is always safe to abuse the rich, and it is brilliantly epigrammatic to refer to the University as a 'hot-bed of conservatism'. But how unfortunate it is that the place where, above all other places, young men and women are brought into contact with the best of the world's thought, where they are trained, however slightly, in those things which democracy must have if it is to succeed, should have fallen under the stupid ban of 'the people'. If there is one thing that the Australian democracy lacks (in particular); it is clearness of political thought. Our system of State education, though *comparatively* good, is meagre; it scarcely takes the growing man past the point at which he has memorised Burns's 'a man's a man for a' that', and has accumulated sufficient of the three R's to read and implicitly believe all the irresponsible rubbish that may be served up by the political journalists of the day. Save in the realm of personal abuse, our critical faculty as a nation is not developed. Criticism as a constructive art is not one of our native products. Therefore, when I say that Mr Tunnecliffe committed a great mistake, I mean that in deliberately widening the gap which separates the University from the practical world of affairs, and in, perhaps, unintentionally, misrepresenting the character of the University student (who is as often as not a rabid socialist of the vaguely theoretical type), he did a great injury to his democratic aims.
>
> The great truth which stands behind it all, however, is the indubitable fact of a chasm separating the University from its political functions. If we are to exercise the influence which we ought to on the democratic thought of the day, we must get right away from any possibility of aloofness. Politics are the supreme profession of public life. Good government is of the essence of social well-being, and we are not going

to ensure good government by adopting the popular political cynicism.
If the average politician strikes us as ignorant, then there is only one
cure, and that is to see that the next generation of politicians will be
a little better. In short, when students think of politics, they must be
prepared to drop many of their *doctrinaire* notions, and come right
down to a serious study of current political problems. We must wake
from our dreams of a Utopia somewhere in the distant future, and
cultivate a closer acquaintance with the wheat marketing scheme, and
the Repatriation question. We must not leave our political economy
behind us as something that Mr Kelly will lecture about to another
class next year; we must endeavour to utilise its guidance in obtaining
a clearer view of political truth. Only in this way are we going to make
the best use of our advantages—advantages which in many ways are
the gift of the State, and which, therefore, ought to inure to the benefit
of the State. Democracy is not mob rule—it postulates a people ready
to govern itself, and capable of governing itself; it will, therefore,
demand of its future leaders something more than a mouthing of
platitudes and a catering to class passions. If democracy is to succeed,
we, the students of to-day and the public men of to-morrow, must
learn to think and not to dream.

This portentous article drew a devastating riposte from Clem
Lazarus in the August 1917 issue of *MUM*. Menzies' pronouncements
on 'the Australian democracy' were punctured with ridicule in verse
based on G.K. Chesterton's famous ode to F.E. Smith:

Aren't they crowding round the portals,
   R.G.M.?
Melbourne's poor, benighted mortals,
   R.G.M.?
Don't they, stamping, struggling, swaying,
   Hungry for the latest news,
Lift their arms in anguish, praying,
   'Give us Robert's saving views.'
Is our shop unequal to it?
   Can we not instruct the mob?
If we don't how they will rue it!
   Won't they, Bob?

And the students in their classes,
   R.G.M.,
Never dream of flops or passes,
   R.G.M.,
No, they clamour to be taught—
   And the Profs., how well they teach it—
Mighty junks of 'World's Best Thought',
   Then they sally forth and preach it.

Look, Democracy is crying;
　　She needs *them* to do her job;
For 'clear thinking' she is sighing,
　　Ain't she, Bob?

What do you know, save the name,
　　R.G.M.,
Of the spirit which, like flame,
　　R.G.M.,
Sweeping through the souls of men,
　　Lifts them spite of wrongs and tears;
Lifts them, purified again,
　　Well above your 'clear' ideas?
Of ideals, and hopes, and aims,
　　You our little world would rob,
For you never get past names,
　　Do you, Bob?

It would soothe me much, I own,
　　R.G.M.,
If you left this theme alone,
　　R.G.M.,
On the Empire pour your gush,
　　Throw the Shop a platitude;
Shower on Mister Hughes some mush,
　　Strike a *loyal* attitude.
Shake your world-redeeming sabre,
　　Dominate the cowering mob,
But Democracy!—and Labour!...
　　—Chuck it, Bob.

                                        S.C.L.

As a prominent member of the Law Students' Society (from which, after repeated debate, women remained excluded), the Historical Society (at which women sometimes spoke but always made the supper), and the Students Representative Council (to which women had been elected by the Arts and Science faculties), Menzies was a major campus personality. He was academically successful. His Bowen Prize essay 'The Rule of Law During the War' was published in 1917. Meanwhile he played a conspicuous part in his local Church Bible Class at North Carlton and then at Kew, preaching on one occasion a sermon on 'The Sacredness of the Secular' which is still remembered by those who heard it. He found time to court several young women, with mixed success. Gladys McLachlan of the Camberwell Presbyterian Church may have been the earliest. She married in July 1916. At the University, Menzies' 'amazing amatory adventures', as *MUM* jestingly described them, included an attachment in 1916 to Norah Crawford, the SRC Vice-President. With conspicuous lack of finesse, his affections were transferred to Phyllis Lewis, sister of Menzies' contemporary at Wesley,

*The Students' Representative Council, University of Melbourne, 1916
(Norah Crawford on Menzies' right; Len Stretton, at rear, makes up the
triangle)*

Owen Lewis. The short-lived engagement that followed was a surprise
to Phyllis's friends, who thought that her vivacity and spontaneity
were ill-matched with Robert's self-importance. The engagement was
broken in 1918 shortly after Owen Lewis was killed in action. Not until
Menzies had begun legal practice did a lasting romance develop with
Pattie Leckie, daughter of J.W. Leckie, a businessman and former state
and federal parliamentarian who became a Senator in 1934. The Leckies
went to the same church as the Menzies. The friendship between Pattie
and Robert blossomed in 1919 and they were married on 27 September
1920. There were three children: Kenneth Leckie (born in 1922), Robert
Ian (1923–1974) and Margery Heather (born in 1928). Apart from
some occasional glimpses of Dame Pattie Menzies (as she was to become)
and one mention of the children, this study will not be further concerned
with domestic matters. The extent to which the Menzies family lived
'happily ever after' cannot yet be discovered or disclosed. Neither
platitudes nor speculation are illuminating; both will be avoided. It
may safely be said, however, that 1920, the year of his marriage, was
one of Robert Menzies' happiest years.

II

THE PROVINCE
OF LAW,
THE LURE
OF POLITICS
1920–1934

AFTER TWELVE MONTHS as an articled clerk with 'a respectable solicitor of some small practice in conveyancing, but with no common law practice', Menzies was admitted to the Victorian Bar in May 1918. He entered the chambers of the formidable Owen Dixon as a pupil, laying the foundations of a respectful friendship that was to last until Dixon's death in 1972. The historian of the Victorian Bar, Sir Arthur Dean, explained how Menzies achieved 'sudden fame':

> ... In 1920, two years after he had been admitted to the Bar, he was briefed, single-handed, by a discerning solicitor, to conduct a case on behalf of the Amalgamated Society of Engineers before the [High] Court. His case depended upon his ability to persuade the Court to reverse previous decisions by former members of the Court upon the doctrine of the immunity of State governmental instrumentalities from Federal interference. The precise issue was whether the Federal Parliament had the power under the Constitution to empower the Arbitration Court to determine disputes between employees of State railways and their Governments. He was briefed to argue that there was such a power. He was opposed by Counsel representing various States: Mitchell, KC, and Latham, Flannery, KC, and Evatt, while

Ham, Leverrier, KC, and Manning, for the Commonwealth, supported
Menzies' case. Menzies' client was successful, former decisions were
reversed, and his triumph placed him at once in the front rank of
constitutional lawyers. The Engineers' Case marked a new departure
in constitutional interpretation.

Judge J.G. Norris has explained how Menzies was able to rise so
swiftly to the top of his profession:

When I came to the Bar in May 1925 *facile princeps* of the younger
generation of stuff gownsmen was R.G. Menzies. Striking evidence of
this fact was that so many men coming to the Bar chose to read with
him. There were at this time three men with whom the majority of
those who had just signed the Roll of Counsel read, viz. Lowe, L.B.
Cussen and Menzies. Lowe had come to the Bar in 1906, Cussen in
1907, Menzies not till 1918. He was himself the first pupil Owen Dixon
had. (Three men only read with Dixon; Menzies, J.B. Tait—now
Sir James Tait, QC—and Henry Baker—the late Sir Henry Baker
of Tasmania). The second woman to sign the Roll, and the first to
read, chose to read with Menzies. She was Miss Beatrix McCay (the
late Lady Reid, first wife of Sir George Reid, QC, a former Victorian
Attorney-General.)

Menzies' distinguished academic course, and more importantly his
personal qualities, would certainly have ensured ultimate success at
the Bar at a time when it was by no means easy for juniors initially
to get work. When, as a raw junior, in 1920, he persuaded the High
Court to overturn its established constitutional doctrine of the im-
munity of State instrumentalities from federal legislation Menzies
made his mark. (The Engineers' Case 28 C.L.R. 129). Henceforward
his progress was rapid. No doubt his victory in the Engineers' case
was made easier by the changes in the composition of the High Court
which had occurred. But it led to early recognition by solicitors of
his outstanding abilities. Moreover he had become known as a junior
skilled in the law of the Australian Constitution. After Latham and
Dixon took silk together in 1922, Menzies was obviously a first choice
as a junior in constitutional cases.

The situation at the Bar in Menzies' early years was one which
provided opportunities for capable juniors, and he was able to seize
them. There had been some four Country appointments, but no ap-
pointments from the Victorian Bar to the Bench (either of the High
Court or the Supreme Court) had taken place since 1906. In that year
Cussen had been appointed to the Supreme Court and Isaacs and
Higgins to the High Court. Madden CJ died in 1918, the year Menzies
came to the Bar, and Sir William Irvine, KC succeeded him as the
Chief Justice of the Supreme Court. In 1919 Starke went to the High
Court and Schutt and Mann to the Supreme Court. In 1920 McArthur
KC and in 1922 Macfarlan KC became Supreme Court judges. George
Dethridge's appointment to the Country Court in 1919 removed from

the Bar a junior with a substantial practice. These changes left real gaps in a practising Bar certainly no more than about seventy or eighty strong. Menzies was, I should say, the man who was best able to meet the need for a junior, competent as a lawyer and capable of dealing with matters of fact. He was a soundly trained lawyer, he had had the inestimable advantage of having read with Dixon, he had demonstrated a capacity to deal with the High Court, and he was equally at home in appellate courts and in trials, whether before judge alone or judge and jury.

His intellectual powers, of course, were manifest. Added to these was his demeanour in court—he was not merely a ready speaker, but his words were carefully chosen and apt to express his meaning. This last played a significant part in his success on matters of law. His arguments were based on a careful preparation of his cases, and these were presented in a form appropriate to the particular tribunal. In trials he was, in my opinion, better before a judge alone than before a judge and jury. While always fair in his advocacy, and he was one who appreciated the strength which candour always lends to an argument, on occasions he failed to conceal his mental superiority to the witness he was cross-examining. The consequence was that he might produce in the jury a reaction sympathetic to the witness whose evidence had in fact been devastated. But in the middle and late 1920s, in my own experience the briefless barristers, as we mostly were, regularly went up to court to listen to Menzies conducting cases. We went in the hope of learning from him, and we did learn much. Most successful counsel are regarded as being either good on law or good on facts. Menzies was good on both.

His practice as a junior was extraordinarily heavy, and he regularly appeared in the High Court, in the Full Court of the Supreme Court, and in trials. By 1929 he must have had the most substantial junior practice at the Victorian Bar. Latham disappeared from practice when he became Attorney-General in 1925, not returning until 1934, and Dixon went on to the High Court in 1929. Wilbur Ham had taken silk in 1927, but with Dixon's disappearance the only other leader available for constitutional cases was Sir Edward Mitchell, KC, then in his seventies. Accordingly, when Menzies took silk not long after Dixon was promoted, he came at once into a very busy leading practice. He continued in heavy practice notwithstanding that he had become a member of the Legislative Council in 1928 and an Honorary Minister in the same year, before he took silk. His own practice at the Bar was substantially diminished from 1932, when he became Deputy Premier of Victoria, Attorney-General and Minister for Railways, but it was still a fairly large one. From 1934 when he followed Latham as member of the House of Representatives for Kooyong his life was substantially, but not exclusively, that of a politician. His appearances as Commonwealth Attorney-General in the High Court and the Privy Council in the 1930s were notable. While he was in Opposition, however, he continued to appear from time to time (I was briefed with him about 1947)

'My learned friend'

but so far as I am aware he did not appear in court after he became Prime Minister in 1949.

He was not merely a man with a large practice. He was, as some such men have not been, a leader who exercised considerable influence over the Bar as a whole. Very early he was elected to the Committee of Counsel as representative of counsel called under ten years, and he remained, as a member before he went into politics and after, while Attorney-General of Victoria and of the Commonwealth. He did not however attend meetings as far as I recall as Attorney, though he did from time to time convey to the committee his opinion. I remember as Acting Secretary receiving a telephone call from him in 1938 in which he expressed strong dissent from the view generally entertained by the Bar in relation to proposed Supreme Court Rules modifying the right to trial by jury. He has always maintained up to the present a real interest in the life of the Bar.

His pupils all became his close friends. They were numerous; most of them had distinguished careers ... He set before them high standards. Like the other two men who in his day were the principal masters of men reading, his influence over the Bar long continued through them and the men who in turn they had as pupils. It probably still does—for tradition is strong at the Bar and its source most frequently unknown.

As his practice grew, Menzies took on a variety of cases. He could not win them all; and, in a lecture delivered in 1960, he revived memories of an attempt he had made in 1926 to argue the view that section 96 of the Constitution did not enable the Commonwealth to attach conditions to grants, entailing the exercise of a legislative authority not otherwise conferred on it:

> In the case of *Victoria v. The Commonwealth*, I myself, as counsel, made a valiant but quite futile attempt to persuade the High Court that this was the position. In the long list of my failures I rate it number one. I remember being supported by a celebrated barrister from Sydney who was such a wit that he ended up by laughing at himself, and having got to laugh at himself, he was involved in laughing at his case, and as that was my case, I wasn't very pleased with him. The case concerned the Federal Aid Roads Act of 1926, My argument in that case, on behalf of the State of Victoria, was that the Federal Aid Roads Act was 'invalid because it was a law relating to roadmaking and not a law for granting financial aid to the States'. I therefore argued that it wasn't warranted by either section 96 or by the legislative powers granted by section 51 of the Constitution. I argued that one must look at the substance of the Act, and that, so regarding it, it was one to provide for the construction of roads, a matter over which the Commonwealth had no general jurisdiction.
>
> This somewhat engaging argument was dismissed by the High Court quite unanimously. That alone makes it stand out like a beacon light in constitutional history. Instead of destroying me in twenty-five pages of well chosen words, they just wiped me out in what I can see at a glance is six and a half lines:
>
>> The Court is of opinion that the Federal Aid Roads Act No. 46 of 1926 is a valid enactment.
>>
>> It is plainly warranted by the provisions of section 96 of the Constitution, and not affected by those of section 99 or any other provisions of the Constitution, so that exposition is unnecessary.
>
> This made it clear that, provided that a law is one providing for a grant to a State, the terms which may surround that grant are matters entirely within the jurisdiction of the Commonwealth Parliament. This view has subsequently been judicially confirmed.

The Australian Constitution, the Commonwealth of Australia itself, was younger than Menzies. Its federal system involved new political relationships and legal problems, many of which were only just beginning to emerge when Menzies went to the Bar. As late as 1932 Sir Harrison Moore was able to write: 'Neither before Federation, nor since, has Australia given heed to federation as an abstract problem of political science . . .'

As a barrister specialising in constitutional cases, Menzies therefore found himself unavoidably confronting not merely technical legal disputes but basic political issues as well. He was obliged to think through, from first principles, the links between the federal and state governments, the intended limits of their respective powers, and the possibilities of either extending or limiting the scope of central authority. In an article that he published in *The Australian Law Journal* on 5 June 1927, Menzies prefaced a brief study of the vexatious section 92 of the Constitution with some characteristic general remarks:

It is probably inevitable that in all documents the particular wording of which has been the subject of discussion in popular assemblies there should occasionally be found phrases of great ambiguity. The round and declamatory statement of a right is often of the highest political value; the audience is made to perceive clearly the central proposition. The subsequent task of interpretation is, however, not assisted by either the roundness or the declamation. The interpreter, while he must not forget the central proposition, must always be chiefly concerned with obtaining that clearness of definition around the edges which is so necessary an element in the determining of legal rights and obligations.

The Commonwealth Constitution abounds in phrases of what one legal wit has called 'lucid obscurity'. Indeed, experience has shown that to such a degree has layman's language of ambiguous import been used that it is a far easier task to secure disagreement among intelligent and informed crities than it is to secure that agreement which is so desirable when dealing with a fundamental law. It is this fact which accounts for the somewhat broken and inconsistent line of constitutional decision, which may be traced in the Commonwealth Law Reports.

The High Court has always maintained the right of overruling its own prior decisions where, in its opinion, those decisions were 'manifestly erroneous'. It is clear that the task of determining at what point the perceived error of an earlier decision becomes manifest is one of the greatest nicety; and the result has been that in practice decisions are overruled upon the simple basis that further consideration has led the Court to a different conclusion.

It cannot be said that this state of affairs has rendered any easier the task of counsel who may from time to time be called upon to advise upon matters of constitutional law; but it at least has the virtue of keeping alive the critical study of the Constitution itself—a study which might otherwise degenerate into a mere tabulation of decided cases.

Tales of Menzies' prowess in the courts are legion. Many lawyers who were at the Victorian Bar in the 1920s and early 1930s have memories of him. One especially perceptive observer was Sir Alistair Adam, who later taught law at Melbourne University and became a Judge of the Victorian Supreme Court:

I was admitted to the Bar in 1928, after a brief post graduate holiday with Starke J.—as his associate, and the depression years which followed made it such a struggle for survivorship among briefless juniors as afforded little opportunity of associating professionally with the by then renowned 'R.G.'. I believe that during this depression I was his junior on only one occasion. That was a Health Act prosecution in the Court of Petty Sessions at Werribee. A Justice of the Peace presided. R.G. rose to announce his appearance with 'my learned friend Mr Adam'. The Presiding Magistrate began writing in his book, then looked up saying to R.G.—'Yes, but who are you?' Bob turned to me and said 'First time in over 10 years I've been asked in a Court who I was.' Although not associated personally in litigation with R.G., I, as a briefless barrister, often watched him in Court with other colleagues, to our great profit. In trials before Judges without Juries he was at his best—a commanding appearance, a strong and clear voice, logical almost to a fault, a master of lucid expression and obviously well prepared in every way. With juries it was a different tale. His self assurance, his effortless superiority and his cleverness and indeed most of his virtues tended to alienate the Australian Jury. His skill as a devastating cross examiner often earned sympathy in a libel action for the plaintiff, the subject of his cross examination, to the pecuniary prejudice of his defendant client. In the late '20s and early '30s, the cases which claimed most of his attention in the High Court concerned constitutional, industrial, taxation and patent law—and until Dixon joined the High Court in 1929—Dixon was his main adversary.

I had no reason to suspect that the unqualified confidence and self assurance displayed by R.G. in Court might have been an act until I heard a speech from him at a dinner given at the Australian Club in honour of Sir Owen Dixon. The High Court had a few days before pronounced invalid Menzies' Communist Legislation. R.G. in his speech told of his early years at the bar and his inferiority complex when opposed to Dixon. He came home from Court quite depressed, and his wife Pattie, so he said, encouraged him by saying 'Bob, always remember that Dixon is not God'. Turning to Dixon in his speech, Bob said—'Now I know how true she was'.

Menzies took silk on 12 February 1929. As an unusually young King's Counsel, he was unequivocally identified as one of a handful of the most eminent barristers of the day. Sir Arthur Dean's assessment was that:

> ... Menzies was a most accomplished advocate, and one of those rare men who achieved success both in trial work and in the conduct of legal arguments. He was superb in cross-examination and could whittle away the evidence of the most hostile witness by aptly framed questions and was, as can be imagined from his subsequent reputation

as an orator, most powerful in his addresses to juries in hard-fought forensic contests. Jury cases were not what they are today—simple issues arising out of motor car or industrial accidents, where conscious falsehoods are not common and where human emotions are rarely aroused. In his day, juries were trying libel actions, fraud actions, actions for malicious prosecution or for breach of promise. It is doubtful whether in all his jury trials, Menzies ever had a negligence case.

In the presentation of legal argument to the Courts, notably to the High Court, he was also outstanding: he knew his law when he came into Court; his argument was well-prepared, and he presented it, so far as he was allowed to do so, in its most attractive way. No Court could turn him from his course. His opinion work, as might be supposed, was considerable. By the time he deserted the Bar for political life he had achieved a dominating position...

One story of his Bar days, though it has been often told, is worth repeating here, if only as an example of his ready wit which later was to find wider scope in Parliament and on the hustings. He was appearing on one occasion in the Full Court for the respondent to an appeal. His opponent, whose confident assurance perhaps outran his talents, was opening the case for the appellant. The papers for the Court had been printed in two volumes, one a slim volume containing the relevant documents, and the other, more bulky, containing the evidence. Cussen, who was presiding, picked up the slim volume but was not aware that there was another. Holding it up, he said to the appellant's Counsel: 'Mr—your appeal book appears to lack viscera.'

'Oh', replied Counsel, 'the viscera will be served up to your Honours later.'

'Yes', chimed in Menzies, 'in the form of tripe by my friend.'

Almost everything we know about the young Robert Menzies suggests that he was destined for a political career. Viewed in the perspective of the half-century since he entered the Victorian Parliament in 1928, his period of full-time advocacy at the Bar looks like a stepping-stone, a necessary pre-condition, rather than a fulfilment. Life in politics would have been impossible for him, had he not been able, for several years, to earn a substantial income and to make that nexus of business and social acquaintanceships which ensured continuing access to the best financial advice and opportunities. He became a director of two investment companies connected with the stock brokers, J.B. Were and Son: the Australian Foundation Investment Company Ltd and the National Reliance Investment Company Ltd. His principal associate in these ventures was the chairman of J.B. Were, Staniforth Ricketson. The two men had neighbouring holiday homes at Mt Macedon.

Menzies was certainly happy as a lawyer. But he later professed to having been afraid that his interests and talents would have been too confined by legal practice. And, as seems hardly surprising in view of the things he wrote as a university student about the duty of educated young men to enter political life, he contemplated spending a limited period in the Victorian Parliament and, according to his own later testimony, hoped to end his working life on the Bench.

It is, however, hard to believe that a man of Menzies' abilities, whose grandfather, father, father-in-law, and two uncles were parliamentarians, had not hankered after all of the glittering prizes of politics. On his wedding day, the officiating clergyman, Rev. J. Ringland Anderson, had predicted that 'the bridegroom of today will one day be Prime Minister of Australia.' And even had he not been fired with that ambition, each fresh triumph in successive academic and legal arenas led ineluctably to the world of politics.

As a specialist in constitutional cases, Menzies' practice naturally brought him into contact with Victorian political leaders. He was briefed for various court appearances, and advised the Victorian Government privately in 1927 on the terms of the new financial agreement with the Commonwealth. Those who knew him in the 1920s recall his prominence in the Constitutional Club, near Selborne Chambers, which was a convivial meeting place for younger Nationalists (as those in the major non-Labor party were at that time describing themselves). He was also increasingly in demand as a speaker at discussion group and right-wing political organisations. He spoke in support of Nationalist candidates in the Victorian state election in April 1927. In June 1927, he spoke at a Nationalist rally in Toorak. W.S. Kent Hughes (a recently elected independent 'progressive Nationalist' Member of the Legislative Assembly) was present. Kent Hughes wrote to his wife that Menzies, whom he admired, had 'made a dreadful mess of "The Uses and Abuses of the Legislative Council". It was painfully obvious that they were forcing him forward to stand at the next elections.'

At a meeting of the Kew branch of the National Federation on 19 September 1927, Menzies and Kent Hughes attacked the 'old guard' for their methods of pre-selecting candidates for parliamentary elections. On December 30, *The Argus* reported that Menzies had 'consented to be nominated' for the East Yarra province of the Legislative Council. The sitting member, J.K. Merritt, had held the seat since 1913. He did not withdraw from the field until the middle of February 1928. A day later, the veteran Nationalist, George Swinburne, who had been a minister twenty years earlier, announced his own candidature with the blessing of the Leader of the Opposition, Sir William McPherson. Under the prevailing Nationalist pre-selection procedures, which Menzies and Kent Hughes had been attacking, it was not unusual for several candidates to stand under the same banner. There appears to have been no ill-feeling between the two candidates. As Swinburne explained sweetly to the press: 'This is the most friendly contest in which I have been concerned . . . The personal issue between Mr Menzies and me, however, is that while he is a very eminent barrister he has, as far as I know, had no experience in politics, financial questions, industrial conditions from inside, and the management of great Government activities.' The contrast with Swinburne's 'wide accumulated experience' was unmistakeable. However cordial were the relations between the candidates, among their supporters a fierce struggle broke out. Menzies was excluded from the platform at the annual meeting of the Hawthorn branch of the Australian Women's National League, the powerful, independent, anti-Labor auxiliary of the Nationalist party. And, having based his campaign in part on the supposed need for young men in politics, Menzies exposed himself to personal attacks on his war record. A small group within the Kew sub-branch of the RSL appears to have instigated a whispering campaign. Questions were asked at public meetings and on 16 May 1928 the issue surfaced in a letter to the editor of *The Herald:*

Mr R.G. Menzies' Candidature
An Elector's Question
To the Editor

Sir,—Of late there has been much propaganda both in the press and on the platform regarding the desirability of having young men in our public life. In particular, Mr R.G. Menzies is appealing to the electors of East Yarra to elect him to Parliament mainly on the ground that the time has come for young men to serve this country.

There was a period between the years 1914–1918 when the call for young men to serve was even more insistent than it is today. During that period Mr Menzies held a commission in what was claimed to be a crack regiment—the Melbourne University Rifles. He also completed his University course in 1915, [sic] and so was in the happy position of having had a military training, his examinations all behind him, no one in the least dependent upon him, unmarried and, further, was of good physical development and health. He did not then heed the call for young men to serve and enlist. Instead he practised at the Bar and, aided both by natural ability and the fact that most of the young barristers who had commenced practice in and before 1914 were in Europe or Palestine, quickly made his mark.

In these circumstances, the electors of East Yarra surely are entitled to know why a man who did not see fit to offer his services in a position when there was little hope of advancement and some risk of life and limb should now be given a position in which there is no such risk and great opportunities for the advancement of a young and able lawyer.

As an elector who has been asked to vote for Mr Menzies, and who has asked the candidate the question on the public platform, I would like to have the answer to the question.

Yours, etc.,
J.R. Hall
386 Lower Malvern Road,
East Malvern.

The response of the candidate was prompt. His statement appeared in the next day's *Herald*, accompanied by a letter from his campaign secretary:

Mr R.G. Menzies' Candidature
Reply to the Electors' Question

Sir,—...

In reply to Mr Hall's letter, Mr R.G. Menzies said today:

'I have already dealt with Mr Hall's question from the public platform and I do not propose to be drawn into a newspaper controversy upon private and intimate matters. In seeking a seat in Parliament I am not asking for a benefit for myself for every factor of personal comfort, personal profit and professional advancement would operate in the direction of keeping me out of public life.

The only thing that I desire to say is that I first became qualified for practice in May 1918, and when the war ended I was reading as a pupil in the chambers of Mr Owen Dixon. Such practice as I enjoy has been entirely built up since the war.

I do not propose to engage in any further discussion.

Mr Hall will, of course, oppose my candidature, but his attack is, I believe, entirely repugnant to the ideals and outlook of the honourable gentleman whom he is supporting.'

Returned Soldier's Support
To the Editor

Sir,—Mr Hall has chosen to introduce a personal note into a campaign that so far has been marked by complete good-feeling, and if it were not for the fact of the prominence given to his letter published last evening, I would refrain from making any comments thereon.

I say this is a personal matter, because the reason why any man did not enlist for service abroad is a matter which he had, in this country at least, to settle with his own conscience. As one privileged to have been a life-long friend of the distinguished family to which Mr Menzies belongs, I claim to have special knowledge of some of the factors which influenced him during that critical period. The determining factors are necessarily of an intimate character, and are not for public discussion, but one fact may be stated. Two sons of this family saw active service in infantry battalions, and a third—the candidate—did not, let me assure the electors of East Yarra, remain home for selfish reasons.

But how, Mr Editor, is such an inquiry relevant? Is it merely a cheap impeachment of Mr Menzies' bona-fides in his expressed desire to render some little community service?

If so, Mr Hall is invited to consult those who have some real knowledge of the candidate and his motives.

Mr Hall may be assured that the intelligent body of returned soldiers today in assessing the worth of a candidate for Parliament look at his character and ability, and if they find both A class, they assume as reasonable men that his explanation for not embarking on active service is at least likely to be a reasonable one and certainly not at this stage a subject for impertinent inquiry.

Yours, etc.,
J.A. Gray, MC,
Campaign Secretary
Late 6th LTM. Battery AIF.
515 Collins Street, Melbourne.

The issue would not die. There were further statements and questions:

Claims of Mr Menzies
Returned Soldier's Questions
To the Editor

Sir,—As a member of the AIF, an elector of East Yarra, and one who claims to be conversant with the views of returned men, I am sure that the question asked Mr R.G. Menzies, through your columns, though considered to be impertinent by his campaign secretary, is one to which most electors will require an answer.

Nobody wishes to have intimate details of another's life, and if Mr Menzies can publicly state that he did not enlist because of physical incapacity, persons dependent upon him, or some other broad and intelligible reason, no doubt his statements would be accepted.

At a time when the thoughts of all AIF men are turned towards the comrades who served with them, it appears to me to be an insult to those comrades, that one who held a commission in the Citizen Forces, and enjoyed the other advantages detailed in Mr Hall's letter, without offering to serve his country abroad, should be seeking election to Parliament on the ground that 'the time has come for young men to serve.'

Mr Menzies, in his reply to Mr Hall, states that he first became qualified to practice in 1918.

He has not denied the statement that he completed all the examinations necessary to enable him to qualify, in 1916. Thereafter, I understand, he only had to serve under articles with a solicitor for a year, without examination, to enable him to practice at the Bar.

Probably he is not the only candidate for the Legislative Council who can claim that, 'in seeking a seat in Parliament, I am not asking for a benefit for myself, for every factor of personal comfort would operate in the direction of keeping me out of public life.'

It is wide of the mark to assert that the intelligent body of returned men would assess the worth of a candidate for Parliament on his character and ability only. I am inclined to think the first question they would require answered would be, 'Was the candidate eligible for war service?' and, if so, 'Did he offer to enlist?'—Yours,

H. Jas. Martin,
37th Battalion, AIF
Emo Road, East Malvern.

Just before the poll, Menzies spoke at Hawthorn Town Hall, directly rebutting the damaging innuendoes that were undermining his campaign. He explained, as *The Argus* reported on May 30, that the three Menzies brothers who were eligible for war service considered the problem in their 'corporate capacity' and decided that two should go and one should stay. He was the youngest and, though it was not an easy position, it was his duty to stay at home. Understandably pained, he concluded that he would never have stood as a candidate if he believed that what he had done called for apology, 'and would never have put myself in the way of attacks such as I have referred to'.

Of 62824 qualified electors, only 14578 voted. Swinburne was returned with a majority of over 3500. He died on September 9. Two days later, *The Argus* reported that Menzies would stand again. He was said to be reluctant to do so, 'but the earnest solicitations and the many assurances of support which he had received could not be refused'. This time the personal attacks seem to have ceased. On October 8, Menzies defeated his Nationalist opponent, E.C. Rigby, by 6899 votes to 4017— in a poll at which only 18 per cent of the electors turned out. Thus, with the direct support of only a tiny fraction of the electorate, began a parliamentary career that was to last for nearly forty years. A disappointingly apathetic constituency sent Menzies to join a group of politicians in opposition for whom, like his friend Kent Hughes, he had little respect. 'Taken in the mass', Kent Hughes had told his wife the previous year, 'our side are a lot of bone-heads.' Kent Hughes' opinions might not have been typical of his contemporaries, still less of his elders. He had been the youngest major in the AIF, served in Gallipoli and the Middle East, won the MC, written a book about the exploits of the Australian Light Horse, been a Rhodes Scholar and an Olympic athlete, married an American, and became a director of his father's printing and publishing business before entering the State Parliament in 1926. One would hardly expect a parliamentary party composed entirely of such glamorous figures. But by almost all accounts, Menzies' parliamentary colleagues were an uninspiring lot. On 2 April 1928, just before he entered the Legislative Council, the Governor of Victoria, Lord Somers, interrupted a recital of racing and polo news to inform the Secretary of State for the Colonies:

> . . . the Opposition, if such it can be called, is feeble in the extreme, its criticisms are colourless and its leadership non-existent whilst such energy as it does possess is devoted to maintaining the identity of the two parties, Nationalist and Country, whose aims nevertheless are identical. At present there appears to be entirely lacking any individual with sufficient breadth of outlook or personality to weld these two parties together.

These were not merely the patronising views of an English aristocrat. Some years later, Frederic Eggleston—who held the same portfolios (Railways, Attorney-General and Solicitor-General) in the Allan-

Sir William McPherson's Nationalist ministry

Peacock Ministry as Menzies was later to hold in the Argyle-Allan Ministry—wrote a scathing description of his ministerial colleagues. His confidential notes have remained unpublished until this day. Describing the man who first invited Menzies to become a minister, Eggleston wrote:

> Sir William McPherson ... was an extremely wealthy hardware merchant of Melbourne, who had been a leader in trade organisation and was elected for Hawthorn at his first try. As a business man, he was the usual combination of canniness and enterprise. He had an intense devotion to making money and a capacity to choose good agents, but without any enlightenment. I had met him at a Conference some years before, when we were discussing employer and employee relations and apprenticeship. I remember his speaking with the greatest scorn of the proposal that apprentices should be given time off to attend a technical school. He was an ardent individualist, but an equally ardent protectionist and he was incensed when the railway workshops set up works which competed against the production of his nut and bolt factory. Sir Harold Clapp told me that his factory having a monopoly had forced him to retaliate. McPherson died with over £300 000 and I think that most of this was made during the war ... his knowledge of the general principles of the State finance was negligible. He took the Treasury as a day to day function, providing the money for conventional requirements on conventional lines, resisting expenditure when he could and gracefully giving in when he could not, without any general picture of the economy of the State or any plan of development. He was excessively mean in little things. He

would delay the signature of a contract or a payment under a contract for a few weeks in order to save interest. The main consideration that guided him was that there should be no increase of taxation or State charges while he was in office as Treasurer. He did not mind increasing expenses, so long as he did not have to meet the charge when in office. Such an expenditure might be ruinous in the long run. It is the reason why our reserve and depreciation funds are so inadequate, why we spend so much loan money on unproductive works without proper sinking funds. I am convinced that McPherson never had a real picture of the State financial position. He was enabled to do what he did and carry on so long without extra taxation because he held office during a period of inflation, while incomes and taxation were rising. This gave him a comfortable surplus at the end of each year and he then surrendered to the urging of his colleagues and brought in a bill for the distribution of the surplus, instead of building up reserve funds. I do not believe that he ever realised how he got these surpluses; he gave the impression that he had produced them by a magic wand. I found out the reason when, as Chairman of the Finance Committee of the Cabinet, I examined the budgets over a ten years' period. I found that rising incomes not only brought many thousands of wage-earners within the taxation field, but raised many thousands of others to the higher tax bracket . . .

. . . Sir William McPherson resigned and the essential increases in taxation had to be introduced by his innocent successor . . . McPherson survived in politics to be Premier for a short term from the end of 1928, when he put out Hogan, until the end of 1929, when Hogan came in in the depression election at the head of a Labour ministry.

The McPherson Cabinet sworn in, 23 November 1928

McPherson is the final refutation of the arguments of those who say that we should have successful business men in politics. McPherson, having built up a thriving business, acquired great wealth rapidly during the war. He attributed this to genius and became, like so many other rich men, extremely arrogant.

Of Sir William Argyle, who was McPherson's successor as Nationalist leader and became Premier as head of the United Australia Party (UAP) in 1932, Eggleston was much less censorious:

Argyle cannot be said to be a successful politician. That was largely through bad luck. He was an intelligent and robust man, with a definite capacity for public affairs, a good administrator. He was Chief Secretary in the Composite Government. This department has a number of sections, such as Health, Mental Hygiene, Pensions, Police, which require technical competence and he was always well-equipped for all these questions and would, given the opportunity, have carried out constructive reforms in many ways, but the times were too disturbed. In his early days of ministerial office, he had a police strike on his hands and, though this was not well handled by the Government, the fault was not his but that of Sir Arthur Robinson. His bearing on this issue was dignified and strong . . .

Argyle's efficiency as a politician was strange, considering that he was dragged into politics much against his will . . . What success he had was due to his competence. But this competence was mixed with prudence. I noticed that in my ordeals Argyle did not stay at my side . . .

Argyle remained in Politics to a rather mysterious end. He was in office in 1932 and stayed there three years, but he had a snake in the Cabinet who after the next election betrayed him and became Premier. Argyle was a man's man, but he had little appeal to the modern electorate. He had also ruined his practice and, as his inherited resources were small, became quite hard up . . .

In such undistinguished company it was hardly surprising that, after only a few months in Parliament, the brilliant young MLC for East Yarra, should be appointed as an Honorary Minister, with membership of the Cabinet. On 25 April 1929, Menzies was featured as the 'Prominent Personality' of the week in the magazine *Table Talk*. 'He is six feet one in his socks', wrote the literary journalist, C.R. Bradish. 'He has a manner that is disinclined to diffidence, a frame that is a tribute to the porridge of his ancestors and a voice that can woo or command'. Bradish spent an hour and a half with Menzies in Selborne Chambers and came away impressed with an intelligence that could 'doff its legal clothes, saunter for a while in the philosophic grove, or wag it with mine in the field of the seven arts'. To his interviewer, Menzies

McPherson's men, with an unrecognisable new Honorary Minister at the rear, 1928

seemed like a country lad who had been blown out of rural obscurity by force of character.

'The only episode worth mentioning' was one, which Menzies himself told definitively in his autobiography, of a visiting phrenologist declaring in Jeparit that young Bob had a great future as a barrister and orator. The boy discovered from his father what barristers and orators did, and resolved to prove the phrenologist correct. Not for the first or the last time was speculative vocational guidance transformed into a determinedly other-fulfilled prophecy.

In politics, wrote Bradish, 'Robert Menzies is a Nationalist paying due devotion to the trinity—the Flag, the Throne and the Constitution'. But there was also a trace of a 'critical Liberal strain' which could have derived from maternal grandfather John Sampson, 'a determined Labor man whose sabbath pastime it was to read allegedly golden passages out of The Worker to his grandson'. What an irony, the reader was invited to notice, that a champion of the workers should have a son, Sydney Sampson, an anti-Labor politician in the Federal Parliament, and a grandson, 'lounging luxuriantly among the waistbands in the House of Cash'.

In the gilded Legislative Council chamber, Menzies was quickly at ease but quickly bored. With no portfolio of his own to administer, he was free to think about any subject that came before the ministry. The condition of the State's railway system and the mounting unemployment problem secured his attention. But, above all, was the political

Table Talk's '*Prominent Personality,*' April 1929

plight of a minority Nationalist government, dependent on an unstable alliance with rural interests, and hampered by a gross gerrymander.

The cleavage between urban and country interests not only divided the Nationalists from the Victorian Country Party and the splinter Country Progressive Party, but also produced deep rifts within the Nationalists' own ranks. While we remain largely ignorant of Menzies' behind-the-scenes activities at this time, we can learn much about his views on the salient public issues. His legal expertise on industrial relations had a special political relevance when the Prime Minister, S.M. Bruce, thwarted in his desire for Commonwealth control of industrial matters, threatened to repeal the Conciliation and Arbitration Act and leave the adjustment of industrial conditions to the States. In a series of articles in *The Argus* in June 1929, Menzies sketched his own criticisms of the federal arbitration system and offered proposals for new regulatory machinery for Victoria. The articles, together with a collection of comments by industrial and trade union leaders, and a reply by the author were reprinted under the title 'Industrial Peace'. First Menzies explained why the 'dramatic and even revolutionary' experiment, initiated a quarter of a century earlier, had failed:

> ... There is no doubt that the Commonwealth power has developed into a curious and anomalous thing. Originally designed to give to the Commonwealth means of dealing with the genuine interstate disputes which were beyond the effective control of any one State, the power has in practice been so freely resorted to and so benevolently interpreted that a section which was intended to permit an emergency action has in fact been treated as justifying the setting up of a permanent wage-fixing tribunal to deal with hosts of matters of a so-called industrial character. The phrase 'industrial disputes', which in 1900 seemed to connote some sort of real conflagration, postulates to-day nothing more real than a polite interchange of stereotyped documents between union and employer.
>
> It is, however, my settled conviction that the real reasons for the failure of the Commonwealth Court lie deeper than this. They can be appreciated only by remembering constantly that the Court has administered a system of compulsory arbitration leading to compulsory awards having the force of law and 'enforced' by an elaborate system of prohibitions and penalties ...

THE DEATH OF CONCILIATION

> Compulsory arbitration kills conciliation. The Court has for years had the power of conciliating the disputants. It may summon compulsory conferences. It may resort to every reasonable expedient for procuring agreement. But if conciliation fails, the dispute is referred into court, and arbitration begins. Few people will need to be told that conciliation in these circumstances is too often a farce. No party will readily concede in conference a point upon which he thinks that he may possibly succeed in court. The conference therefore becomes

little better than a 'clearing of the decks' for action. This defect is accentuated by the fact that a Court system requires advocates, and advocates sometimes—shall I admit it?—play to the gallery, and give the client his money's worth of fight . . .

Compulsory arbitration is inherently unsound. It treats employers and employees as divided into hostile camps, and it brings them to court as litigants. Imperfectly understood legalistic notions are imported into the adjustment of essentially non-legal problems. The means of fixing industrial conditions being the warfare of the industrial Courts, employers and employees tend more and more to engage in elaborate organisation possessing an almost military character. Modern, international ideas are growing in the direction of amity and disarmament. Men and women of humane outlook are beginning to doubt the accuracy of the old and cynical maxim, 'If you wish for peace, prepare for war'. But under a system of compulsory industrial arbitration the co-operators in industry achieve a state of so-called peace—frequently merely the calmness of exhaustion—only after having prepared for and passed through the tumult of battle.

THE FAILURE OF COMPULSION

Compulsory arbitration does not compel. Some years ago the late Mr Justice Higgins, always a courageous observer of facts, stated in court that no unionist was under obligation to accept work upon the conditions prescribed by an award. The cry of anguish which went up seemed to indicate that somebody had propounded a heresy. Yet the learned judge was plainly expressing what was obviously true. Arbitration Courts cannot compel people to work or to give work. Awards of Court merely contain a code of provisions which must be observed by employer and employee should a contract of employment be entered into. The entering into that contract is a purely voluntary affair.

Even when the contract is entered into, the prescribed law, the industrial award, does not and cannot bear evenly upon both sides. An employer may not pay less than the prescribed wage; if he does he may be effectively prosecuted or sued. But an employee may refuse to work unless he be paid more than the prescribed wage; he may back up that refusal by leaving his employment or by acting in concert with fellow-employees so as to produce a strike. What remedy has the employer? Apart from merely academic theory, he has none. You cannot with propriety or even utility prosecute individual workmen. Industrial law must always operate primarily as a law restraining employers . . .

Again, let us suppose that the system of penalties was in fact calculated to operate so as to restrain both sides. Would such a system work? I am convinced that it would not. The ultimate effectiveness of any law, as I think Nathaniel Hawthorne once pointed out, depends upon its ready acceptance by the majority of reasonable people. Do reasonable people really think that striking or locking-out or breaking industrial awards is a penal or criminal matter in the sense that violating the statute law of the land is a penal or criminal matter? I think not. The almost complete failure of the penalty system, except in so far as it is directed against simple breaches of award by employers, is the strongest corroboration of that opinion. . . .

Compulsory arbitration involves some sort of judicial system. Otherwise it will be difficult to ensure reasonable impartiality and a proper degree of competence in the assessing of witnesses and the weighing of evidence. Yet, and I say it with unfeigned respect for the many learned and eminent men who have occupied the Industrial Court benches of Australia, the judicial machinery is grotesquely inappropriate to the regulation of industry . . . The work of a judge is to decide what the rights of contending parties are. To enable him to make that decision he is armed, not only by the arguments of counsel, but also by his own training and experience, with a knowledge of existing legal standards. In a word, he ascertains, interprets and applies the law; he does not make it. The work of the industrial arbitrator is precisely the opposite. He is made arbitrator so that he may decide what the rights of contending parties shall be in the future. Broadly speaking, he applies no fixed standards; he acts as a legislator, not as a judge.

It will be seen at once that the judicial and the legislative functions are as distinct as possible. A training in the one is no necessary qualification for the discharge of the other. Yet we like to imagine that when we set up our so-called 'courts of arbitration' we are in some mysterious fashion introducing judicial principles into the settlement of industrial troubles. The diversion into purely social and economic problems of men who have passed their lives in the study and practice of the law while it may be a success in individual cases of great versatility, has been one of the strangest features of the whole business.

REGIMENTING INDUSTRY

Federal arbitration has tended to convert local disputes into national disputes. This is due partly to the limits upon the constitutional power; to get before the Commonwealth Court it was and is necessary to produce a two-State dispute. It is also, I think, inherent in any system of Commonwealth control of industry. Central control of the diverse industrial affairs of a continent will always tend to produce a centralised industrial organisation, and the whole tendency of both is to magnify every industrial disturbance by increasing the area over which its influence will be felt. We get a certain regimentation of industry. The results are all utterly unfavourable to industrial peace. Disputes become cumbersome because they involve others instead of being isolated from others. Delays occur, and delays are productive of misunderstanding, irritation, and more disputes. When at last the central power does operate it produces the foolish and dangerous spectacle of a remote and overworked tribunal interfering in the minutiæ of an industry the problems, financial position, and significance of which it is frequently, through no fault of its own, ill-equipped to understand.

It will be retorted that the transfer of all industrial power to the Commonwealth would enable it to do two things beloved of all candidates for Parliament—co-ordinate and decentralise—and that decentralisation of tribunals would meet the difficulty I am now discussing. All that need be said is that if our experience counts for anything no Commonwealth Parliament is likely to be able to resist the definite centralising force which invariably seems to accompany the exercise of any Commonwealth legislative power. In Federal systems the central Government has usually, and perhaps not unnaturally, shown itself much more adept at gathering up than at distributing.

AUTOCRACY IN UNIONISM

Federal arbitration has converted trade unions into vast federal bodies, and is by so doing destroying industrial democracy ... Knowledge is power, and the private member of a union who has lost touch with its affairs is no match in general meeting for the official who knows those affairs intimately ...

In the federal unions, then, power has become more and more concentrated into the hands of a few. The few no doubt frequently owe their positions to fluency of tongue or aggressiveness of outlook. Their knowledge of their trade may be rudimentary and their appreciation of the real problems of their co-workers imperfect. But the important consideration is that they have the power, and that that power, largely placed beyond the reach of direct and effective criticism, grows more autocratic with the passing of time. The plain unionist, just as competent as any of us to form a sound opinion if given the materials, is thus deprived of the information which is the necessary ingredient of wise action, and is counselled to express himself, as recent strikes only too painfully indicate, through the natural instinct of mass loyalty.

LEVELLING UP

Under Federal arbitration there is a tendency to think that interstate competition ought to be eliminated. The consequence is that Federal Courts become adept at the process of levelling, and that levelling is as a rule a levelling-up ... under this previous levelling system, the industrial experiment of one State has every prospect of becoming the general standard of the Commonwealth. Our costs of production may rise, our tariff barriers rise, the purchasing power of our money diminish, our export trade fall, but we have the mournful comfort of knowing that it has all happened in the sacred name of uniformity. Do I violate any orthodox faith when I suggest that a little interstate industrial competition might help to produce not only efficiency but sanity?

The Federal Court has for many years proceeded upon a basic wage so high, so unrelated to economic or family facts, that the skilled workman has never been able to procure adequate financial recognition of his skill. If the basic rate is too high you cannot afford to pay the skilled man as he should be paid. This has resulted in a falling off in the number of competent tradesman, grave apprenticeship difficulties, and a general lowering of standards. Our industrial progress requires to be stimulated just as much by the financial recognition of excellence in the workman as by the financial recognition of business ability in those who are the managers and controllers of industry.

Following his analysis of the defects of the Conciliation and Arbitration system, Menzies wrote an article dealing with the Victorian practice of appointing wages boards, with equal numbers of employers' and employees' representatives under an independent chairman. In many cases, the boards produced what amounted to compulsory arbitration by the chairman. Their proceedings tended to be insufficiently publicised, nor did they have any mechanism to take account of the public interest. They also perpetuated gross anomalies between industries in the same localities. What was needed, according to the headlines on Menzies' concluding article, was 'A New Conciliation System. Public to be Represented. Voluntarism the Basis':

I am convinced that industrial peace lies along the path of voluntary agreement—of collective bargaining producing a set of industrial conditions which, just because they represent the combined will of the parties, will have every prospect of being loyally observed by them. But before we come to the point of agreement there are two matters upon which the State must, I think, afford a definite minimum standard. One is the living wage, the other the normal weekly hours of work.

THE LIVING WAGE

At the present time our basic wage, so-called, is a theoretical and illogical thing. It credits the average worker with a wife and with children who are in a very large number of cases fictitious. It proceeds upon an uncertain standard of sustenance and comfort. In the result most people have an uneasy suspicion that it is too high and that in consequence industrial tribunals have, as already pointed out, been unable to give to the skilled worker the proper extra reward for his skill which the maintenance of craftsmanship demands. The only purpose of fixing a basic wage is to ensure that in a civilised country no industry shall pay a wage so small as not to permit of a reasonable standard of civilised living. The State must provide for the fixing of a wage minimum for that purpose.

I would to that end establish an expert tribunal with first-class economic and financial qualifications to ascertain and declare what weekly amount of money would cover the cost of living of the lowest-paid adult unskilled labourer with actual average family responsibilities. The amount so found, with periodic adjustments in accordance with the Statist's figures, would become the living wage below which it would not be competent for any agreement to go. This would make it possible to pay real and substantial margins for skill. Unless those margins are substantial there will be no inducement to men to acquire skill in a trade, and the dearth of apprentices will become more acute every year.

A 48-HOUR WEEK

The weekly hours of work are not, having regard to the all-round moderateness of hours in this State, so clearly a matter for State intervention. But I think that a useful purpose would be served if the State, for the guidance of industry generally, declared in conformity with enlightened opinion the world over, that 48 hours should be the normal work week ... Let us accept this test. Let us prescribe 48 hours as the normal, and give a direction to wage boards that a departure from that normal, either up or down, shall be made only for good special cause ...

NEW INDUSTRIAL COMMITTEES

The sort of thing I have in mind may be summarised as follows:

NAME.—Industrial committees. The name 'wages board' or 'special board' conveys too narrow an idea of function.

FUNCTION.—The function of each committee should be to agree if possible upon all questions of wages, hours, and working conditions in the particular industry with which it is concerned, and to record that agreement; to meet periodically for the free discussion of grievances, the financial position of the industry, and so on.

STRUCTURE.—There should be equal numbers of elected representative employers and employees. A chairman of standing and independence should be selected by agreement of the parties from a panel of qualified persons nominated by the Governor in Council. Three competent persons of high standing and economic and financial experience should represent the public and be nominated by the Governor in Council. These 'public representatives', as I shall call them for brevity, would sit on more than one industrial committee, and would be therefore permanent, salaried, and independent.

Now let us see how such a committee would work ... The parties to any agreement are the representatives of employers and employees. The chairman has no vote, but he is charged with the duty of exhausting all efforts to procure agreement. The parties know that a failure to agree will not simply mean the intervention and decision of a third party, but will mean an absence of regulation of the industry and even a resort to direct action. They therefore have every sort of business inducement to agree.

PROTECTING THE PUBLIC

The public representatives will ... assist discussion by affording a means of economic information: for this purpose they will have recourse to a central economic bureau, the statist's office being reinforced to that end. . . . They will, by virtue of serving on a number of industrial committees, be able to act as industrial liaison officers, and so by their advice obviate the creation of irritating anomalies. . . . They will protect the interests of the public in one of two ways. Should the parties make an agreement which, in the opinion of the public representatives, is in effect an agreement to exploit the public, the duty of those representatives will be to report accordingly, with full reasons, to the Governor in Council, who will then have power to suspend the agreement, give publicity to the report, and remit the whole matter for reconsideration.

Should the parties fail to agree the duty of the public representatives will be to report the fact of disagreement, the precise points of disagreement, the relevant contentions of the parties, and the view of the public representatives of what would be an equitable and proper basis of settlement. The Governor in Council will make the report public, and in the event of a strike or lock-out public opinion, which is after all the final judge in these matters, will be formed, not upon partisan propaganda, but upon precise official information.

NO PROHIBITIONS: NO PENALTIES

I can hear somebody say, 'But this scheme contains no prohibition or provision for prevention of strikes!' I agree. It does not. The Commonwealth act has contained prohibitions of strikes for years; they have been a dead-letter. We have strikes every year, and they are ultimately ended by public pressure, not by the law. I regard strikes as instances of almost incredible folly; but I cannot regard them as inherently criminal or illegal. Indeed, one cannot help feeling that industrial life will be healthier when we are saved from the demoralisation of strikes against the law. This is, politically speaking, an age of mutual interference. But I believe that in the industrial field the duty of the State, once certain minima have been assured, is to clear the way for and provide machinery for free collective bargaining, and then to stand aside.

One or two observations of an ancillary character must be made. To facilitate agreement and to make representation of parties effective we should need machinery for the registration in each industry of unions of employers and employees. Where such a union was registered I would give it the sole right of electing the representatives of its side on the industrial committee. Once an agreement was made and filed I would have no system of penalties . . . But I would make the agreement operative over the whole industry—a common rule—and prescribe that its provisions should be enforceable by action in the ordinary way in the civil Courts.

I commend these ideas, imperfect as they are, to the consideration of thoughtful men of all parties . . . I appeal to them to make their views known.

There was a spirited response to this appeal for the expression of
views. The industrialist, Mac Robertson, commended Menzies' wages
board proposals as 'sound and practical'. The President of the Employers' Federation, T.R. Ashworth, generally concurred. For the
Chamber of Commerce, R.B. Lemmon was against the Arbitration
Court but in favour of 'some kind of properly constituted authority'
to periodically 'declare' a basic wage. The Professor of Commerce at
Melbourne University, D.B. Copland, welcomed proposals that involved a minimum of state activity and urged the creation of an 'expert
body' to review economic conditions, declare a minimum wage, and
provide guidance to industrial committees. While businessmen mostly
seemed to endorse the Menzies' scheme, criticism came from H.J.
Richardson (the Chairman of over forty wages boards), from the
secretary of the Australian Council of Trade Unions, and from the
General Secretary of the Australian Workers' Union. The leader of
the Federal Parliamentary Labor Party, J.H. Scullin, insisted that
handing industrial matters back to the States would be a retrograde
step. However:

Mr Scullin agreed that there should be more conciliation and less
of the spirit of litigation for the prevention and settlement of industrial
disputes. Conciliation had not been used sufficiently in later years,
while the courts, with the case for each side being conducted by
advocates who were highly skilled in legal subtleties, had produced
serious effects. In spite of that, however, the Federal Arbitration Court
had achieved many great successes in maintaining industrial peace.
It must be remembered that industrial tribunals were set up because
of the existence of shameful 'sweating'. Fair employers, unable to
compete successfully with 'sweating' employers, were forced to reduce
wages against their inclinations. The fixation by law of industrial
conditions was a protection to fair employers as well as to employees.
To set up an authority to fix conditions of labour without legal power
to enforce those conditions would be futile. Much emphasis had
been laid upon the value of collective bargaining, but that was a
protection to the employees against unfair conditions only when they
were very strongly organised, and could strike a hard blow by direct
action. What the Legislature set out to do more than a quarter of a
century ago was to afford protection to all workers, and the public
conscience was aroused mainly by the cruel conditions under which
women and children were forced to work. Employers could not be
forced to keep their establishments open against their will, neither
could employees be forced by law to work; therefore penalties for
lock-outs and strikes were of practically no value, and merely created
bitterness. In saying that, Mr Scullin said, he was quite in agreement
with Mr Menzies, but it was a different matter when it came to a
question of enforcing an award or agreement.

INDUSTRIAL COMMITTEES

Discussing the proposed industrial committees, Mr Scullin said that the constitution of such bodies as suggested by Mr Menzies was on the old lines of wages boards, with the exception that Mr Menzies proposed to add three persons whom he described as 'public representatives'. Mr Scullin could not see how those additional people could serve any practical purpose. If advice or information were required from competent persons it could be obtained in the ordinary way of evidence. The only other important purpose which it was proposed that they should serve was to report to the Governor in Council (which was really the Ministry of the day), who would then have power to suspend an agreement. Apart from that those public representatives would have no power. The only powers that they would have in the event of representatives of employers and employees failing to agree would be to report the matter to the public. Surely something more than that was required. Round-table conferences were good. The spirit of conciliation should be encouraged as far as possible, but when a conference failed to reach an agreement there must be legal authority to fix the industrial conditions in each industry.

As a preface to the first of his arbitration articles, *The Argus* pointed out that they were 'contributed by Mr Menzies in an individual capacity, and must not be regarded as committing the State Ministry of which he is a member, to the adoption of the views expressed in them'. The disclaimer may only have been a formality. Yet ten days later the young Assistant Minister, and two of his colleagues, had severed themselves from the Government on grounds that implied a deep gulf of principle and political philosophy. 'POLITICAL SENSATION' cried *The Argus* headline on 2 July 1929:

The sudden resignation of three members of the Cabinet yesterday, on the eve of the opening of the State Parliament, has caused a political sensation. The Ministers who have resigned are Messrs. Menzies and Saltau, two Honorary Ministers from the Legislative Council, and the Secretary of the Cabinet (Mr Kent Hughes).

The resignation followed a difference of opinion between these three members and their colleagues on the policy which should be adopted towards the co-operative freezing works of the State. In response to applications for help from the works, which have already been freely assisted from the Treasury, a majority of the Ministry proposed to make a bank guarantee against losses up to £60 000 to enable the works to operate in the coming season. On the ground that this proposal was uneconomic, and was prompted by a desire to yield to political considerations, Messrs. Menzies, Saltau, and Kent Hughes resigned ...

Although so dramatic a development was not expected, it has been known for some time that difficulty was being experienced by the Ministry to agreeing upon a policy in regard to the freezing works, and the matter has been the subject of several keen discussions in Cabinet in the last month. In an announcement last night, Sir William Mc-Pherson said: 'I regret having to announce that Messrs. Saltau and Menzies have felt obliged to retire from the Cabinet, and that Mr Kent Hughes has decided to relinquish his position as secretary to the Cabinet. The reason for this action is that they differ from the other Ministers in the policy agreed on in respect to the country freezing works. These works, in which the Ministry has a very great financial interest, have applied for a renewal of the guarantee which was given to them last year to enable them to open. The Ministry, after mature consideration, felt that to withdraw the guarantee at the present juncture would mean the closing of the works and the absolute loss of the money which has already been advanced by the Treasury. The Ministry is of the opinion that such guarantees which, in the past, have been granted without Parliamentary sanction, should be submitted to Parliament for approval, but in this instance, when the season is advancing, time does not permit of this procedure being followed. It has been decided therefore that while the existing bank guarantee will be renewed for this year, early in the session a bill will be submitted to Parliament to provide that, before any Ministry can in future pledge the credit of the State by a bank guarantee, Parliamentary sanction must first be obtained. The view the retiring members of the Cabinet took was that the Ministry should not give any such guarantee.'

In a personal statement to the press, Menzies explained his position:

Though I am in the main a supporter of the general policy of the Ministry, I have felt compelled to resign upon what I regard as a vital matter—the public finances of the State. Everyone must realise that unless the strongest measures are taken to check the financial drift, which has been going on for some years, a day of reckoning will come. If it does come, I can see no escape from largely increased taxation as the only means of 'squaring the ledger'. As it appears to me one of the main causes of our financial disorder is the growing disposition to hand out public moneys to large or small sectional interests, not upon any reasonable business footing, but as a result of acute political pressure from and bargaining with aggressive minorities. The decision of the Cabinet to give a further guarantee to the Amalgamated Freezing Company has disappointed my hope that that disposition would be at last checked. The record of the company and of its predecessors has been one of consistent failure. Though co-operative in name, it is ludicrously non-co-operative in its working, for it has many shareholders who are not producers, and it has substantially failed to secure the patronage of the lamb-raisers whose interests it is supposed to reflect. In short, it is an ordinary trading concern which has failed to succeed. Notwithstanding this, various governments have for years made large advances to it under the guise of guarantees. These have, as might have been expected, failed to put the company on its feet. Today the amount owed to the State is £514 000 and the State's prospect of recovering more than a few pounds is negligible. Had it not been for political pressure, it is incredible that such a dissipation of the public money could have occurred, for no reliable assurance has been, or can be given that these purely seasonal inland freezing works, with their imperfect selling organisation in London, can ever be carried on competitively at a profit. The shadowy suggestion made in some quarters that the existence of these works has kept up the price of lambs for the producers (who in the main have consistently refused to patronise them) is unsupported by any real evidence and must be dismissed. Yet Cabinet now proposes to make a further guarantee of £60 000 for the ensuing season. Good money will thus be thrown after bad.

I am happy to say that I have the warmest possible regard for the Premier and for other members of the Ministry, who have accorded to me as a newcomer to politics every consideration. But, and I say it with unfeigned regret, I cannot regard this decision as anything else than a yielding to political considerations which have for too long been allowed to impair the proper appreciation of the grave responsibility which rests upon Parliament to administer the public money with due regard to the fact that the public has provided it. Unless that principle is recognised, not only in this particular instance, but generally, economy is impossible.

The address-in-reply to the Lieutenant-Governor's speech gave the ex-minister an opportunity to elaborate on his reasons for resigning. The official record of the Legislative Council debate on 24 July 1929 reveals not so much sadness and disillusion, as cleverness bordering on open contempt for his former colleagues:

> ... As one with no first-hand experience of freezing works, I was forced, as we all are in the last resort, to come to an opinion on the impressiveness of the evidence before me. I saw abundance of evidence to the effect that these works had been carried on with disastrous losses and prospects of success so small that they were not worth considering. On the other side, I saw no evidence whatever that any amount of good money thrown into their laps, or hands, in the years to come would ever do any real good to the producers of this State. In other words, I found myself endeavouring to balance what appeared to be solid, reasonable, practical arguments against mere speculations which seemed to be inspired by hopes, or by interests, and not by the facts. Hope springs eternal—in-deed it does—in the political breast, particularly, one may say, in the breast of the smallest but most active party in politics at the present time. I was greatly comforted to find in my *Hansard*, which as a dutiful junior member of the House I read with respect, that my own views on this matter were adequately sup-

ported, and indeed emphasized, by the Leader of the Government in this House. I can do no better, I think, than read a short passage, some of which has been read before in the course of this debate, and to say to this House, 'There is my authority for such action as I took.'

The Hon. H.I. COHEN—You did not discover that, because I drew your attention to it.

The Hon. R.G. MENZIES—I hope that the honorable gentleman will not discuss Cabinet secrets. What I desire to say is this: that the views I am about to read seemed to me to put the case so admirably and so convincingly that I found no option but to dissociate myself entirely from the action contemplated by the Government, and, as sometimes happens, the disciple outran the master in action. But I will read the words of the master, which may be found on page 1690 of last session's *Hansard*. My learned and honorable friend, Mr H.I. Cohen, was engaged in a discussion of the Stamps (Sheep Duty) Bill. In point of fact, at the moment he was engaged in a very acute consideration of the position of the Amalgamated Freezing Company (Victoria) Proprietary Limited. He referred, with one of those historical gestures of which he is such a master, to what had happened on a previous occasion when he was in a Government, and then said—

> I could then see no justification for the making of loans which have resulted in such enormous losses to the Government of this State. It is appalling to think that sums amounting to £477 000 should have been sunk in concerns of this kind, especially when there at no time appeared to be any more than a remote prospect of the money being recouped to the Government.

At that point my honorable friend, Mr Kiernan, always, so to speak, hot on the scent when the Leader of the House is speaking, very pertinently interjected—

> What was the reason for advancing, the money?

Guileless Mr Kiernan! One can almost hear him putting that question. 'Let me know all about it', he begged. 'I do not care to go to my own people for information. What do you say about it?' The reporter inflexibly goes on—

> The Hon. H.I. COHEN.—I shall try to be candid in answering that question. The money was advanced for much the same reason as this Bill is being brought before us to-day—for political reasons; certainly not for reasons of State. It is imagined that a few votes may be won by the granting of this particular concession. That is what I candidly think. I do not like to express an opinion of that sort, but as I have been asked for the reason I have given my opinion.

The Hon. G.L. GOUDIE.—It may be that weighty arguments have been used on the other side.

The Hon. R.G. MENZIES.—Since?

The Hon. G.L. GOUDIE.—Yes.

The Hon. R.G. MENZIES.—I am indebted to Mr Goudie for that suggestion. Weighty arguments may have been advanced since, but I have not heard them. If the Leader of the Government in this House has heard them, I shall be interested, and so will Mr Jones, in hearing them, too. Mr H.I. Cohen concluded his reply to Mr Kiernan's question with a heroic gesture. 'Nothing on earth', said the honorable gentleman, 'would induce me to lend one shilling of the money of the State for all the votes in the community.'

The Hon. E.L. KIERNAN.—You will notice that he said 'nothing on earth'.

The Hon. R.G. MENZIES.—Does Mr Kiernan think that some supernatural circumstances have intervened since? However, there the statement was, admirably put, convincing to me at least. Sharing the honorable gentleman's opinion that nothing on earth should induce me to become associated with such a method of securing political support, I thought that, as far as I was concerned at any rate, there was only one path open to me. I look forward with the very greatest interest to the explanation by the Leader of the Government in this House of what new circumstances have arisen since the making of that speech to render a course undesirable then an entirely proper one to-day. . . .

Having taken a stand on an issue of public morality, Menzies warmed to the theme in a federal election campaign speech which was headlined in *The Age* on 10 October 1929: 'MACHINE POLITICS . . . THE DUTY OF ELECTORS, ABSURD ARGUMENTS OF PARTY DISCIPLINE, RETURN MEN WHO THINK FOR THEMSELVES':

The maintenance of the public school spirit and ethics in after-school life, particularly in politics, was urged yesterday by Mr Menzies, MLC, in a lively speech which he delivered at the Old Trinity Grammarians' (Kew) luncheon held at the Hotel Australia.

Mr Menzies urged a greater and more widely intelligent public interest in politics, and stressed the importance in the public interest of returning to Parliament candidates who were prepared to think for themselves, unfettered by decisions made for them by outside bodies.

While, he said, it was important to run a business or a profession well, the most important business was to run the country well. There-fore, whether one liked it or not, the people in whom was placed the responsibility of running the country were the most important people in it. But what did many electors do about it? They stood aside from politics. They joined in the condemnation of politicians, and they cast a vote in mechanical fashion. There appeared to be an idea that politics were something that really intelligent people need not bother themselves about. They simply voted according to what in their particular family circle was considered good form. The representative who recorded in Parliament merely the decision made for him by other people was no good to anybody. Electors should see to it that we put into Parliament only those who had the faculty of thinking for themselves and the determination to exercise the dictates of that faculty. The topical question was how that was to be ensured. At present political campaigning seemed to mainly centre around the activities of two groups—on the one hand those who rushed round the country saying what a fine fellow their candidate was and giving expression to any degree of fulsome praise, and on the other hand those who went round raking up all that could be found to say against the candidate. (Laughter.) The accepted right way to make a good political speech appeared to be to stamp vigorously on the platform and say something of a highly defamatory character about someone else. (Renewed laughter.) If a candidate were able to say more uncomplimentary things about his critics than they were able to say about him, apparently he was to be regarded as a great fighter—a successful campaigner, irrespective of his attitude in dealing with the actual political issues at stake. Unless one had a previous knowledge of the political situation one would gather from an association with the present campaign that the great problem was whether Mr Maxwell was a decent man, whether Sir A. Robinson was a political hack, whether Mr Scullin was a dangerous man, and whether Mr Theodore made money out of mining interests in Queensland. (More laughter.) The real issue was a mystery to about 80 per cent of the people. In public school life it was not the fashion to abuse the other side. You were generous. You believed in fair play, and you assumed the other fellow's motives were as sincere as your own, and you realised that contests would be conducted with the greatest of vigor, but with no ill-will whatever. (Applause.) But apparently when one left school those ideas were to be left behind, whereas if the public weal were to be the accepted standard, such ideas were to be carefully nurtured and preserved in our ordinary life and our politics. (Hear, hear.) Without a general and intelligent interest in politics there could not be that intelligent opinion without which democratic government must prove a failure. The issue at the present campaign was whether the fixing of wages and conditions in industry ought to be carried out by the Commonwealth or by the States. It was a fundamental question of constitutional structure. With a Parliament that could be trusted to judge all cases simply on their merit we would have gone a long way to get rid of those absurd complications of parties and the absurd arguments of party discipline. (Hear, hear.)

Enough Victorian Members of Parliament behaved in the way that was thus recommended to bring down the McPherson Government on 23 October 1929. An adjournment motion on unemployment and the plight of the Mallee was moved by a Country Progressive Party member and carried, thirty-four votes to thirty. The ensuing manoeuvres between the various non-Labor fragments—the Country Party, the Country Progressives, the Nationalists, and a tiny group of Liberals—resulted in a dissolution, defeat for McPherson at the polls and in the House, and the creation of a Labor government, the ninth Victorian Ministry since 1923. One of the few Nationalists to emerge happily was Menzies. He had conducted a vigorous campaign, not only on his own behalf but in concert with a group of 'younger Nationalists' led by Kent Hughes and A.H. Clerke. His 'brains', 'punch', and 'imagination' attracted favourable press comment. And he took the opportunity of the election to transfer from the Legislative Council to the Legislative Assembly seat of Nunawading (the other Nationalist and Liberal candidates obligingly withdrawing from the contest). Within a very short time after entering politics, Menzies was now playing a major role in Nationalist party affairs. Inevitably, such rapid fame stirred jealousies. *Table Talk* was gently euphemistic in pointing out on 28 November 1929 that he was 'a forthright young man who says what he means and does not appear to be courting popularity'. As far as other Members of Parliament were concerned, this was a massive understatement. Moreover, the more he pronounced judgement on the way in which politicians ought to behave, the more he laid himself open to ridicule for presumptuousness and pretention.

On 6 December 1929, C.J. Dennis immortalised one of the young MLA's more precious utterances in some verses published in *The Herald*. In a homily to his parliamentary colleagues, Menzies had said: 'If every politician in Victoria had pinned over his shaving mirror the words "How can I do a better job in the next 12 months?" they might actually begin to do a better job in politics.' After four mocking verses, Dennis asked:

> Can practise e'er perfection gain
>   In such a game as this?
> Do qualities that men may gain
>   Make up for what they miss?
> Whether they learn them newer tricks,
>   Or sink in a weary groove,
> Can sanguine youth in politics
>   With years hope to improve?

'Sanguine youth' would no doubt have preferred not to be laughed at. However, Menzies had opted for what in the 1970s was to be known as 'a high profile'. He needed publicity, and had to take the risk of caricature. In retrospect, his resignation over subsidies to freezing works might seem a disportionately excessive reaction to a predictable event. But he may not have been too distressed at finding an issue of principle that served to separate him in the public eye from the older generation of conservative politicians. Better still, a cynic might reason, he had been able to launch an attack on rural interests which would not offend the powerful city commercial and financial leaders whose support he could not afford to alienate. Menzies and his ally, Kent Hughes, had reached a point of decision. They had acted in protest against what Menzies described in November 1929 as 'a slovenly, dangerous and in some ways dishonest policy'. Menzies worked closely with Kent Hughes in organising a group of 'younger Nationalists' to provide speakers and workers to support Nationalist candidates.

Before the end of the year, *The Argus* was reporting that a 'large and valuable force' had been created and that the new organisation had linked up with the National Federation. The Young Nationalist Organisation was launched formally in March 1930—'an inner and active body of members who will be qualified to undertake active political campaigning'. The leaders included Arthur Clerke, an ex-Rhodes Scholar who was Kent Hughes' campaign secretary in 1927; J.A. Gray, a Hawthorn City Councillor who became MLA for Hawthorn in 1930, having been President of Swinburne Technical College since 1927. Clerke, Menzies, and Kent Hughes were members of the Constitutional Club. Gray, who ran Menzies' campaign for the Legislative Council in 1928, was a fellow member with Kent Hughes of the Naval and Military Club. Among the earliest recruits were Thomas Maltby, later premier of Victoria, James Fairbairn, Trevor Oldham, and J.A. Spicer. On 9 June 1930, *The Argus* published a letter from the chairman of the Organisation, T.S. Nettlefold, a Melbourne City Councillor, with interests in cement, insurance, and retailing, who, like Menzies, was a member of the Savage Club. Perhaps embarrassed by his age (he was 51), Nettlefold was replaced by Menzies, who took the title of president, in March 1931. Nettlefold wrote

The formation of the Young Nationalist Organisation affords a splendid opportunity for younger men to give expression to active Liberal or Nationalist ideals, and it is hoped that this opportunity will be availed of by many men, who perhaps felt in the past politically lukewarm. Never was there a time in the history of Victoria, when we needed more to discard a doctrinaire belief in the efficacy of State action. More and more thoughtful men must be coming to realise that leaning on the State will never get us through our difficulties. The cure for most of our troubles must be the effort, initiative, and independence of individual citizens. I believe that youth is the natural period of individual effort, and I therefore think it imperative that Nationalism as an active element in the political life of the State must summon its youth to its service. I urge the young men of this community to believe that our political problems are their problems in particular, for they must see the matter through. If they believe that all our troubles are to be solved by the handing out of money by the State, that the right way to permanent success is that the State as a whole should grant subsidies to its various sections, then Nationalism as I understand it can have no appeal for them. But if they believe that we can achieve our full growth as a people only when every section has learnt to stand on its own feet, then Nationalism has an urgent claim to their support. The Young Nationalist Organisation movement comes at the present time with an extraordinary wave of enthusiasm, almost unknown in political circles. At all meetings the attendance has been excellent, and almost every member who has been invited has been in attendance. We are working in co-operation with the National Federation, and Messers. Menzies, MLA, J. Spicer and R.A. Braford have, at the invitation of the National Federation, been selected to represent the Young Nationalist Organisation on the Federation. Leaders of hundreds have been selected, which hundreds include both metropolitan and country centres, and vigorous young Nationalists have been selected as leaders. In the past, young men interested in Nationalist politics have been somewhat neglected. All this will now be altered, and every inducement will be given to any young men interested in the welfare of his country to join up with the Young Nationalist Organisation.

Like a latter-day Praetorian Guard, the Young Nationalists were limited to 440 members—their basic structure was groups of ten and a hundred, half being in the country and half in the city. A young man who led one of the country 'hundreds' was Chester Manifold. Nearly fifty years later he remembered attending Arthur Clerke's speakers' classes and addressing street-corner meetings on Friday nights. There would be three or more speakers. An inexperienced man would make a noise and talk long enough to attract a crowd. He would be followed by someone who knew more. Finally, when there was a large enough gathering, a star like Menzies would begin. Although he gave the impression of being supremely assured and imperious, Menzies was actually a very nervous speaker. Manifold remembered going to meetings with Menzies who would 'walk around the block for three-quarters of an hour before the meeting, he just couldn't eat anything, couldn't talk normally to anybody'. The result was usually a speech of great power, commanding rather than engaging, but the work of a craftsman who knew what he wanted to say and could say it the way he wanted to be heard.

What was Menzies' message? As the country lurched further into depression, he clung to orthodox remedies and exhortations. Compared with the more advanced Labor proposals of Premier Jack Lang in New South Wales and E.G. Theodore, the controversial Labor Treasurer in Canberra—proposals that were in the end too advanced for most Labor supporters—Menzies' diagnosis and prescriptions for the Australian economy from 1930 onwards sound like a strange echo of the nineteenth century.

To an audience of National Federation supporters at Rushworth in July 1930, he said:

> The only sound way to relieve the position is by exporting goods ... Australian manufacturers must eliminate waste and reduce costs of production.

'Reducing costs of production' was, of course, a euphemism for cutting wages. Menzies favoured both reducing wages, which he called distributing the sacrifice, and lengthening hours of work. He did speak of sacrifices by capital as well as labour as part of a common front to reduce costs; but he was less insistent and less specific about the nature

An unequal contest: Young Nationalist honesty pursues E.G. Theodore's inflationary balloons, June 1931

of capital's sacrifice, apart from his favourite programme of diminishing government assistance. In February 1931 he said that the Labor Government's policy was being shaped by a left-wing group whose first objective was the destruction of capitalism. He explained that the technique being used to attack 'the existing order of society, the existing financial structure, and the general well-being and good name of Australia', was inflation of the currency, printing and circulating more bank notes. It was a technique supposedly invented by Lenin.

When the Scullin Labor Government in Canberra found itself frustrated by the Commonwealth Bank, which denied it the credit it needed, it suggested a new central bank that would be more susceptible to government control. Menzies sprang to the defence of the Governor of the Commonwealth Bank, Sir Robert Gibson. He described Gibson melodramatically in May 1931 as 'a gallant old man who single-handed almost, was carrying the financial responsibility of the nation'. Few people were probably aware that Menzies was not merely commenting on the Bank from the standpoint of a concerned politician. Privately, in his professional capacity as a barrister, he was also acting as legal adviser to the Bank. When the Country Party and the Labor Government joined to pass a bill to guarantee farmers a payment of three shillings a bushel for wheat, Menzies advised the Bank to resist the Government's request for funds to cover the guarantee. The scheme was unconstitutional, he said, because it infringed section 92 of the Constitution.

So the Bank refused to co-operate in a plan to rescue farmers from their desperate situation. This was January 1931. By April, Sir Robert Gibson had reached the point of threatening to provide no further financial assistance of any kind for the Government. Meanwhile, Menzies denounced the plans of New South Wales Premier Lang to repudiate state debts as 'unveiled dishonesty and criminality'. As for the Federal Treasurer, Theodore, a man whose past personal financial dealings in Queensland were not above suspicion, Menzies branded his expansionary proposals in late April 1931 as 'infinitely more subtle, infinitely more attractive, and infinitely more dangerous'.

When we find Menzies talking the language of conservatism and the economic orthodoxy of the early twentieth century, we may be inclined to accept it as a predictable phenomenon, something that demands little comment. Yet, if we ask about the company he was keeping: who, when he attacked the 'pernicious doctrine of inflation', shared his views? When he called for sound, safe people, and cautious, responsible policies, who and what did he have in mind? If we ask these questions, the answers are instructive.

The first clue lies in the coincidence between Menzies' attitudes and suggestions on economic policy and those of significant Melbourne financial and commercial interests. There were times when parts of his speeches seemed to be compiled from a stockbroker's newsletter.

In October 1930, he preached the doctrine that Australia had been borrowing too much money for ten years. Australian orators, he said, had become so fond of talking of 'our vast natural resources' that they had persuaded themselves that our resources could be taken along to the pawnshop.

In August 1930 at Blackburn he told a joint meeting of the powerful Australian Women's National League and the Nationalist Federation that government spending and individual spending had to be curtailed —possibly the worst policy that could have been proposed. He wanted to see ministerial salaries, and those of MPs and public servants, reduced, instead of throwing all the burden on 'the industries which are our only hope of financial salvation'. If this sounded like a sort of capitalist's catechism, the emphasis became even sharper the following year. In May 1931, according to contemporary press accounts, Menzies delivered the extraordinary judgement in the Albert Hall, Launceston, that the only thing standing in the way of a £30 000 000 loan in London was that the Labor Government lacked the courage to 'cut down the public service'.

It is hard to know just how seriously to take the reasoning of Menzies' arguments that recovery was impeded only by squeamishness about slashing bureaucrats' salaries. But Menzies did call on people to support the renegade Labor man, J.A. Lyons, as leader of the newly formed United Australia Party and as an alternative Prime Minister on the ground that only a Lyons Government would make public servants bear a little of the burden being borne by the unemployed. And only this sight of public servants suffering, he implied, would restore the confidence of English investors enough to re-establish Australian credit.

In the end, public servants, as well as old age and invalid pensioners, did take cuts in their incomes. However, there was a different group in the community—the holders of securities and government bonds—whom Menzies believed to be in a special, almost inviolate, legal position. His view was set out in a memorable letter written from his retreat at Upper Macedon. The federal and state governments had agreed on a plan to impose a 25 per cent property tax on any holders of ordinary securities and government bonds who refused to convert their bond holdings into new bonds. This was, in a sense, a harsh measure. But it was surely consistent with the idea of sharing the burden. Not so, said Menzies:

> Who will lend new money to a Government which says 'we will take your money on such-and-such terms but we may later, if occasion arises alter those terms as we think fit'? The argument that bond interest is on the same footing as pensions or wages will not bear examination. Pensions are not contracts; they are voluntary payments, and they may be altered at will. Wages are payments for current or future services and they must always be fixed from time to time in the light of economic circumstances. Bond interest is payment under national contract for money which the nation has already received and spent.

So, hands off the bond-holders! Menzies' letter was published in *The Argus* on 27 May 1931. Probably very few people noticed that the penalty tax on investors was also denounced one day later in a special issue of the weekly newsletter of the Melbourne stockbroking firm, J.B. Were and Son.

By this time, Menzies was not just a business partner of Staniforth Ricketson. The two men were the central figures of the group that first came together in December 1930 to assist the Labor Government's Acting Treasurer, Lyons, in a campaign to persuade bond-holders to convert their bonds into a new government loan: Kingsley Henderson, architect and businessman; Ambrose Pratt, journalist; Sir John Higgins,

The Bulletin's *readers meet the Victorian Young Nationalist leader, 1931*

formerly a leading figure in wool marketing; C.A. Norris, general manager of the National Mutual Life Association; Ricketson, and Menzies. These six men decided—on their own initiative, without informing the Nationalist party organisation or their backers in the National Union—that they must prevent economic collapse and possible civil disturbance by destroying the Labor Government.

Their plan developed in stages. First, they persuaded Lyons to defect from his own party with a promise to help him to become the leader of all the non-Labor forces. Eventually Lyons supplanted Sir John Latham as leader of the combined right-wing parties, won a decisive electoral victory and became Prime Minister at the head of the new United Australia Party—an amalgamation of the old National Party and the ephemeral 'All For Australia Leagues' with unacknowledged assistance from the New Guard's patriotic clandestine force. The Country Party would not join the Nationalists. Their leader, Earle Page, told his colleague Archie Cameron that 'the mob behind the

Lyons-Nationalist coalition are all big Melbourne manufacturers and
stockbrokers, and would have no more mercy on us than on Latham,
whom they have buried alive'.

Probably the most quoted speech of this phase in Menzies' career
was an address on 'Politics and the Church', reported in the Melbourne
daily papers on 4 May 1931. One sentence was to be quoted again and
again by left-wing propagandists, because it seemed to epitomise the
attitudes of a man and a class incapable of understanding the plight
of their fellow countrymen. 'If Australia was to surmount her troubles
only by abandonment of traditional British standards of honesty,
justice, fair play and honest endeavour, it would be better for Australia
that every citizen within her boundaries should die of starvation during
the next six months.'

A man who made statements like that could not avoid becoming a
celebrity. Not only did the Victorian press report his speeches, his
political engagements, and his courtroom appearances, they assumed
that their readers would also be interested in anecdotes about his private
life. Nowhere was this phenomenon better observed than in country
newspapers. For example, on page 2 of *The Pyramid Hill Advertiser* on
Wednesday, 28 October 1931, the big story was about preparations for
the town's 42nd annual agricultural show. There was news of a visit of
the Better Farming Train (a 'stupendous' touring exhibition and band
of lecturers), an enterprising pilot 'reaping a harvest in the skies' with
joy-rides, and a camel whose owner, 'a patriarchal Afgan from the
great wide interior', also offered rides. But the action story of the day
was 'A KC's Exciting Travelling Experiences':

Mr R.G. Menzies KC will have reason to remember his recent visit
to Pyramid. Before leaving his home at Kew on Saturday morning to
catch the northern train at Spencer Street, his young son expressed
doubt about getting there on time, and sure enough he missed it. The
'man in grey' thought he would have a chance to overhaul the train
by car at Diggers Rest, so with a garage employe pressed into service
he hurried off to catch the rattler; but at Diggers Rest the train was
still ahead of them. In no ways deterred, and determined to succeed,
Mr Menzies then made up his mind to board the train at Gisborne,
and dashing along the bitumened highway at 60 m.p.h. he arrived at
that station 16 minutes to the good. The commencement of the home-
ward journey on Sunday was equally exciting. He left hurriedly without
refreshment after PSA service with the party of Bendigo singers,
intent to catch the ten to seven train at Bendigo. The road through
Campbell's Forest was new to all of them, and it may be conceded they
did not do so badly to cross the railway line at Tandara instead of Myer's
Flat. At Raywood they were short of petrol and only half-an-hour left
them to reach Bendigo railway station dead on time. The bowser-
keeper failed to respond to their summons, so off they went to find at
Eaglehawk that the barest possible chance to register success or failure
was to make a back-way rush from the Borough to Golden Square

railway station. Churchgoers might have mistaken them for a bandit party by their pace and alert demeanour, but, all of this withal, they succeeded by a margin of only a few seconds, and Mr Menzies took a breathless departure from his greatly-relieved companions who had been earlier apprised of the very important fact that the eminent KC had an important case to defend in the city early Monday morning. When the car was examined as to the petrol supply the register showed 'empty'! Had they refuelled at Raywood they would undoubtedly have missed the train.

At thirty-seven years of age, after barely four years in politics, Menzies' position within the Victorian wing of the United Australia Party early in 1932 was immensely powerful. It was a matter of public comment before the downfall of the Hogan Labor Government that there was a growing struggle to wrest control of the Party from Sir Stanley Argyle. In successive issues of the magazine *Today*, the former Nationalist minister, Frederic Eggleston, commented sympathetically:

> Menzies is by far the ablest man who has come into Australian politics for the last twenty years, but ambition is a big flaw. Argyle, rigid and inelastic as he is, will make a fine leader, and Menzies a magnificent lieutenant. Menzies would have found it difficult to lead

Sir Stanley and Lady Argyle: 'competence mixed with prudence'

a House which hates intellectuals, resents arrogance and is incapable of
appreciating brilliance. Any attempt on his part to lead at present
would probably break instead of making his career.

(30 April 1932)

Menzies in particular has impressed everybody as possessing the
quality of statemanship as nobody else here since Watt left Victoria.

(14 May 1932)

I say this with the utmost admiration for Menzies' talents, but his
judgement as a statesman will be very much discounted if he urges
his personal claims at the present moment. He is the type of man who
at present can have far more influence as a loyal lieutenant than as a
leader. In a grudging, jealous House his very ability is an offence, and
the small men who predominate will take a delight in thwarting him.

(28 May 1932)

In January 1932, *The Labor Call* informed its readers that 'the
oracular legal gentleman' who usually advocated self-dependence had
recently been chief spokesman for a delegation to the Victorian Labor
Government on behalf of the Fruit Growers' Cool Stores Association.
The object of the mission was to seek a reduction of interest on money
due to the government and the deferment of the next three payments
of interest and principal on the loans to the cool stores under the Fruit
Act.

Of course, all politicians are forced to interpret their principles in
the light of circumstances. When the Hogan Labor Ministry was defeated in Parliament over the Premiers' Plan in April 1932 and at the
ensuing election, a combined United Australia Party (UAP)–Country
Party Government was inevitably bound on a compromise course.
Menzies, at the head of a bloc of sixteen Young Nationalists was probably the most powerful individual in the Government. He became
Minister for Railways, Attorney-General, and Solicitor-General, having
been prudent enough not to try to depose Sir Stanley Argyle from the
leadership. The Argyle Ministry was formed on May 19. On June 15,
Menzies was elected Deputy Leader of the UAP, beating the previous
Deputy Leader, Ian Macfarlan, twenty votes to thirteen. Yet, notwithstanding his authority and influence, there were political embarrass-
ments which *The Sydney Morning Herald's* special correspondent in
Melbourne was able to report with some relish on June 29:

Wisely, the Argyle Ministry has decided not to try to build up a
reputation upon a crowded legislation programme, but rather to concentrate administratively upon the work of cutting down governmental
costs. The Budget, which it has promised to submit earlier than usual,
will be awaited with interest. In the Lieutenant-Governor's speech at
the opening of the session on June 14 was included a warning that
public grants to sections of the community could not be expected
from the Ministry. This was a good beginning, and in consonance

UAP leaders Argyle, Menzies and Ian Macfarlan, 16 May 1932

with the task of cleaning-up generally, which the electors have en-trusted to the non-Labour groups, but unfortunately the Ministry has stultified itself at the outset. On the very day the speech was delivered it introduced a bill to authorise the guaranteeing of bank advances to enable country meat-freezing works to operate. There was no excuse for this apostasy. For many years the country freezing works have been a source of heavy loss to the Government. Several years ago, in an endeavour to make unfortunate enterprises self-supporting, the four works—at Ballarat, Bendigo, Donald, and Murtoa—were placed under the control of an Amalgamated Freezing Company, which has tried to stem the heavy losses by carrying on only the Ballarat and Bendigo works. In spite of this measure, the losses continued, and the enterprises are hopelessly in debt to the Government. It was because of a decision to guarantee again the Amalgamated Freezing Company, in the face of these losses, that Mr Menzies and two other Ministers resigned from the McPherson Cabinet three years ago. On this occasion the Argyle Ministry has attempted to put a better face on the matter by introducing a bill to sanction the guarantee, instead of, as hitherto, doing the business by administrative act. But such a course is maladroit as well as weak. The Ministry should have the courage of its decision, good or bad, and not try to shelter behind its Parliamentary majority. The acting Labour leader, Mr Tunnecliffe, astute debater as he is, and not without a spice of malice, did not miss the obvious chance of twitting Mr Menzies with constructively condoning on this occasion what he had resigned office for previously. Mr Menzies, noted for hair-trigger repartee, did not hit back, except to hint that Mr Tunnecliffe was mistaken in supposing that he had changed his convictions.

THE TASK OF MR MENZIES

Mr Menzies could not very well have blurted out the truth—that on this occasion, being the acknowledged leader of the Young Nationalist wing of the party, he could do much better service to his principles by remaining in the Ministry and using his powerful influence to check the aspirations of country Ministers who wish to adhere to the bad old methods of bribing large sections of voters by giving them assistance from the public funds. . . . The freezing works episode is not particularly big in itself, especially in comparison with some of the problems to be faced, but it . . . illustrates strikingly the contest which is going on below the surface in Victorian non-Labour politics between the new and the old points of view. One of the outward and visible signs of this contest was the elevation of Mr Menzies to the deputy leadership of the United Australia party. Although there is no such office as Deputy Premier, and the choice of Mr Menzies as deputy leader by a majority of the party does not necessarily add anything to his stature in Cabinet, it is generally recognised that Mr Menzies will be Deputy Premier should the occasion arise. The Chief Secretary (Mr Macfarlan) who was formerly deputy leader, and unsuccessfully contested the position with Mr Menzies on this occasion, acted as Deputy Premier recently, but both Sir Stanley Argyle and Mr Menzies were out of the State at the time. The virtual choice of Mr Menzies as Deputy Premier has a further significance. It emphasises that the representation of the United Country party in the Cabinet is of a different nature from that of composite Ministries of the past. The Country Party leader is not an 'equal in all things', he is simply the holder of a portfolio.

Charles Meeking joined *The Age* as a reporter in 1923. At the time Menzies again entered the Victorian Government, Meeking covered what was then called the western round, which embraced the Railways Department but not the Attorney-General's Department. In an interview he recalled his first encounter with the new Minister:

I thought I had better go and see this new Minister and I went up full of despondency because even at that stage I had become cynical about ministers, and asked him a few leading questions on various themes at that time—bus competition with railways and so on—and to my great astonishment, instead of hedging and saying he'd get a report or he'd let me know, he answered them directly, very adequately, grammatically, which was a change for the Minister. And having given me four or five stories nobody else had come up with—nobody else had thought of it—he said 'Are you walking down Collins Street' and I said 'Oh yes' and that was that.

I went in to see him one day at the Railway Department when he was Minister for Railways and he said 'Look Meeking, I'll show you something interesting'. He opened a drawer and produced a little book and showed it to me. He said 'I was given that when I was dux of the fourth grade in Jeparit'. He said 'The headmaster said to me in giving it to me at the end of the year "you know Robert, you might be Prime Minister of Australia one of these days". And he said 'Look at me, Minister for Railways, I ask you!' So I said 'Cheer up, you might be.' 'Oh', he said, 'I wouldn't think. . . .' But I haven't the slightest doubt that he did.

The Minister for Railways inherited a department whose financial position was described by the Chairman of the Railways Commissioners as 'a matter of very grave concern'—about a third of all government loan funds were spent on railways. Estimated revenue for 1931–1932 was the lowest since 1919–1920; and 'working expenses' had to be slashed by a third. As revenue plunged, more and more railway workers were sacked. The wages of those who remained were cut. A strike began in the Government's Wonthaggi coal mine, in protest against a severe wage cut that had been made possible by a hastily conceived legal manoeuvre to set up a state tribunal. Menzies, cabling from Sydney on 21 June 1932, had pointed out to the Premier that if a tribunal were set up, the Government 'can probably have onerous federal award cancelled.' The plan succeeded. *The Labor Call* commented retrospectively on 31 May 1934, that 'the miners in Wonthaggi have never known a Minister who has been more callously indifferent to the hardships and sufferings of others.' It was an unenviable reputation.

Attacked from the left by trade union and Labor leaders, Menzies was also locked in perpetual conflict with his Country Party colleagues and those in his own party who, in his view, were too ready to surrender to Country Party pressure. On 25 November 1932, after what was generally seen as an ignominious retreat by the UAP on the inclusion

The Argyle Cabinet, 1932

of new and renewed mortgages in legislation to reduce interest payments, *The Sydney Morning Herald* correspondent drew attention to tensions within the Ministry:

> Those behind scenes in State politics are well aware that in spite of the assertions of unanimity in the Cabinet room, the Ministry is by no means a happy and united family. The Premier (Sir Stanley Argyle), although an honest and a well-meaning man, is not a strong leader . . . The Attorney-General (Mr Menzies), who is more intimately identified with the Young Nationalist wing, and, in country members' minds at least, with city interests, has been the chief apostle of inflexibility in the matter of not interfering with private mortgages. It would be more than human if the country members of the Ministry—and more particularly United Country party representatives in the Ministry—regarded with kindly tolerance the attitude which they deemed so unsympathetic toward the troubles of land settlers who largely comprise the mortgagor class. Mr Menzies, too, is not as popular in the House as he might be because of his stinging repartee, and his rather high-and-mighty attitude on political questions generally. Mr Macfarlan, another legal member of the Cabinet, whom Mr Menzies has displaced both as Attorney-General and Deputy Premier, is more personally popular in the House. There have been indications in the shape of promised legislation that the Ministry is disposed to conciliate the Country party by fathering legislative measures which are fundamentally opposed to the principles of the United Australia party. . . .

As Attorney-General, it was Menzies' duty to consider various proposals for legal reform and changes in the laws relating to the legal profession. Two examples from the archives of the Victorian Government are revealing. Late in 1932 the suggestion was made that much time and money could be saved if people who pleaded guilty to technical offences (breaching of licensing or traffic regulations for instance) should be fined according to a fixed schedule rather than brought to court. There was a subtlety involved in the question: from the point of view of the Government, the costs to be considered included the costs of legal aid. The Chairman of the Bench of Metropolitan and Suburban Magistrates, A.M. Cook, argued powerfully against the arbitrariness of a scale of fines. On legal aid he suggested that:

> . . . persons who have not been previously convicted of an indictable offence, or who have not been—say once or twice (as may be thought fit)—previously convicted, or in any case where some important question of law is involved, may, in the discretion of the Attorney-General, be granted assistance.

Cook's extraordinary recommendation—effectively denying aid to a large number of citizens—was minuted by Menzies: 'I agree in substance with this report.'

In August 1933, Menzies was joined by Ian Macfarlan, as a sub-committee of Cabinet, to report on the law relating to defaulting solicitors. Somehow, in their consideration of the problem, they overlooked the one class of person whom they might have been expected to be protecting—the solicitors' clients:

We have considered this question with some care, and have had the advantage of discussion with the President and Secretary of the Law Institute, and also with Mr C.H. Lucas, solicitor, who takes a view different from that entertained by the Law Institute as a whole.

We find that the general feeling among solicitors is that some steps ought to be taken to restrain the unauthorised or criminal use of trust moneys, but that previously suggested means of dealing with this problem by establishing a special Compensation Fund to be contributed to by all solicitors is thought to be unjust.

We agree with this view. We are of opinion that to tax honest solicitors for purpose of establishing a fund to meet the defalcations of dishonest solicitors is not only inherently unfair but gives rise to invidious distinctions between the legal and other professions. We are of opinion that it is much more useful to go to the root of the recent troubles which have manifested themselves in connection with the misappropriation of trust moneys, and make some effective provision for the segregation of trust moneys from other moneys which may be in the hands of a solicitor or other person in the position of a trustee. We have always entertained the view that the best deterrent to dishonesty will not be the existence of a Guarantee Fund, but will be the extreme probability of a conviction if criminal proceedings are launched. The institution of criminal prosecutions will be greatly facilitated, in our opinion, if the law is amended so as to provide that it shall be a criminal offence for a solicitor receiving trust moneys to pay them into any other than a trust account, or to pay them out of such account except under the terms of the trust or trusts. Such a law would be simple, and prosecution for its breach would be a matter of no great complication. Most of the cases which have come before the courts in recent years have been cases in which trust moneys were mingled with the solicitor's own funds, thus causing confusion in the first stage and dishonesty in the second.

We are further of opinion that additional security would be afforded if it were made the duty of every solicitor to register annually for some nominal fee with the Law Institute, and to provide, as a condition of each renewal, an affidavit stating that he had duly dealt with trust moneys during the preceding twelve months. The advantages of this course would be that a second prosecution for perjury could also be launched in cases of dishonesty, and that the whole matter could be dealt with by an amendment of the Law Institute Act.

We have given some thought to a suggestion which has been made that there should be a compulsory audit of solicitors' trust accounts. After hearing the views of the Law Institute we are satisfied that this course is impracticable, having regard to the very large expense which would be involved in having the exhaustive kind of audit which would be necessary if any real protection were to be given to the public.

In the days when he was creating the Young Nationalist Organisation, Menzies stressed the importance of direct contact between politicians and the public. He had always believed in the potency of reasoned presentation of arguments to the electors. As a minister, therefore, it was not surprising that he accepted a wide variety of speaking engagements. He defended the Government in his own electorate, and he also undertook the rigours of country speaking tours, provocatively taking his message into the heart of Country Party territory. In February 1933, before embarking on a series of speeches in country areas, Menzies addressed a public meeting at the Lyric Theatre, Box Hill. There, *The Box Hill Reporter* noted on 10 February 1933, 'the attendance was very good considering the warmth of the weather, and the speaker was listened to with keen interest and attention throughout'. The speech on this occasion provides a summary of salient political issues as well as a characteristic example of the application of Menzies' philosophy and style to unglamorous contemporary problems:

Mr Menzies said the session was taken up with many contentious measures. One night was insufficient to tell of everything, and he would select four topics about which some legislation was carried into effect.

Unemployment

Unemployment was a problem that occupied almost 50 per cent. of the time of Cabinet, which had held a record number of meetings since it took office. The problem had two aspects, (a) adminstrative and (b) legislative. Administration was in the hands of Mr Kent-Hughes, whose humane and orderly methods earned compliments from all sides of the House. He had been responsible for the Act put through last session, which consolidated all previous Acts and incorporated some new features, notably the establishment of some sort of family obligation on similar lines to Commonwealth action relating to pensions. The new legislation would work more satisfactorily than anything we had before, and it firmly established two principles—(1) That relief is best dealt with by local committees, which know the conditions and the people who are getting it; (2) that relief should only be given in exchange for work.

The Minister is now engaged in organising the funds in such a way that there shall be no imposition and compiling records of every individual case so that there should be no injustice. This strict control of the funds, coupled with some measure of recovery in the general conditions, has resulted in the reduction from 45 000 to between 20 000 and 30 000 in the numbers of people drawing sustenance . . . Loan money had been used to accelerate the absorption of men into industry . . .

Closer Settlement

People in Melbourne were inclined to think that land settlement questions were of secondary importance to them, but when they remembered that the State was losing about £1 000 000 per annum it would be seen that closer settlement was of vital interest to everyone. Money had to be borrowed to make up the losses, and interest on this borrowed money had to be found by the individual taxpayer. The Lands Department, and particularly that section of it relating to closer settlement, had been in a state of chaos for a number of years. The State had undertaken the task of settling returned soldiers and civilians on land. In addition to the cost of the land, advances were made to these settlers for improvements, stock and, lately, to an amazing extent, for sustenance. It was not surprising, therefore, that interest far exceeded revenue, and it was to the credit of the Argyle Government that it had tackled a problem that no Government for the past 10 years had attempted.

The elimination of political interference with the administration had been the first objective of the Ministry. A commission had been formed to consist of three permanent and two part-time members, who would have control of the administration of closer settlement, and would be in a position to administer the Act as they thought fit and on business lines, free from the influence excepted by the average country member of Parliament who was constantly under pressure from his constituents to seek special concessions in individual cases.

Another principle adopted had been the basing of settlers' payments on their ability to pay ... It was proposed to base his payments for the next five years on his special circumstances, and after that a complete revision of his position would be made, the land revalued in the light of experience of what it might reasonably by expected to return, thus giving the settler a manageable debt in place of an unmanageable one, and a chance to pull through.

Mortgage Interest

In 1931, continued Mr Menzies, an act was passed compulsorily reducing the rate of mortgage interest on their existing mortgages by twenty-two and a half per cent. or 4/6 in the £, provided the reduction did not bring the rate below 5 per cent. This was portion of the Premiers' Plan. He had opposed it at the time, not because he was a mortgagee, as some people seemed to think, but because he believed that the way to hinder financial recovery was to start tearing up contracts ... However, this Act had been passed and applied to mortgages existing in October, 1931. He had pointed out that it would cause a lot of trouble in the future, which it had. For instance, some mortgages had only, perhaps, three months to run; these got the benefit of the reduction for a short time only. The Act did not legislate for renewals and new loans. Other mortgages had, perhaps, three years to run; these got the benefit for a much longer period. He protested that this was unfair. One member suggested that the Act should provide that the reduction

should apply to the renewed mortgage three months later. This might
have been a brilliant suggestion if there was any way to compel a
mortgagee to lend or renew. If carried out it would have meant that
before lending or renewing the mortgagee would increase the interest
rate by 25 per cent. to provide for the compulsory reduction of $22\frac{1}{2}$
per cent. In the interests of the mortgagor it was finally decided not
to deal with contracts that might come into existence in the future,
but to apply it merely to contracts then in operation.

A concerted move was made by that section of the Country Party
not in the Ministry to force interest reductions on all mortgages renewed
since October, 1932, and what they partly succeeded in doing was to
put into the Bill a provision that every mortgage which had run out
and been replaced by a new mortgage between the parties should
carry the reduced interest. They said, 'It is not fair that one man
should have three years' relief, while another should only have three
months relief.'

The question should be looked at in this way—If Parliament can
come along and alter contracts, how long will anyone be able to borrow
money on mortgage at all? During the session he had letters from men
prominent in the financial world; one said that he had a client prepared to lend £5000 on a certain rural security, everything had been
fixed up, but when the lender read of the Country Party amendments in
the paper he declared the deal off. Prior to this class of legislation in
New South Wales between four and five million pounds per annum was
being invested in real estate mortgages; to-day it had dwindled to
about £400 000, and the only thing that astonished him was that there
was £400 000, for he had still to meet the man who is prepared to
lend money on the flexible contracts we have introduced.

'I am not worried about flexible contracts in the interests of the
mortgagees,' declared Mr Menzies. 'I understand that 90 per cent. of
my electors are mortgagors—I am one myself. I am concerned with
the interests of mortgagors. I am thinking of the interests of the man
who cannot exist unless he can borrow money to carry him on. How
many men on the land could have got on if they had not been able to
borrow money? It is the mortgagor's policy I am advocating, not a
mortgagee's.'

One country member remarked that he was not concerned about
the people who were going to borrow, but about those who had already borrowed. This might strike some people as very ingenious, but
was it honest? How many mortgagees had obligations themselves?
Some people seemed to think that mortgagees are wealthy fat men.
(Laughter.) Did they never think that the mortgagee had obligations
himself? Some people had invested perhaps £500 for three years because they had some obligation to meet at the end of that time, but
Parliament did not consider that aspect. Mr Maurice Blackburn
moved an amendment to apply the same relief to the mortgagee in his
dealings with his creditors, but he (Mr Menzies) told him that perhaps
this did not go far enough, for there was still the creditor's creditor

and so on. It was like the old song of the man who was chasing his son round the room. (Laughter.)

He was concerned with doing justice, and when justice was the objective they could not deal with one section only. One could not go down into the complicated fabric of business obligations with a broad sword to cut the tangle without causing an infinitely greater tangle. That sort of thing might be done once, but if it was to be done year after year it would be as well to give up the pretence that any contract ever made is worth the paper it is written on. They might think his attitude an academic one, but most of the things that keep society together were rooted in academic ideas. 'If I wanted to introduce Communism, and I had the powers of a Mussolini,' said Mr Menzies graphically, 'I would merely pass one small Bill to abolish contracts, and you would soon have the chaos of Communism.'

The only way to get people to lend money was to persuade them that their rate of interest was certain. This had another advantage, for where interest was certain the rate was low; high interest rates were the result of uncertainty.

'We will, in the next few years,' he added, 'see how these theories work out, and I hope the experience will not be too tragic for mortgagors.'

Transport

The question of transport would take nearly two hours to explain in detail, said Mr Menzies, so he could only touch on some of the main features.

The first thing to note was that as soon as any Government began to deal with transportation problems, the motoring interest rushed to arms, and simply inundated members and Ministers with all sorts of protests. One form of protest was a triangular piece of paper cut from an advertisement, which between 500 and 600 people had forwarded to him. Among others, the protest took this form: 'This is an iniquitous attempt to take away our living. Everyone ought to be allowed on the road; it is the King's highway.'

These were picturesque arguments, but they could not live on that kind of thing and hope to govern a country. One of the first things that would impress itself on anyone who became Minister of Railways was that the transport problem was one that could not be run away from very much longer.

Were those people who asked for the freedom of the King's highway prepared to grant it to the greengrocer? The unrestricted use of the road by motor carrying interests was equivalent to allowing the greengrocer the right to use the footpath on which to get up his stock in trade and compete, rent free, with the regular shopkeepers who paid rent and other charges. Were those in retail trade prepared to let this doctrine of 'freedom of the road' take hold in all its ramifications?

In the Victorian Railways, £75 000 000 was invested, and this was the concern of everyone. These railways, many of them, were put down more for the purpose of developing the country rather than as strictly business-like ventures; in operating them the Commissioners had to provide many services which the motor carrier was free of. The railways had to provide and maintain their own tracks, build stations and equip them, provide safety devices, a regular schedule and pay men a rate of wages as fixed by arbitration. None of these obligations or restrictions applied to the carrier who expected to use the road for nothing. This was not a rational state of affairs. Every country of importance in the world had found it necessary to regulate transport and had either passed the law or were in process of doing so. . . .

Some people put forward the suggestion that competition should be met by the railways in the ordinary business way, viz., by reducing freights and fares to attract business. Well, this had been done, and for a year an energetic officer had been going round making special arrangements, and the very type of people who asked for 'business methods' were the first to protest against 'unfair tactics'.

The railways had to carry bulky and heavy goods, such as wool and wheat, at low freights, and the only way to make up the deficiency on this was by getting a large amount of carrying at higher rates. Private transport came in and skimmed the cream of this high grade freight and left the railways the task of carrying the bulky unprofitable-in-itself freight. This sort of competition was the easiest in the world; all the motor carrier had to do was to get the railway freight book and go round quoting 5/- a ton less. He did not have the expenses and upkeep of a permanent way, and working for himself in the majority of cases could work even 24 hours a day if he cared to while railway employees' hours and pay were strictly regulated.

If the transport problem is not dealt with the time would quickly arrive when the railways will be left with only the bulky low freights, and wheat and wool freights will have to be raised or the railway system lost altogether. Such was unthinkable, nor was it possible to raise freight on heavy primary produce. The time had come, therefore, not to crush competition, but to regulate it and restrict it.

Much inexpert criticism had been levelled at the Victorian Railways, but he could say they were most efficiently managed, and he only hoped that the critics managed their own businesses as efficiently as the railways were run. It was true that last year the loss was £700 000, but this was largely due to circumstances outside the control of the management. For instance, half of it was on account of overseas exchange, a factor obviously outside the scope of the management to deal with. For the present year the ratio of working costs to revenue was the lowest it had even been, and it was doubtful if there was any railway system in the world that had a better ratio. In fact, an impartial observer had said that the economies effected in railway working last year were to be numbered among the great financial feats of the world.

Questions

Men are being called up for relief work on the railway line at Hartwell at rates that give them £1 17/4 per week. Do you consider this a living wage?—I consider it is much better than the 12/- per week they would get for sustenance.

You claim to have reduced the number drawing sustenance by 25 per cent. How long does your Government expect to take to put the other 75 per cent back in work?—The Government can only find money for relief employment by taxation or by loan. Loan money this year was £2 500 000, and I do not favour its increase; in fact, it ought to be reduced. Moreover, I would like to know where the Government could get more loan money, as we have reached our limit with the banks, and a public loan last year was not very successful. If the money is to come from taxation, the present unemployment taxation would have to be raised four times, and this would not meet with much favour.

Would you favour a Bill fixing the maximum of 5 per cent as the mortgage interest rate for the next three years?—Not unless you can find some means to compel people to lend money.

Menzies' country speaking tour in early 1933 provides fascinating evidence of the tedious ritual and flattery that a political 'star' had to endure. Everywhere he went, the young minister was preceded by publicity—which appeared almost verbatim in each newspaper—announcing that 'Mr Menzies, who is recognised as one of the most forceful and logical speakers in the Commonwealth, will deal chiefly with . . .' whatever it was hoped was the dominant local issue. Occasionally, the local press would capture for posterity a moment of banality that would otherwise have been unmemorable and unrecorded. Thus *The Gippsland Mercury*, on 3 May 1933, described a small gathering in Sale, under a delicious, triply ambiguous headline, 'CIVIC RECEPTION—Tendered Minister for Railways':

In the Mayor's parlor on Thursday afternoon a civic reception was tendered Hon. R.G. Menzies, KC, Attorney-General and Minister for Railways. There was a representative gathering over which Cr M.T. Cullinan presided, in the absence of the Mayor, who was attending a municipal conference. An apology was received from Mr G.H. Wise.

After the loyal toast had been honored, Cr Cullinan said it was his pleasure and privilege to extend a welcome to the Minister, more especially as he occupied so exalted a position as Attorney-General, which carried with it great power and responsibility. His position as Minister for Railways probably appealed more to the rank and file, as they all had more or less interest in the railways. . . . It was highly desirable for Ministers to visit the country districts and discuss public questions apart from the turmoil of an election. The people were anxious to hear the Government's proposals in regard to road transport —a question of much concern to the Railway Department. He hoped the Minister that evening would be greeted by a bumper house and that the people would be satisfied with the Government's activities.

Cr Hagenauer was pleased to add a few words of welcome, and was proud to join hands with the legal profession. When both professions were joined together the welfare of the people was in good hands.

Cr Cullinan said they were pleased to have with them Mr W.D. Leslie, who was recovering from a very serious accident. Mr Leslie was an old councillor of the town.

Mr Leslie said he endorsed the remarks of the previous speakers. He was deeply interested in Mr Menzies who was a very clever young man. He knew Mr Menzies' father well, and he had done a lot of good work. As Cr Cullinan had said, he was a very old councillor, and was born in Sale, and claimed to be a senior. The Mayor had acted rightly in according the Minister a reception.

Cr Rolland welcomed Mr Menzies as head of the legal profession and one of the most honored members. He was sorry an election was not on as he enjoyed listening to Mr Menzies' repartee. As a councillor and member of the legal profession, he welcomed Mr Menzies, and hoped he would be able to enlighten the people on the Government's proposals in regard to transport.

Mr Menzies said he much appreciated the welcome. When visiting country districts his difficulty was to choose a subject local people were most interested in. Cr Cullinan had given him the cue in this respect when he said the Sale people were anxious to know the Government's intentions in regard to road transport. He would endeavor to throw some light on the transport question that evening. Parliament was indifferently reported in the Press, and it was desirable that the Government's views on various questions should be presented to electors during the recess. He had strong views in that regard. He had been credited with entertaining views that he had never heard of. He invited criticism. If he were Minister for Railways who ought to know more than the man in the street. That was true of Parliament generally. Members of Parliament should not be mere sounding boards. They should be in a position to give expression to their own views. A good healthy exchange of ideas or a good healthy argument was good to arrive at a proper understanding. He again thanked them for the welcome.

The major piece of legislation with which Menzies was entrusted was a Transport Regulation Bill, introduced into the Legislative Assembly in August 1933. The Bill established a Transport Regulation Board to license commercial motor vehicles for passenger and freight operations in non-urban areas, and to recommend the closure of uneconomic railway lines. Designed as a feasible, non-political, transport regulatory system it ostensibly preserved the State's massive railway investment but actually afforded many opportunities for displacing rail with motor transport. The licence fees themselves were nominal. Menzies' second reading speech on August 29 took two hours. *The Age* noted that it *was* a speech, not the increasingly familiar 'recital from a statement

prepared by departmental officers'. Of all the parliamentary speeches
Menzies made, at federal as well as state level, none displayed greater
mastery of detail or fluency of argument. Although the printed word
barely conveys the atmosphere of contemporary debate, Menzies'
robust humour and complete assurance are clearly evident in the
Victorian *Hansard*:

> It is being said in certain quarters, and by some persons interested
> and otherwise, that legislation of this kind is calculated to impose a
> burden on the primary producer, that it is placing all the difficulties
> of transport regulation on his shoulders, and conferring all the advan-
> tages of transport regulation on those who, presumably, live in the
> metropolitan area. I should have thought that by this time it would be
> well known to the public that the central feature of any transport
> regulation Bill that can be introduced now is that it is designed to
> preserve the position of the primary producer. The position of the
> primary producer ... is integrally bound up with the railway system
> of this State, and any attitude which merely permits an unregulated
> transport war to continue would inevitably lead to the grave impair-
> ment of the railway system, and through it to the grave impairment
> of the real interests of the man on the land.
>
> ... Either the general taxpayer, who includes the man on the land,
> will be called upon to provide increasing sums of money year by year
> to recoup railway losses, or, alternatively, the man who depends on
> long haulage by train—he is the man on the land—will be required
> to pay increased freight. There is no escape from that grim alternative
> —increased taxation or increased freights, unless we treat this problem
> as one of great magnitude and urgency, and endeavour to put it into
> a coherent condition.
>
> The second matter to which I want to direct attention, and it is
> somewhat allied to the first, is this: The Board points out in paragraph
> 64 of its report and in a map, which honorable members will find as
> an appendix to the report, that the State of Victoria embraces an area
> of 56 000 000 acres, of which 34 900 000, or 62 per cent, lie within 8
> miles of a railway line. The map contained in the report shows that
> in a singularly graphic way. It is worth while bearing that in mind.
> We are not being invited in legislation of this kind to consider the
> position of a railway service which exists only spasmodically in the
> State, but the position of a railway service which is almost ubiquitous
> in the State and which brings 62 per cent of the area of the State
> within 8 miles of it. I am reminded by the Premier that if you omit
> some of the practically inaccessible mountainous region in the eastern
> part of the State the percentage becomes higher. If that region were
> omitted, 75 per cent of the Scale could be regarded as within 8 miles
> of a railway line.
>
> The third matter to which I wish to refer as a matter for comment
> at this stage is the claim, which I have always believed to be a false
> claim, that commercial motor revenue pays for the roads, and that

commercial motor vehicles have some kind of purchased vested interest in the roads on which they travel. I have always had, and I am sure many honorable members have had, the greatest doubt about that claim. We have always entertained the view that the community provided roads, and that those roads were being used for the erection of what amounted to private franchises without adequate payment by those who held the franchises, and that contention is abundantly supported by a very interesting examination conducted by the Board, the result of which is set out in paragraph 149 of its report . . .

There we have what is in the nature of a judicial finding on this matter, and it completely disposes of the claim that has been made that commercial motor transport has, so to speak, purchased the right to use the roads at its own sweet will. The Board . . . realizes that motor transport is a necessary element in the transport economy of the State, but it also recognizes that that place ought to be defined, and that there ought to be some effective regulation of that element, with some effective means to eliminate the unnecessary competition that goes on in many places, and the community waste that is occasioned as a result.

The fourth matter I wish to mention is that this Parliament has, on one or two occasions, endeavoured to deal with this problem by rigid means as opposed to flexible means. At the end of 1929 it passed an Act which had the effect of prohibiting the use of certain commercial vehicles on the five main highways of the State. That might be described as an interesting experiment, but in the opinion of the Board it has failed . . . It is for that reason that this Government last year, as it does in the Bill I am presenting to honorable members, made provision for control by a licensing system, and not by some definite rigid parliamentary prohibition. It appears from what the Board says that the ban on the five main highways has been a failure.

Mr HOGAN.—It was a failure because people were allowed to break the law.

Mr MENZIES.—If the honorable member will have enough patience to hear what the Board says on the matter, I think he will be rather inclined to agree with it. In paragraph 179 of its report the Board, referring to the Motor Omnibus Act of 1929, says—

> Under the Act licensed ommibuses of this class—

That is, light motor omnibuses with seating capacity for less than six passengers.

> are free to operate on any route in Victoria with the exception of certain sections of State highways.

The Board then refers to what I have called the five main highways. In the following paragraphs the Board says—

> 180. The restrictions in regard to highways were intended to protect railway passenger traffic on main lines to the principal inland towns. They constitute a recognition of the effect of highway construction. . . .

181. Speaking on these restrictions, one witness asked rather pertinently, 'Why was the road ever put there?'

182. The restrictions have failed to prevent competition with the railways for passenger traffic between Melbourne and the provincial centres. Driven from the highways, these omnibuses have sought other routes over roads which, in many cases, are not suitably constructed to carry this class of traffic, and which are maintained largely at the expense of the municipalities.

Mr HOGAN.—The omnibuses have not been driven from the highways. They are running on them to-day.

Mr MENZIES.—I will not enter into any contention with the honorable member as to whether it is possible to obtain 100 per cent of efficiency in the policing of the existing law, but most honorable members will agree with me from their own experience of these matters that it is a common thing to find vehicles which have been driven off the five main highways zig-zagging to their destination along side roads and back roads, submitting those roads to a type of traffic they were never designed to carry, and submitting the passengers whom they convey to a considerable amount of discomfort. I am not criticizing the passing of the Motor Omnibus Act of 1929.

Mr SLATER.—If it had not been passed, there would be no passengers carried by train from Ballarat and Bendigo.

Mr MENZIES.—I said I am not criticizing the making of the existing law, but I do agree with the Board in thinking that it is far better to have a general system of control by licensing through the instrumentality of a Board if you can get it, than to mark out certain particular routes in order that they may be the subject-matter of parliamentary prohibition.

The fifth point I wish to make is that motor transport itself is urgently in need of a Transport Regulation Act. The Board has discovered that many men operating on the roads and performing useful and necessary services on the roads are being exposed to a type of competition which is calculated to destroy the services which they are rendering. Men who, during the ordinary course of events . . . are performing a steady public service along some roads, at not very remunerative rates, find themselves at those particular times when revenue is good—at holiday times or on special occasions—subjected to competition from all sorts of people who arrive only when the cream of the traffic is to be obtained; and from the point of view of the regular road operators it is an important thing, as the Board points out, that there should be some protection, some security of tenure, that will enable a man to make a reasonable capital investment and to give reasonable service to the public. It appeared from the investigation the Board made that in connexion with road transport services there is almost a complete want of proper costing. It is almost impossible to determine whether a particular road service is operating at more than cost or at something below cost . . .

Mr MENZIES.—Proper costing is by no means a universal habit, but, however far it may exist in the case of ordinary commercial undertakings, it is clear from the report of the Board ... that this industry is suffering not only from a want of proper costing, but also from working conditions which are to a large extent unregulated.

The sixth matter I wish to mention is this—a good deal of dissension has occurred from time as to what the railways of this State are losing through this particular form of competition, and all sorts of airy estimates have been made by partisans. The Board, however, gave particular attention to the matter, and it is very valuable to have its findings. It appears from paragraph 383 of the Board's report that the Railway Department estimated its losses in respect of passenger services, as a result of the competition of tramways, metro-politan omnibuses, and country commercial road passenger services, at £270 000. That does not include any losses caused by the owners of private motor vehicles.

Mr Cook.—Have the motor interests disputed the figures?

Mr MENZIES.—The Transport Regulation Board investigated the matter, and I shall refer to what it says. Paragraph 387 of the report reads—

> We regard these figures as well within most probable limits, and therefore think the Department's estimates of loss are reasonable.

Mr Frost.—The amount would not extinguish the deficit.

Mr MENZIES.—It would not, but it would be a comfortable thing to have that amount. Honorable members will understand that we are talking in terms of revenue and not of net profit. Nobody says that, by any legislation that we may pass, we are going to prohibit this competition. To a large extent, competition of this kind in places where it is desirable and economic will go on, but this is an interesting indication of how much business is being lost, and on what area, so to speak, the Board would be able to work. I have been dealing with the passenger traffic, and the Railway Department estimated the total loss caused by the services mentioned as £270 000, of which the tramway competition was responsible for £90 000.

Mr Hogan.—That would be only the railway trams.

Mr MENZIES.—This includes the metropolitan tramway services. It is an estimate of the loss that the railways have sustained through the competition of other forms of transport. The total loss is estimated to be £1 030 320, the great bulk of which is due to private motor cars, and is irrecoverable for the purposes of this legislation. In the metro-politan area, as the honorable member for Warrenheip and Grenville will understand, the tramways are conducting many services which in no reasonable sense are in competition with the Railway Department; the estimate to which I have referred, however, is based on the factor of competition, and not merely upon the total volume of business which the tramways may be doing.

Mr Lind.—You do not say that the tramways are not coming into competition with the railways.

Mr MENZIES.—No. The estimate of the Railway Department is that it is losing £90 000 through that source. The position in regard to goods traffic turns out to be much more serious. Paragraph 391 of the Board's report says—

> In the course of our inquiry, we have obtained from depots, road operators, and other sources, information not available to the Railway Department regarding the road traffic in wool and other commodities, from which we find that the annual loss of gross revenue from diverted goods traffic is at present not less than £400 000, and probably exceeds £450 000.

I refer to these figures because it is as well that we should understand clearly that we are not dealing with a theoretic problem but with an actual problem that is to some extent in its infancy, and with a new form of transport which, exclusive of the vehicles in private use, is responsible for a loss of revenue, which the Transport Regulation Board says is something in the vicinity of £750 000. It is worth having that fact in mind when we hear people suggest that we are talking about trifles and seeking to invent a new and terrible machine to deal with a comparatively non-existing problem.

The seventh of the preliminary matters I deal with is this: There have not been wanting bold advocates who, following the good rule of advocacy, assert roundly that the railways are losing £1 000 000 per annum on the suburban services. Of course, a man, I suppose, gets a reputation for being a profound authority on a matter if he repeats with sufficient force and often enough that the suburban railways are losing £1 000 000 per annum. I regret to say that that statement is used with particular vehemence in the country districts, and for a reason which is obvious. If the railways are losing £1 000 000 on the suburban services, and the total deficit is £1 500 000, the country user of the railways is being bled to the extent of £500 000 to enable the suburbanites to have low travelling fares. It is a pretty argument.

Mr LIND.—You allow the suburban people to have extravagant services, while the country people suffer.

Mr MENZIES.—Exactly. The honorable member has heard something of these stories.

Mr LIND.—I have seen some of these things.

Mr CAIN.—If the Minister questions him sufficiently, the honorable member will admit that he is an advocate of the point.

Mr MENZIES.—He will not, after he has perused the report of the Transport Regulation Board. I also wish to draw the attention of the honorable member for Essendon to what the Board says on the very important question of the losses on the suburban railways. The Board had an investigation made, and according to paragraph 400—

> The loss disclosed by the investigation is £80 860 compared with the total loss as shown in the railways accounts of £1 193 977 over the whole system before allowing for the recoup from Government subsidy against loss incurred in connexion with the reduction of freight charges for certain classes of agricultural produce.

Mr COOK.—The country lines show the greatest losses.

Mr MENZIES.—They do. This is the irresistible conclusion to be drawn from what the Board says.

Mr TUNNECLIFFE.—The Railway Department said it could prove whatever we wanted it to prove.

Mr OLD.—This may be a rough approximation.

Mr MENZIES.—I am reading what the Board says. In the first place, if I may say so, the Board has had the advantage of a prolonged investigation of this question which has not been enjoyed by any honorable member.

Mr CAIN.—Thank God for that!

Mr MENZIES.—Perhaps the word 'enjoyed' is out of place.

Mr LIND.—The Board did not leave the city. It refused to go into the country.

Mr MENZIES.—I do not know what has come over the honorable member. He was orthodox on this matter last year.

Mr LIND.—I have seen things.

Mr MENZIES.—His heterodoxy has overcome him in the recess.

Lieut-Col. KNOX.—Did the Board go into the country districts?

Mr MENZIES.—I shall answer the inquiry later, for I am now dealing with the question of suburban fares. Paragraph 403 of the report states—

> Upon all the facts, we are satisfied that in the operation of the suburban services there is no loss sufficient to affect the question of transport regulation.

Mr McLACHLAN.—What were the actual losses sustained through the street railways?

Mr CAIN.—The honorable member means Bourke-street trams.

Mr MENZIES.—I mentioned the losses a little while ago, and it is disturbing to have to repeat statements. It is rightly pointed out that any calculation of the losses on the suburban railway services must be in the nature of an estimate; it is not capable of precise mathematical ascertainment.

Mr HYLAND.—The Railway Department does not keep separate figures.

Mr MENZIES.—That is what I shall try to explain if the honorable member is interested. The explanation is this: There are many factors, particularly items on the assets side of a railway system that are common to country and suburban traffic. It is not possible with mathematical accuracy to apportion those items, and to determine how much of the capital expenditure in the suburban radius ought to be attributed to the country services, and how much of the maintenance in the suburban radius should be attributed in the country service.

Sir STANLEY ARGYLE.—In other words the Gippsland line does not stop at Dandenong.

Mr MENZIES.—That is so. I should like to remind the honorable member for Gippsland East that the railway, like any other business, must determine charges with some relation to the volume of business. If there is highly concentrated traffic over the suburban lines, the charges will be different from those made on a 200-miles line running into the country. I was engaged in pointing out that, in a calculation of this kind, because of the difficulties mentioned, there must be assumptions. These assumptions were made and checked by the Auditor-General, and the result brought out satisfied the Transport Regulation Board as being substantially within the limits of probability, and that it is within a reasonable distance of the actual result if it were possible precisely to determine this matter. It is worth emphasizing this because it helps to dispose of the talk that the suburban railway system is being pampered at the expense of the country service. Two honorable members are rather concerned that the Transport Regulation Board did not take evidence in the country. They seem to think that it was a Parthian shot to fire at me. I point out that this Parliament, to which those two members belong, authorized the Board to make a report by a certain date. The general feeling of this Parliament was that if we were going to get a report, we should get it as soon as was reasonably consistent with the proper investigation of the matter. To bring in a report on general principles no Board needs to travel to the country, but when a Board has to determine whether a car should run to Gippsland East or to a particular country district, it must go to that point and investigate the matter on the spot, because it will be a matter of detail. However, on a matter of principle, no Board would be justified in constituting itself a peripatetic body.

Mr LIND.—It was a bit bigger.

Mr MENZIES.—The Board heard a number of witnesses, including 35 from country districts. Among the districts represented by witnesses were Frankston, Lilydale, Ballarat, Omeo, Warburton, Daylesford, Wangaratta, and Yarrawonga. In the circumstances, to contend that the investigation is worthless because the Board did not travel around the country is to fly in the face of one of the most logical and well-considered reports that it has been my fortune to read.

Mr COOK.—Who said the investigation was worthless?

Mr MENZIES.—I am glad to say that the honorable member did not.

Lieut-Col. KNOX.—You are the only person to say that.

Mr MENZIES.—Perhaps not worthless but not so valuable.

Lieut-Col. KNOX.—You are only putting up a bogy and knocking it down yourself.

Mr MENZIES.—The main thing is to knock it down, because it is a poor sort of bogy, anyhow.

The eighth matter—and I refer to this because I have seen some references in the newspapers and some expressions of opinion from some country members regarding it—is the question of railways capitalization. The question of writing down, or should I say transferring, railways capital, is one which is becoming almost a perennial. There are very strong arguments in favour of transferring some portion of the railway capital account to the general Treasury account; but there are also very weighty arguments against that course. That is a matter which deserves the most careful independent consideration on the part of the Government, and which will get it. But you cannot offer any writing down of railway capital as a substitute for transport regulation. That is the point that I wish to make, and it is the only aspect in which this question becomes material, and the Board itself draws attention to that fact in a very interesting chapter of its report, that is headed 'Over-capitalization of Railways'. I recommend the chapter to the consideration of honorable members as containing an acute criticism of the proposals which have been made. In paragraphs Nos. 407, 408, and 411 . . . will be found stated in a convincing fashion the proposition that you cannot avoid transport regulation merely by making some provision for the writing-down of capital. As honorable members know, if we were to write down railway capital by £30 000 000 to-morrow, we would at once and thereafter need to make provision in the railways account year by year for certain charges which had not previously appeared.

Mr Cook.—And the problem would still be there.

Mr MENZIES.—The problem of regulation would still exist.

Mr Cain.—And the interest would still have to be paid.

Mr MENZIES.—The interest would still have to be paid, and that is a matter always worth while remembering, and, I am afraid, sometimes forgotten. Finally, so far as these preliminary observations of mine are concerned, I direct attention to the summary which the Board makes, in paragraph 549 of its report, of the injurious effects of the present unregulated system. They are put very briefly, and I think they are worth recording:—

(1) Uncertainty in business due to instability in transportation charges, both of railways and road motor, combined with discrimination between users of transport with its inevitable unfairness.

(2) Loss of capital by the community caused by the reduction in the earning capacity of the assets of the railways system in State ownership and of commercial motor vehicles in private ownership.

(3) Interference with the correct adjustment of the rates structure of the railways, with consequential loss of State revenue and detrimental effects on primary industries.

(4) Reduced standard of working conditions in the road transport industry.

I am glad to say that the Board has investigated that aspect of the matter.

(5) Increased risk to life and property on and in the vicinity of roads.

Mr Hogan.—Did you read the paragraph about over-capitalization?

Mr MENZIES.—I referred to it by number. I did not occupy the time that would have been involved in reading it, because I have already taken some considerable time in explaining matters, and I did not want to weary honorable members by lengthy citations. I have expressed briefly the views that the Board has put on that question. There is one other matter which the Board mentioned, and which I think is worthy of the attention of a Parliament in Australia. It is mentioned in paragraph 503 and following paragraphs of the report. This question of regulation has something to say to the question of national security and the question of national defence. We must never leave out of sight —as the Board points out—when considering this question, that our railway system in this State is an Australian railway system, and that the material which it calls on, and the man power for which it is responsible, are Australian materials and Australian man power. The motor industry with all the services that it has to perform in this State, is, as the Board has pointed out in language that was grossly misunderstood by somebody a few days later, an exotic—an exotic in the true sense of that word. It depends upon materials which are not native to this country. Its fuel supplies are overseas fuel supplies, and it is worth while having in mind matters of that kind when we are considering the national significance of any particular form of transport with which we may be dealing.

I want to make one more observation before pointing out the clauses in this Bill, and it is this: a good deal of ill-founded criticism has already been engaged in on the assumption that it is proposed to increase the taxation on motor vehicles. A paragraph in the Board's report was torn from its context, and made the subject-matter of those allegations, but the Board, in fact, reported on the question of transport regulation that fees ought to be as far as possible nominal, and that principle has been accepted by the Government in the Bill that I am introducing. It is not proposed to use this measure as a means of taxation. If the general financial policy or position of a State requires that there should be increased taxation upon any subject-matter of taxation, that—I think honorable members will agree—is a proper subject for special legislation, and it is not—as the Board has pointed out—a proper aspect of transport regulation. The result is that it finds no place in this Bill. As honorable members will see, we provide for a fee to be paid by the holder of a licence the fee to be of an ordinary nominal character. An amount is stated in the Bill, a maximum amount of £5; but the proposal is associated with a definite proviso that no more money is to be raised by licence-fees under this legislation than would be necessary to pay for the administration of it. In other words, this is not a revenue-raising piece of legislation.

Steering through a barrage of interjection, the Minister for Railways went on to expound the bill in great detail. It was a tour de force—the performance of a clever man, well-briefed, confident and at the height of his considerable powers. Words with which Menzies once praised the batting of Patsy Hendren could equally well have been applied to himself: 'Not for him a tedious and negative defence letting the runs come, as it were, by inadvertence. His was the defence of attack.' Over forty years later it is not difficult to see why this man saw himself, and was seen by very many of his contemporaries, as destined for a sphere of action wider than Victoria's 56 million acres.

In mid-November 1933, Menzies' colleague, Wilfrid Kent Hughes, jolted the Victorian political world with a series of articles in the Melbourne *Herald* with the title 'Why I Have Become a Fascist'. Disillusioned with the traditional parliamentary system, Kent Hughes argued for greater economic control by the State and streamlining of antiquated electoral and parliamentary machinery. At a weekend conference of Young Nationalists in Healesville on November 26 and 27, Kent Hughes—then President of the organisation—developed his views. Menzies attended, supported by P.D. Phillips, to counter the drift towards 'Fascism'. Brian Penton filed two candid stories in the Sydney *Daily Telegraph*. The first appeared on November 27, under the tendentious title 'Fascist Youth Has Its Say':

> The hundred or so budding politicians—mostly enthusiastic amateurs and all Young Nationalists—who came to this pleasant vale yesterday to decide what was wrong with Parliament, began their diagnosis in fine style.
>
> The ears of politicians all over Australia must have tingled at the outrageous things that were said about them and the Federal member for the local seat of Indi (Mr Hutchinson), who had to listen to it all, sat uncomfortably on the platform in pallid, wretched isolation, a pitiful object to behold.
>
> One Mr Davies had just appealed to our profoundest longings for social improvement, by telling Mr Hutchinson that as there were people who could go to a sewage farm and smell nothing, so there were people who could sit in the Federal Parliament and swear that the atmosphere was sweet as the airs of Healesville.
>
> At that point Mr Robert Menzies (Attorney-General in the Victorian Government and a great force in the Young Nationalist movement) rose, and laid about the critics with a heavy hand.
>
> There was not much wrong with Parliament, he declared, and that put all the embryo Fascists sadly out of countenance.
>
> Mr Kent Hughes, who provided the real motive for the conference by confessing Fascist aims a few weeks ago, tried in vain to rally the young idealists.
>
> ### BEST OF FASCISM
>
> 'I believe we have got sufficient genius to take the best of Fascism and adapt it to our own needs', he said. 'Anyway, if the parliamentarians don't make Parliament efficient some force outside Parliament certainly will.'
>
> The Young Nationalists slept on that, and showed a little more spirit when they resumed under Mr Menzies' eye this morning.
>
> 'Parliament is on its last legs', declared a spirited youngster named Stafford from St Kilda. 'No motion we pass is going to alter that. Executive government is replacing representative government. It's no good talking of putting better men in Parliament when they only become rubber stamps if they get there.

'With half an eye you'll see that the most efficient Governments in the world at this moment are non-democratic: so instead of attempting to reform Parliament we ought to consider seriously with what institution we could displace it.'

IGNORANT MAN

And Mr Stafford went on—

'Talk about the value of committees and boards of experts working in harness with Parliament is waste of time for we know that when experts and politicians conflict (as they do constantly) the politician, usually an ignorant man, always wins.'

Mr Menzies saved all his radicalism for a speech on the relation of government to industry.

'The State's duty, if it finds that prosperity and private enterprise are incompatible', said Mr Menzies, 'is to regulate private enterprise drastically, and even perhaps to eliminate it.'

'We have let unrestricted competition in milk distribution and in transport waste our substance. We have kept farmers inefficiently producing wheat for which there was no market!'

Then came Mr Kent Hughes again.

'Call the principle by which we propose to remedy the situation Fascism, or call it something else', said Mr Kent Hughes: 'the fact remains that we agree.'

And so ended a conference which someone described as 'the first step along the road to Fascism in Victoria'.

On his return to Melbourne, Penton reflected on what he had heard, and the subeditors made amends on November 28 with the headline 'No Mailed Fist at Healesville':

Having seen the Young Nationalists in action and duly pondered their weighty views on affairs in this vale of tears and trouble, I opine that Melbourne need not fear to awake one morning and find Mr Kent Hughes or any of his co-conspirators shaking a mailed fist from the windows of Parliament House. They are not that kind of Fascists.

They don't wear any uniform except plus fours, horn-rimmed spectacles, public school blazers and the lapel badges of their get-together organisations.

They don't read subversive literature or take revolver practice in the back yard.

In fact I doubt very much whether they are Fascists at all. Rather they strike me as young men with high hopes of making a better world, who find that crabbed age, having taken possession of the nicest benches in Parliament, refuses to budge, thus inhibiting their flights of fancy and aspiration.

Most of them do not really think the community could get along without Parliament: they merely think that man would be cheerier, the weather better, and bread cheaper, if there were more Young Nationalists in Parliament.

But they are as timid as two-day kittens, thinking of the forthcoming party meeting at which the Premier, the hard-headed old Scotsman, Sir Stanley Argyle, will no doubt want explanations for the conspiracy of Healesville.

NOT HIDEBOUND

The conference had more the back-slapping atmosphere of what the Americans call a chautauqua than the fanatic purposefulness of a band of revolutionaries. They changed their opinions frequently—were for and against Parliaments, were for and against private enterprise, were for and against the party pastors and masters according to which of their heroes was stamping the rostrum at the moment.

Still it is as well to remember that these youngsters have considerable influence in the Victoria UAP through their groups of ten in each electorate, which have given them a majority in the Government and on the party excutive. Also they have three of the party's outstanding personalities, the arguments of whom will decide whether some muted form of Fascism or Parliamentary reform is to become a party plank in the near future.

The most talkative of these at the conference was Mr P.D. Phillips, a barrister, and a lecturer in modern political institutions at the University.

He is an energetic academic given somewhat to patronising himself out of difficulties, and to exchanging heartly backslaps with his legal confrere, Mr Robert Menzies, another of the triumvirate. . . . Mr Kent Hughes took a back seat at the conference, though his articles on Fascism in the press recently were the motive behind it. He has more commonsense than Mr Phillips, but baulks at following his ideas right down to their burrows.

He hopes that there can be Fascism without dictatorship, with a board of experts and consumers sitting at peace in double harness with Parliament. But if the worst comes he thinks it still will be for the best, and that people will let themselves be regimented to the noble work of the totalitarian state without censorship, secret police, or the suppression of minorities.

CHANGED VIEWS

He is an agreeable fellow, an ex-Rhodes Scholar, a nephew of a High Church canon, and a fervent believer in the good intentions of human kind. . . .

Mr Robert Menzies, Attorney-General in the Victorian Ministry and a leading barrister, is a bird of an altogether different feather.

Political theorising is sheer poppy-cock to him. Being a Minister with probably a career in Federal politics ahead of him, he has no grudge against Parliament.

He has a shiny plump surface, a good bump of self-esteem, and the glib adjustability of a competent advocate. Till recently he was a dyed in the wool Benthamite, and champion of private enterprise, but his Government has had to interfere with transport and milk distribution, and his address to the conference was more a political speech justifying these measures than any probing after fundamentals.

His remedy for any little weakness Parliament might manifest was to abolish Hansard. Plainly he came to the conference to squash a budding enthusiasm roused by Kent Hughes' manifestoes, and with the help of Phillips, succeeded in side-tracking any impulse for quick action into a vague resolution that the discussions at the conference be referred to the executive for report.

One or two of the rank and file thought Parliament was doomed or ought to be, but, otherwise the most revolutionary suggestions for reform were as follows—

National councils for each industry elected by State Governments; standing orders should be altered, Governments to resign only on defeat over no confidence motion; elective Ministries; proportional representation; a council to report to Parliament on each measure, so that politicians should be better informed; only selected second reading speakers; Government by mediaeval guild system; a law to permit Young Nationalists to speak on street corners.

I wondered, listening to them, how much of their zeal would survive six months in Parliament, a cynical view substantiated by the fact that, of the sixteen Young Nationalists in the State House, only three attended the conference.

For several months in early 1934, Sir Stanley Argyle was too ill to perform his duties as Premier. Menzies was Acting Premier until Argyle recuperated from a serious operation and returned in mid-May 1934. The press had predicted widespread dissension over the leadership if Argyle had been unable to resume. And, if Menzies had won, friction between the UAP and Country Party was generally expected. However, Menzies was not confining his interests to Victoria; his ambitions were national, as many observers had long supposed.

Continuing experience and reflection on the federal system convinced Menzies that the growth of central power in the Australian Commonwealth was ineluctable. He believed that there had been a 'silent revolution' in which centripetal forces of self-interest, and defence and economic needs, had been strengthened by judicial interpretation. The financial sovereignty of the Commonwealth—as exemplified by 'the most drastic piece of legislation in Australian history', the Financial Agreement Enforcement Act of 1932, empowering the Commonwealth to appropriate state revenues—implied the subjection of the States. Menzies' analysis of the altered federal balance of power led him to change his mind on industrial law. Early in 1933, he told the Australian Institute of Political Science Summer School that he favoured eliminating the conflict of state and federal jurisdictions by amending section 51 of the Constitution to give the Commonwealth power to legislate generally in industrial matters. This proposal, *The United Australia Review* noted, 'publicly marks the conversion of Mr Menzies to a principle which he has previously opposed'.

In the midst of all the centralising tendencies, Menzies discerned one feature whose consequences were 'extraordinary and anomalous'. Concluding an address to Blennerhassett's Commercial Educational Society of Australasia at the Central Hall, Little Collins Street, Melbourne on 8 June 1932, he had said:

> ... I do not wish to be taken as making a jocular remark about that very unpopular place, but I believe that the creation of a remote Federal capital in Australia ... may have most serious results on the personnel, and consequently upon the prestige, of the Federal Parliament. The power of a Parliament does not depend merely upon the words conferring that power: if I have succeeded in making myself at all intelligible, I will have shown you, I hope, that the power rests far more upon public sentiment than it does upon mere words, and that the centralising of power in a community depends upon something more than the mere form under which the distribution of power occurs. I leave it to this audience to speculate as to how far it is likely that we shall be able to attract to the Commonwealth Parliament the best brains and the best characters year after year: I may say myself that I have the gravest doubts about it. Like many people in Australia, I feel that when in a country like this, which does not possess to any real extent a leisured or a moneyed class, that when you make the scene of Government remote from ordinary human activities, you unconsciously expose it to artificial influences, to unbalanced influences and to very dangerous influences, and that you have a tendency to convert the whole business of government into a profession. I would have no objection to that if we regarded the very great profession of politics as one which calls for cultivation and training, but we do not. We regard it—and there is a great deal to be said for it—as a sort of amateur business, and so long as we do that it will be perfectly clear that to make the seat of Government remote from ordinary human undertakings will have the effect of dissuading many of the best brains we have from engaging in Australian politics at all. That is one very powerful force which may operate against any increase in Federal power. You may have thousands of people who will say—'Yes, as a matter of pure reason, I think the Commonwealth should have the power to do so and so, but as a matter of instinct—while the Parliament is at Canberra I think I will be on on the safe side and keep that power for the States.' I think that the detachment of Canberra may have an anomalous effect: it may mean this—that all those powerful centralising agencies to which I have referred, will have their logical result and will produce accretions of power to the Commonwealth, while at the same time, the existence of

a remote capital will have the effect of diminishing public interest in the people who are exercising that power: so that in a rather paradoxical fashion you may have an increase in power with a diminution of public interest—and I cannot imagine anything more dangerous than that.

'One day in 1934, Menzies found among his letters a personal and confidential letter from the Federal Prime Minister, Joseph Lyons.' In this fairy-tale fashion, one biographer began his account of how Menzies was invited to replace the Federal Attorney-General, Sir John Latham, inheriting Latham's seat of Kooyong as part of the bargain. The official version of this momentous transfer from state to national politics tells us that Menzies declined Lyons' offer. He was concerned at losing contact with his wife and children. He could not afford to move his family to Canberra or to cut himself off from the income he earned at the Victorian Bar. He did not wish to place on his wife the burden of looking after his two sons (one of whom, in particular, had been unwell) and small daughter while he was 'in exile' in Canberra. So he said No.

The reader of Menzies' memoirs may be forgiven for being less surprised at the ensuing dialogue than the author appears to have intended:

> My wife at once said, 'Why on earth did you do that?' I replied that my reason was that I did not want to be cut adrift from her and the children. Whereupon she said, with measured clarity, 'In what place can you give the greatest service to the country; here or in the National Parliament?' Well, there could be only one honest answer to that question and I gave it. 'Right,' said my indomitable wife, 'you'd better ring Mr Lyons up right away, and say that you have changed your mind!'
> And that's how it all happened. . . .

It is curious that Menzies should have so transparently transferred to his wife the responsibility for this decision.

The fact is that Menzies' move to federal politics had long been contemplated by Lyons—and was firmly in Menzies' own mind at least as early as February 1933. The move depended on the retirement of Chief Justice Sir Frank Gavan Duffy who was to be replaced by Latham. In a letter to Stanley Bruce on 20 February 1933, Richard Casey explained that Menzies, with whom he had lunched a fortnight earlier, was expecting to be offered Latham's seat and the Attorney-Generalship when Latham left the Ministry, probably in August. According to Casey, Menzies was pretending to toy with the idea; but Casey believed the offer would be accepted if it came. Menzies continued to play the coquette when Lyons spoke to him a few weeks later about what would happen if Latham left Parliament. Meanwhile, however,

Gavan Duffy unobligingly clung to the Bench. It was not until mid-1934 that Latham, who had been ill, stood down, for reasons 'entirely private in character', to resume his practice at the Bar and wait for Duffy's eventual retirement the following year. Right to the end, Menzies played hard to get. The Melbourne press ran stories of how he would not nominate for Kooyong until 'satisfied on many matters of Federal policy'. *The Age* on July 12 said that his friends were convinced that he would not contest Kooyong. Menzies' views on the immorality of offering bribes for vote-catching purposes were recalled. But the particular issue—a rural rehabilitation scheme involving adjustment of debts at the expense of creditors—trampled on Menzies' known commitment to the sanctity of contracts. The wealthy Senator Sir Walter Massy-Greene had warned the Defence Minister, Sir George Pearce, on July 9: 'I doubt if Menzies is going to be the help to you that some people think he is. Anyway, I think you can make too great a sacrifice to get Menzies.' Massy-Greene saw Menzies as the most intransigent of the group of Melbourne power-brokers of the National Union who were about to negotiate with the Prime Minister on the land valuation and debt adjustment proposals. As he told Pearce on July 14:

> ... I do not know whether you are aware of the fact that Menzies was just as bitter in his opposition to the reduction of interest on bonds as he appears to be in regard to this proposal. That he was utterly wrong in ninetenths of what he said at that time in regard to the bond events have abundantly proved and it may not be out of place to remind him of it. I had a long talk to him on Tuesday night and I told him that I was not fully in the confidence of the government, but I assumed that this debt proposal was only part of a more or less comprehensive plan and I put to him this question—
> I said I assumed, though I did not know, that in some form or other the government proposed to raise the local price of wheat. I asked him what was his answer to the political question which would inevitably be put—'Are you going to let the mortgagee off scot free whilst asking the man on the dole to pay more for his bread?' To that Menzies had no answer, except to say that contracts should not be broken.

Following a conference between Lyons, Richard Casey (the Assistant Federal Treasurer), and Pearce, a compromise was reached, and Menzies was sufficiently appeased to allow himself to be elevated to Canberra.

His departure from state politics was marked by a public audit of his qualities in the magazine *To-day* on 1 September 1934. The writer discerned both great strengths and serious weaknesses:

The Private Ledger
ROBERT GORDON MENZIES
Legislative Assembly, Victoria

CREDIT

With remarkable unanimity the newspaper prophets and quidnuncs are proclaiming Robert Gordon Menzies the coming man in Federal politics. And this, despite the fact that he is not yet a Federal member!

This Victorian barrister-politician, who has just turned 40, has already gone a long way.

He has made the most of his advantages, and they were no slight advantages. He was born with brains, in circumstances that allowed him the best possible education. Appearances, as he grew up, were all in his favor. Beneath his barrister's wig you see the straight features and mobile lips that might have made the possessor a matinee idol. The slight tendency to embonpoint, as he approaches middle-age, is hardly a drawback.

In Australian politics—in any politics—such men are rare.
The father of Robert was James Menzies, formerly MLA for Lowan, in the Western District of Victoria. The boy received the rudiments of education at a State school. Later he went to Wesley College, and to Melbourne University.

A brilliant scholar was this young man. He was also industrious. He took his MA degree with the highest honours in Law. In May, 1918, he was admitted to the Victorian Bar.

Robert Menzies embarked on the difficult and often disappointing profession of a barrister with a fair wind behind him. In University debating societies he was a leading light, and the gift of speech, plus his academic qualifications, made him much sought after by solicitors looking for a likely junior. He was further helped by his association with Owen Dixon, now a High Court Judge, in whose chambers he read for six months.

At an age when most young barristers are wondering what is to happen to them, Menzies was enjoying a large and lucrative practice. He was junior to Owen Dixon in many important High Court cases, and, when his senior went on the Bench, much of the work in which both had been engaged was taken over by Menzies.

His friends and admirers told him he should go in for politics, where he was sure to come to the top. He was quite willing. In 1928 he made his entry by winning a seat in the Victorian Legislative Council. He had hardly arrived there when he was appointed an honorary minister in the McPherson Government.

... he entered the Victorian Legislative Assembly by way of Nunawading, a Melbourne suburban seat with strong Nationalist leanings. A new Cabinet was formed with Sir Stanley Argyle as Premier, and Menzies, at the age of 38, found himself Attorney-General and Deputy-Premier.

He was the youngest man in the Ministry, and, by common consent, the ablest. His prestige as a constitutional lawyer, combined with his platform ability, made him the outstanding figure in Victorian politics.

DEBIT

Appearances count for much in public life. Your undersized, squeaky-voiced man of genius has a hard job to get a hearing. But everyone, whether in court or at a public meeting, was willing and anxious to hear 'Bob' Menzies, because his natural gifts as a speaker were enhanced by the symmetry of his appearance.

That he has in him the makings of a constructive statesman—a man strong enough and far-seeing enough to take a new and unpopular road should the need arise—has not yet been shown.

His path so far has been made easy. He has not had to go without He does not know what it is to wait, and struggle, and strive for the necessities or the prizes of life. He has been associated at the Bar, and in politics, with the moneyed interests of Australia. He is the darling of those prosperous financiers and businessmen who see in the Labour movement only an uncouth manifestation of a force that threatens the comforts and luxuries of the nicest people.

If Menzies is not a snob, he has had every inducement to become one. If he is not one-sided in his outlook; if he can see more in Australia than certain vested interests, it is because he has risen superior to his environment. But has he risen superior to it?

'No man,' said Lord Melbourne on one occasion, 'can be agreeable to his fellow men, or achieve anything worth while, unless he realises that he is a fool.' Against the illimitable background of the unknown, the wisest man is but a stumbler in the dark.

A danger to Menzies' future is a certain intellectual self-sufficiency that tends to make him look down on the rank and file, and, what is far more perilous for a politician, to let them see that he is looking down.

Every politician in Australia, no matter what his creed or party, is dependent on the votes of ordinary people. These ordinary people can respect ability, but they dislike what they consider superior airs. W.M. Hughes could do anything with them in his heyday, because, while he had a lot of ability, he had no superior airs.

Robert Menzies is being rushed forward a little too precipitately. Already he has had several consultations with the Prime Minister, Mr Lyons, and it is an open secret that one of the matters discussed between them is the composition of the next Federal Cabinet.

The electors do not like these arrangements behind their backs.

Another possible hindrance to Menzies is his known objection to composite ministries. If, as is quite likely, the Country Party holds the balance of power in the next Parliament, it is by no means certain that they will fall in with the programme mapped out by Mr Lyons for the Melbourne barrister. It is believed in Melbourne that if Dr Page comes into the new team, Mr Menzies will stay out.

III

AMBITION
AND ASCENT
1934–1940

UNTIL THE GENERAL ELECTION of September 1934, the United Australia Party (UAP) Government had an absolute majority. Menzies campaigned vigorously in Queensland and New South Wales as well as Victoria. His new private secretary, Alfred Stirling, was struck by the number of people seeing his chief in action for the first time who identified his style and manner with that of the former Prime Minister, Stanley Bruce. Menzies' eloquence was not sufficient to stem the erosion of support for the Lyons Government.

The Prime Minister, having lost his absolute majority, announced the composition of a reshuffled UAP ministry on 12 October 1934. Menzies was appointed Attorney-General and Minister for Industry. The Industry Department scarcely existed. It had responsibility for the enforcement of Arbitration Court Awards, and its officers were absorbed into the Attorney-General's Department. Frederick Stewart, although designated Minister for Commerce and Industry, was actually entrusted with the Ministry's employment plan. Senator T.C. Brennan was Minister without Portfolio assisting the Minister for Commerce and was meant to be the real controller of the Commerce Department. Three weeks later, a coalition government was formed, and the Commerce portfolio was transferred to the Country Party leader and Deputy Prime Minister, Dr Page. Brennan remained as Minister 'assisting'.

The Lyons Cabinet at Government House, November 1934

In a press release describing the members of the new federal ministry on 16 November 1934, the Government's official spokesman wrote that the 'Attorney-General and Minister for Industry, Mr R.G. Menzies, is one of Australia's leading barristers. Still a young man, he has combined wide ministerial experience in the Victorian Parliament with a brilliant legal career.' Curiously, it was Menzies' activities and judgement as the Government's senior legal officer which were to cause some of his main difficulties in Canberra. First, however, he was to have the pleasure of making his own interpretation of the Constitution the policy of the Commonwealth. In response to a query from the head of his department, George Knowles, he reaffirmed Latham's restrictive view of the Commonwealth's appropriation power. But he acquiesced good-naturedly in the High Court judgement on the Federal Aid Roads Act of 1926—against which he had argued unsuccessfully for the Victorian Government—which enabled the federal government to make conditional grants to the States under section 96 of the Constitution. Four days later he took the opportunity to concur with the views of Latham on another subject, communism. In a letter to the Prime Minister on 12 November 1934, he concluded:

I agree with the views expressed by my predecessor as to the distinction between violent utterances against the existing order and proceedings which really challenge in a definitely dangerous manner the foundations of government. However reprehensible the former type of utterance may be, it may, during the heat of an election campaign, be ignored, but the government has a definite responsibility to suppress the advocacy of the overthrow of established government by force or violence. The measures taken by the government since 1931 have caused the advocates of communism to pursue their tactics with the greatest caution and reserve and I do not propose the depart from the principles laid down in this regard by my predecessor (Mr Latham).

These neat principles, as enshrined in the Immigration Act, were used by the Government—with the Attorney-General as major spokesman—to justify the exclusion from Australia of the principal guest of the Congress Against War and Fascism, Egon Kisch. The day after Menzies' memorandum was written, the Czech journalist leaped from the deck of the liner *Strathaird* to the wharf at Port Melbourne, breaking his leg. Although he was reputedly proficient in thirteen languages, Kisch was given a dictation test in Scottish Gaelic—a blatant and risible attempt to find a non-political justification for declaring him a prohibited immigrant. Kisch's subsequent perambulations and litigation brought down a torrent of contumely and mockery on the hapless Menzies, who was pictured as an enemy of peace and free speech.

To add to the Attorney-General's discomfiture, a long and complicated parliamentary debate took place on 30 November 1934 on the question of whether the Attorney-General should engage in private practice. The issue was raised ostensibly on the ground that, while he was Victorian Attorney-General, Menzies had represented the Shell Oil Company against the Commonwealth during the Royal Commission on Petrol. Making no concession to the view that a minister might be more selective in his choice of clients, Menzies affirmed the right of the Attorney-General to practise privately. He had, of course, behaved perfectly properly as a state minister appearing against the Commonwealth. But, in this incident, as in many other episodes in his life, there was an abrasive cleverness about his reply. He did not seem able to allow himself to hint at contrition. His strategy was always offensive.

In the 1940s and 1950s Menzies was an ogre figure of the political left. He was depicted as the rich upholder of capitalist tyranny. This bogy image dates back to the days of the Wonthaggi coal strike when he was Minister for Railways. It was inflated by his behaviour over the civil liberties and immigration issues raised in the case of Egon Kisch. And it was further reinforced by his unqualified support of the free enterprise system throughout the depression and its aftermath. Menzies' stern economic orthodoxy was exhibited in his first speech in federal parliament. On 2 November 1934 he told the House that they must not place too much faith in public works for the relief of unemployment: 'We do not advance the easy theory that the present troubles of Australia or of the world are due to monetary factors.'

The Government promised to investigate the causes of unemployment, especially those causes susceptible to direct Commonwealth or concerted federal–state action, drawing from Labor critics the understandable remonstrance that they had already had three years to carry out enquiries. Unabashed, the new Attorney-General drew from his stock of debating perorations a theme he had used before in the university and the state political arena:

> May I conclude by saying something which honorable members may choose to regard as a criticism, but which I choose to regard as a perfectly frank admission. I make it as one who, it is true, is a completely untried member of this House, but has had some experience of both office and opposition in another Parliament. When we are not in office, we all too frequently regard the task of thinking as unnecessary, and, indeed, as irrelevant; and when we are in office we are so busy that we have little time for thinking. The result is that thinking about large problems tends to be discounted, and any government which says boldly in a policy speech or a Governor-General's Speech, 'We propose to think', is at once accused of having idled for years past. I wish to take this opportunity to say, as I suppose it is permissible for me to say, that the members of the Lyons Ministry are to be congratulated.

Menzies, of course, believed that he has capable of thinking even when the pressure of work was heavy. He knew, as a succession of private secretaries—Alfred Stirling, Trevor Heath, Theo Mathew, Peter Heydon, Charles Kevin, Corbett Tritton, and Cecil Looker—learned, that he had the good barrister's ability quickly to assimilate a brief and assemble an argument. John Ewens, who had joined the Attorney-General's Department in 1933 and in 1978 became a member of the Law Reform Commission, remembers: 'Menzies was short, sharp, and to the point, You'd put up a paper . . . and it would come back—"No", "Yes". That was all that would ever be written.' But, outside his office, Menzies characteristically seemed to prefer verbal combat to contemplation. He relished debate; and his style was notable more for its ridicule of opponents than for constructive approaches to current political problems. Sometimes his polemical manner was better demonstrated in correspondence than in more discursive platform orations. A good example is his reply to T.L. McCrohan, a spokesman for The Australian Association of British Manufacturers, who had written in January 1935 a letter protesting about Menzies' purchase of an American car. Menzies devoted about 800 words to demonstrating, with added rhetoric and ridicule, that his Chevrolet was '92% British manufacture', gave more employment in Australia, and was cheaper than any comparable British car. He would, of course, have preferred, if his diminished means had permitted, to buy a more expensive English vehicle.

Four months after his elevation to the federal ministry, Menzies embarked on his first trip to Britain, via Cairo, Rome (reportedly to examine the Italian system of government and if possible—it wasn't—to see Mussolini), and Paris. (In Egypt, Enid Lyons, who was travelling with her husband, was unimpressed with the pyramids which she compared unfavourably with the 'mountains of Kalgoorlie . . . built shovelful

by shovelful by the men who won the riches from the golden mile'.)
Unlike those of his contemporaries whose military service, academic,
or business careers, and other interests had taken them out of Australia
in earlier years, Menzies' knowledge of the world beyond Australia's
shores was all second-hand and third-hand until his forty-first year.
More than any other major Australian political figure of 1935, his
experience was limited, insular, and bookish. His manners and attitudes
had never been subjected to the searing privations of war. He had
escaped the enlightenment of prolonged contact with other races and
nationalities. His picture of England was romantic and literary, un-
clouded by irksome memories of British officers at Flanders and
Gallipoli or British civil servants in London.

On this visit Menzies was too junior to meet the King, but he had
a busy round of official duties and informal engagements. He came into
contact with 'the City'—the London financial community, the bankers
and brokers upon whose calculations of profit so much of Australia's
prosperity seemed to depend.

Menzies met David Lloyd George and, despite total political
disagreement, found himself bewitched by the Welsh wizard. He spent a
weekend with the secretary to the British Cabinet, Sir Maurice Hankey,
finding him 'wise and well informed'. Of Hankey's technique of self-
effacement, he noted 'perhaps History does not take too kindly to that
sort of man'. With Hankey, Menzies met Winston and Clementine
Churchill for the first time on 26 May 1935. Winston, as Menzies never
failed to remember, was floating on his back in a heated outdoor swimming pool: 'After a while he reared himself up, took a piece of cotton
wool out of each ear and, scowling heavily, came ashore.' Tea with
Churchill and General Sir Ian Hamilton, the Gallipoli commander,
was a time to listen to older men's tales. But there were younger men
and fresher subjects, like broadcasting. The Director-General of the
British Broadcasting Corporation, Sir John Reith, had a visit from
Lyons, and Menzies followed a few days later. Reith's memoirs, *Into
the Wind*, based on his voluminous diaries, provide a sympathetic
glimpse, first of the Australian Prime Minister and then of the Attorney-
General in candid mood:

> The Australian Broadcasting Commission was in an unfortunate
> position; he [Lyons] was uncomfortable about the privately owned
> B class stations on which advertising was permitted. He was more
> uncomfortable at the end of the conversation. I said that unless he did
> something now he would be sorry later; the B class stations would
> become so powerful that no one would touch them. He asked if I
> could visit Australia and look into the situation. I suggested that since
> many of the B class stations were press owned and therefore had con-
> siderable political influence behind them this might be an unpopular
> move; they would assume that my recommendations would lead to
> some check on them; if he really wanted me to go I would try to manage
> it, but he had better ask somebody else from England as well—perhaps

someone associated with the press. His attorney-general, Menzies, came to see me about it a few days later. He thought Lyons was putting the cart before the horse in urging me to visit Australia. He himself was apprehensive about the B class stations, but the problems and dangers were not generally understood by the Cabinet. If it were suddenly raised by an announcement of my coming out there was bound to be trouble. A year later Menzies told me I had been quite right about the B class stations getting beyond control. The Postmaster-general had made a fighting speech, but then everyone had got cold feet about the next election, all as foretold; the idea of my being invited to visit Australia had put the wind up people. I asked if they were ever going to deal with the problem. 'No', he said 'we haven't the guts.'

Menzies was one of a large number of Australian ministers in Britain who attended King George V's Silver Jubilee celebrations and held several 'informal' talks with other dominion leaders. The main official purpose of the group was the discussion of British policy on meat imports. The Attorney-General also briefed Wilfrid Greene, KC, who was appearing on behalf of the Commonwealth Government before a Joint Select Committee considering whether or not to receive a petition of Western Australia for secession from the Commonwealth. Menzies personally appeared before the Privy Council in a patent case relating to multi-ply paperbags used for cement—this was a private brief, probably the first time an Attorney-General had taken such a case during his tenure of office.

On 17 May 1935 there was a lunch with Anthony Eden, British Minister for League of Nations affairs, the first meeting of the two men. At Westminster Hall, where he was leading the Australian delegation to the Empire Parliamentary Association, Menzies replied to the toast of 'our overseas colleagues' by the British Prime Minister, Stanley Baldwin. 'Will our Parliaments survive?' he asked:

I believe that they will. No son of the race can stand, as I have had the privilege of standing, on the fields of Runnymede, on the drive of Great Hampden House, in Westminster Hall, whose rafters still ring (if sound be indestructible, as the scientists tell us) with the voices of Cromwell, of Edmund Burke, of Stanley Baldwin, of the great lawyers whose courts for centuries opened out of this room, without realizing with dramatic force that the growth of Parliament is in truth the growth of the British people; that self-government is here no academic theory, but the dynamic power moving through 800 years of national history.

In speeches like this, and at other gatherings—with the Devonshire Club, and with 'Australian' bankers at the Savoy—Menzies made a big impact on the British press. He was widely tipped as a future Prime Minister of Australia. 'Robust, cultured, self-confident', the *Daily Express* said on 23 March 1935; and what is more he 'exercises regularly in a gymnasium'! There was an honour to receive and a pilgrimage to make before the trip was over. He became the only Australian other than Billy Hughes to be an honorary Master of the Bench of Gray's Inn. And he trekked to Aberfeldy and to Weem, Perthshire, 'from which I think my grandfather, Robert Menzies, emigrated to Australia', and was met by members of the Clan Menzies Society (six of them named Robert) and shown the Menzies mausoleum in the old kirkyard.

In a farewell interview in London, Menzies intimated that his experience of 'foreign affairs' in the previous few months had been 'a liberal education'. The lack of interest in foreign affairs in Australia was 'not only discreditable but dangerous'. The chief new thought he had had on imperial matters was the need to pay more attention to inter-dominion problems, and he foreshadowed an intention to explore ways of developing relationships with Canada and South Africa. Two years later, in a Coronation Week speech to the Bendigo Commerce Club, he mentioned that he had attended the 1935 Football Association Cup Final at Wembley Stadium. The behaviour of the crowd fascinated him, especially its reaction to the arrival of the Prince of Wales. The band struck up the national anthem and: 'Everyone of the 93 000 stood up like a shot in one united instinctive act, hats came off, and everybody stood looking dead to the front . . . 93 000 people brought into complete silence when the band was playing "God Save the King".' Taking comfort from what he construed anachronistically as 'instinct which has come down to them over a thousand years . . . the ingrained habits of centuries', he concluded that if he had been 'a Bolshevist' with pamphlets to distribute he would have gone home very depressed.

The return journey to Australia was by way of Canada where Menzies met the Prime Minister, R.B. Bennett, and the Minister of Defence. He discussed problems of American shipping competition in the Pacific, where the heavily subsidised Matson Line had exclusive rights to carry cargoes from Honolulu to San Francisco and other American ports. Having taken pains to brush up his French, with the assistance of the fluent Alfred Stirling, Menzies made a point not only of visiting Quebec and Montreal but of talking to the French-language newspapers. He arrived back in Canberra in September, after brief calls at New York, Washington, Chicago, and San Francisco.

Having seen the world for the first time, Menzies could now speak with greater authority on international and imperial themes. On 6 October 1935, he addressed the Victorian branch of the Australian Institute of International Affairs on the impressions he had gained while he was overseas. On British attitudes to Germany, he had noted that:

. . . there were two points of view existing in or near Whitehall, which in some respects were diametrically opposed. It was interesting to notice that in each case they were expressed with the greatest possible authority, and to wonder how they could be reconciled, and which point of view, if either, would win in the long run. For example, in one quarter there was obviously an intense distrust of Herr Hitler. Indeed, it would not be going too far to say that there was in that quarter a profound conviction that Herr Hitler was working to a set, pre-determined programme, that this reassertion of military, naval, and air power was merely a preliminary to the conducting of offensive operations in two or three years' time in an easterly direction, and that these offensive operations in the east and south-east would in due time be followed by offensive operations in the west, and that any discussions of a friendly kind that Herr Hitler might have with England were merely designed to drive a wedge between British and French opinion and to create the necessary amount of disunity on that western flank of his to make his task of attack in the future a smaller one. I have not the slightest doubt that this point of view at that time was that Germany was the great enemy to be feared, that Herr Hitler was not simply a person who in good faith was seeking to restore the self-respect of the Germans by giving them the amount of armament which would accord with their self-respect, but that he really was aiming at something far beyond that. I several times asked questions, because from my own point of view the whole problem seemed to depend so much on the view one took of Herr Hitler. If he were merely restoring national self-respect in Germany, endeavouring to get rid of that feeling of repression and subjugation which followed on the treaty, then one result might follow. He might, on the other hand, be raising what might turn out to be a Frankenstein. He might be setting out on a deliberate course which was designed to end in war, every detail of which was being planned in the direction of ultimate war.

The English public point of view, which attitude, I think, was very strongly in the direction of the first of those views, that is to say, that you cannot keep a good man down, so as to speak, and that Herr Hitler ought to be treated as acting in good faith until something to the contrary was proved. The result of this divergence of opinion was such as to produce what some people regarded at that time as a certain hesitation in British foreign policy, a very natural hesitation, after all, because under those circumstances what any English foreign minister would seek to do would be, as a member of the Cabinet put it to me just before I left England, to keep the whole position as fluid as possible, in order to prevent it crystallising in any unfortunate way as between groups and sections.

Another subject on which Menzies developed his thinking while he was away was what he called, in an article published in *The Australian Quarterly* for December 1935, 'The Relations Between the British Dominions'. He confessed that he now had a better understanding of why the Balfour Declaration of 1926 which stated that Britain and the Dominions were autonomous, united by their allegiance to the Crown, and freely associated in the British Commonwealth, was regarded as so important by Canada and South Africa. Canada's French-Canadian minority and the 'constant lateral thrust' of American influences made a formal declaration of independent self-government appealing to the Canadian mind. As for South Africa, Menzies believed that the Balfour resolutions had 'converted General Hertzog from being the active leader of a separatist and republican movement into being a friend of Great Britain and a loyal adherent of the British throne'. While recognising that acknowledged independence may have helped to stabilise and reassure Canadian and South African public opinion, Menzies did not mask his own belief that the passing of the Statute of Westminster 'has almost completed a process of organic disintegration'. Many Australians, he said, regretted it as 'unnecessary and legalistic'. What did Australians think of their relationship with Great Britain? Characteristically, he described Australian sentiment in a way that was implicitly prescriptive:

> My own view is that the average Australian is well content to be closely associated with Great Britain and is not inclined to devote very much attention to considering the exact legal status of his own Government. He believes in Great Britain; he believes in the British Empire; he finds any reference to the 'British Commonwealth of Nations' something of a mouthful and not altogether self-explanatory; he knows that in the last resort Great Britain will not seek to interfere in the domestic problems of Australia; and he is normally quite content to leave it at that.

In Parliament on 9 October 1935, Menzies affirmed that one thing had definitely not been set aside by the Balfour Declaration and the Statute of Westminster—'our common allegiance to the common Crown'. Foreshadowing the view he was to take in September 1939 when war erupted in Europe, he asked: 'How is it possible, with one king who makes peace or war, for the Crown to be at war in relation to Great Britain, and at peace in relation to the Commonwealth of Australia?' Menzies ridiculed the notion that one king could be at peace and at war at the same time. Professor Berriedale Keith had said, in his latest work on the subject, 'For a dominion to declare its neutrality in a war to which the British Crown is a party would be tantamount to secession'. 'This', said Menzies, 'entirely represents my own considered view.'

There were other areas in which Menzies had, by the mid-1930s, a 'considered view'. He was firm in his support for the basic economic structure of the country. Notwithstanding the cataclysmic upheaval of the depression, he saw no reason to believe that increased government intervention would materially assist economic recovery. His attitude to business in the post-depression years was summed up in a defence of the Broken Hill Proprietary Company, to which his father had been a consultant, in Parliament in October 1935. By then economic recovery, especially in manufacturing industry, was well under way, although unemployment remained at 300 000. And only about 55 000 of the unemployed were on relief work rather than the dole. When Labor spokesmen attacked BHP for making excessive profits and ill-treating its employees, Menzies had nothing but praise for its 'superb management'. When the militant left-wing leader, J.A. Beasley, complained that BHP took its profits out of Australia, Menzies answered without hesitation: 'I like to see companies profitable; the more prosperous they are, the better.' He went on to admit what great entertainment he had when the names of shareholders in companies were read out by witchhunting Labor MPs—the entertainment was so great 'because I hear so many names of my friends read out'.

Until December 1935, the position of Deputy Leader of the United Australia Party, which had been vacated by Sir John Latham, remained unfilled. Lyons had intended to promote Menzies' candidature—and, according to Dame Enid Lyons' testimony, his original plan was 'after a short term of office' to step down as Prime Minister in Menzies' favour. However, New South Wales' interests backed the Minister for Defence, Sir Archdale Parkhill, for the deputy leadership; and it was reported that Menzies would not seek the position although he would accept it if this were the general wish. By late 1935 the balance of forces had altered. The field of candidates had been restricted to ministers, thereby excluding the popular South Australian ex-minister, Charles Hawker, and W.M. Hughes, who had been forced to resign a month earlier because of controversy surrounding publication of a book he had published on defence and foreign affairs. After a preferential ballot, Menzies defeated Parkhill, with R.G. Casey and T.W. White trailing.

Menzies returned to England early in 1936. During this visit, he cemented a friendship with the British Foreign Secretary, Anthony Eden. When Eden was much troubled by Britain's acquiescence in Mussolini's conquest of Abyssinia, he found in Menzies a sympathetic companion. In *The Eden Memoirs:* 'Facing the Dictators', Lord Avon remembered dining with the visiting Australian Attorney-General one evening in mid-June 1936. Menzies 'gave a vigorous report of the backing which was being given to me in the Dominions. He begged me not to worry unduly, but to go ahead confident that I should get fair support for a decided line.' Notwithstanding these comforting words, Eden remembered that 'such reflections did not prevent these days from being very unhappy ones for me'.

Eden may not have recalled when he wrote his memoirs that Menzies had told an all-party meeting of MPs in London on 20 May 1936 that sanctions against Italy should be dropped—they were not helping Abyssinia, and 'nations are not yet ready to fight for an idea'. This rugged realism was also exhibited in a defence of Australian tariff barriers; although London was a fairly safe place to say that a policy of preference to Britain was in no sense an expression of hostility to Japan. At Whitsun, Menzies stayed with Lord Swinton, with whom he continued discussions on an imperial airmail scheme. Australia reluctantly accepted a British plan to use seaplanes around the Australian coastline, instead of using local flights over land.

Troublesome as the international scene may have been, it did not prevent the Australian Attorney-General from enjoying the society and scenery of Britain. A weekend with the Scottish Conservative MP, W.S. Morrison, led to a chance meeting with the whimsical J.M. Barrie. Menzies thought that the handsome and eloquent Morrison would some day be Prime Minister. (He became Speaker of the House of Commons and at Menzies' invitation, Governor-General of Australia.)

In a series of articles published in the Brisbane *Courier-Mail*, 9–15 July 1936, Menzies commented on the Englishman ('he is the most civilized and I believe the wisest man in the world'), the Englishman's dress ('sartorially the drabbest'), the beauties of the Cotswolds hills and villages ('the average inland Australian village of comparable size would exhibit all the rawness of wooden houses and iron roofs, dust and bustle, and a dry sweep of plain beyond'), the haunting charm of Hadrian's Wall, and the secret of London's architectural distinction, Portland stone.

As if to give the lie to those who were to say that he had been overwhelmed by the English, fatally entranced by aristocratic hostesses and majestic buildings, Menzies injected both humour and sensible warnings about British oddities and afflictions. As he described English institutions and customs, their dominating characteristic was anachronism—bathrooms without showers, kitchens without refrigerators, butchers' shops with glassless windows, and itinerant milk vendors. And as for the kind of black felt hat worn by Londoners, including his new friend Anthony Eden, it was 'first worn by undertakers' representatives and practising members of the Black Hand'. In education, a subject in which a life-long interest was gathering momentum, he found Winchester a fine public school; but he observed that there were 'too many narrow chests and round shoulders in England'. And the 'old school tie' was, he thought, over-exploited—a subtle qualification from a man who frequently invoked the 'public school spirit'.

The English were unpredictable and eccentric in some ways. Nevertheless, their 'moral philosophy' was supreme, and they were 'of our own blood. And we can't say more than that, can we?' One thing Menzies could and did say, in an article for London's *Daily Telegraph* on 15 June 1936 was that the British must 'rid themselves of any lingering old-fashioned idea that "these colonials" are inferior persons of aboriginal habits and outlook and deplorable manners, whose true function is that of being the hewers of wood and drawers of water for their more favourably placed relatives in the British family.' The sentiments were refreshing, although the language could have been better chosen.

The main purpose of Menzies' trip was to appear before the Privy Council on behalf of the Commonwealth Government. The case related to the legality of joint federal–state marketing schemes for primary products. The Privy Council ruled that the schemes were incompatible with section 92 of the Constitution. As a consequence, the Lyons Government sought to gain a full Commonwealth trade and commerce power, but failed to secure the necessary majorities at a referendum

in 1937. Menzies' Privy Council appearance was notable not merely
because he lost the case but because of a parliamentary debate on the
propriety of his having accepted a simultaneous brief from the Victorian
Government.

Labor speakers, led by the barrister, Maurice Blackburn, and
including John Curtin, argued that Menzies was in breach of section
45 of the Constitution. He was, they said, receiving indirectly a fee of
£2000 for services rendered to the Commonwealth, thereby contravening
section 45 and rendering his parliamentary seat vacant. Both Billy
Hughes and Lyons defended their absent colleague. Hughes, in particular, seemed to enjoy the opportunity to rebut statements that 'reflect
grossly upon the personal character of my colleague, holding him up
as a grasping and avaricious man who is ready to sacrifice public
interests for his own pecuniary gain'. Although the Labor Party pressed
the matter to a division, they did not pursue it further.

Menzies returned to Australia on the *Strathaird*. One of his fellow
passengers between Marseilles and Bombay was a stowaway duck.
Refused permission to disembark at Malta, Port Said, Port Sudan,
and Aden, the duck's prospects were bleak. The Australian Attorney-
General was asked for a legal ruling on whether it could be landed in
Australia. The opinion offered was 'too evasive to be comforting', a
travelling companion later remembered. And Donald, as he had inevitably been christened, was put ashore at Bombay more decorously
than Egon Kisch had made landfall at Fremantle from the same ship
two years earlier.

The Attorney-General's portfolio gave great scope to an ambitious
and able minister. There were legal and constitutional aspects to a
large part of government business. Menzies, therefore, had a basis for
intervention on most issues that interested him and many that did not.
He was usually appointed to Cabinet committees set up to draft official
statements or legislation on trade and foreign affairs as well as domestic
subjects. The 1935 Cabinet minutes show him involved in considering
Empire Air Schemes, the Administration of the Transport Workers'
Act, National Insurance and Employment, the parliamentary rights
of the member for the Northern Territory, as well as reporting himself
on problems relating to section 92 of the Constitution. In 1936 he was
discussing shipping competition in the Pacific, Farmers Debts Adjustment Acts, Terms of Employment, section 92 again, the League of
Nations Covenant, the New Hebrides, a prohibited migrant (Mrs
Freer), Wool, the Tenure of Justices of the High Court (contrary to
the stand he was to take in 1977, he advocated a constitutional amendment to have federal court justices retired at the age of 72), tariffs on
motor cars, patents, and the Statute of Westminster. The agenda for
1937 included such topics as the Meat Agreement with Britain, alleged
unrest in the Navy (he was deputed to warn the chairman of the Newspaper Proprietors' Association that 'action would be taken' if inaccurate
press statements were repeated), problems of newsprint manufacture,

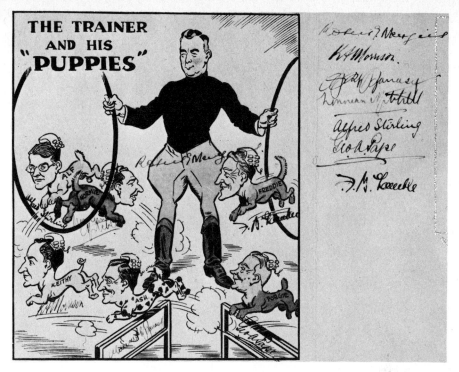

Menzies and his former pupils: Keith Morrison, Maurice Ashkanasy,
Norman Mitchell, Alfred Stirling, George Pape, Frederick Gamble,
illustration from a dinner menu, 7 February 1936

shipping rates, Mrs Freer again, the Inter-state Commission, and
Darwin Cyclone compensation. Next year he was confronted by 'the
case of Mrs Freer', Trade Diversion, Secondary Industries Research,
Dutch Air Mail, Waterside Workers' employment, Qantas Airways
Agreement, Immigration Policy, Tenants' Rights in Canberra City
Leases, and the Government's election policy speech. From this by no
means exhaustive inventory, one Cabinet submission—recommending
an inquiry into the desirability of reduced hours of work—stands out
for its constructive, if cynical, approach:

DEPARTMENT OF INDUSTRY

HOURS OF LABOUR.

1. Before dealing specifically with the point on which Cabinet has
asked me to submit a recommendation. I desire to point out that there
appears to be a misconception in some quarters concerning the industrial powers of the Commonwealth.

The Dominion of Canada has recently passed laws designed to
carry out the provisions of Treaties and Conventions, even when the
subject matter of those Treaties or Conventions is one normally a
matter for the provincial legislatures and not for the Dominion Parliament. Because of this, some people have suggested that the Commonwealth of Australia might directly control working hours by ratifying
the I.L.O. Conventions and then legislating for their effectuation. I
want to make it clear that the domestic jurisdiction of the Common-

wealth of Australia is not enlarged by any Treaty or Convention to which it may become a party. There is no express power in the Commonwealth Constitution, as there is in the Canadian, to pass laws for the carrying out of Treaties ... Except in relation to inter-State and overseas trade, the Commonwealth's only jurisdiction is through the Commonwealth Arbitration Court, which cannot competently be directed by the Commonwealth Parliament as to what working week it is to adopt as a standard or in any particular case. In a sense, therefore, any inquiry by the Commonwealth may be said to be unreal, since the only legislatures who have power to legislate directly upon the subject of working hours in Australia are the State Parliaments, and these Parliaments may quite possibly take little notice of a Commonwealth inquiry not instigated or participated in by themselves. Nevertheless, if the Commonwealth is to give a lead on what is undoubtedly a matter of first-rate national importance, it should conduct an inquiry, presenting the results of that inquiry either to the State Parliaments for their guidance or to the people of Australia with a request for the extension of the Commonwealth's industrial powers.

2. For a great many years the world-wide agitation for the reduction of working hours was avowedly based upon considerations of health; the forty-eight hour week was evolved as something which came very close to the standard at which the exhaustion of the worker was reduced to a reasonable minimum. My personal view is that any case for the reduction of working hours below forty-eight per week (except in the case of special classes or occupations) must rest not upon considerations of health but upon other and modern economic and social considerations. As I see the problem, any up-to-date consideration of this question in Australia must take into consideration the significance of hours of labour in relation to—

(a) *Employment and unemployment.* Will a greater volume of employment be possible if hours generally are reduced? Will a shortening of hours by compelling business economies, still further encourage the tendency to mechanisation, and so aggravate the unemployment problem rather than cure it? Has there been such a rapid improvement in the mechanical arts that some re-distribution of the world's work in point of time is inevitable?

(b) *Increased leisure.* Should not the harnessing of natural forces render a greater amount of leisure for mankind both natural and desirable? Is increased leisure a good thing? What steps is the community taking to provide facilities for the rational use of leisure?

(c) *Costs of production.* Will wages be reduced with reduced hours? If they are not, what will be the effect on costs of production? What will be the effect of this on the Australian consumer? Do these factors outweigh any positive advantages which may be found to result from a reduction of hours?

(d) *The export industries.* What will be the effect on these industries of any added costs through reduction of hours? To what extent will our capacity to compete in the foreign markets be affected? Is it possible to reduce hours in Australia without regard to what may be done elsewhere, particularly in competing countries?

(e) *Tariff protection.* Can increased costs in Australian industries be provided for by increased protection? What will be the effects of such increased protection on the Australian economy?

(f) *Exchange.* Will it become necessary to deal with any of the results that may be arrived at under previous headings by further raising the exchange rate? What will be the results of such action?

3. If it is decided to conduct an investigation into these and many other related matters which will suggest themselves, I recommend that the terms of reference to the inquiring body should be as wide as possible; for example, "to inquire into and report upon the question whether any and what general reduction of working hours in Australia is desirable and/or practicable, having regard to the social economic and national interests of Australia as a whole".

4. I suggest that this inquiry should not be conducted by a Royal Commission of the ordinary peripatetic kind. My experience of Royal Commissions is that for the most part they are extremely slow, unduly expensive, and afford a much too easy rostrum to cranks and self-seekers. I therefore recommend that the inquiry should be by a Committee of a relatively expert kind . . . it should, in my opinion, include—

The Chief Judge of the Commonwealth Arbitration Court;
Some Judge or officer representing State Industrial Tribunals;
Two manufacturers;
Two primary producers;
Two representatives of employees in manufacturing industry;
Two representatives of employees in rural industry;
A Commonwealth Treasury Officer;
An economist;
A medical man;
A housewife;
A customs officer.

5. The Committee would need to be armed with efficient secretarial assistance and would have access to the mass of printed material which already exists on this subject. Some provision would need to be made for fees, particularly in the case of employees' representatives who may lose wages. The Committee should be given power to control its own procedure subject to a direction that, as far as possible, the Conference method should be followed, that the sittings should normally be held in camera, and that witnesses should be called only in special cases.

Robert G. Menzies.
Minister for Industry.
20th November, 1935.

Cabinet accepted Menzies' proposal, and the appointment of Chief Judge Dethridge of the Arbitration Court was announced. John Curtin, for the Labor Party, indicated a lack of enthusiasm for an inquiry that seemed like a device to justify inaction. The Ministry refused to meet demands by the Australian Council of Trade Unions and the Australian Workers' Union for larger representation in the proposed conference. The unions refused to participate, and late in April 1937 Lyons announced that the conference would be abandoned. In Menzies' absence overseas, Labor moved an inevitably unsuccessful censure motion on the Government. R.G. Casey announced that the Commonwealth Government would ratify the 40-hour convention adopted by the 1935 session of the International Labour Conference if and when it was ratified by the States. In July 1937, Menzies robustly condemned the ALP's policy of a 40–hour week as 'a piece of pure political humbug'. It was, he concluded, the task of the Arbitration Court, not the Government, to fix hours.

As Attorney-General, Menzies had no specific responsibility for initiating welfare legislation or for developing economic policy. In December 1935, however, he was appointed a member of a Cabinet sub-committee, with R.G. Casey, Archdale Parkhill, and H.C. Thorby, to examine proposals for a scheme of national insurance. But when Lyons, following a pre-election pledge in 1934 of a national housing scheme in conjunction with the States and local government, proposed that the Commonwealth should play a part in the provision of low-cost housing, Menzies evidently pronounced that the federal government had no power to do so. Dame Enid Lyons recalls:

Joe was very keen to establish a Department of Housing . . . He was spending a Sunday in Sydney [in July 1936] and he used to see a great deal of Tom Murray who was a friend of his—a very outgoing sort of extrovert, not the sort of person that normally you would have thought Joe would have taken to, but this man, he was just overflowing with the milk of human kindness, and he was associated with politics. But . . . he spent the Sunday with Tom. Well, Tom Murray's Sunday began, he'd go to Mass, he was a Catholic, then he'd start off on a round of his old friends who were in trouble, and there were people there, Joe said, from way back in the days when Tom was desperately poor . . . his father died when he was 12, and he took over the earning for the family, his mother had several children beside himself, and he'd made a wealthy man of himself . . . If he knew of any of those in trouble in Sydney, Joe said, he went to hospitals. They went to . . . a sanitorium for tuberculosis [Boddington Chest Hospital, Wentworth Falls, New South Wales] and he said in a letter to me: 'I believe inadequate housing is at the root of it all.' There were young girls there, 'now wrecks with scarcely a hope'—they'd come mainly you see from the slums of Sydney. He said 'That is something I want to establish.' But Bob Menzies said that it was unconstitutional, it was constitutionally not possible . . . and Joe, respecting his opinion as a constitutional lawyer, didn't go further with it. And of course, don't forget he'd probably be the only one in the Cabinet with that view.

If Lyons was, in some ways, a subdued radical, his Attorney-General was a wavering conservative. His passion for liberty and legality, combined with a sense of the ridiculous, could lead him to overturn the Minister for Customs' banning in 1936 of the works of Marx, Engels, and Lenin. He stayed the hand of those of his colleagues who wanted to ban the Communist Party—merely expressing Communist opinions should not, he insisted, be made an offence. The more Menzies thought about the powers of the federal government, the more convinced he became that many of the Constitution's impediments to national action had to be removed. These stirrings of vision were possibly invigorated by the widening horizons of overseas travel and the additional minister-ial responsibilities he enjoyed as Acting Treasurer and Acting Minister for External Affairs when his colleagues were absent. Still, for all the maturing of political grasp and conviction, Menzies seemed to be im-prisoned within an image of aloof superiority, of contempt for his

Murdoch's marionettes—the Lyons government as seen by Stan Cross of
The Argus, ca 1936

associates and opponents. The Melbourne *Herald,* commenting on a parliamentary incident, in which he had said he did not have the time to explain to a member what could readily be studied in textbooks available in the library, said on 12 November 1936 that a reputation for flippant, witty, smartness in public life was never preferable to one for 'unalloyed sincerity and earnestness'. Stung by the imputation that he lacked sincerity and earnestness, Menzies protested to Keith Murdoch that the article was defamatory. The flurry subsided, but the behaviour that was at the root of the trouble was not significantly abated.

Politics was not everything to Menzies. In an Australian Broadcasting Commission radio broadcast in October 1942 he admitted that 'in the days before the war no visit to Sydney was complete for me without a precarious perch and half an hour's good talk among the impedimenta in Norman Lindsay's studio; a dinner with a notable host, with Lionel Lindsay, Syd. Ure Smith, Charles Lloyd Jones and Will Ashton for good measure'. In a preface to a book on the life and work of Ashton, published in 1961, he said: 'for the whole of my adult life I have been in a small way a collector of Australian art'. He had also sought to ensure that his fellow Australians would be aided in their judgement of contemporary painting and sculpture by the establishment of an Academy of Art. Thus, in endorsing artistic conservatism and seeking to combat what he was later to call 'the spurious and the merely fashionable', he managed in 1937 to stir up more heat and expostulation on the subject of art than on any piece of legislation or national policy pronouncement. A book by Adrian Lawlor, obscurely titled *Arquebus,* chronicled the beginning of the controversy:

QUININE

Mr R.G. Menzies, being invited by Mr James Quinn, the liberal-minded (if Royal-Academical) President of the Victorian Artists Society, to 'open' the Society's 1937 annual show, saw fit on that occasion to ease his chest of certain 'humours' concerning the goodness of the art of the past, the badness of the art of to-day, the desirability of officialdom in art, the excellence of art-academies in general and the implied benefits that would accrue to art and artists in Australia by the establishment of an academy of the kind in this country.

Now it happens that Mr Quinn, who has had the advantage of long residence in Europe, had invited the Melbourne Contemporary Art Group to send their work to this exhibition. Thus an entire wall of the Gallery pullulated with pictures in the modern manner; and some, if not all, of the painters of these pictures were present among an audience that found itself being exhorted by Mr Menzies—at least by obvious implication—to look with favour on *this* picture and with abhorrence on *that.* Mr Quinn thereupon sprang to his feet and delivered himself with un- or at least extra-presidential emphasis in repudiating any sympathy that he might be construed by the unwary as harbouring for these sentiments; which gesture stands, in the circumstances, doubly to his credit as a man and as an artist. Now this must have been a dramatic moment; and I could wish that I had been considered important enough to have been sent an invitation to be present.

The 'Argus' report of the proceedings (discreetly 'subbed') makes light enough of what must after all be considered an historic event.—

Argus, April 28.—

Mr Menzies was introduced by Mr Quinn. 'You all know,' Mr Menzies said, 'of the proposal to form an Academy of Art in Australia. I must admit that I was the prime mover in this idea. I feel definitely that some authority and body should be formed here as in other countries. Every great country has its art academy. They have set certain standards of art and have served a great purpose in raising the standard of public taste by directing attention to good work.

'This exhibition indicates that the Victorian Artists Society is encouraging people in every type of painting,' Mr Menzies said. 'Experiment is necessary in establishing an academy, but certain principles must apply to this business of art as to any other business which affects the artistic sense of the community. Great art speaks a language which every intelligent person can understand. The people who call themselves modernists today talk a different language.' . . .

Mr Menzies no doubt thought that this was the end of the matter. . . . He had, in short, done his bit for society and the sort of art that society (especially Colonial society) is accustomed to—and was there anywhere a worm that would dare?

Well, there was. Mr Norman Macgeorge looked at his 'Argus', took another look, transmogrified himself into a splendid worm—and turned.

Here is his letter to the Editor:—

Argus, May 1st.—

Sir,—Mr R.G. Menzies, at the opening of the Victorian Artists Society's exhibition of pictures on Tuesday night, made a comparison between the traditional school of painting and the so-called 'modern' movement, and said that it was a pity that the modernists did not use a language that the public could understand. Mr Menzies, as everyone knows, does not approve of 'modern' art, and the 'Royal Australian Academy', of which he admits the paternity, is obviously intended as a disciplinary measure to those whose conception of art is not his, and not the conception of those artists whose works he would doubtless have us all emulate, and after whose names a string of letters will assure the public that it is getting the only genuine article. Does Mr Menzies think, then, that art should be non-progressive, and that we should forever be content with representational painting? Is there no room for the 'modern' artist who disdains the well-worn paths and seeks to express what he thinks rather than what he sees? I have before me a set of illustrations in black-and-white and colour of an exhibition of Canadian art which, after a tour of the other British Dominions, will be sent to Australia. The funds for this enterprise have been provided by the Carnegie Corporation

of New York, under the terms of the British Dominions Fund, and the
exhibition is being sponsored by the National Gallery of Canada through its
director, Mr Eric Brown. The pictures to be sent are all of the 'modern'
variety that apparently Mr Menzies so cordially dislikes, and it will perhaps
surprise him to find that most of their painters write R.C.A. (Royal Canadian
Academy) after their names.—Yours, etc.,
Norman MacGeorge.

This was a very courteous worm. Nevertheless it had definitely
turned.

ACADEMIC

Even so, the matter might have been allowed to lapse here and be
forgotten within a day or two at most, if—prompted by that evil genius
Lucifer alone knows—Mr Menzies had not given vent in the 'Argus'
on the following day to a further spate of opinionative 'blah'.
My *Argus* cutting for May 3rd reads:—

The Federal Attorney-General (Mr Menzies) repudiates the suggestion
that he supported the formation of a Royal Australian Academy 'as a disciplinary measure to those whose conception of art is not his'.

'Mr Macgeorge has been misinformed about the object of the proposed
Australian Academy', Mr Menzies said yesterday. 'It is true, however, as
Mr Macgeorge claims, that I find nothing but absurdity in much so-called
"modern art", with its evasion of real problems and its cross-eyed drawing.
It is equally true that I think that in art beauty is the condition of immortality
—a conclusion strengthened by an examination of the works of the great
European masters—and that the language of beauty ought to be capable of
being understood by reasonably cultivated people who are not themselves
artists.

'I realise that an academy should find room in its membership for all schools
of artistic thought provided they are based on competent craftsmanship',
Mr Menzies said. 'So much do I realise this truth, which I take to be the basis
of Mr Macgeorge's letter, that at the outset when mentioning the academy
idea to a committee of artists, I stipulated that I would take no steps to further
it unless this principle were adhered to.

'The published list of those invited to join the proposed academy is the
best proof that this principle has been followed', Mr Menzies said. 'The list
was selected by artists of the highest standing. My only function has been,
and is, as an uninstructed lover of fine painting and drawing, to do as much
as I can to help obtain for Australia the benefits of an artistic organisation
which has been invaluable in England.'

Now the formation of an academy *is* 'a disciplinary measure', and
it is in this sense that Mr Menzies referred to it in his address at the
V.A.S. private view.

'I was the prime mover in this idea', he said. In short—and it
couldn't be shorter—he *is* the Academy . . .

PROBLEM

I notice, though, that Mr Menzies, takes delicate care not to name
specific names when traducing modern painters; as when, for instance,

he says: 'I find nothing but absurdity in much so-called "modern art", with its evasion of real problems and its cross-eyed drawing.'

Does he refer to Cezanne here?

(I once, as a mere juryman, saw Mr Menzies blast away the craftily-built tissue of his legal opponent's twelve-hour argument, reduce the defendant to a heap of untidy rubble, shatter absolutely the morale of 'the lady' and pulverise the whole case to flying splinters, all within the quarter of an hour. But the really extraordinary thing about this exhilarating display was that it was entirely impromptu—'the lady' herself having unwittingly given him the lead by the spiteful ejaculation of one small and quite irrelevant word. I wonder if Mr Menzies will remember the word—'wig'?).

Is it possible, then, that a mind that is brilliant in one direction can be merely obtuse in another—can look, for instance, at a Cezanne and see nothing but 'evasion' where the setting—to say nothing of the working out—of the 'problem' was sufficient to bring any painter with knowledge enough to read the canvas, down to his two humbled knees?

Or is he by any chance thinking of Picasso?—But Picasso has kept a whole world on tip-toe during these thirty years with problems posed and problems solved and new problems sought, found, cleared up and flung in the discard, until it is no mere hyperbole to say that he carries in his paint-box more problems than all the other painters in the world lumped together. Problem, problem? What *does* Mr Menzies mean?

One observes, moreover, that in the same breath he speaks of himself as 'an uninstructed lover of fine painting and drawing'. But since Cezanne was the first painter of his time and Picasso is the greatest living draughtsman, and these two men, each in his age, are the main founts of 'modernism', and only a painter can fully understand the qualities of the one, only a draughtsman the qualities of the other, and Mr Menzies is, on his own admission, 'uninstructed', and . . .

MARVELLOUS

Mr Menzies's 'conclusion', as he calls it, that 'in art beauty is the condition of immortality', finds me all complaisant and agreeable; but when he adds that this conclusion of his was 'strengthened by an examination of the works of the great European masters', I can only marvel at him. For how many months, pray, was he in Europe? . . .

As to his dictum that 'beauty should be comprehensible to all', he is, of course, on extraordinarily difficult, not to say dangerous, ground here. I shall consider this complex question in more detail elsewhere . . . contenting myself meanwhile with one modest repique: Beauty *is* comprehensible to all—which is precisely why we all of us argue about it.

Further contributions that flowed in from well-known artists, self-advertisers, the anonymous and the pseudonymous (including 'Aubrey Beardsley Epstein', who quoted with approval the remark of a gentleman

'Even if it were good I wouldn't like it') added to the merriment of an inconclusive debate. Menzies' Academy, although it was not extinguished at birth, never achieved the commanding position its title suggested.

Menzies' caution, if not his conservatism, was further evidenced in mid-1937. The Government had many of its members overseas in 1937— so many that the Acting Prime Minister, Dr Page, cabled Lyons on May 13 that 'sickness or absence of one will make it impossible suspend standing orders. Think you should expedite return home of some of our men at earliest possible moment.' No one came home early. But the Opposition agreed to grant two months' supply, sufficient to last until Parliament met again at the end of August. On July 3 Page reported to Lyons who was returning to Australia on board RMS *Orford*:

> Session completed and we establish from the beginning moral superiority over opposition who went away much depressed. Sydney men especially have completely lost defeatist attitude which distinguished them last month stop Stewart now satisfied with government policy and in fact urged early election while we are in the boom.

This news heartened Lyons, who was further pleased with the announcement by Menzies, as Acting Treasurer, of a budget surplus. But pleasure at the good figures was dampened by Menzies' beam-wireless message to the ship-bound Prime Minister: 'Strongly urge you not to make any observations on last year's results which would commit you to any particular policy.' Worried about pension payments and the costs of a possible new scheme of national insurance, Menzies evidently feared promises, or even hints, of benefits that could not be delivered.

Lyons waited until late October before holding an election. The campaign was notable, among other things, for a revealing exchange in a meeting at Balwyn on October 8, where Menzies was asked: 'Can Mr Menzies point to one particular bill passed during the last three years of any great benefit to the people?' He replied:

> I believe the real services a Government performs are of an administrative order. Arrangements made in relation to the export of mutton, lamb and beer from Australia in the last few years are worth literally millions of pounds.

The audience, dissatisfied with his classic credal conservatism, chorussed the destination of this revenue: 'To Angliss!' (the meat millionaire). The wider electorate was also disenchanted with the government. The United Australia Party lost four seats; the Country Party gained one, and obtained an extra seat in the Cabinet. Early counting of votes in Kooyong went so badly against Menzies that he feared the loss of the seat. His majority of nearly 16 000 was slashed to 1600. In a private letter of 17 November 1937 to Stanley Bruce in London, Richard Casey

TO LONDON AGAIN, The Argus, *23 March 1938*

attributed Menzies' 'very close go' to the fact that people had 'the idea that he has a contempt for the average man, and they don't like it.' Thirty-five years later, in a letter to Dame Enid Lyons, Menzies admitted that the election made him realise that 'for three years I had been largely an absentee on the business of the Nation and that I must keep in better touch with my constituents'. In the post-election reshuffle, Menzies remained as Attorney-General and Minister for Industry.

In March 1938 Menzies once again set off for Britain, this time to discuss immigration and revision of the Ottawa trade pact. His travelling companions included Dr Page and T.W. White. Page later recalled:

We travelled by ship. This was, in fact, the last of the substantial ministerial delegations to set off by sea, the four days' journey by air

henceforward replacing the leisurely six weeks at sea.

We joined the ship at Fremantle and were immediately informed that an incoming oversea liner which had called at Bombay was in quarantine because of the presence of several smallpox cases. Most of those who had not previously been vaccinated received injections before we sailed, but Menzies left the job to me as we were crossing the Indian Ocean. He had a tremendous reaction, his arm swelling to enormous size, and became too sick to leave the ship at Bombay, where the Bombay Ministry was anxious to discuss mutual problems with us.

On arrival at Suez we motored across the desert in blazing heat to see King Farouk. We arrived at Easter time and the King, who had been well coached concerning the personalities of our delegation, welcomed me warmly with appropriate words, cunningly introducing my second Christian name (Christmas), derived from a maternal aunt. 'It's Easter time', he said, 'yet Christmas is here.'

He thought Menzies was the author of a book on experiences as a prisoner of the Turks in the First World War, which was in fact written by White. The book was entitled *Guests of the Unspeakable*, and the King asked Menzies what had made him think of this unthinkable term. Menzies hastened to give White full credit for his literary efforts.

After a pleasant audience with the King we called on his royal uncle, an elderly man who had often visited Australia to race his horses and who employed an Australian jockey in Egypt. He astonished us by congratulating us on our advanced policy of exterminating the Australian aborigines, which he seemed to think had been a great success; he expressed the opinion that Egypt had made a mistake by not doing the same. Nothing we could say to the contrary could convince him that our policy was, in fact, the reverse, and we left, basking in his admiring glances at the statesmen who had achieved so much.

There had been a plan that Menzies should break his journey in Italy and call on Mussolini. But news reached him that Mussolini was unlikely to see him, although the Foreign Minister, Count Ciano, would almost certainly do so. Menzies told Britain's Secretary of State for Dominion Affairs, Malcolm MacDonald, that his illness had delayed the preparatory work of the delegation. Consequently, he felt that he 'should remain with the other Ministers all the way to Plymouth and London'.

The Attorney-General, accompanied by Peter Heydon of the Department of External Affairs, arrived in England at the end of April 1938. On May 8, *The Sunday Times* described him as 'among the first six speakers in the Empire'. This sort of flattering appraisal—he would 'inevitably' become Australia's Prime Minister—reverberated in newspaper columns and society gossip. 'I have no doubt at all', Menzies told Australian radio listeners on June 20, 'that there are plenty of people

left: The Australian Attorney-General leaves the Dominions Office, London, for lunch, 17 June 1938

in Australia who are writing or saying that those fellows of ours in London are ... succumbing to a clever combination of duchesses and tea parties.' Tragically, the people at home were right. Awareness of the disease was no cure. The impulse to dazzle was unquenchable. And a reputation for wit needed constant refurbishing. The measure of Menzies' self-confidence by 1938 was his remark to a *Sunday Times* reporter about the prolific use of notes by British speakers. He could understand why a Prime Minister making an important announcement must read a prepared statement. 'But why did Winston Churchill make a completely prepared speech at the Academy Banquet the other night? ... words can only come to life when the speaker gives them birth at the moment with his brain.' (Nearly a year earlier the Launceston Chamber of Commerce in Tasmania had been informed that Winston Churchill filled the House of Commons when he spoke, but that MPs listened to him for his entertainment value. 'He walks into the House carrying a book looking like a railway guide, in between the leaves of which is the typescript which he will read with great dramatic effects, obviously prepared the night before.') So much for Churchill and, by implication, for his judgement of European affairs.

Having disposed of Churchill, there were English cricket writers to vanquish—the British press seized on a sarcastic aside, in a broadcast to Australia about 'the brilliant contributions made to insular prejudice and Empire disunity by most of the cricket writers of the London evening press'. Unrepentant, Menzies extended his attack, late in June, in an article for *The Daily Express* on his first visit to Lord's. At Lord's there was a sightboard at only one end, a primitive scoreboard, and a crowd that was not technically well-informed—'it applauds good fielding and fortuitous fielding with equal courtesy'.

Cricket's shrine had no terrors. But other arenas were more disturbing. Three weeks after Menzies reached Britain, events in Czechoslovakia grew ominous. Alfred Stirling, Menzies' former secretary who was now External Affairs Officer in London, spent a whole Sunday morning at the Attorney-General's flat briefing him, and returned in the afternoon with a fresh batch of telegrams from the British Government. Menzies read the telegrams, shut his eyes momentarily, and then said quietly, 'This is a terrible state of affairs'. Finally he outlined his own views on the policy that ought to be adopted. At a meeting of dominion representatives with the British Foreign Secretary, Lord Halifax, in the afternoon of May 25, Menzies expressed his puzzlement at the attitude of the Czech President, Benes. 'He had frankly been unable to understand what his policy had been. Was it bluff, and if so, was it not almost a suicidal bluff?' Sir Earle Page, the senior Australian minister at the meeting, stated that what Australia wanted was 'a politically satisfied Germany which would be ready to take her share in the peaceful development of the world'. Page asked a question which pointed clearly in the direction of further appeasement: 'Would the German Government be satisfied if they got the Sudeten Germans, and if they would be satisfied, would it not be wise to give the Sudeten Germans to them?' The official report of the discussion noted Menzies' reply to this question. He 'wondered whether the German Government would ever stop short of the rest of Czechoslovakia'. Two months later, having watched Test cricket at Nottingham and backed the Derby winner, Menzies took the opportunity of studying German opinion and plans at first hand. Alfred Stirling went with the party and on 3 August 1938 sent a report home to Lieutenant-Colonel Hodgson, Secretary of the Department of External Affairs:

GERMANY

VISIT OF MR MENZIES TO BERLIN, 27TH TO 31ST JULY, 1938

The Rt Hon. R.G. Menzies, KC, MP, Attorney-General and Minister for Industry, left London for Germany by air on Wednesday, 27th July, and remained in Berlin for four days. Mr Menzies himself described his visit as being undertaken for the purpose of general observation at first hand, and with a view to contacts with representative men in Germany. The visit attracted considerable notice in both the London and German press. The 'Times' Parliamentary Correspondent on 28th July, commented that 'it was a minor landmark in the progress of the Dominions towards an individual European policy'.

The Attorney-General was accompanied by Mrs Menzies, and his staff comprised Mr Heydon, Private Secretary, and Mr Stirling, who had been seconded for the visit. The Minister took an early opportunity of establishing contact with the British Ambassador in Berlin, Sir Nevile Henderson, with whom he had long conferences on each of the four days of his visit. The Ambassador gave a dinner at the Embassy on 28th July in honour of Mr and Mrs Menzies.

The German Foreign Office put a senior officer at the Minister's disposal throughout his stay in Berlin. Calls were made on several departmental heads at the Wilhelmstrasse. Among those whom the Minister saw were Herr von Weizsäcker, the State Secretary for Foreign Affairs, Herr von Woermann, Assistant Secretary and lately Charge' d'Affaires in London, Herr von Rintelen of the Western European Department, and Herr Wiehl, director of the Trade section. Before leaving London Mr Menzies also saw the German Ambassador, Herr von Dircksen. Dr Schacht, President of the Reichsbank, gave a luncheon for Mr Menzies on 28th July, at which the British Ambassador, the State Secretary, the other directors of the Reichsbank and representatives of all the leading German banks and industrial organisations were present. A dinner was given jointly on 29th July by Herr Brinckmann, head of the Reichswirtschafts Ministerium, and Herr Herbert Goering.

Among others with whom Mr Menzies had discussions during the course of his visit were the Financial Adviser to the Embassy, (Mr G.H.S. Pinsent of the United Kingdom Treasury), the British Counsellor, Sir G. Ogilvie-Forbes, the Military Attaché, Colonel Mason MacFarlane, Sir Edward Reid, director of Baring Bros who was in Berlin in connection with the recent financial negotiations, and the South African Minister to Germany, Dr Gie.

Although the principal object of his visit was to observe the political situation, Mr Menzies also made arrangements to see something of German industry. A visit was paid to Siemensstadt, and a whole morning was spent in inspecting the Siemens works, an organisation employing some 120 000 men and women. The Minister first saw over the Metallwerk and Kabelwerk which turn out cables for heavy and light-current engineering and the accessories necessary for their installation. A visit was then paid to the Dynamowerk where the largest electrical machines are manufactured, including the alternators which have supplied Ireland with electricity since 1929. The staff club houses and dining rooms, and the colonies of workers' flat, houses and gardens in the vicinity of Siemensstadt, were all inspected, and a lunch was given by the directors at which Mr Menzies spoke.

To see something of the work of smaller industries Mr Menzies visited the Lindner works at Wittenau. Here machine tools are manufactured, a particular feature being the use of the latest optical measuring instruments as part of the actual process of manufacture instead of their being applied only to the finished piece.

Mr Menzies also drove out into the country to see examples of the new State highways which radiate from Berlin all over Germany, and to try the 'Arvus' track, where a speed of just under 100 m.p.h. was reached. On the way a visit was paid to the recently erected Olympic Stadium, the swimming pool and open air theatre, which form part of the 'Kraft durch Freude' movement, and the Tempelhof airport.

Mr Menzies left Berlin on the evening of Saturday, 30th July, by air for the Netherlands. He spent two days at Amsterdam, making brief journeys to the Hague and Haarlem and renewing contacts made on his visit to the Netherlands in June, 1936. The party returned to London by air on Monday, 1st August.

The British Ambassador in Germany, Sir Nevile Henderson, was greatly impressed by Menzies' level head and common sense. In his memoirs, *Water Under The Bridges*, published in 1945, Henderson compared Menzies favourably with Stanley Bruce. Like Bruce, he found Menzies to have 'a breadth of vision which seems, since the first World War ended, to have become a lost quality in England'. The Ambassador, who has been anathematised for forty years as an appeaser of Hitler, evidently found Menzies' opinions in harmony with his own. Someone who was less interested in Menzies' opinions—which he described as 'a lot of twaddle'—was the Duke of Gloucester, who sailed with the Australian delegation as far as Port Said on their voyage home. The Duke announced with great relief to some fellow passengers, whom he surprised by joining for deck tennis, 'anything to keep away from Menzies who had kept him up till 3.00 a.m. with his stories!'

Menzies' secretary during this last pre-war trip, Peter Heydon of the External Affairs Department, has left vivid recollections of his chief at this time:

I was his private secretary in Australia for 4 weeks before we went abroad; we were $5\frac{1}{2}$ months abroad, including nearly 9 weeks on the water going to and from London; and then I had 8 weeks with him in Australia before I went back to the Department. I was essentially appointed as his private secretary because he thought it was a good idea to give one of the young men in External Affairs experience abroad. His previous private secretary was leaving him to go into private business. He wanted to have Theo Mathew, but Hodgson, the Secretary of the Department, said he could not be spared. When Menzies asked whether I was available Colonel Hodgson was able to say that I could be spared quite easily. I enjoyed the trip immensely and both Menzies and his wife contributed to this.

I have always felt there was another factor in this. I hope this does not sound immodest, but the Department of Defence, just after Sir Frederick Shedden had become Secretary, did dangle a position in Defence in front of me and, having had some unfortunate exchanges with Colonel Hodgson, I was seriously thinking of accepting it. But when Mr Menzies offered me this trip abroad, operating on the principle of a bird in hand being worth two in the bush and at the same time fundamentally thinking I would rather continue in external affairs work than go to Defence, I went off with him.

Menzies was very satisfactory in many ways. He was, of course, a man of great intellectual power; he was of great precision of mind; he had a real sense of the dignity of his office. Like Sir George Pearce and Lord Bruce, he wrote short letters—sometimes short letters are harder to write than long letters, but on the other hand if a minister consistently writes them they make life for his private secretary much easier. In the office there was more warmth and friendship and humanity than perhaps in an office run by Pearce or one run by Bruce. On the second or third day I was with him he asked me if I would go abroad, and it is worth recording on an occasion like this, I think, that he said: 'Well, would you like to come to Britain and Europe with me this northern summer?' I said I would and he said: 'I wanted to look at you for a few days and, of course, I also wanted my wife to meet you because, after all, we will be travelling together, and you have passed her test.' I learned later from Mrs Menzies, as she then was, that— on the second day I was with him I had to go with them in the car, which she was driving, down to look at a sister ship of the 'Strathmore' (which was then the best ship on the run) and in which they were going to Europe. She gently asked me whether I was a good sailor and I said I was a fairly good sailor, or something equally innocuous, while my pulse rate rose sharply. She had thought that I had already been told I was going to Europe and I had not, and she said that her husband gave her a dig in the ribs leaving a bruise which took some weeks to disappear.

But all that was warm and friendly. In many ways Menzies was a very considerate chief. If we went to Sydney on an official visit, my family was there and he was undemanding on hours; when I was with

him in London he made sure I had the Whitsun weekend for a trip to
Europe and when I told him the plan I had worked out—it was 6
days—he said: 'Well, congratulations on creating a record. That is
the longest weekend I have ever heard of, going from one Wednesday
afternoon to the following Wednesday morning.' In London he took
me to Gray's Inn, where he was a bencher; he took me to dinner there
and to a Ball which I saw described somewhere as the last great ball
in London before the Second World War! It was about two months
before Munich! Whenever they had large parties that included me they
were always careful in introducing me to people I would be interested
to meet. We went to a luncheon given by the British Government and
Menzies made a point of introducing me to 2 or 3 of his Cabinet
friends, and so on . . .

There is no doubt that at this time one thing dominated Menzies'
thinking. He thought he would be a good Prime Minister of Australia,
he wanted to be Prime Minister of Australia and all his political actions
were largely tested against that particular framework of reference.
This does not make him unique. At any one time in a national parliament in any democratic country there are a number of people whose
mental processes are exactly like that. But, for all that, Menzies in
those days, compared with the later years when he was thought of as
being remote and Olympian and out of touch with the cities of Sydney
and Melbourne, did have a lot of very warm friendships. This was one
thing in which he was different from both Sir George Pearce, who had
very few close friends really, and Mr Bruce. I can think of people now
—the late Judge Stretton, Judge Campbell, Jack Gray, MLA, Mr
Villeneuve Smith, QC, of South Australia, J.R. McGregor, the wool
merchant of Sydney, Syd Ure Smith, Tim Clapp of the Australian
General Electric Company—these men were warm friends of Menzies
in the same way as they would have been if he had never been in politics
but just knew them as friends and neighbours in an ordinary professional and suburban setting.

Another thing that was very likeable about Menzies and did induce
loyalty from subordinates was the way in which he insisted on frankness
by his staff with him. A day or two after we left Fremantle going to
England his wife was not well and she went to bed early. He and I
after dinner were sitting in the lounge drinking coffee and talking and
Menzies suddenly said: 'I think such-and-such a situation is very
interesting. It seems to me that the main essentials in it are 1, 2, 3.'
I have forgotten what the situation was. He said: 'What do you think
of that?' I said: 'Well, I would make certain reservations, sir.' and I
made them, 1, 2, 3. He said: 'You are a humbug. Those are not reservations; they are denials. You think the exact opposite of what I believe.
Now let that be a lesson to you. Never attempt to dissimulate with
me. You are my private secretary; you are not a clerk who handles
papers. We have a relationship of confidence. I expect, of course, you
to observe the rudimentary courtesies and I would not want you to
be disagreeing with me in front of members of the public, but when

we are together we will be frank.' This meant a great deal for the working method of his office.

The other thing I would say about it too is that, being essentially warm and generous, Menzies was somewhat temperamental ... one day in seven if Menzies were depressed he was touchy and difficult. He was a sort of, I might say, a perverse sabbatarian ... it was not that he took a day of rest but a day came when he was different from his normal ebullient self. But this is natural enough in a man who was great responsibilities, strong feelings, great ambitions and also, of course, had opponents and a lot of difficult situations.

'I am looking forward very much to getting back home again. As you know, the pleasure of these overseas visits can be grossly exaggerated.' As if implicitly rebutting unspoken charges that he was being over-impressed by the 'duchessing' of British and European political and social leaders, Menzies had told Joe Lyons on August 6 of his eagerness to leave the scene of his current successes.

On his return to Australia, the Attorney-General began to beat the drum of Australian nationalism. There were still people in Whitehall

'I have been Mr Lyons's Attorney-General for four and a half years ...
I have never seen anyone who looked less like a man who had been "dumped"
or faced the slightest prospect of being "dumped".'
Menzies in Burnie, Tasmania, 10 February 1939

and Westminster, he told reporters in Melbourne on 11 September 1938, who thought that dominion views on foreign policy were 'a matter to be ascertained after the United Kingdom decision—a sort of ratification, useful to have, but not essential'. What was needed, he said, was debate preceding decision, a 'family conference'. (In London, when he spoke on this theme, the British newspapers had not at first reported his remarks. By the time he made his farewell statement the desirability of 'closer and franker consultation' had become the keynote of editorials.)

On the European situation, Menzies was widely quoted as believing that it was 'in reality more balanced than it was six months ago'. To a reporter from *The Yorkshire Post* he had said on August 8: 'It is surely a truism to say that nobody in Germany wants war . . . ' Further:

> The principles of the totalitarian State, as Germans freely admitted to me in Berlin, are not suited to the British genius, but I do hope that we British people will not too easily accept the idea that because personal liberties have been curtailed in Germany the result is necessarily a base materialism. There is a good deal of really spiritual quality in the willingness of young Germans to devote themselves to the service and well-being of the State.

Before leaving London he had said in an interview to an Australian Associated Press representative: 'I do not believe that war is possible in Europe . . . The new Rhineland defences cancel out the Maginot line immobilising both the French and German land forces'. This happy revelation was now followed by a warning that it would be a mistake to take sides too hastily over the Czechoslovakian problem; Germany's menacing behaviour had to be seen in its context. *The Sydney Morning Herald* reported his statement on September 12:

TRUCULENT GERMANY

A great deal of Germany's intransigent and occasionally truculent attitude to-day was due to the fact that she was convinced that other nations thought she was always wrong. Mr Menzies said 'Germany thought in effect that she might as well be hanged for a sheep as a lamb.'

In a mad world, cool heads were more precious than the wagging tongues of partisans. It was the business of the British people to provide the cool heads and uphold the national reputation for judicial fair play, and when thinking of fair play the case of Germany might be cited.

Germany had done things which were abhorrent to British people, and Germany had constantly misunderstood the easy-going British character. She had deprived herself of the stimulus of ideas by making people think and say the same thing. She had, so British people thought, delusions of persecution and she attached a dangerous significance to the element of force in her national philosophy.

OTHER SIDE TO PICTURE

There was another side to the picture however. Germany might never have had a dictatorship if a little more sympathy and understanding had been extended to her by the Western Powers during the chancellorships of Stresemann and Bruning.

After the Great War, Germany found herself hemmed in and disarmed. No peaceful attempt to have her grievances examined seemed to succeed. The provisions in the covenant of the League of Nations for a revision of the Treaty of Versailles seemed a dead letter in these circumstances and Hitler became her leader. He adopted the principle of 'doing it first and arguing about it afterwards'.

Mr Menzies said that there were credit entries in the Nazi ledger, although the philosophy of the movement was repellent to the British mind. He still believed, as he did two years ago, that Germany held the key of the world's peace. If Germany could be persuaded that no nation had designs on her and that the other nations were prepared to give her justice, the twin evil spirits of suspicion and hatred, which were making her such a dangerous neighbour, might be driven out.

Menzies' determination to drive out the evil spirits took the form of resolute support for Neville Chamberlain's policy of concession. The Acting United Kingdom High Commissioner cabled to London on September 14:

From long private conversation with Menzies following Cabinet meeting last Monday and from short interview with the Prime Minister this morning I am satisfied that the Commonwealth Government remain strongly of the opinion that almost any alternative is preferable to involvement in war with Germany in the event of the latter forcibly intervening in Czechoslovakia.

Having made a plea for family conferences and debate before decision, Menzies was quick to demonstrate that Australia could be trusted not to be irresponsible or unruly. With the assistance of Richard Casey he drafted a telegram for Lyons to send to the British Prime Minister, expressing great admiration for Chamberlain's initiative and courage: 'As we have approved of your policy we have not thought it necessary to encumber you with our advice . . . ' The cable went on to urge that 'before a ruinous, and perhaps inconclusive, war is permitted, consideration should be given, not to the value of what has already been conceded, but to the value of the actual points now in difference.' The senior British diplomat in Canberra, Percivale Liesching, was so appalled at this message that he cabled at once to say that he was convinced that it was 'very far from representing the core of Australian majority opinion' which he believed was more inclined to take a firmer stand against Germany.

Many Australians did share Menzies' attitudes. But there was a vocal strand of opinion that labelled his pronouncements pro-German.

At an Old Scotch Collegians' Association dinner in Melbourne on
Saturday, 15 October 1938, Menzies replied to his critics, saying that
because one saw another person's point of view, one did not necessarily
agree with that view. He went on to develop one of his recurring themes
about the inadequacies of his fellow countrymen. It was typical of
Australians, he is reported to have said, that they were reluctant to
engage in uncomfortable thought. Politicians were often regarded as
eccentric and self-seeking. Yet 'Australians who could not bother to
exercise a vote sometimes had the effrontery to proclaim their disdain
for the Government of Italy or Germany'. In the fascist countries, 'the
enthusiasm for service to the State, although it perhaps went too far,
could well be emulated in Australia'.

No episode more memorably illustrated and reinforced the cleavage
between Menzies and his left-wing opponents than the 'pig iron' dispute.

For a quarter of a century, largely as a result of repetitive hostile
propaganda which, in later years, usually became good-natured raillery,
Menzies was known throughout Australia as 'Pig Iron Bob'. It is unlikely that any Australian who was politically conscious by the 1950s
could hear or see the words 'pig iron' without immediately thinking of
Menzies. For the generation which had been directly involved in the
politics of the 1930s, and was to experience the long, anxious, and
bloody war against Japan, the memory was deeper and more painful.
What the 'pig iron' episode meant to one unforgetting section of the
Australian people was pungently expressed in an anonymous letter
posted to me from Brisbane in November 1976: 'Menzies gave iron to
Japan for bullets to fire at Australians'. Legends cannot be dissolved
by facts. Nor is it the purpose of this book to determine the truth about
every incident in Menzies' career. But, on a subject so obviously important in the making of the public image of the post-war Menzies, it is
essential to have some understanding of what both participants and
well-informed observers thought had happened. The original incident
was clearly recounted in a book published in New York in 1940. Jack
Shepherd had been commissioned by the Institute of Pacific Relations
to write a study of *Australia's Interests and Policies in the Far East*. He
completed it less than a year after the events he described. After explaining the Australian Government's concern not to antagonise Japan
unnecessarily, Shepherd went on:

> So firmly did the Australian Government set its face against unilateral
> sanctions against Japan that it even sought to prevent private action
> to curtail exports of war material. The first of these attempts was the
> refusal by Sydney waterside workers on January 25, 1938, to load
> cargoes of tin scrap, on the ground that the metal would probably be
> used in the manufacture of munitions for the China war. This boycott
> was continued for more than four months, and early in May it spread
> to the Melbourne waterfront where cargoes of tin and iron scrap were
> waiting to be loaded. At first the Government sought to end the boycott
> by gentle persuasion. The acting Attorney-General, Senator McLach-

lan, warned members of the Waterside Workers' Federation that their action was not 'conducive to international peace', and appealed to the men not to take action which might be regarded as offensive to a foreign power. Members of the Government and others questioned the utility of barring metal exports to Japan while allowing wool and other produce to be shipped freely. Wool could be used to clothe soldiers and wheat to feed them . . . but, then, any attempt by Australia to impose general sanctions against Japan would not only be futile but dangerous. Furthermore, the complete cessation of Australian exports to Japan, it was urged, would entail greater economic difficulties than the country could well afford. Even some union officials indicated that 'officially they disapproved of the action taken by members in refusing to load ships'. But despite all argument the men stood their ground. . . .

By May when a final effort to persuade the waterside workers to 'leave matters of foreign policy to the Government' proved unavailing, it was announced that the provisions of the Transport Workers Act would be applied on May 25, in those ports where the boycott was still in force. This Act was one, designed originally for use in breaking illegal strikes, which empowered the Government to apply a licensing system to transport workers. Its application in this case would have meant that in the ports of Sydney and Melbourne all stevedores would be required to take out licenses, but that none would be issued to those participating in the boycott. The 'Dog Collar Act', as it was called by the trade unionists, had been applied before with results disastrous to the waterside unions, and so, at the last minute, in meetings of the unions concerned in Sydney and Melbourne, the boycott was abandoned. The Government then refrained from instituting the licensing system.

The same problem arose again in a more serious form, at Port Kembla, when on November 15, 1938, a rank and file meeting of waterside workers refused to load the *Dalfram* which had come to pick up the first of a series of shipments of pig iron ordered from the Broken Hill Proprietary Company for Japan. Only a few weeks before the Sydney unions had been deterred from applying a similar boycott by a renewed Government threat to invoke the licensing system, but since no non-union labor was available in the new industrial center of Port Kembla, the men there apparently felt themselves in a stronger position to challenge the Government, and risking application of the Transport Workers Act, decided themselves to apply 'working-class sanctions' against Japan.

As on previous occasions . . . the Government sought, first by persuasion and then by threats of licensing, to end the boycott. At the end of November, an ultimatum was presented to the men . . . in which the Government expressed its intention of invoking the Transport Workers Act if the loading of the *Dalfram* were not resumed within a week. In announcing the Government's determination the Attorney-General, Mr R.G. Menzies, declared that 'the men's persistent refusal to load pig iron for Japan raises an important issue. The question is not whether the waterside workers are right or wrong in their views on what the international policy of Australia should be; it is whether that policy is to be determined by the duly constituted Government of the country or by some industrial section. There can be no doubt that if international relations are to be sensibly and peaceably handled no responsible Government can submit to dictation by a section of its people. The Government has, therefore, decided that it must take steps to enforce its authority.' Mr Menzies claimed that the action taken at Port Kembla was 'inconsistent with the principles of democratic Government'. The Port Kembla men stood firm, and the Federal committee of the Waterside Workers Federation sent a reply to the Attorney-General, intimating that while it had no wish to interfere with the Government's policy, individual members of the Federation were free at all times, under the existing Federal award, to choose which employer they wished to work for. Their present action was, therefore, not inconsistent with the principles of democratic freedom. The policy of the waterside workers was endorsed by a conference of 17 trade unions, and there were threats of a general strike involving 4000 employees of the Port Kembla steel works. The conference called upon the Government to withdraw its ultimatum and the trade union movement to rally to the support of the waterside workers; it declared that 'to supply iron in any form to Japan is injurious to the national and defense interests of the Australian people'. . . .

The Government then felt itself obliged to bring the licensing system into operation. So solid was the feeling in Port Kembla, however, that no volunteers presented themselves for licenses, and the *Dalfram* remained unloaded. There was no general strike, but the Australian Iron and Steel Company, a subsidiary of the Broken Hill Proprietary Company, which controlled the steel works at Port Kembla shut them down, throwing 3000 to 4000 men out of employment. This action was evidently taken to reinforce the Government's effort to break the boycott. Steel for Japan formed only a relatively small part of the output of the Port Kembla mills, and although with the licensing system in force and no applicants presenting themselves for licenses, iron and steel for other destinations could not be shipped direct from Port Kembla, it could readily have been sent the short distance to Sydney by rail. The men dismissed from the steel mill persisted, despite the loss of their own employment, in their support of the waterside workers' boycott.

By this time the matter was attracting national attention and there was ample evidence that the boycott had a degree of public support which went far beyond that of the organized labor movement. Even the conservative press expressed sympathy with the motives of the Port Kembla watersiders if not with their method, and expressed doubts as to the wisdom of the Government's attitude . . . Questions were being raised as to the legitimacy of applying the Transport Workers Act in the Port Kembla case; the Act was originally designed to prevent *illegal* strikes but there was considerable doubt as to whether the *Dalfram* strike was illegal. The Government's embarrassment was increased by demands from the unions that a Federal referendum be held on the question of the export of war materials to Japan. The trouble threatened to extend to the Sydney waterfront when waterside workers there refused to handle two other small shipments of pig iron destined for the East, but the two ships involved sailed with other cargo when calls for labor to load the pig iron proved unsuccessful. Even though actual boycotting was confined to Port Kembla the issue had now become one in which the Government felt its own prestige to be involved, and so in an effort to break the deadlock, the Attorney-General himself visited the center of the disturbance early in January.

... According to reliable reports, Mr Menzies went so far as to tell one deputation 'that he agreed that there should be a complete embargo by all countries on the export of goods to aggressor nations, but added that it would be dangerous for Australia to take the drastic boycott steps suggested by the unions. Such an action, he said, would be provocative and might possibly lead to war. Australia could not afford to adopt such an isolationist (*sic*) policy.' He reiterated the Government's contention that the action of the boycotters was in effect an attempt to dictate the Government's foreign policy which the latter could not tolerate: 'nations like Japan, which are accustomed to a high degree of authority in their governments, have difficulty in understanding how, in a country like Australia, one policy can be announced by the government and another policy be acted upon by a section of the people ... If the government is to be defied, the result will be that unofficially Australia will have imposed sanctions against Japan in relation to her Chinese war ...' He, therefore, suggested, as a basis of settlement, that the men should load the *Dalfram*, submit their views on the supply of raw material to aggressor nations to the Government, and that the Government would then reconsider its policy in this respect and discontinue the licensing system. On the other hand, union spokesmen argued that already Japan was Australia's potential enemy and that 'they would not load any pig iron for Japan when they knew it might be used for the manufacture of rifles to shoot down Australians eventually.' It was denied that the boycott involved any attempt to dictate to the Government on matters of foreign policy. One union official contended that wharf laborers in America and England had taken the same stand as the Port Kembla workers, and that Governments in those countries had not felt obliged either to assume responsibility for the action of individuals or to take action against them: 'If it is good enough for Mr Chamberlain to do this, why is it not good enough for Mr Lyons?' Another charged the Government with being out of step, both with Australian public opinion, and with the policy of other friendly nations.

Although during the next few days a settlement of the immediate issue of loading the *Dalfram* was agreed upon between Mr Menzies and a committee of trade union leaders in Sydney, along the lines Mr Menzies had suggested at Port Kembla, it is a significant indication of the determined attitude of the rank and file that for some time they refused to accept the advice of their own officials and it was only when they were eventually convinced that the Government was likely to change its policy and adopt the recommendations in favor of a future embargo on the export of war materials to Japan that they agreed to load the *Dalfram*. Under the terms of settlement the licensing regulations at Port Kembla were lifted, and the Prime Minister and the Attorney-General agreed to meet trade union representatives in Melbourne on January 24 and discuss the question of an embargo on future exports of pig iron. This meeting duly took place, but on February 14, after a meeting of the Cabinet, the Prime Minister announced that it had been decided to reject the union proposals.

The declaration of policy which accompanied the announcement was particularly important: 'The Government, while recognizing and sympathizing with the humanitarian motives which actuated the unionists is unable to accede to their request. The Government is compelled to view the position from the widest national aspect. It has to consider the effect of any interference with the ordinary flow of trade upon other industries and upon other Australian interests. To single out one commodity and one nation would amount to a discrimination wholly contrary to the declared policy of the Government to preserve and maintain friendly relations with all countries. Further, it must be apparent that in the present unsettled state of the world such an act might be fraught with grave consequences. It has been said that we should impose a ban upon exports to Japan because of Japanese action in China. The Government is not prepared to impose sanctions upon any country, except in conjunction with other countries.'

There was bitter disappointment among the waterside workers who, without any hope of gain for themselves, had for nearly three months sacrificed their own livelihood in order to make their contribution to the checking of an aggressor nation. They had clearly hoped that the representation of their leaders to the Government would bear some fruit and lead to the imposition of nation-wide 'sanctions' against Japan. But the Government decided to adhere to its original policy and, apparently feeling that further struggle was useless, the men of the waterfront indicated their intention, on February 17, to load future shipments of pig iron 'under protest'.

One incident during the course of the dispute, which illustrates the extraordinary lengths to which the Government was prepared to go in suppressing criticism of its policy, was the closure without warning of the trade union-owned radio station 2KY, Sydney, after a news commentator had accused the Postmaster General of ordering a censorship of telegrams to Port Kembla and the tapping of trade union telephone lines. The Postmaster General immediately had a writ served ordering the closing of the station, and Post Office engineers cut the connection between the studios and the transmitters in the middle of a commercially sponsored program. This action evoked strong protests not only from the trade unions but from a wide variety of sources including the conservative press. The ban was removed three days later, on December 24, after the station authorities had published an apology in the press, saying that they believed to be untrue their commentator's statements regarding the censorship of telegrams and the tapping of telephone wires. Whatever the truth may have been regarding censorship of telegrams and telephones, the shutting of the radio station was in itself an arbitrary and unprecedented action which in the words of the *Sydney Morning Herald* savored 'too much of dictatorial censorship to be palatable to a freedom loving community'.

From a detached, academic review of the issue, it is difficult to appreciate the full impact of the pig iron dispute in the Australian workforce. Something of the flavour of the trade union response is captured in an unpublished *Brief History of the Australian Waterfront and the Waterside Workers' Unions 1902–1947*, written by the watersiders' leader, Jim Healy, as a report to the union's federal council and subsequently distributed to union branches:

The truculence of Japanese officers on visiting ships led to several incidents, particularly in Sydney, so it was not surprising when in 1938 Sydney members refused to load tin clippings and scrap iron for Japan, on the grounds that this would assist the Japanese war lords to continue their aggression against the Chinese nation. The Government of this day, led by Mr J. Lyons, intervened in the matter and as a result of local discussion the Sydney Branch decided to lift the ban.

However the decision made by the Lyons Government to lease the Yampi Sound Iron ore deposits and to export pig iron from New South Wales to Japan caused the South Coast Branch to refuse to load the SS 'Dalfram' with pig iron for Japan. This action appealed to the mass of the Australian people and support was forthcoming from all quarters.

Sir Isaac Isaacs, the late Governor-General, expressed his appreciation and support for the action which he later recorded in his book 'Democracy and our Constitution'. The Lyons Government however, decided to throw its full weight against the South Coast Branch. The provisions of the Transport Act were extended to Port Kembla and blood curdling threats were made against the waterside workers. However, the greatest degree of solidarity was built up among the local workers, with the result that the Government was not able to get one application for a license under the Transport Workers' Act to work on the waterfront. The full support of the Federation was thrown behind the South Coast members after the Federal Committee of Management had visited Port Kembla and discussed the position with the local workers . . .

Subsequent conferences with the Government, at which the Federation was represented by Bill Brodie (Branch President), Ted Roach (Branch Secretary) and Jim Healy (General Secretary) led to an agree-

ment under which the Government agreed that no more pig iron would
be exported after the 27 000 tons which had been contracted for, The
Transport Workers' Act would be lifted from Port Kembla forthwith
and no victimisation. After that contract no more pig iron was in fact
exported from the South Coast.

The terms of the agreement were observed, with the result that the
amount of pig iron obtained by Japan was strictly limited and, in view
of the subsequent attack on this country by Japan in 1942, the correct-
ness of the stand taken by our members was emphasised up to the hilt,
and the conservative Lyons-Menzies Government was exposed as a
government unable to protect the best interests of the Australian people,
because of its overseas commitments and its general concern for those
who exploit for profit.

This is the same Government which has by its policy torn up the
protection provided in the terms of surrender imposed on Japan at
the conclusion of hostilities. It has agreed to a resurgence of Japanese
militarism, the rebuilding of Japanese industry and the restoration of
the governing class which was directly responsible for the savage attack
made on the defenceless port of Darwin on February 19th 1942 when
waterside workers and seamen were sent to their death without warning
and in a most horrible manner. Yet these guilty men are still left to
govern our destiny and to commit our sons to further wars solely with
a view to retaining their rights to exploit our National resources and
our young manhood for their own private profit.

When considering the legislative record of the Lyons Government, it is
essential to remember that federal powers were by no means as extensive
as they were to become after the Second World War. Judicial interpretation of the Constitution, the degree of antagonism between the
national Government and the States, the remoteness of Canberra, the
state and metropolitan orientation of the press—all these worked
against the development of Commonwealth consciousness. Richard
Casey, in a moment of pessimism, wrote to Stanley Bruce on 28 January
1936, saying that 'one gets rather a sick headache in the contemplation
of the next ten years. The amount of energy that is going to be wasted
in the State v. Commonwealth struggle is appalling.' Casey was tempted
to withdraw from politics altogether until the balance of power had
swung by 'the merciless logic of events'. Meanwhile Menzies increasingly
became concerned about expanding the areas in which a federal government could act. In the budget debate on 22 November 1938, he posed
the question 'Why has there been, in the past, such reluctance on the
part of the Australian people to amend the Constitution?':

In the first place—and I say this as one who has had experience of
these problems both in a State parliament and government and in the
Commonwealth Parliament and Government—there is a common
fallacy that the States are sovereign bodies, and that any proposal to
increase the power of the Commonwealth is, therefore, almost a

sacrilegious attack on State sovereignty. Let me be frank, and say that I have, no doubt, in the course of my life, used the expression 'sovereign States'. I think many of us have, but I say quite deliberately to-day that, on an examination of the matter, I can imagine no greater fallacy than this theory of sovereign States. Sovereignty in this country belongs to the people of Australia. . . . because this is a democratic community which carries out its desires through various agencies. Wherever there is popular federal government and there are two governing agencies, no one of them exercises sovereignty, but . . . we must get away from the somewhat rhetorical atmosphere in which there is talk of sovereignty, and realize that the problem of the distribution of power is a direct, common-sense problem of which authority we are to entrust with a particular task.

The second answer I suggest to the question is this: In the past, we have, I think, underrated the real difficulty of explaining constitutional changes to the people. We have, on far too many occasions, had relatively hurried campaigns. It is not a criticism of the people of Australia to say that, after most of these campaigns, most of the people have had to go to the poll with no clear idea of what the issues were. The people of Australia are of an intelligence second to no other people in the world, but they are entitled—indeed, they are bound—to be given ample opportunity to understand the changes suggested. Therefore, if we believe that in certain respects, or in all respects, additional powers should be given to the Commonwealth Parliament, we should make up our minds that there is a price to be paid, namely, a sustained attempt by us to make everybody in Australia, as far as possible, understand what the issue is. We must have longer periods of preparation; otherwise, we shall find that the people, as always, will say, when in doubt, 'I vote No'. That is not an unhealthy attitude of mind; it is a perfectly reasonable and natural state of mind.

The third answer is that, far too frequently in the past, Constitution alteration proposals have been regarded as party political matters to be determined, not by one's opinion regarding the Constitution, but by one's opinion of persons sitting, for the time being, on the Government benches. . . . From my point of view, there is only one question: Should the people of Australia take power through our Commonwealth Parliament to carry out certain functions? If they do, the people will have their own rights, in their own way, to decide which party shall sit on the Government benches. That is a matter which they will determine every three years, or perhaps more frequently, but the result of constitutional changes will endure for generations, and will affect Parliament for generations. We must forget party if we would deal with these organic questions.

The fourth answer is this: I have detected many times, as have other honorable members, an instinct in the average voter in Australia to feel that, in this welter of governing authorities, his primary loyalty is to his State. We have all encountered this. . . . And so, year after year, and referendum after referendum, we hear well-meaning people, otherwise intelligent, saying that the real question is, 'Why should the States give more power to the Commonwealth?' whereas the real question is, 'Should we, the people, who are superior both to Commonwealth and States authorities, entrust this power to this parliament or to that?' If that were properly understood, a great deal of the difficulty that attaches to this feeling among the people would disappear. Nothing is so calculated, I believe, to thwart a real attack on great problems as the necessity for determining, with the assistance of lawyers, not only what the remedy is, but also which is the right doctor to apply the remedy, the Commonwealth doctor or the State doctor. Our most vital problems and most imminent dangers affect us as a nation, and I believe, as, I think, other honorable members believe, that only a national spirit, a new and vigorous national spirit, can meet them with success.

There were few political controversies or crises of the late 1930s in which Menzies was not involved. He was a top attraction at meetings all over the country. His words were assured of wide publicity. During his period as a federal minister he spoke on several occasions on the theme of threats to democracy, the regrettable apathy of the electorate, and the need for greater national efficiency and discipline, and for better leadership in public life. These speeches were always delivered in abstract terms. If personalities were mentioned, it was almost certain to be the European dictators, Hitler or Mussolini, not the benign Joe Lyons.

Thus, in August 1936, Menzies warned the Melbourne Commercial Travellers' Club that there were only three democracies left in 'the old world': Great Britain, France, and Switzerland. (As an aside, he delivered a withering rebuke to the United States, which 'long since withdrew herself from any sense of responsibility toward the affairs of the world.') For Menzies, the great danger in Australia was the refusal of people to take an intelligent interest in public affairs. Yet, simultaneously, he felt there was a developed habit of taking all troubles to the state. 'If we are afflicted by pestilence, fire, flood, or drought, or even by our own laziness, we go to the Government and ask for help . . . we cannot go on for ever with a system under which we all want to be on the list of beneficiaries and do not want to be on the list of contributors.' Embroidering on this sermon for the Millions Club in Sydney in November 1936, Menzies warned that a dictatorship could happen in Australia if 'the best men with the most brains, fortitude, and possessing the finest character' did not enter Parliament. And in Goulburn on 15 June 1937 he argued that when criticism of public men degenerated into slander, it produced demoralisation and opened the way for dictators. He spoke wistfully of British politics where he believed the 'leaders gave other leaders credit for being honest in their convictions'. In Australia on the other hand, 'the moment a man begins to achieve a position in public life, every little tongue and every little dirty mind begins to look round and try to find something about him; whether he beats his wife, or whether he is a chronic "boozer".'

This series of utterances culminated in an extraordinary proposal, published on 11 September 1937, after scenes of uproar in the House of Representatives, that drastic changes be made in the law relating to parliamentary privilege. As a result of years of reflection, Menzies contended that:

(1) When a Member of Parliament made an offensive statement and subsequently withdrew it, the offensive statement should not be recorded in Hansard, and its publication in the press should be prohibited;

(2) That where an offensive statement was made and upon challenge was not withdrawn, no parliamentary privilege should attach either to the making of the statement in Parliament or to its publication in the press.

The press exploded. *The Canberra Times* discerned a 'dictatorial mind' at work in 'the chrysaloid stage of fascism'. And even the normally friendly *Argus*—whose controlling group included Menzies' former business partner, Staniforth Ricketson—said that the adoption of these suggestions would be a 'retrogressive measure.' In Parliament, F.M. Forde (Deputy Leader of the Opposition) and Frank Brennan (an ex-Attorney-General) led the attack on 'a definite threat against the privileges of Parliament by a responsible Minister of the Crown'.

Menzies defended himself on shifting ground, arguing that the privilege of free speech should not give rise to 'privileged blackguardism' and that, in any case, he was only speaking in a private capacity. No one else could be blamed, any more than they could be charged with responsibility for a speech a year later, which precipitated the political climax of Menzies' recital of variations on the theme of the need for leadership. Dame Enid Lyons remembered:

Towards the end of October 1938, Menzies made a speech that has become among politicians one of the most famous ever made in Australia. It brought to a head, if not to a conclusion, long-held suspicions. It aroused bitter political antagonisms, and led eventually to the making of a Prime Ministerial statement by Sir Earle Page. This was so violent that he later regretted it but Dame Pattie Menzies never again acknowledged him. By permission of the House, it was withdrawn from Hansard and replaced by a more restrained version.

Menzies' speech, delivered at the Constitutional Club in Sydney, is remembered not so much for its content as for what was generally accepted as its intent. Its subject was leadership, but it was regarded not as a contribution to serious thought on a matter of public moment but as a further attempt to denigrate the Prime Minister. This was certainly the light in which I saw it.

Joe and I customarily breakfasted in bed while we read the morning papers. At that hour, beside the local *Canberra Times*, only the Sydney papers were available—the *Sydney Morning Herald* and the *Telegraph*. All three carried reports of the leadership speech. Suddenly I was electrified.

'Joe', I exclaimed, 'Have you seen what Bob Menzies said in Sydney yesterday?'

'Yes! Why?' he answered mildly.

'Why?' I almost shouted. 'Why? Can't you see it's a direct public hit at you?'

'Not at all', he replied. 'Bob wouldn't be guilty of such a thing. It's just the way it's reported!'

'Don't be a fool, Joe.' I adjured him. All my fighting blood was up. I could not accept any theory of mis-report or misinterpretation. The attack on Joe's leadership had for weeks, yes, even months, filled columns in the daily press. He would be a naïve person indeed who would expect such a speech at that time to be taken at its face value, and Bob was not noted for naïveté. I was brimming over with righteous wrath.

Joe went off to the office somewhat disturbed by my tirade, but still clinging to the belief that the speech had been made without malice. This view met with little acceptance at Parliament House. However, when Menzies reached Canberra, he sought an interview and immediately stilled any stirring of doubt Joe may have felt.

'There was no need to tell me that', he said, when Bob protested his innocence of any ulterior motive. 'You didn't even have to mention it!' And he meant it. Which of the two men was the more relieved it would be difficult to judge; Menzies because he had wanted to be believed, or Joe because he had wanted so much to believe.

In January, after the Christmas holiday, the Cabinet went to Tasmania, and a happier mood prevailed than had been known for a long time. Members enjoyed the climate and the scenery, and Menzies was at his charming best. He even made a speech in praise of Joe, pledging his loyalty.

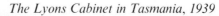

The Lyons Cabinet in Tasmania, 1939

With Menzies' apparent restlessness causing growing curiosity and concern about his motives, some of his colleagues began to watch his activities with particular care. If Menzies' ambition were to displace Lyons, there were some impediments to be surmounted. The Minister for Trade and Customs, Lieutenant-Colonel T.W. White, had travelled to England and back with Menzies in mid-1938. On October 25, he wrote in his diary of 'a most sensational week'. On the Monday evening he attended a Chamber of Manufactures dinner at the Hotel Australia. The President of the Chamber was flanked by Menzies and by the New South Wales Premier, Bertram Stevens, who had been described privately by R.G. Casey in February 1936 as 'breaking his neck to get into Federal politics—to become Treasurer and then Prime Minister'. White recorded:

Owing to Stevens's recent announcement that he intended to enter Federal politics, and Menzies' utterances lately on leadership, I asked the President if he were announcing them as Federal and State heavyweight champions in the manner of a stable announcer. Menzies as usual spoke well, and Stevens indifferently. I had to lead the replies for the Guests, and discounted something of what M. had said by stating that a good general average in standards among the people was better than consideration of those who believed themselves specially ordained to lead the people. I also spoke of manpower and got as close as I could to recommending compulsory training.

Left Mascot next morning in DC2 Douglas, and being half an hour early had a good look around this stupendous machine. M. and Moore were also on board. The day was cloudy and as we approached Canberra there was indifferent visibility. The hostess informed me that they did not intend to land at Canberra but would put us down at Wagga. I protested and declared that there was sufficient visibility to see the ground if he flew round carefully. This was done, and, although there had been heavy rain, the pilot who had gone well east of Canberra circled and put us down safely enough on a very wet aerodrome.

There was immediate Cabinet which lasted until a Party Meeting at 11. Matters were rather hectic as Menzies' speech the day before at the Constitutional Club, saying that leadership was wanted in the country, had led to speculation as to whether he was criticising the Prime Minister, and Price in the Party room asked who were the other contenders. He moved a resolution of support for the Prime Minister, which was rather discomfiting for M., but there was no opposition. The House had met, knowing that the Opposition intended to present a censure motion on the lamentable lack of leadership. The Prime Minister asked leave to make a statement and announced that news had just been received that a DC2 plane from Adelaide had crashed into Mt. Dandenong with the loss of life of all those on board. The House was staggered at the information and when Curtin read his motion of censure the House immediately adjourned, conforming with the usual practice of consideration for a day.

Just at the tense moment when the air was rather electric after the setback to M., Bell, the Speaker, came in and informed me that Charles Hawker, Member for Wakefield, had been in the crash and was killed. The news shocked everybody. Ministers drew off to Cabinet and all sat around listlessly as the news sounded too tragic to be true. . . . Hawker was one of the brightest minds in our Parliament. Badly wounded, an eye knocked out, and wounds in the spine paralysing him for some two years, during which he obtained a law degree at Cambridge, by sheer pluck he had defied his disabilities and with irons on his boots, managed to get around. I had been quite a close friend and he had several times been at our house. A stern critic of the Government, he had been Minister for Markets in 1932, but through making a promise at election time that he did not favour an increase in Members' salaries, resigned his portfolio when a motion for an increase was before Parliament at the end of 1932. He was the spiritual leader of the 'squatter' group in the House—McBride, Fairbairn, and others following him always slavishly.

In the week following Hawker's death, deep divisions opened up in the Cabinet. White's diary provides a vivid account:

November 1st (Cup Day). There is considerable comment that Cabinet should be sitting on Cup Day, it being almost unprecedented. The clamours for Cabinet reconstruction and the criticisms over Defence made the meeting essential and discussion soon began on Compulsory Training which had been declared against the previous week, but which it was felt still necessitated discussion; and undoubtedly the public feeling seems to be veering round to universal service again. Casey had declared for it previously and now back-pedalled, apparently not to displease the Prime Minister who is honestly pacifist at heart. Cameron declared he would have to consider his position if something of the sort was not carried.' The Prime Minister challenged him on this and his bluster died away to some feeble excuse. This time I wrote a note to Hughes who sits alongside me after he had again as before declared against compulsory training. I had told him last week that the returned soldiers would be disappointed to know that he as a former advocate of universal service was not now supporting it. This time I asked him had he seen the article in 'Mufti' giving a resolution carried by returned soldiers in favour of universal service and informing him that this would bring him down if they knew his attitude. He snarled and shouted and I told him he could read it out to Cabinet if he liked, which he did, and there were high words between us both. He said I must have written it when I pointed out what a backslider he was on compulsory service, of which he was once the champion. The Prime Minister intervened on Hughes's behalf, so I told him that I had already made up my mind that I could not remain in a Cabinet that could not support universal service and that I had thought it over well and intended to withdraw, and I left the room. There was apparently consternation because I had, first, Perkins, my Assistant, then Casey, and then Page persuading me to come back, each of them contending that my resignation would mean an election, happening during a censure motion and that in an election the Government stood a big chance of defeat, and Casey contended that he almost certainly would lose his seat, having National Insurance on his hands. I had a letter partly written out, showing that for years I had disapproved their defence policy, and I thought the time had now come when there had to be efficient and universal service. However, after long representations, particularly by Page, I decided that for the sake of the Government I would return, but made it perfectly clear where I stood. A long statement on defence had been prepared by the Secretary of Defence and into this I had inserted on the matter of military service the following:—

> An intensive drive will immediately be made to bring enlistment in the Militia Forces up to a strength of 70 000. It is hoped that volunteers will be forthcoming now that the urgent necessity for adequate manpower is realised. Full co-operation by the people and all political parties is necessary to reach this total if the voluntary system is to be retained.

We sat all day and late into the night, one of the typical Cabinet days of 12 to 15 hours; and at the evening session had the opportunity of interrogating General Squires, the English Lt. General who has been made Australian Inspector-General of Forces for a term of two years, the Admiral, Sir Ragnar Colvin, and Air Vice Marshal Williams.

I was satisfied to find that in almost every respect they agreed with the proposals I had been putting forward, namely, universal service, a capital ship, a small standing army and more and more aviation.

The House sat through Wednesday, Thursday and Friday, with intermittent Cabinet meetings. The lobbies are very active with the newspaper men and their speculations on the new Cabinet. The Argus, very much followed by the Herald, is featuring Menzies as being the great brain sighing for leadership and a paragon of all that is wonderful as a patriot and statesman. Casey is usually bracketed with him and undoubtedly these two, who are very personal grata with the Argus, are their selected deputies in all things.

An amazing sidelight to the Cabinet manoeuvring is that Menzies had given out to the press that he would probably resign if scope were not given to his great ability or if compulsory training were not introduced. My temporary resignation apparently upset his plans, though I am sure nothing would drag him from the Treasury benches while he thinks he has a hope of leadership.

A few days later White recorded what he believed to be the end, for the time being at any rate, of Menzies' leadership ambitions:

5th November. . . . On Wednesday we had an interesting Party Meeting that might have had interesting consequences. Menzies' talk on leader-

ship had aroused a section of the party to espouse his cause and it was
soon put forward in rather an electric atmosphere, after some criticisms
had been voiced by Gullett that he was dissatisfied with the Prime
Minister's leadership and he thought he ought to make way for somebody else. There was a little wordy by-play between the two of them
and after another one had spoken I got up and suggested that, although
it was unusual for a Minister to speak in a Party Room, I thought it
proper to say that at this moment I believed we had no other leader than
our present leader and that anybody who imagined he was specially
ordained to lead the Party was flattering himself. I pointed out that I
stood pat for universal training but that a via media had been worked
out to endeavour to obtain the 70 000 recruits essential for defence by
the voluntary system, if it was to be retained. This settled the attack
that apparently Menzies was going to launch, and except for one other,
Senator Wilson, a new arrival from South Australia, there were no
direct attacks upon the Prime Minister.

It is important to understand that Menzies had genuine grounds
for impatience with Lyons. Not only had he to contend with a Prime
Minister whom he considered ineffectual, he could guess, if he did not
know, that there were manoeuvrings, involving Lyons, to impede his
own succession to the leadership. Lyons wanted to retire in 1937, but
was persuaded by powerful United Australia Party backers to lead
the party through the next election. The leadership question was,
nevertheless, becoming urgent. A wide field was possible. Until his
death, it had always been possible that Charles Hawker might emerge.
Billy Hughes still commanded a strong following. Casey, with an eye
to the future, could hardly afford not to run. There was also some support
for T.W. White. All of these parliamentary contenders stood in Menzies'
path. Outside Parliament there were other possible candidates. Bertram
Stevens and S.M. Bruce were the two most fancied outsiders; and
Sir Sydney Snow pressed Lyons to form a 'triumvirate' with them.
Meanwhile, the Melbourne interests that had sustained Lyons and
originally sponsored Menzies were no longer so committed to Menzies.
He had not proved as amenable as had been hoped. Even Keith Murdoch
found Menzies a hard man to promote. The Attorney-General had a
curiously disconcerting way of discouraging adherence while in fact
eagerly seeking it. Whatever caused this—'utter laziness or pride' were
the alternatives suggested by Murdoch to Clive Baillieu on 4 January
1939—it seemed that the public was beginning to dislike Menzies. 'Each
week now he is becoming less likely as Prime Minister.' Many years
later, Bruce told his biographer, Cecil Edwards, of a conversation with
Menzies early in 1939:

I asked Menzies to lunch at my flat at Toorak and after lunch we
had a long talk. I told Menzies frankly that I thought he was making a
serious mistake in the attitude he was adopting towards Joe.

I pointed out to him that Joe was a marvellous election leader, with the tremendous appeal he had to the people of Australia and the confidence they felt in him. I told Menzies that I recognized Joe was not competent to run a Government between elections; however, if you had a certain winner at election-time it was quite possible to steer Joe so that the Government would carry on efficiently between elections.

To this, Menzies' reply was that Joe was utterly impossible. I asked him for some evidence of that as, when I had worked with Joe and more or less from the background steered him, I had found him one of the most pleasant and amenable people I had ever had to work with.

Menzies said he had done his best to help Joe and used to discuss with him every move that the Government was going to make. On one occasion he had seen Joe about three o'clock in the afternoon. They had discussed some problem that confronted them and arrived at a decision. On the adjournment of the House the same night, Menzies heard Joe announce a policy on the subject they had been discussing which was diametrically opposed to what they had agreed upon.

Menzies' comment was: 'How can you work with a man who behaves like that?' My reply was that one of Joe's weaknesses was that he was always swayed by the last person he talked to. Was I right in assuming that after Joe had made his statement, Menzies went to Joe, very angry, having made up his mind that it was hopeless to try to help him, and that from that date the breach widened? Menzies admitted that was so.

I replied that in my view he had made a fundamental blunder. What he should have done was to have followed Joe into his room, reminded him that he and Joe had agreed to an entirely different line in the afternoon, and pointed out that it was impossible for Menzies to help if that sort of thing happened. The result would have been that Joe would have been contrite beyond words, and would have eaten out of Menzies' hand ever after.

I do not think I succeeded in convincing Menzies but from my experience of Joe, which lasted over a considerable period when I returned to the Government as Minister without Portfolio and helped Joe in the absence of Latham during the difficult days with Lang, I am sure my opinion was right.

Peace had not come to the Cabinet. Following a re-shuffle on 8 November 1938, Thomas White had resigned in protest against the creation of an alleged inner Cabinet from which he was excluded. In a statement issued shortly afterwards, White said that 'the steadily growing influence of two prominent Ministers upon the Prime Minister, and their ambitions toward leadership were apparent and feared by those who value democratic ideas.' White was not alone in his dismay at the developing cleavage and contest for the succession to Lyons. The 'two prominent ministers' were Menzies and Casey. They were soon to be even more antagonistic.

Frank Green, Clerk of the House of Representative from 1937 to 1955, was a friend from boyhood of Lyons. Green's memories of the events of late 1938 and early 1939, culminating in Lyons' death, were tinged with bitterness. Green believed that, had he lived, Charles Hawker might have emerged as Lyons' successor, and he was a sharp observer of the Cabinet's leading personalities:

Early in 1938 as Treasurer Richard Gardiner Casey (later Lord Casey) had introduced the National Insurance Bill which, after weeks of debate and obstruction by certain Country Party members, was finally agreed to by both Houses. . . .

The officer appointed to the Treasury to administer the Act was a Professor of Economics, James Brigstock Brigden. Under him he had a staff of competent officers, together with a public relations organization consisting of a number of able journalists whose duty it was to explain to the business community and the public generally their obligations and their benefits under the Act. So far the Melbourne financial group which controlled the United Australia Party had taken little interest in National Insurance; having put the Lyons government into power it felt safe in assuming that it had nothing to worry about from legislation, but when large business firms began to receive material from the public relations branch of the National Insurance Department they realized that this new scheme was going to cost them something. The Prime Minister was therefore instructed not to proclaim the Act without the permission of this financial group—generally known as 'the Temple Court Group'—Temple Court being a building in Collins Street which housed finance firms and other large business headquarters.

The Treasury's position was most humiliating, not only to Lyons, Casey and other ministers, but also to Professor Brigden who, after the months spent by his staff in informing the public how the scheme worked to the advantage of everybody, now had to go to work to re-educate the people to believe that, after all, the scheme was a gigantic failure. . . .

Menzies resigned from the Cabinet in protest against the failure of the Government to proclaim its own Act. Earle Page's autobiography declares that this action by Menzies is inexplicable. History should find no difficulty in explaining it. Menzies had found a reasonable excuse for breaking with Lyons, who had almost reached the end of the road, and there was no advantage to be obtained by remaining loyal to him.

Although in power himself later for eighteen years, Menzies never took the trouble to proclaim the National Insurance Act, which is still in the Statute Book. . . .

Following Menzies' resignation there came a Cabinet re-shuffle by which Casey's status was raised; this was believed to indicate that Lyons was about to resign and Casey would succeed him. This appeared to cause a Cabinet split, and Cabinet meetings became ineffective. No decisions were made, and ministers spent the time baiting each other. I visualized the position when on two occasions Lyons walked out of Cabinet and came to my room, as he explained, 'to get out of the way'.

He and I had been close friends since our student days in Hobart, and when he came to me from the Cabinet room I could see that he was under great nervous tension, and almost hysterical. He said on the second occasion he wanted to resign and end the torture, but was being urged to wait for something to take place. I gathered that he had been offered an appointment by the British Government and was awaiting details of the terms and conditions before he resigned as Prime Minister.

On the day before the Good Friday of 1939 Lyons sent for me. When I went to his room he was dressed for travelling, and at his suggestion we had a drink together. He said he was going to Sydney to have a rest during Easter. Of course, he could have rested at Canberra, but he appeared to have reached such a state of nervous strain that he was under great tension and could not rest anywhere. He spoke of his worries, saying: 'I should never have left Tasmania; I had good mates there, and was happy, but this situation is killing me.' A few minutes later he was on his way to Sydney by car, but along the road he had a heart attack and died in a Sydney hospital a day later.

Menzies' considered his resignation to have been justified by a pledge he had made on 17 December 1938 in a circular letter to his constituents to 'incur any quantity of temporary unpopularity' in defending National Insurance. But his departure was widely interpreted as a stab in the back for Lyons. However, the Prime Minister was an incorrigibly magnanimous judge of his colleague's motives, and he did not therefore treat Menzies as an enemy. Even when pressed by his wife and political associates to recognise that his leadership was being deliberately undermined, he refrained from criticism. Thus, he told J.A. Perkins, the Minister for Trade and Customs, that he fully understood Menzies' position and that Menzies had assured him that he would continue to support the Government. Perkins made a point of publicising this conversation, which he said had taken place just before Lyons' death; and *The United Australia Review* reported it to the party on 1 August 1939.

Some of those who felt that Menzies had behaved disloyally towards his chief also believed it was the anxiety caused by Menzies' defection that contributed decisively to Lyons' fatal illness. First among those who held this view, bitter and deeply distressed, was Earle Page, who had become Acting Prime Minister. On the death of Lyons, the Governor-General summoned Page to form a government. Page agreed to serve until the United Australia Party had elected a new leader; and he gave notice that he would not join a Cabinet led by Menzies. Five days after becoming Prime Minister, Page initiated moves to persuade Stanley Bruce to return to Australia. In his autobiography, Page quoted the cables and transcripts of key telephone conversations:

On 12th April 1939 I cabled Bruce at Los Angeles in the following terms:

As you can understand Lyons' sudden death has left political complications which in my opinion should be solved, if a solution is practicable, at the earliest possible date.

I think that the only way in which an election can be avoided is for you to return to Australian politics in UAP ranks. No need to stress to you how important it is to have in power Government which has confidence of whole people and co-operating whole-heartedly with Britain.

Personally, I would be prepared to resign from Cowper to enable you enter Parliament immediately. Glad urgent advice your ideas and whether proposal acceptable to you. Regards.

In reply Bruce cabled:

Greatly appreciate offer but I would not entertain the suggested resignation. Following are my views. I am not prepared to return to politics as member of any political party.

Seriousness of situation and necessity for united nation if you and Casey after necessary consultation decide I could materially assist this end and safe seat available to which I could be elected immediately as independent I would be prepared to return Australia and enter Parliament. This decision is dependent on you and Casey being prepared join me in that event of my having to form Government and on your being satisfied in such an event I would have the support of your respective parties.

R.G. Casey was fully in accord with my point of view. He consented to join me in a radio-telephone conversation with Bruce on the morning of 18th April, the day on which decisive meetings of both the Country Party and the United Australia Party were scheduled. . . .

BRUCE: My point is that I am not prepared to come back and go into party politics. If there is a real demand from the people and all parties, I would be prepared to form a Government on the basis that, in the national crisis, I am asked for by all parties. That I should be in a position to ask the Labour Party or anyone I wished to work in my Government and it would not cut across any particular section.

CASEY: I had not up to the present thought of anything but a straightforward invitation from the UAP and Country Party for you to return to Australia and re-enter politics, and that there had been a demand from both parties that you come back to help the Government, and that preparations were in hand for you to contest a seat and immediately assume office.

BRUCE: I do not know that it would be wise to commit yourself as to how it is all going to be done at the moment. I think we might keep to this point. That you and Page have been in touch with me, you have put the question up to me, and I would be prepared to return to Australia and go into politics, and that I have said I would be prepared, but that I am not prepared to affix myself to any party.

CASEY: Just what does that mean exactly?

BRUCE: I am not prepared to come back and say I would be coming back as a member of the UAP. If there is a national crisis and there is a demand for me to help, I would be prepared to come back, and if the people elect me I am prepared to go into Parliament, and I am prepared, if it so falls necessary, to form a Government, but I am not prepared to accept the position where there has to be a certain number of seats allotted to a particular party. I am not prepared to accept the idea of my followers meeting in separate parties. If the Country Party likes to meet on its own, they can do so in their own room, but when they meet me, I would insist that my followers have to meet me. I absolutely won't look at the thing on the basis of coming back as the leader of any particular section. I am quite prepared to come back if a seat is found for me in Parliament, and I am prepared to do this only on the basis that I appeal for support to anybody to come into my Government. That is the thing that is the absolute condition of my coming back.

PAGE: Do I understand that you would be prepared to come back if there were an absolutely safe seat found for you immediately and that you would to some extent take your chance of later being able to form a Government on the lines you suggest? We could not commit so far ahead in that way. We could not say now that under those conditions we could absolutely certainly ensure that you would form a Government. I think it would be a million to one chance that the public would demand it, and I am satisfied we can find a seat for you under those conditions, but personally I think that the attitude you take of being willing to take a chance in that connection would strengthen your hold on the people, would strengthen the possibility of getting the whole nation behind you.

BRUCE: That is my attitude, Page. That I would be prepared to come back and that I am prepared to say I will come back and go into politics if a seat can be found that will accept me without my pledging myself as a supporter of any party. As to what the future may hold, I do not ask for any guarantee or anything else.

PAGE: Under those circumstances, it seems to me that the right course would be to proceed along the lines of electing the leader of the UAP, but to have in mind that such a leader would be prepared to accept the conditions that you laid down now. I myself unreservedly accept them as leader of the Country Party. It seems to me that in the UAP room a leader ought to be chosen there who would be prepared to act likewise.

BRUCE: It boils down to this, that at the moment I am the High Commissioner in London. You told me of all that. I said, 'Yes, I am prepared if I am acceptable to any electorate to return to Australian politics', and because of that my plans have been altered. I am returning to Australia. I am still High Commissioner and if it works out that a seat can be found, I am prepared to accept it, but it would have to be entirely dependent on how the situation works out.

PAGE: We will have to think this thing out. I think the right course will be for the UAP to have the matter before them and postpone the election of a leader until they have had time to consider this. Where will you be in the next two or three days and when are you reaching America?

BRUCE: I can get a cabin on the same boat I came over in, which leaves on the 25th April and I get to Australia on 15th May . . .

CASEY: We have our party meeting in an hour or so this morning. I would propose to read them out a summary of what we have been saying this morning. It is essential that there is no possibility of doubt in anyone's mind as to the position. Page can answer now presumably for his party, but nobody can answer for our party until after our meeting today. Then we will have to decide whether we will elect a leader of the UAP in the interim, and it would seem to me that, if the party accept, as I would tremendously hope they would, what you have suggested, that the Government should be carried on by Page in the meantime. It is no good our going through the mumbo-jumbo of getting a UAP Prime Minister for six weeks. Don't you think that is the best thing to do?

BRUCE: Yes, I think so. You can go to your party and tell them that you have been talking to me and that if there is a feeling in Australia that they want me to come back and lend a hand, I am prepared to come back and give any help to Australia in the political arena, provided that I am not hampered or hindered by being tied to any semblance of party politics.

CASEY: You come back to be Prime Minister if you come back at all?

BRUCE: I do not make that a condition. I have been told that I am wanted to come back as a leader and I am prepared to do that purely on the terms that I am elected to a seat not as a member of any party but as a member of the National Parliament.

CASEY: That point has got to be cleared up. That will be cleared up, presumably today, tomorrow or the next day—within three days. . . .

The Parliamentary Country Party met at Canberra on the afternoon on 18th April, immediately following the conversation with Bruce. . . .

There was a full attendance. In addition to myself, Thorby, Hunter, McEwen, Gregory, Paterson, Prowse, Anthony, Badman, Thompson, Collins, Fadden, and Nock were present from the House of Representatives, with Abbott and Cooper from the Senate.

After we had resolved to send a letter of sympathy to Dame Enid Lyons, I outlined the position which arose at the Prime Minister's death and the circumstances under which the Governor-General issued to me a commission to form a Government. I also gave the Party an account of the negotiations with Bruce following my offer to vacate Cowper, with an intimation that Bruce, while willing to return on specific conditions, was unwilling to contest my seat.

As a result of the discussion that followed, the meeting carried the unanimous resolution: 'That in view of the international position and the need for a united national effort for defence and development the Country Party unanimously approve of the suggestion for Mr Bruce to return to Australia to form a government with a Cabinet drawn from all parties or members who are willing to co-operate to that end.'

Prowse, Hunter, Paterson, Anthony, Gregory, and Abbott expressed support for the action taken in opening negotiations with Bruce. Fadden, while agreeing to the motion, opposed my resignation from Cowper.

The following further resolution was carried with the agreement of all: 'That in spite of past harmonious co-operation in government with the United Australia Party and a willingness to continue similar co-operation to maintain stable government, the Party is definitely unable to co-operate in a government with the Hon. R.G. Menzies, KC, as its Prime Minister; nor is it willing to give any undertaking to support such a government if it be formed.'

The United Australia Party met the same day to discuss the leadership. . . .

In a further conversation with Bruce on 19th April, I reported progress. . . .

PAGE: Yesterday at the UAP meeting Menzies was chosen leader after three ballots. He narrowly defeated Hughes and Casey and White dropped out early. Subsequently they discussed this question (of Bruce's return) which Casey put before them, but they failed to show much enthusiasm. When Menzies came to see me last night, I had already put it to my own party, which was unanimously in favour of it—not a dissenting voice. I asked Menzies where he stood in regard to this matter of your return and although he did not put the thing out of court altogether, he was not at all enthusiastic. I believe they were going to throw the thing out in the UAP meeting, but I persuaded Casey to get the thing deferred; but I am sure within a few days there will be an irresistible increase in the demand from the public.

I told Menzies, of course, that I won't serve under him. I told him the Country Party was unanimous in that regard. This, of course, is an added reason—that I wish you to return. I told the members of the Cabinet before the meeting that that was the position of the Country Party and that it ought to be conveyed to Menzies before the election of leader. I did not wish to say it myself, because it might seem as if I were wishing to dictate to them who their leader should be. There is now a move to try and secure an election of the leader of the Government by a vote of the combined parties, in which it is quite possible that some other man than Menzies would be chosen as the head of the Government, which would really conform more or less to the type of Government which you were contemplating yourself.

BRUCE: Whose suggestion was that?

PAGE: It had come from Casey and is in Cameron's mind and it has been put to quite a number of people like Spender. It is being canvassed today. My party went rather far in their statement when they carried a resolution regarding their refusal to co-operate in a Government with Menzies—they also added that they would not support a Government which was led by him as UAP leader. That is going to make Menzies's position rather difficult with the Governor-General.

BRUCE: Yes, it is. He really cannot carry on. I am not clear about the attitude of the UAP.

PAGE: I do not know that very clearly. Casey can tell you better. I think the way Menzies had put it to them is that, if they have to get a man who is not in Parliament, they are admitting they are bankrupt of statesmanship, which is perhaps the truth. . . .

Bruce then asked for a radiogram of the Country Party statement of 18th April, and I read the statement to him.

BRUCE: I entirely accept that.

PAGE: It is what was said to the UAP . . .

BRUCE: Then the attitude of Menzies and Hughes was really 'Oh, to hell with this'?

PAGE: No, I think Hughes might possibly be right on this, but there is no question about Menzies's end. But the position now is that Menzies has been elected, although he has not got a majority support in the party. It took him three ballots to win and there is no question in my mind that he will lead everyone to political suicide. The feeling of my fellows is that they must take to the raft at once rather than sink in the same boat with him.

BRUCE: Yes, I think you are right. It is a most extraordinary position . . .

I had already indicated to my fellow Ministers and my Party that I would resign the Prime Ministership as soon as the UAP elected a leader. My preference was to resign as Prime Minister and make a

statement in Parliament in my capacity of Country Party leader. The
Country Party evening meeting of 18th April supported this procedure
without dissent. But Curtin, alive to the political possibilities of a
first-class clash on the floor of the House, declined to sanction an
adjournment of Parliament to permit me to discuss my resignation
with the Governor-General, without a full statement of my reasons
for the course I proposed.

I had no option but to move the adjournment of the House on 20th
April, and state my reasons, as Prime Minister. . . .

Unable to contain his emotions, and unpersuaded by more cautious
advisers, Page attacked Menzies in Parliament with unparalleled venom
and ferocity. (Several senior officers of the Australian Broadcasting
Commission agreed that even the news summary of the speech was in
such bad taste that it should not have been broadcast.) *Hansard's*
modified version still reeked of calculated, fervent antipathy:

Every one realizes that to-day we are perhaps on the threshold of
war. During the last four or five weeks actions have been taken by
certain aggressor countries, which, if permitted to continue, would
undoubtedly finally lead to Australia having no option but to fight in
self-defence. More recently, extraordinary steps have been taken by
other nations, such as the United States of America, for instance, in
an endeavour to assure the peace of the world. It seems to me that if
a wartime government is to function—and that may be the position
at any time, although I hope not—it must function in such a way as
to secure the greatest possible measure of co-operation in the community. The Australian Government needs a leader with not merely
the qualities I have mentioned, but also the three essential qualities of
courage, loyalty and judgment, in such degree as will ensure that the
people of Australia will give the last ounce of their energies and resources in a united national effort to ensure our preservation. Therefore, as the Leader of the Country party, which had been associated
for so many years with the United Australia party in the government
of this country, . . . if the leader of that party was to become the leader
of a united national effort, I was entitled to consider whether he possessed the qualifications necessary for his high office. I had to ask myself
whether his public record was such as to inspire the people of Australia
to the maximum unstinted effort in a time of national emergency.
Because of that I was reminded of three incidents in the public career
of the newly elected Leader of the United Australia party. The first of
the three happened only 24 days previously, when, honorable members
will remember, the right honorable gentleman tendered his resignation
as Attorney-General in the Lyons administration. . . . At this time,
when all our efforts were being strained to put the defences of this
country in order, the right honorable gentleman insisted on resigning
from the Government because he differed from its attitude towards
national insurance. . . .

The second incident is this: Some 24 weeks ago he went to Sydney, where he made a speech on leadership; that pronouncement was regarded by the public and the press of Australia as an attack upon his own leader. I do not say that it was; I merely say that it was construed in that way.... I come now to the third incident: Some 24 years ago the right honorable member for Kooyong was a member of the Australian Military Forces and held the King's Commission. In 1915, after having been in the military forces for some years, he resigned his commission and did not go overseas.

Mr JAMES.—That is dirt!

Sir EARLE PAGE.—I am not suggesting that the right honorable gentleman had not the best possible reasons for his action.

Mr JOHN LAWSON.—Then why did the right honourable gentleman mention the matter?

Sir EARLE PAGE.—I am not calling into question the reason for the right honorable gentleman's action, nor would I question the reason of any other individual in similar circumstances. All I say is that the right honorable gentleman has not explained, to the satisfaction of the very great body of people who did participate in the war, his reasons, and because of this I am afraid that he will not be able to get that maximum effort from the people of Australia to which I have referred.

Page concluded by informing the House of Bruce's willingness to return to Australia if, by so doing, it would be possible to bring into existence a 'non-party government of the Commonwealth'; and he announced that he would tender his own resignation as Prime Minister that afternoon. Then Menzies, his arm in a black sling following a fall the previous day, rose to reply. After a few introductory words, he turned to the attack that Page had made:

. . . We all agree, irrespective of party associations, that the Commonwealth is, at the moment, called upon to deal with difficult problems. Most of us believe that those problems can be attacked successfully only by a concerted effort. I, in consequence, and in spite of some temptation during the last two days, have preserved complete silence on subjects that are now matters of notoriety, although I have heard whispers occasionally about the reason for the refusal of the Country party to co-operate with me in the formation of a government. I should have been very glad to avoid having to say anything about that matter even if that refusal had been persisted in, because my own view is that in the interests of Australia the door might have been kept open. If that door had been closed for reasons of high policy, I could have respected those reasons. But the door has been closed, bolted, and barred, presumably, for reasons which are not only offensive and personal, but also paltry. I shall say something about those reasons in their turn, and I shall speak, Mr Speaker, with due restraint—

indeed with more restraint than I might have felt disposed to display on another occasion.

The first reason that has been adduced for the refusal of the Country party to co-operate with me, as Leader of the United Australia party, is that I resigned from the Lyons Government on the issue of national insurance. But honorable members know that I resigned from that government because, only a few weeks ago, I had given a specific pledge in writing to my electors. . . .

Is it a contemptible thing for a man to keep his word? Is it the mark of a coward for a man to keep his word on an issue which is far from popular? I have no apologies to offer for my resignation. On the contrary, I regard it as one of the more respectable actions of my public life.

The second reason given exhibits an amazing effort at ingenuity on the part of the right honorable gentleman. Having, I think, looked the matter up, he said that 24 weeks ago—I have forgotten the date— I made a speech to members of the Constitutional Club in Sydney on the subject of leadership. I do not know whether any honorable gentleman was present on that occasion had heard the speech, but I can say now that not one word of it do I wish to retract. The burden of my remarks was that the dictatorships owed no small portion of their success to two things—one was the leadership, the undivided leadership, which they enjoyed; the other was the undivided loyalty to that leadership which existed inside their countries. I went on to say that whilst I despised the doctrines of dictatorships and would resist them to the utmost, the test of a successful democracy was leadership, and loyalty to that leadership. After I had said that I actually went out of my way to add that it was a homily which I was addressing to myself and every other person in Australia who occupied any public position involving leadership of the people. I am not responsible for the manner in which my views may have been twisted. . . . into an attack on my late leader. All I can say on that point is that conversations which I had with my late leader and friend were completely inconsistent with any suggestion that he regarded my speech as an attack upon him. After all, is this not getting down pretty low? If we are to be held responsible not only for what we say—I am always prepared to accept responsibility for my utterances—but also for the gloss which some person who may or may not have heard a speech puts upon it, that will be the end of all pleasure in public life. I invite every honorable gentleman in this chamber to ask himself: 'How should I like that standard of judgment to be applied to me?'

I come now to the third ground of attack, which, I may add, is no novelty. It represents a stream of mud through which I have waded at every election campaign in which I have participated. The attack is 'You did not go to the war.' That is a statement which, I daresay, has occasionally been directed to some members of the party led by the right honorable gentleman.

Mr GANDER.—Yes, and in the Government front rank. 'Shoot 'em down, Thorby'!

Mr MENZIES.—There are certain people who regard it as their ordained mission in life to pry into the private reasons for the actions of other people; to put them up against a wall and say, 'Why didn't you do so and so?'. Presumably prying in this fashion, the right honorable gentleman discovered some facts concerning my action at the time he mentions, but failed to discover others. He said, with all its deadly implication, that I resigned a military commission a year after the Great War broke out. If he had investigated a little further, he would have discovered that I, in common with other young men of my age, was a trainee under the then existing system of compulsory training, and as such, in common with other young men, I took my chance of being a private, a sergeant, a lieutenant or an officer of any other rank. When my period of universal training expired, my activity in connexion with the system also expired. I did not resign anything. I served the ordinary term of a compulsory trainee. I was in exactly the same position as any other person who at that time had to answer the extremely important questions—Is it my duty to go to the war, or is it my duty not to go? The answers to those questions cannot be made on the public platform. Those questions relate to a man's intimate, personal and family affairs, and, in consequence, I, facing those problems, problems of intense difficulty, found myself, for reasons which were and are compelling, unable to join my two brothers in the infantry of the Australian Imperial Force.

Mr FROST.—It is the business of no one but yourself.

Mr MENZIES.—I say that. After all, this kind of attack is very disagreeable. It is the sort of attack that is made, and in my case has been made, time and again; but I am foolish enough to believe that the only judgment as to a man's capacity, a man's courage, a man's fortitude that has any relevancy to his public conduct is the judgment of the people who have known him and worked with him. Members of the United Australia party are familiar with me; they know my many faults; they are acquainted with such poor qualities as they may think that I possess; they believe, and I am conscious of the honour that they have done me in expressing that belief, that I am capable of leading them, and I am vain enough to hope that I have capacity enough to discharge that trust, and that in the discharge of it I shall exhibit none of those miserable attributes that have been suggested by the Prime Minister in the most remarkable attack that I have ever heard in the whole of my public career.

Page's account resumes:

. . . I had not abandoned hope that Bruce would return to Australia. I discussed the situation with him further on 21st April relating briefly the speeches in Parliament . . . .

PAGE: The papers have tried to make a tremendous fuss about this thing. My own feeling is that before many weeks a very definite demand will be made that Menzies and I should resign from the leadership of our parties to enable a new man to come along. My own feeling was to avoid this thing being done. I discussed the question with the UAP Ministers and told them exactly what would happen before the election of leader took place. . . .

BRUCE: What was Menzies's reply?

PAGE: He said on National Insurance that it was a matter of principle on which he resigned. He did not explain what he is going to say when he has to bring it before the House. He had made no real attack on Lyons and had explained the matter to Lyons at a special party meeting which had been called for that purpose.

BRUCE: The UAP are so far apart. Will Menzies be able to carry on?

PAGE: When I saw the Governor-General I told him the position which was then known to everybody. My opinion was in the circumstances that Menzies, having been elected leader, was entitled to an opportunity to form a Government, because if a UAP man had been there on Mr Lyons's death he would have had a chance to name the successor. I suggested the Governor-General should see Mr Curtin, as he had the largest party numerically in the House, and he should be allowed to consider the position. I also told him that the Country Party was prepared to serve under another member of the UAP, if necessary. I do not know on what terms Menzies was given the Commission as Cabinet will not be sworn until next Wednesday. It seems to me that the elements of trouble will be tremendous. I would not like to be in his position because the UAP have only twenty-six members, one more than a quorum.

BRUCE: What is Mr Casey doing?

PAGE: He is just sitting back . . . I have a personal regard for Menzies. I felt it had to be done and the only straight and courageous thing to do was to put it beyond any dispute.

The Government will be sworn in on Wednesday and will be a UAP Government. Menzies says that he will co-operate with the Country Party despite my speech.

BRUCE: Was my name dragged into it at all?

PAGE: I just mentioned that the offer had been made by me, but you were not discussed at all . . .

BRUCE: Well, I do not think there is anything we can do in the matter. I think your statement admirable and understand perfectly what the position was.

In a personal letter to Menzies on 4 October 1939, Bruce, who had never seriously intended to return to Australian politics, confided that there was 'no doubt that Page was your fairy god-father, if you had the slightest desire to be a Prime Minister'. Page, he said, had taken the only possible course which would make the job a 'sitting certainty' for Menzies. Defeating the 78-year-old Hughes by twenty-three votes to nineteen was hardly an impressive victory. Nevertheless, once Menzies had been elected UAP leader, however small his majority, he was certain to be invited by the Governor-General to form a ministry. He was; and he did. *The Sydney Morning Herald*, having told its readers on April 17 that there was 'very grave doubt' about Menzies' ability to command the loyal support of the Country Party, had urged a Bruce Government. But the *Herald* recognised on April 19 that Bruce's terms were unlikely

Kate Menzies, Isobel Green, Syd Menzies, James Menzies, Robert Menzies,
Frank Menzies, Les Menzies, 1939

to be met, and admitted that Menzies' election as leader of the UAP did 'no more than justice to the standing he holds of his own merit in the party and in Parliament.' Page's attack was excoriated in a long leading article as 'despicable'. Menzies' sixteen-man, all UAP, Cabinet—the largest since Federation—was praised; and the Prime Minister himself was portrayed by 'A Political Observer' under the headings 'Brilliant Intellect' and 'Adherence to Principles':

> Ever since his election to the Commonwealth Parliament, Mr Robert Gordon Menzies has puzzled his supporters, and often driven them almost to despair. No one has ever doubted his intellectual strength. No one has ever questioned his ability as a debater of singular brilliance. No one has ever denied that he is one of the best public speakers in Australia.
>
> Yet in spite of all these great qualities, he has done and said things that made seasoned politicians shudder, shake their heads woefully, and murmur that a man like that would never make a successful politician. There was even the time, not long ago, when it was freely predicted that he would never command sufficient support to win the leadership of his party, let alone win the Prime Ministership.
>
> Well, he has confounded those wiseacres by gaining the leadership of the United Australia Party, and at the moment the Prime Ministership seems to be within his grasp.

NEVER PLAYED TO GALLERY

Perhaps, after all, he has the qualities that go to make a successful politician. On the other hand, it may be that we are on the dawn of a new era in Australia—an era when forthrightness will count more than politics and adherence to principles more than the ability to bend to every breeze of expediency.

Mr Menzies has always, when he has been convinced of the soundness of his convictions, displayed an unwillingness to bow to popular clamour. He has never been able to play to the gallery. He has never been able to tickle the ears of the groundlings. And this is precisely what has worried the supporters of his party—particularly those outside the Federal arena—because in the past it has always been assumed that these qualities, lacking in Mr Menzies, are essential to the winning of elections. Apparently a majority of the Parliamentary members of the party are now prepared to stake their political future in a leadership which will, if necessary, run the gauntlet of public opinion confident that in the end right will prevail.

OUTSTANDING QUALITIES

Mr Menzies has other qualities that lift him high above the other members of the Federal Parliament. His keen analytical brain dissects a problem instantly, and he is able to expound an argument with crystal clarity. His speeches in the House on international affairs remain as treasured memories in the minds of those who were privileged to hear them. His repartee has the speed of lightning and the force of a sledge-hammer. He can turn a phrase with astonishing facility. His wit is in the tradition of Wilde and Whistler. As an after-dinner speaker he is without a peer in Australia. As a raconteur he is almost faultless. As a mimic he is the equal of many professional actors.

His ready wit has often got him into trouble.

He simply cannot help himself. His mind is so agile, the ready answer comes so promptly to his tongue, that he is unable to restrain himself.

On one occasion he was addressing the House on the Government's policy regarding economic sanctions against Italy. A prominent Labour member persisted in interjecting.

'What about the Pact of Paris? What about the Pact of Paris?'

Mr Menzies stood it for a few minutes. Then turning to the Speaker, he said:

'I do not wish at this stage to enter into a recondite legal argument with my honourable friend.'

'There you go with your superiority again!' complained another Labour member.

Mr Menzies turned again to the Speaker.

'I submit', he said, 'that in the circumstances it was justified.'

THE ALLEGED ARROGANCE

Mr Menzies has been accused of arrogance and superiority, and even his best friends admit that his demeanour often lends colour to the accusation. Like many men of considerable intellect, he cannot suffer fools gladly, but it is a mistake to assume that he is always arrogant, self-confident, cock-sure. He is often shy and nervous, and the apparent air of self-assurance is a cloak that frequently hides extreme nervousness. He has told friends that for more than two years after he took his seat in the House of Representatives he never made a speech there that was not preceded by mental torture. Some of his best speeches in London were made in similar circumstances. The experience is not unusual with accomplished public speakers but the knowledge that Mr Menzies suffers from it occasions surprise to those who do not know him intimately.

He has also been accused of over-ambition, and when he entered Federal politics there were not wanting those who predicted that it would not be long before he would begin to undermine the Prime Minister. That was in 1934. Four and a half years have passed. Yet, until recent months, when he began to express open criticism of certain aspects of the Government's policy, there had never been any suggestion that he was other than loyal to his chief. When the United Australia Party balloted for the election of a deputy-leader, there was intense rivalry for the position, and no inconsiderable amount of canvassing for support took place, but Mr Menzies, who was one of the candidates, refused to lift a finger to win votes. He told a colleague that he would be elected on his merits or not at all. He won.

HIS FEDERAL DEBUT

. . .

He stepped on to the Federal stage under the best auspices, and he was regarded as the logical successor to Mr Lyons. Yet, until recently, his popularity had steadily waned. Last year, it was, perhaps, at its nadir.

Now he has staged a remarkable come-back, due largely to his uncompromising stand on national insurance, while his recent settlement of the Port Kembla waterside dispute did much towards regaining for him popular favour, for he handled the affair with tact, firmness, and understanding, winning the admiration not only of the employers, but, strangely, of the men and their leaders.

Only the future will show to what extent he possesses the qualities of leadership necessary to hold a party together in times of stress. If he can overcome one great disability he will go a long way towards achieving success. A very shrewd political judge once said of him—

'The trouble with Bob is that he is not quite clever enough to hide his own cleverness.'

In the troubled times that lie ahead he will probably have his hands too busy to worry about hiding anything, and the chances are that he public will like him for it.

In a broadcast talk to the nation on 26 April 1939, the new Prime Minister talked about his alleged defects. 'I come to you as one who

has been freely accused of...aloofness, superiority, and what not...
In fact, I am a singularly plain Australian.' If, as he stressed, he was not
'born to the purple', how was Menzies' accession to be treated by the
conservative party which he now led? His position in Victoria was
strong. In New South Wales his base was less secure. Nevertheless, the
UAP monthly journal, *The United Australia Review*, came out on 1 May
1939 warmly in praise of 'A Brilliant Australian' who was 'The New
Force' in Australian politics:

The New Force

During the month of April Australia lost a beloved Prime Minister
who had gained to a unique extent a general popular esteem based as
much on his likeable personal qualities as on his long term of successful
leadership. The events that followed that national bereavement, notwithstanding that some of them were regrettable, have culminated in
the formation of an all-UAP Ministry, presided over by one whose
career abounds with evidences of exceptional ability and mental equipment capable of affording leadership both vigorous and statesmanlike.

Consternation was felt amongst supporters of the United Australia
Party when the leader of the Country Party threw the javelin of non-
co-operation into the Federal arena. But this has been succeeded by
the feeling that the government of the country will go on under vigorous
leadership and that a group of able young men from UAP constituencies
will have the opportunity to win their ministerial spurs. That opportunity may not have come their way for some considerable time if the
course of political events had kept flowing placidly.

There is a prevalent hope that the estrangement of the Country Party
is but temporary and based only on the personal prejudices of one or
two individuals. Sir Earle Page's scurrilous personal attack on Mr
Menzies recoiled on its maker. So much so, that, ever since, the leader
of the Country Party has been engaged in a peregrinating campaign
of justification among his own supporters. Perhaps one should say
his erstwhile supporters, for not one has openly endorsed his stand;
two members withdrew from his small Party, and the New South
Wales and Queensland Country Party organisations have made declarations which can reasonably be interpreted as warnings to an intran-
sigeant group against hostile action that might precipitate an election.

The dignified manner in which Mr Menzies rebuffed his attacker
and the statesmanlike manner of his utterances since then give assurance
that his Government's actions are not likely to be either provocative
or injurious to the Country Party's true interests. Those interests can
only be further damaged by its own leadership.

Happily, reading between the lines, it can be discerned that the
Central Council of the New South Wales Country Party has declared
for support of the Menzies Ministry so long as no legislation is introduced that conflicts with established Country Party principles.

That being the case, there is a disposition to regard the reconciliation of UAP and UCP interests in a fresh coalition as a distinct possibility of the future. The long and continuous reign of the Lyons Government was based on a mutuality of interests between the two anti-Socialist Parties. The record of the Stevens Government was founded, and is being continued, on the same foundation. The times are such that the nation must be considered to be in a state of emergency. Therefore, no-one having the security of the nation at heart would advocate the widening of the present division that exists in the Federal Parliament.

None of these considerations, however, should be allowed to stand in the way of the Government carrying on with the essential needs of the Commonwealth. Nor have they been allowed to deter Mr Menzies acting with vigour and resolution, not only in the choosing of his team and in the allocation of their duties, but in the enunciation of the main policy principles which he has laid down as guiding flags for his Cabinet. Security against external foes and social justice within—those are the two main pillars of the Federal UAP policy. And they cannot be faulted by any Party, whatever its name.

Already it is being said that Mr Menzies has created a deep impression in political circles by the manner in which he has taken over the job of leadership. Already he has given indications that he has the capacity to introduce into Federal politics a force that will be appreciated in a time that calls for positive action.

Associated with the 'new force' were a wife, children and parents, all of whom found themselves further exposed than ever before to the glare of publicity and unsuppressed curiosity about their domestic arrangements. 'The New Chatelaine of Prime Minister's Lodge', as *The Argus* called her on 24 April 1939, was by now no stranger to public life. Reprinting *The Argus* article on 1 May, *The United Australia Review* chose a slightly more subdued title:

WIFE OF THE NEW PRIME MINISTER

As the new mistress of the Prime Minister's Lodge at Canberra, Mrs Menzies will find that her public duties have greatly increased, but she has already shown, since her husband first entered Parliamentary life in 1926 that she can discharge these duties charmingly and capably. During their tours abroad, Mr and Mrs Menzies have met most of the distinguished people in British politics, and Mrs Menzies has everywhere made firm friends by her sincere manner and her quick understanding.

The eldest daughter of Senator John Leckie, Mrs Menzies was educated at Fintona, Camberwell, and at the Presbyterian Ladies' College, East Melbourne. Of a quiet but attractive personality, Mrs Menzies dresses with more than ordinary good taste. Simple and direct in manner, she has developed a good platform style and has helped her husband in many ways during his political campaigns.

Mrs Menzies is on the committee of the Children's Hospital, and was for some time president of the Canterbury auxiliary to the Royal Melbourne Hospital, and a bazaar for this auxiliary's funds was held recently at her town home in Howard Street, Kew.

Mrs Menzies is, however, better known as a wife and mother, and her three children, Kenneth (17), Ian (14) and Heather (11), have claimed much of her time. In the holidays their Macedon home is filled with the children's friends.

One art which appeals greatly to Mrs Menzies is the ballet. First she was drawn to it by her young daughter's distinct flair for ballet dancing—and later Mr and Mrs Menzies also travelled out from England with the members of the Russian ballet company. At present Madame Dorati, wife of the ballet's principal conductor, is Mrs Menzies' guest.

Mrs Menzies is not greatly interested in sport, but she is regarded by her immediate friends as one of the best women car drivers in the Commonwealth, and one of the best drivers of either sex anywhere. The Prime Minister and his wife almost always travel together. Mrs Menzies has accompanied her husband abroad twice—and she has also accompanied him on air flights. But when they were flying to Germany during their recent stay in England Scotch caution suggested that they should take different planes—and they flew one after the other to the Continent!

Mrs Menzies is by descent a Macgregor—and in the days of the clan wars Macgregors and Menzies often found themselves on opposing sides in an argument. But to-day there is no stauncher supporter of the Prime Minister than the charming woman who now becomes the first political hostess of Australia.

When Mr and Mrs Menzies go into residence at Prime Minister's Lodge, Canberra, their children may be there only at holiday time, for Kenneth and Ian are boarders at Geelong College (Kenneth is a lieutenant in the cadet corps), and Heather is at Ruyton, Kew. . . .

Anticipating the trend of political events by several hours, an admirer of the new Prime Minister sent a beautiful basket of bright red berries to his mother, Mrs James Menzies, of Kew, the morning before he became Prime Minister. The basket bore a card on which was written, 'To the mother of our Prime Minister.'

Mrs Menzies and her husband, who was in State politics for some years, will celebrate their golden wedding this year.

Menzies, as much private testimony and many public polls were later to attest, was attractive to women. He had successfully courted the politically important Australian Women's National League since the Young Nationalist days. As Prime Minister, it became necessary for him to listen and respond to a much wider range of women's voices. *The United Australia Review*, 1 August 1939, recorded an early encounter:

WOMEN'S WANTS
Prime Minister Under Fire
THE DELICATE QUESTION OF DIVORCE

In his visit to Sydney at the beginning of July, the Prime Minister received eloquent and numerical testimony as to the extent and variety of women's organisations in this State. Following on the meeting at which he was greeted and extolled by 800 women at the invitation of the UAP Organisation, he met, on July 3, a gathering of women representatives of 25 organisations of differing shades of opinions. Speakers representing each body read statements of their objectives and views on current problems.

Although he made no claim either to the wisdom of Solon or to the judgment of Solomon, Mr Menzies made some convincing declarations on the far-reaching requests that were made, and cleared the air in regard to others.

No 'Free' Money

The 'Australian Women's Party' asked why the Government did not instruct the Board of the Commonwealth Bank to issue whatever money was necessary for public works, free of interest, 'so lifting from the backs of Australians the intolerable load of interest and taxation'.

Mr Menzies confessed that he was still old-fashioned enough to believe that the money the Government provided must be provided by the people. The millenium had not arrived and he would not encourage the idea of unlimited free money—to encourage such an idea would be to inflict the gravest injury on the wage-earners.

Divorce And Domicile

The united Associations of Women and the Federation of Women Voters had urged that women should have the right to retain their own nationality on marriage; and that married women should have the right to establish their own domicile. Other organisations urged that the Commonwealth should enact uniform divorce laws.

Mr Menzies said that it had not been possible to get uniformity of action with other parts of the Empire on the question of nationality of married women, but the Cabinet would consider the matter to see whether it could offer any constructive suggestions to the other Dominions.

The question of divorce laws was one that affected very large masses of public opinion, he added, and on such questions, which intimately concerned people's religious views, it was necessary to be particularly careful. He said he would not make any rash and off-hand declaration, although he clearly recognised the advantages that would follow on uniform divorce laws throughout the Commonwealth.

On the question of domicile, he would see whether legislation was practicable and effective without simultaneous Federal divorce legislation. It would be difficult, he said, to pass uniform domicile laws and yet leave divorce jurisdiction with the States.

Not Reckless

Replying to a suggestion that Australia should impose economic sanctions against aggressor nations, Mr Menzies said Australia could not act alone.

'To take this course, while holding a continent with 7 000 000 people, we would be the bravest, in fact, the maddest, people in the world,' he declared.

If there was a collective economic move by nations opposed to aggression, Australia would join it.

To other suggestions Mr Menzies replied as follows:—

Abolishing Arms Profits.—Mr Menzies said this would mean that the Government would have to expend millions to undertake the manufacture of war materials itself. Profits were being strictly limited.

Equality of Sexes.—Mr Menzies said women could not be expected to do the same work, under the same conditions, as men.

One basic wage for men and women would mean a wholesale revision of awards, the rates for which were fixed on the basis of a family of four.

Question of Power

Answering other points raised by the organisations, Mr Menzies said that a number of the matters mentioned, including matters of health, were problems with which the Commonwealth had no constitutional authority to deal. The powers of the Commonwealth Government, were extremely limited and in some cases almost absurdly narrow.

Other suggestions showered on Mr Menzies included the following:—

Soroptomist Club: People Northern Australia with Syrians.

Australian Youth Council: Create special department to deal with youth employment.

Racial Hygiene Association: Establish segregation farm colonies throughout Australia for the mentally deficient.

Labour Women's Central Executive, A.L.P.: National insurance to include pensions on a non-contributing basis.

The Arts Club: Restrict jazz music over radio.

International Peace Campaign: Prohibit war toys.

W.C.T.U.: Abolish the wine bounty.

Thus fortified for his task of leading the nation, Mr Menzies that night caught the train for Melbourne, carrying with him lasting recollections of the versatility and ubiquity of the Sydney women's movements.

Whether he introduced unilateral sanctions, abolished profits from arms sales, or prohibited the sale of war toys, there was nothing an Australian leader could do to affect the great upheaval which threatened Europe from the moment that Menzies became Prime Minister. Menzies'

At war, 1939

priorities and budget allocations in 1939 clearly reflected a heightened fear that war could not be long averted.

The Prime Minister's belief in the indivisibility of the Empire in wartime was already well-known. It encountered no opposition within his ministry. Thus, as war seemed increasingly probable, military, air force, and naval planners were able to study the Australian War Book with growing certainty that their prospects of action were inseparable from those of their British counterparts. Confident of the acquiesence

of his Cabinet, Menzies embellished the last weeks of peace with porten-
tously rhetorical speeches and broadcasts. Behind the scenes, public
servants prepared all the necessary documentation for a declaration of
war, and the Prime Minister himself dealt with a tricky question posed
by the acting Chief of the Naval Staff, Captain John Collins:

> . . . Our ships were at sea flying the White Ensign. The question was
> whether they could consider themselves at war when they received the
> signal from the British Admiralty that hostilities had commenced
> against Germany, or should await a further signal from the Australian
> Naval Board. There could be some delay in getting approval to send
> this, and enemy ships might be encountered meantime.
>
> Secraphones had been fitted between Navy Office in Melbourne
> and Parliament House in Canberra at 'Munich' and these had proved
> invaluable. I called Mr Menzies (as he was then) on the scrambled
> line and put the problem to him. After a few seconds' thought he ap-
> roved the suggested signal authorizing HM Australian ships to act on
> the Admiralty War Telegram if and when received. Thus 'Australia
> was there' even before Britain officially declared war.

In his remarkable book, *The Government and the People 1939–1941*
—one of the finest works ever written on twentieth-century Australian
politics—Sir Paul Hasluck has chronicled Menzies' wartime premiership with compassion and clarity. Hasluck's sympathy for the man in
whose Cabinet he was later to serve is undisguised. Yet his pages leave
no doubt that from the time when Menzies told the Australian people
that it was his 'melancholy duty' to inform them that Australia was at
war, to the day nearly two years later when he 'lay down the Prime
Ministership with natural regret', Menzies was engulfed by the torrent
of events. Neither his talents nor his accumulated experience provided
sufficient protection. Before tracing the landmarks in Menzies' decline
and fall, it is appropriate that we should catch a revelatory glimpse of
him a few months after the German invasion of Poland had precipitated
European war. At the end of 1939, at 45 years of age, he was entrenching
himself in the highest post that his country had to offer.

Although he was still a relatively young man, Menzies as Prime
Minister enjoyed a stature and dignity that made it natural for him
occasionally to reflect in public on the changes he had observed in his
lifetime. It is, of course, almost a defining characteristic of conservatives
in any period and in any society that they should express misgivings
about the way in which their social environment has changed. And
Menzies was no exception. He could deliver a persuasive oration on
the benefits and burdens of 'progress'. An opportunity to do so came
at a 'conversazione' held by the Sydney division of the Institution of
Engineers on 18 December 1939. The Prime Minister's presence at this
meeting at the Wentworth Hotel brought the largest attendance that
the Institution had ever had. Disarmingly, Menzies began his address by
apologising that preoccupation with 'other things' had made it impossi-

ble for him to prepare as he would have liked to do. His speech would, therefore, be discursive, and might be regarded as 'a few thoughts about engineers'. In these 'few thoughts', which were published the same month in the Institution's *Journal*, he confessed to some conventional doubts about whether the world had become a better place as a result of engineering innovations. But he also allowed some glimpses of personal tastes and values that less frequently found their way into his public statements:

He often thought, he said, about what had been done by engineers, even during his own lifetime. Whatever foundations had been laid by the pure scientists before 1894, the year of his birth, engineering accomplishments during the years that had passed since that date had revolutionized the mechanics of life, if not human nature.

He thought, first of all, about light. Modern lighting was not usually regarded as being within the revolutionary category, but from the days of flickering candle lights events had so moved until through the miracles of electrical engineering means of turning night into day at a touch had been provided. The Prime Minister said he thought that the effect of this progress in the world, on industry, on private habits and the general conduct of the community was phenomenal.

Mr Menzies referred next to the internal combustion engine. He recalled the use by judges 'and other eminent people' of horse drawn vehicles moving at 'devasting speeds of eight or ten miles an hour'. Mr Menzies told his audience of a Judge of whom it was said that he never drove along Bourke Street, Melbourne, in the crush of traffic without saying to his coachman, 'drive carefully, but if you must knock something down, knock down something cheap'.

Nowadays, he said, the insurance man with his 'knock for knock policy' had made it almost a comfortable thing to knock people down, but whether that was the case or not the truth was, said Mr Menzies, that those of his own generation had never quite adjusted themselves to the new kind of world in which they found themselves.

The Prime Minister said he was born in a little town 240 miles from Melbourne and, as a small boy, he could remember the effect produced when Melbourne newspapers were received three times each week and only two days late. To-day, he said, he could reach that place in five hours driving over a first class road, but he confessed that he did not, neither did he go to other interesting places in Australia simply because he had never accustomed himself to thinking of places one hundred miles or so away as being easily and comfortably reached in two or three hours.

The old notions of distance were giving place to newer ideas which, in a country like Australia, would most likely produce a first class social revolution. The fluidity of movement which was rapidly taking shape in Australia would, he thought, have the effect someday of producing a genuine Australian spirit. There were, he thought, tremendous advantages in these almost fantastic developments in transport.

Mr Menzies recalled a remark by Mr Stanley Baldwin (Earl Baldwin) who once said 'you must never make the error of confusing acceleration with civilization'.

It was a great blunder, said Mr Menzies, to assume that, because with the aid of motor cars, aeroplanes and such like, people could move so much faster than was possible in earlier times, an intrinsic contribution to civilised life had been made. At the same time, he said, engineers with their capacity for objective thinking had produced these means of rapid movement and in challenging fashion had said to the world, 'These are what we have given you, see what kind of use you can make of them.' The engineer, in other words, had done his job but he was not sure, said Mr Menzies, that the rest of the world had done its job in relation to engineering achievements.

Another of the revolutions of the past forty years, the Prime Minister said, was the development in the use of the telephone which had had a very interesting effect on the manners of life. A sharp distinction between Australia and England is noticeable in the matter of the telephone. In England the people write letters, in their own handwriting, much more than is the case in Australia where the telephone and typewriter is relied on to a far greater extent. In this connection Mr Menzies referred to the practice of the earlier Prime Ministers of England, who after meetings of the Cabinet, would write a full report of the decisions reached, in their own handwriting, for the information of the Sovereign.

No Prime Minister of the present day, he said, writes an account of anything in his own handwriting, he usually takes what is placed in front of him, signs it and hopes for the best. That is a revolution, said Mr Menzies, brought about by the invention of the typewriter.

Another interesting sidelight in this connection is that to-day a Foreign Minister of Great Britain is engaged in negotiations with fifty different countries almost every day. At one time such a Minister received elegantly worded despatches brought by special messenger after journeys of from two to four weeks, and himself wrote leisurely replies to be returned in the same way. To-day, said Mr Menzies, there are brought into his room piles of cipher copies of almost instant communications from fifty countries. All of them require not consideration over a few days or a week or two, but within an hour the Minister is required to despatch something that will be prompt, clear and satisfying. The effect that such conditions have had on the tempo of government is a remarkable feature of modern life, and perhaps one of its dangerous features.

The Prime Minister said he had never sat in the office of a Foreign Secretary of Great Britain and talked to him about affairs of the moment without thinking 'what a hag-ridden man he is compared with his predecessors of a past century'. George Canning was able to write a little verse occasionally, things moved in such a leisurely and respectful way. No foreign minister to-day wrote verse. He was very thankful indeed to write prose that would keep his country out of war or further the interests of his country in some place or another.

The Prime Minister said he had been reminded of another thought he would like to express by something the Chairman had said at the outset of the meeting. The Chairman had spoken of the engineer being concerned with pieces of steel, bits of wire, lumps of concrete and other inanimate things. While that was quite true, Mr Menzies said, he envied the engineer the capacity he had for making, with such inanimate things, something that would be capable, centuries hence, of stirring the emotions of man. That was one of the great things the engineer had the opportunity of doing in life. He was, in that sense, not a mere fabricator of inanimate things, but a creative artist. Like a painter or a sculptor, he was able to do something that would be arresting in the world one hundred years hence, and the value of his work on that account, should not be underestimated.

Mr Menzies referred again to England 'that most delightful of countries', and said that what had always stirred him in England was seeing the buildings, bridges and so on made by men, the engineers of the past. The odd, strange and wonderful thing about such things, he thought, was that they enabled a much better understanding of the people than would otherwise be possible.

Mr Menzies told his audience of an experience he had had whilst at Chequers, the home of the British Prime Minister, on one occasion. He was standing with Mr Malcolm MacDonald, the present Colonial Secretary, on a hill overlooking the country towards Oxford. It was an entrancingly lovely scene into which Mr MacDonald had introduced visions of early engineering efforts. He had pointed to the old Roman road to Wendover and had mentioned that it was the 'Ickneald Street' of the Saxons. Although, of course, the road surface had been changed Mr Menzies said, he saw in that scene a perfect engineering summary of British history.

In that same district he had seen also the marks of the old trenches, built by the Saxons in order to resist the Roman invader who came to Britain in the time of Caesar.

The Prime Minister said he had referred to that experience because he wished to emphasize that engineers were not toiling simply in the inanimate. He said he had always believed that there was nothing so ennobling to a profession as a belief amongst its practitioners that there was something more than earning a living in what they were doing. He said the thought that if all had a consciousness, that what they were doing, though at times prosaic, dull and mathematical, was going to make its mark somewhere in the world and would leave something that in time would become animate and a means of interpreting the present to future generations, that all would practise their work with more vigor and success.

Mr Menzies said he believed the remark by Mr Baldwin that acceleration is not civilization, and that scientific success must not be confused with real progress of the spirit which represents civilization to be profoundly true. He was not altogether sure, however, Mr Menzies said, that the engineers who in so short a time had given the world such wonderful things, had had regard to the danger of creating a Frankenstein monster. He had sometimes wondered if they had not, perhaps, encouraged the belief that civilization was proved by the possession of faster aeroplanes, faster motor cars, larger ships and bigger buildings.

There was good reason to know, he said, in the events of the last few months, that a country may have all these things and still be fundamentally uncivilised. A country may have the greatest Air Force in the world, a vast army with the last degree of mechanization, the most skilled engineers and the most brilliant organization and yet be so unaware of the rights of the human being that it may be regarded as uncivilized.

It was a good thing to remember that achievement should not be exaggerated. It would be a good thing if the reasons for the possession of all such things were examined. They were the mere mechanics of life and did not, intrinsically, have anything to do with the utility or the beauty of human lives at all.

The Prime Minister went on to say that what he admired in the engineer more than anything else was his completely objective approach to a problem. The engineer was in the habit of saying 'here is a problem, I must find a solution'. He was not concerned with designing a machine merely to develop a theory, but to build something that would stand the stresses and strains imposed upon it.

To the engineer, Mr Menzies said, nothing is good or bad except in the practical sense. That was as it should be so long as he was acting as an engineer. If he was told to produce a gun, an aeroplane or a submarine, it was his duty to do so as well as he could, but when the engineer ceases, for the time being, to be an engineer, and becomes just a citizen then it might be well to consider that while the objective approach would produce the results aimed at, the results could be good or bad, useful or destructive, according to the way in which their consciousness and the conscience of the community had encouraged the approach.

The work that had been done should not be exaggerated. It had been very clever but it was not yet known whether the world was better or worse because of it. There was no doubt that the world could be better for it but whether it was or not would depend more upon the engineer as a citizen, than upon the engineer as an engineer.

Whilst it was not wise to exaggerate achievements, they should not be minimised, and engineers should not forget that at a time like the present, when the work of engineers was being blown into destruction all over the world, there could be no reason for despair.

On the contrary, the very orgy of destruction that was taking place in the world was a challenge to the engineer more than to anybody else, because a world in a state of ruin must also face reconstruction. A world in which genius was being employed to destroy, was inevitably a world to which sanity would return, and genius would be directed to the work of re-building. However drastic, or however mild, may be the experience of the Australian people in the present struggle, genius would be required for the work of reconstruction.

At the present time, the Prime Minister went on, the business of Government in Australia was to convert everything from peace to war, and to organise and plan in time of war things that people would have been very reluctant to engage in the time of peace. It was the business of Government at the present time, to concentrate industrial, engineering and scientific resources, generally, in the production of things that would destroy and that would themselves be destroyed in the very fact of destroying other things. But whilst this was going on, as it must, because there was a cause to be won and it could not be won except through such things being done, some thought must be given to that reconstruction which would be required after the war was ended.

The business of reconstruction and of laying down foundations for new effort, of setting up plant and providing motive power, is an engineering job.

Although, said the Prime Minister, there must be no distraction from the task of winning a war in which, through no fault of its own the British Empire had become involved, it was necessary that some thought, and later, increasing thought, be given to the work of building up in Australia, organised industrial resources which will ensure that the machine will serve its real purpose of enriching the community and of making the people happier and more prosperous. In such great and challenging work, the engineers of Australia would be called upon to play an even more commanding part in the future than they had played in the past.

In concluding his address the Prime Minister said he envied engineers their part in the work of building Australia. People like himself, he said, were able to help in a way, they could speak a word here, make a decision there, and perhaps exercise some influence, but it was the engineer who was privileged to undertake the real work of building the country and of establishing memorials for the guidance of future generations.

To speak a word here, make a decision there, and perhaps exercise some influence—who would believe that a Prime Minister's ambitions could be so modest? Anyone who knew anything of the agenda of the War Cabinet would be hard to convince. Nevertheless, while the war was far away in Europe and the Middle East, it was not easy for either the Government or the people to grasp its implications. Schemes covering manpower and munitions production, the training of air personnel, the defence of Australia's shores, and a thousand ancillary and complementary problems were discussed and gradually implemented. By early 1940, Menzies was even discussing 'peace aims' with his ministers. He found them, as he confided to Stanley Bruce in London, 'with one or two exceptions, quite unresponsive':

There is, as one might perhaps have expected, a growing feeling among them in favour of the so-called realistic approach, and an almost pathetic belief that the dismemberment of Germany would alter the German spirit and outlook. This seems to me to be a tragic misconception and I shall continue to work upon their minds but the process will be slow.

My impression from your various communications is that Chamberlain and Halifax are very largely in accord with your own views, while Winston is opposed to them. I cannot tell you adequately how much I am convinced that Winston is a menace. He is a publicity seeker; he stirs up hatreds in a world already seething with them and he is lacking in judgment, as witness his recent speech on the position of the Neutrals.

One cannot help sharing to the full your obvious fear that, unless some reasoned view can shortly be arrived at, it will become impossible, and that unless it has been formulated the heat of battle and the bitterness and privations of war will inevitably lead us to another Versailles. I have for a long time believed (though I admit to being wise after the event, and I have no criticism of the treaty-makers under the circumstances in which they met) that in 1919 the Allies had a choice of two practical courses. They could have said, as I think Foch would have liked, that they were going to keep Germany subdued by sheer force of arms and convert her into a sort of slave state; on the other hand they could have said that the war being over they were going to forget it and that instead of exacting reparations they would be prepared to grant even financial assistance to Germany to restore the world's trade, and with it the world's good-will and happiness. I know that the second course would be regarded by many people as 'sappy sentimentality', and as ignoring the brutality of the German spirit, but after all we have tried to alter the German spirit by force. Is it not possible that it might be more effectively altered by conspicuous generosity following on conspicuous defeat? In effect, of course, the Allies took neither course, they alternated between an intransigent French policy and a 'pussy-footing' Henderson policy, and so they made the worst of both worlds.

It is a great pity that the political waters here are so muddy because there is nothing that I should like better than a direct exchange of views upon these matters with members of the British Government.

At the risk of repeating myself, I must say that the policy of conquering and dividing is hopeless; that it completely understimates the virility of the German people and ignores the fact that such a policy breeds a fierce desire for revenge and must inevitably produce results like those of 1938 and 1939.

It is true that we must be careful not to cause a division in the united front which exists at present between Great Britain and France. But like yourself, I have a feeling that the problem cannot be postponed forever and that, if it were deferred until the peace negotiations after the war, divisions might then occur which would be even more dangerous in a Europe enfeebled by years of war than they would be at present.

The one aspect of your letter about which I feel real doubt relates to the degree of particularity with which we should state our aims. My own view is that, during the currency of the war at least, our statements should be as general as possible, the objectives of a community of nations freely, honourably and equally negotiating with each other being put in the forefront, but the particular questions relating to such matters as economic adjustments, access to raw materials, etc., being left for future consideration.

Your remarks about Russia seem to me to be most appropriate. I cannot doubt that if the war lasts long enough there will be a rapid spread of Bolshevism in Germany and in the Danubian States. Under these circumstances a new alignment of nations in which not only Great Britain and France, but Germany and Italy, combined to resist Bolshevism is by no means impossible, and so long as it is a possibility it must affect our view as to the nature of the war objectives which we now state to the German (and incidentally to the Italian) people.

As you say, no nation will indefinitely be prepared to shoulder the burden of giving effect to a repressive military policy. It is perhaps more easily contemplated at present, when the full burden of war expenditure has not been felt, than it will be later on when people will realise vividly that an indefinite continuance of the war burden will mean an indefinite postponement of social amelioration and growing dissatisfaction on the part of ordinary men and women, with results that cannot be foreseen. So far as Australia is concerned, there would be a violent unwillingness to continue the burden of armaments for the mere purpose of keeping some other great power in a state of submission. The fact is that we British people, while we are seldom magnanimous to our friends are invariably magnanimous to our enemies, and the more experience people have of war the stronger and not the weaker will that feeling be.

Your summarised reasons why a policy of repression is impracticable are entirely in line with my own ideas. Two years ago, I would have said that the idea of an international force to keep the world's peace was hopelessly academic. But when this war is over, I think the nations will find themselves immeasurably more disposed to accept it than they ever have been before. When I say this I am referring not only to the air force, but to an international army and navy. None of the three is, I think, practicable if the war comes to an inconclusive end, but an unequivocal defeat of Germany, accompanied by great financial and commercial and nervous exhaustion in all the relevant countries, might, in my opinion, provide the right atmosphere for its establishment.

One cannot, of course, shut one's eyes to the fact that the latent fear in our minds in Australia is that when this war has been finished we will need to prepare for another and defensive war against Japan. Personally, I do not rate this possibility very high, but I would feel more satisfied about it if I really believed that the British Foreign Office had a practical and realistic view of the Far-Eastern position. One's instinctive judgment is that the Japanese have a marked inferiority complex and that a real gesture of friendship with some real assistance in the settlement of the Chinese question, accompanied by a proper recognition of Japanese trading ambitions, might very easily produce peace in the Far East, particularly if Japan was, by that time, feeling the impact of Russian Bolshevism.

Speaking without much knowledge I have had a feeling that America's approach to these matters has been over-sentimental and that much good work is to be done in persuading America that she has her real interests in common with the British Empire in the Pacific and that a generous understanding would be more effective than prejudice and a series of somewhat pontifical moral reproofs.

Your remarks about the relative merits of a future international organisation upon a world or a regional basis appeal to me very much. Right through the Abyssinian trouble, I felt that the failure of the League was not due to its attempting to do too little, but to its attempting to do too much. The view of the League that I had, therefore, would indicate that it should be remodelled in such a fashion as to make it workable. Nations will much more readily undertake obligations in relation to an area in which they have an immediate interest than in relation to an area some of the countries in which are remote. As you say, regions might in some instances overlap. For example, Australia has an immediate and vital concern in the Pacific, it also has a mediate but none the less vital interest in any region of which Great Britain is a member.

These remarks, of course, apply with special force to any organisation in which direct obligations affecting peace and war are to be assumed. You are no doubt right in saying that the solution of economic and social problems requires a collaboration of all the principal nations on a world basis. I have read your practical proposals for such economic and social adjustments with great interest, but I feel that any attempt to be precise in relation to them would be doomed to failure because it would prejudice acceptance of the general scheme by diverting the discussion to particular issues.

I am a good deal concerned to know just how I should move in this matter. As you point out, the Dominion Prime Ministers might easily exercise a desirable influence in the direction of rationalising our war effort and not letting it degregate into a more 'hymn of hate'. But misunderstanding both in our own countries and in the enemy country might easily arise. Several newspapers in Australia are already quite disposed to criticise me violently for having what they believe to be a philosophic approach to a matter in which they think my proper function is a mixture of swashbuckling and rhetoric. The Germans, in their turn, would be quick to seize upon anything which they could construe as a weakening of the Allied war effort or as a desire to obtain peace without victory.

If only a kindly Providence would remove from the active political scene a few minds which are heavily indoctrinated by the 'old soldiers' and by the 'Versailles' point of view, my task here would be easier.

Providence was not in a kindly mood in 1939 and early 1940. The Australian people seemed strangely unready for war. The Government had appeared to waver between a policy of 'business as usual', designed to avert dislocation and disharmony, and rapid mobilisation of men and resources. Inevitably, it attracted criticism from people who thought both that it was doing too much and too little. Personal criticism of the Prime Minister was severe. J.V. Barry, QC, a colleague from the Victorian Bar, wrote to him on 27 May 1940 that the 'continual malicious sniping' to which he was being subjected was 'revolting to one's sense of fairness and feeling for the decencies of controversy'. Much of the sniping was predictable party polemic and dealt with issues of ephemeral interest. But it was possible to see a pattern in the sporadic and varied attacks on the Government's errors and omissions. There was a widespread belief that what was wrong was inextricably bound up with the character and personality of Menzies himself. In a powerful attack on the mentality of the 'phoney war', the editor Brian Penton, in *Advance Australia—Where?*, castigated strikers, profiteers, and other complacent

A joke shared? Arthur Fadden with the Prime Minister, January 1940

citizens who chose men as political leaders for their 'acquiescent, commonplace mentalities' and then beat them over the head for not imposing discipline on the nation. He then went on to identify the weaknesses of the Prime Minister:

The Government was a collection of fair-average talents led by an exceptional man—Robert Gordon Menzies. . . . His special gift was enunciating, anatomizing a problem; his special weakness was his belief that a problem enunciated was a job done. He really believed that when he said Australia was going to manufacture planes, guns, tanks, these commodities began at once to roll off the line. He had a lawyer's faith in the magic cantrap of words, which he used more gracefully and incisively than any politician Australia had known. But before Australia began to get planes, guns, and tanks out of her factories in quantities commensurate with her danger, she had to solve a colossal social and industrial problem. The mediocrities with whom Mr Menzies surrounded himself in Cabinet were unable to tackle these problems— to buck the rich vested interests on their own side who must be driven into line, to command the trust and support of the other side, notably of the big industrial unions, who also must be disciplined to service. Mr Menzies's own history was not an asset. He had gone to Germany and come home favourably impressed by many of the changes he saw. He had fought with wharf-labourers who refused to load scrap iron for Japan and compelled them to resume this doubtful traffic, which mocked our professions of pity for China's suffering. He had echoed most of the optimistic platitudes of the Chamberlain Government.

These first two years the war brought only defeats—he and his Government had to take the discredit for these. They brought Chamberlain down, they helped to bring Menzies down, too. In the meantime, they pointed criticism at his incapable colleagues and his halting administration. In the current state of Australian mind any administration would have fumbled the ball. Menzies tried to say so, but, great as his powers of expression were, he could not get near the people. Too proudly he wore the mantle of 'the superior man', whose leadership he invoked with a profound insight into the defects of Australian democracy. When that man came forth to lead us he would be less conscious of his superiority than was Mr Menzies. Superiority mixed with humility was the only kind of superiority this paradise of the average was likely to accept. So, for two years Mr Menzies talked down to the people about their duty, and life went on very much the same as in peace-time, only better.

Unravelling the causes of Menzies' decline and fall is a major task. No historian in the last twenty years has attempted it. The available sources—both written and oral—make it possible to throw light in corners which were dim or in shadow in Hasluck's account. With the passage of time, some restraints and inhibitions have been relaxed. Fresh testimony has been recorded. The former Labor minister, John

Dedman, for example, argued in an instalment of his memoirs in 1967 that the circumstances surrounding his own election to the House of Representatives early in 1940 were vital to Menzies' future:

The decision to send the sixth division overseas was made by the full cabinet towards the end of November.

In announcing this decision to the parliament Menzies stated that 'adequate assurances have been given with respect to the capacity and availability of the Royal Navy, which is after all our first line of defence, to give to us protection against any major aggression'.

John Curtin reacted by moving an amendment that no expeditionary force be sent overseas. He 'preferred to have some clearer exposition of what was to be the ultimate alignment of nations in this struggle before consenting to the stripping in any degree of the manpower resources of this country'.

In January 1940 the sixth division embarked for overseas.

In the same month, Casey resigned from the ministry to become the first Australian minister to the United States.

I am sure Menzies blundered in sanctioning this appointment. Casey was an experienced and senior minister whose portfolio (Supply and Development), created only nine months earlier, was one of the most important in the ministry. The Washington post could have been filled by someone equally capable of undertaking the tasks pertaining to that office—Sir John Latham, the chief justice, was later to represent Australia in Japan. Casey's appointment, which entailed a by-election in Corio, was the first of a series of events which finally led to the defeat of the Menzies government and the accession to office of a Labor government.

In the Corio by-election at which I was the Labor candidate, Curtin stated that the Labor party would support the sending of reinforcements to the sixth Division, but would oppose any more divisions being sent overseas. Menzies made it clear that he had no intention of introducing conscription for overseas service. Both leaders outlined plans for stepping up the war effort. Menzies coined a slogan—'The eyes of Hitler are on Corio' and the UAP candidate another—'Vote for the Australian-born returned soldier'.

I now think that the election, which resulted in my obtaining a majority of 3000 votes, was won largely on an issue unconnected with the conduct of the war.

Late in 1939, the government had entered into an arrangement with Australian Consolidated Industries for the manufacture of motor cars in Australia. There was no doubt that this arrangement was inimical to the interests of the Ford Motor Company, the largest industrial firm in Corio and the pride of Geelong city. The transactions became the subject of even greater criticism when it became known that the managing director of ACI had leased a racehorse to the Minister for Customs, who had negotiated the arrangement.

Years after I had retired from politics a former executive officer of the Ford company informed me that during the last week of the campaign, the managing director of the Ford company instructed his subordinates to muster every vote they could for the Labor candidate.

How the arrangement with ACI was not vetoed in cabinet by Mr Casey, who was vitally interested both as the member for Corio and as minister for supply and development is something of a mystery. The loss of Corio and the resignation of the Minister for Customs compelled Menzies to reconstruct his ministry by bringing into it some members of the Country Party. In doing so he agreed to permit the Country Party members of his cabinet to vote as individuals when the agreement between Australian Consolidated Industries and the government come before parliament. They did so. Immediately after the election, it was announced that another division—the seventh, would be recruited for overseas service.

It must here be conceded that the first six or seven months of the war constituted a period of great difficulty for whoever happened to be Leader of the Australian government. Although the people were almost unanimously in agreement that the forces of aggression launched by Hitler had to be halted, they were uncertain about the extent and form of the contribution Australia could or should make. . . .

Could anyone else have given a better leadership to the people than did Mr Menzies during those early months of war? Perhaps his use of the phrase 'business as usual' on one occasion was unfortunate but the fact is that the people were not then ready to submit to that high degree of direction by the government which is a *sine qua non* of an all-in war effort. Only under a dictatorship could the tempo of the war effort have been greatly accelerated at that time. No leader in a democracy can pursue a policy very far in advance of public opinion; if he does he will soon be displaced and in Australia an election was due towards the end of 1940.

As the prospect of a general election loomed in mid-1940, one issue seemed to epitomise the allegations of government muddle, indecision, and opportunism. Since early in the war there had been rumours that petrol rationing was to be introduced. Although ministers denied any such intention, the permanent head of the Supply Department was working out a scheme under which private motorists would be restricted to 2000 miles a year or 40 miles a week, and commercial vehicles would have an annual range of 2500 to 15 000 miles depending on type. On 11 July 1940 the Minister for Supply, Sir Frederick Stewart, announced that this drastic scheme would operate from September 1. In a hard-hitting book published by the Sydney *Daily Telegraph* in October 1941, the ensuing events were scathingly recounted:

 . . . Sir Frederick Stewart left for Sydney the night he announced the scheme, but his announcement caused a nation-wide uproar from the motoring and petrol trades and from private motorists. Sir Frederick spent the next few desperate days trying to square off. Eventually he admitted that the scheme he had announced had not been entirely approved by Cabinet, but he expected Cabinet to approve.

The Cabinet, however, got the jitters, and Sir Frederick Stewart asked his department to draw up an alternate scheme, more liberal than the original.

In the meantime Mr Menzies . . . tried to calm the upset public mind. He announced that all the Cabinet had decided was that petrol rationing be introduced to cut consumption by $33\frac{1}{3}$ per cent. Mr Menzies added: 'The particular method of achieving this result has never been before Cabinet, and the proposals announced on July 11 were merely recommendations by the Petrol Control Board.'

On August 17, the Federal Cabinet decided to introduce a petrol rationing scheme giving private motorists 4000 miles a year instead of the original 2000 miles a year proposed. This scheme—the first real rationing scheme introduced in Australia—began on October 1 instead of September 1 as originally intended. The next cut was on March 31, 1941. By this time the tougher Senator McBride had replaced Sir Frederick Stewart as Supply Minister. Under the new scheme private motorists suffered mostly. They were reduced from 4000 to 3000 miles a year. On February 14, 1941, Senator McBride said that the scheme introduced on October 1, 1940, had not resulted in a $33\frac{1}{3}$ per cent cut on pre-war consumption. He said: 'The new scheme is aimed at ensuring that consumption is cut back to this level. The decision was based on Cabinet's knowledge of the grave deterioration in the war situation which makes it vital to reduce petrol consumption and build up emergency stocks.'

As the situation got worse the Cabinet planned more cuts.

The next big cut was on June 1, 1941. This reduced rations all round by 20 per cent. Plans had also been made in May, 1941, to reduce rations for business and pleasure cars from August 1. Between June and August, 1941, various schemes were introduced to cut civilian consumption to 12 000 000 gallons a month for August and September. . . .

Long before France fell a group of departmental heads and economists associated with the Government worked far into many nights preparing a review of Australia's resources and urging policies to increase and organise these resources. . . .

Experts of the war departments are still preparing plans—for diversion of manpower, for increasing the production of munitions, for improving price control, to mention only a few of the big problems— and hoping that one day we will have a Government strong enough to be unpopular and get these matters straightened out.

A new figure appeared on the political scene in the spring of 1940. Dr H.V. Evatt stepped down from the High Court Bench to enter the electoral contest because, he said, he believed it 'essential that nothing should stand in the way of a fresh effort to give Australia victory in war

followed by social advancement and high standards of living in the peace
which is to come.' Evatt's determination to do something useful in the
war was unmistakeable. His speech at Hurstville on 4 September 1940
was trenchant in its criticism of his old legal rival and his Government.
This was Evatt at the height of his intellectual power, with strong
political conviction and enthusiasm to serve. The indictment of the
Menzies Ministry's performance, and of the Prime Minister's personal
responsibility, was formidable. These extracts are from the carefully
revised text of Evatt's speech at Hurstville, as released to the press for
publication the following day:

> The crucial question is whether Mr Menzies should be appointed
> to direct Australia's efforts or whether it is not better for the Empire
> and Australia that the Commonwealth Government should be en-
> trusted to the Labor Party under the leadership of Mr John Curtin.
>
> At the outset it should be emphasised that there is agreement between
> us all as to the absolute necessity of Australia's maintaining and im-
> proving her war effort. The great issue between the parties has arisen
> because of the almost universal distrust of the ability of the Menzies'
> Government to co-ordinate and improve Australia's contribution to
> the struggle in which our lives and fortunes are engaged. . . .
>
> I have not the slightest personal feeling against the present Prime
> Minister. Tonight I shall criticise him firmly and strongly but honestly
> and only in relation to his public acts, his public administration and
> his public leadership of the Australian people. His administration is
> after all only a loose fusion—or confusion—of UAP and UCP. The
> UAP has a somewhat different policy in each State of the Common-
> wealth. Similarly with the UCP. For instance, in Victoria, Mr Dun-
> stan's CP Government exhibits liberal tendencies. . . .
>
> . . . The truth is that the Menzies' administration has little to keep
> it together except the fear of the Labor Party. It would seem to follow
> that it is not reasonable to expect unified command and true adminis-
> trative co-ordination from such a coalition.
>
> In point of fact it is notorious that the administration of the Govern-
> ment has been characterised by vacillation and incompetence. I do
> not think it is necessary to describe every administrative bungle of the
> Menzies Ministry—that would take a week or more—but I shall refer
> to one or two of the most glaring cases. Several months ago while
> France was collapsing the Sydney press almost unanimously con-
> demned the Government for instances of gross slackness and negligence
> in the departments of the Army, the Air and Munitions. . . .
>
> . . . At that time Mr Menzies was, as he still is, the responsible Minis-
> ter for co-ordinating the essential services of defence. . . . I would
> refer you to the very remarkable series of exposures published in the
> Sydney 'Daily Telegraph'. They created a profound sensation through-
> out Australia. They proved a state of shocking unpreparedness com-
> bined with fatuous complacency on the part of those responsible. The
> substantial truth of the exposures was practically admitted on all

sides, and the so-called explanations of Ministers made the position seem even less defensible. As a result the outcry throughout Australia was so unanimous and persistent that undoubtedly some improvements have since been effected.

But today Australians must ask themselves—who is it who was politically responsible for the self-satisfied and indolent attitude which had caused Australia to be placed in such imminent peril? Unfortunately the blame was not pressed home to its final source. The Press blamed Mr Street, Mr Fairbairn and Sir Frederick Stewart. Why is it that, in this extraordinary Federal government, whenever maladministration of negligence is revealed it always seems to be pre-arranged that the person to take the blame is the subordinate minister but never the Prime Minister. Here we come to the very crux of the present political crisis in Australia. . . . In times like this we need a leader such as Mr Churchill. Mr Chamberlain and Mr Menzies are shown to be quite inadequate in face of the tremendous crisis of war. . . .

The policy of Mr Menzies' Government seems always to be subject to amendment or sudden reversal. Witness the notorious attempt to control the press. Even these press regulations have not been entirely abandoned, and if they are carefully studied in their amended form they show that great powers may still be exerted against independent papers under the guise of protecting national security. Similarly with the bungle over petrol rationing. I do not know whether any such rationing was or is necessary. If it was necessary it should have been introduced carefully and systematically and many months ago. The whole thing fills patriotic citizens with nausea. . . .

When Mr Menzies says 'Yes' he means 'Perhaps'. When he says 'Perhaps' he means 'No'. When he says 'No' you can't even be sure that he doesn't mean 'Yes'. This kind of administration is absolutely indefensible, and it must be ended. In time of peace it may be a good joke. In time of war, where every hour counts, it is a national tragedy.

. . . I firmly believe that when the history of these times comes to be written, it will be found that never before in Australia's history has there been a ministry so irresponsible and inefficient as the Menzies Government. It is irresponsible because through his publicity officers the Prime Minister has developed the habit of throwing responsibility for Cabinet decisions upon individual Ministers whenever such decisions turn out to be unpopular. In this way Sir Frederick Stewart was forced to take the odium for the wretched mess of the petrol rationing scheme in order that Mr Menzies should go scot-free. Sir Keith Murdoch was forced to take the blame for the attempt to muzzle the press although it is certain that the Prime Minister knew all about the matter beforehand. In the same way Mr Cameron had to carry the baby for the wheat muddle, Mr Hughes for the atrocious handling of the coal dispute and Mr Spender for the financial swing towards deflation. In all of these things the Prime Minister took care to throw the blame for the joint decision upon the individual Minister.

But Mr Menzies now comes before the people in an even more deceptive guise. He says, and how well it sounds, 'Give us a national ministry, I am a generous man, I am even willing to give Labour a few well-paid portfolios. How good am I'. Let us examine this a little more closely. Mr Menzies suggests that this is the great issue of the election.

Let me make one or 2 points clear. Labor believes that, in an emergency like the present, the best brains of the nation should be invited to come to the assistance of the nation. It is evident that unless Mr Menzies shares that belief, all his talk of a national ministry is sheer political hypocrisy. The question therefore arises—does he want the best brains of the nation to serve the Australian people in their hour of need? Or, on the other hand, does he want to exercise power autocratically and tyrannically with a Cabinet of 'Yes men' around him? When Mr Theodore was willing to assist in Australia's financial organisation and Mr Spender had suggested his name to the conference of State Premiers, Mr Menzies allowed Mr Theodore to be rebuffed, humiliated, and almost insulted. It would seem probable that Mr Menzies did not want the assistance of a man of brains. When Mr Dunstan was patriotically minded to enter the Federal Parliament and surrender his post and prestige as State Premier, did Mr Menzies welcome him, or scowl at him? Then there is the case of Mr Stevens . . . he was Premier of this great State for a longer period than any other man and . . . he had the courage to resign his seat in Parliament and offer his help to the nation. How did Mr Menzies receive his offer? He buttoned up his overcoat as though Mr Stevens had been a pickpocket and let his select claque of publicity officers humiliate Mr Stevens in the eyes of the Australian nation. I mention these three cases because the political party was different in each case. One was a Labor man, one was a UCP man and one was a UAP man. Mr Menzies wanted none of them. Like the Turk he was not content with his throne and his right of ruling, he could bear no one to be near him.

If this represents the true attitude of Mr Menzies to proved ability it is fair to conclude that his cry of a national ministry is a sham and a pretence. I say deliberately that a national ministry under Mr Menzies is an absolute impossibility, that responsible government cannot exist while he remains Prime Minister, and that the sooner Labor is put into office and power the sooner we shall return to responsible government with a ministry carrying out the people's will fearlessly, quickly and as an undivided unit. . . .

But the case against the Prime Minister does not end even there. The whole question of a national ministry is a fictitious question. For Mr Menzies' real object during the last few months has recently been revealed in the remarkable speech of Mr Cameron at Bairnsdale. It would seem that Mr Menzies was so intent on retaining office and power that he actually proposed to invoke the aid of the Parliament at Whitehall to pass a special Act for the amendment of the Australian Constitution. Under our Constitution, the House of Representatives can endure for three years, but no longer. The Constitution can only be amended by popular referendum. As Mr Menzies well knew that the people of Australia would never agree to extend the life of the House of Representatives, he thought that his political friends on the other side of the world might come to his assistance. But he seemed to have reckoned without his host. Mr Chamberlain was no longer in power, and the great War effort of England was under the entirely new management of Mr Churchill and Mr Attlee, the Leader of the Labor Party. It is certain that English Labor would never have been a party to destroying the democratic rights of the Australian people to elect their representatives every three years. The inference is that it was only when he was finally baulked in this attempt to abrogate our constitutional rights, that the Prime Minister, anxious to retain office at all costs, decided upon a snap dissolution in which he would assert that Labor was obstructing his patriotic endeavour to form a truly national government. He wrote a marvellous letter to Mr Curtin. Mr Menzies will tell you that it is very easy to write a marvellous letter and make all sorts of charming assertions in it provided you are quite certain what the answer to your letter will be. If a young man knows for certain that a girl will reject his offer of marriage he can easily produce a letter that sounds sincere. So with Mr Menzies' letter. He knew that Mr Curtin was bound by the decisions of a representative Labor Conference to reject any coalition or fusion with Mr Menzies . . . I advise the Australian people to have nothing more to do with such transparent political manoeuvres. Labor will be the national ministry of Australia. Remember that Mr Menzies is staggering along to the polls with no budget for the ensuing 12 months, and no policy save a string of platitudes. We don't know how his ministry would exercise the taxing power except that, from past experience, it would seem that it would be quite prepared to cast further and heavier burdens upon the middle classes and the workers by increasing sales tax, petrol tax and other forms of indirect taxation. It is a public scandal that, although there has been 12 tragic months of War, no war-time profits Act has yet been passed. The Menzies Government represents the interests who hope to make large profits out of war. Let us see to it that they do not succeed.

As Mr Menzies has failed the middle classes, so he has been adamant against the just claims of industrial labor. He admits that industrial labor is loyal. How typical of Mr Menzies to make himself the judge of the loyalty of the workers! . . . If he admits that Labor is loyal, why does he use, or abuse, the National Security Act by imposing unfair restrictions on the personal freedom and liberty of the munition workers? Today munition workers are not allowed to move freely from job to job even although their housing conditions are disgraceful. Discontent is so rife that the great Amalgamated Engineering Union has had to call a special stop-work meeting. This is the selfsame policy of intimidation and bluster which was pursued throughout the coal dispute . . . for 11 or 12 weeks and caused great economic loss. Mr Menzies must be taught to realise that the Australian people cannot be driven by methods of repression or by threats of legal punishment. . . .

Mr Menzies has failed, just as Mr Chamberlain failed. Each man was sincere. Each man was so anxious to avoid war that he took inadequate steps to prepare against it. Each man was consumed with a conviction of his own indispensability. Therefore, in spite of great qualities, each man failed to produce national unity in the face of the common enemy. It may be that each man did his best. But in each case that best was not nearly good enough.

I believe that most of what I have said will be immediately accepted even by UAP, and certainly by UCP supporters. Few persons can be found to defend the Prime Minister's administration. All they can say is 'Who else is there?' Ladies and gentlemen, fancy our beloved Australia being governed by a 'Who else is there' Prime Minister! But the question is so easy to answer. Who else is there? John Curtin, Leader of the Labor Party, a lover of Australia, a lover of liberty, and a fighter for social justice.

One of the undercurrents of dissatisfaction with the Menzies Government was the persistent story that he favoured Melbourne over Sydney whenever the interests of the two cities were in conflict. Among the first people to write to Dr Evatt when he emerged as a Labor candidate was a troubled accountant from Beecroft in New South Wales:

11–9–40

Dear Sir,

Last night I heard the Arch-Parochialist Menzies at the Town Hall —He is a parochialist because his main effort (to my mind) from his entry as P.M. has been to keep the Capital in Melbourne at the expense of *Australia*, not Sydney alone.

He beat Hughes 21/19 for the UAP Leadership and on becoming PM, elected his ministers—Casey *Supply*, Street *Defence*, Fairbairn *Air*, Gullett *Information*, and one or two others. Kept the *Treasurership* for himself—

My point is that every big spending department under the enlarged defence scheme on which millions (55 at that time) were to be spent, had as its minister a Victorian.

He created the Supply Department and immediately proceeded to spend lavishly on buildings to house it in Melbourne, not in Canberra. I read in the papers that the plans are now prepared for a building to cost £50000 to house a scientific research laboratory in Melbourne (not in Canberra) so increasing difficulties of transfer to Canberra.

I am informed, and believe that Melbourne war factories are kept going at full pressure (or nearly so). While any shortness of material labour organisation is reflected in factories in Sydney and elsewhere.

At this stage let me say that I have been voting UAP (under different names) for some 20 years now, but recognising that for the benefit of Australia that 'Menzies must go' I seek a party prepared to commit itself to govern from Canberra, and to progressively and quickly transfer to Canberra all government departments, is the official Labour Party prepared to do this—A start could be made with Supply Department. The research bureau could be established at Canberra where it belongs and other departments transferred in order. The expense would be as nothing to the advantages gained for Australia in war effort by a population (other than Victorian) in a satisfied frame of mind—one could write on for hours of points which occur but I have no hours to spare —I will endeavour to get into Mr Curtin's meetings and hope to hear soon an announcement of government for Australia from Canberra.

Yours faithfully,
W. Thatcher

What worried Mr Thatcher worried many other people as well. But, in addition to those who were genuinely upset by manifestations of apparent bias, there were more potent critics who placed their own interests before those of the nation—men whose lack of patriotism and lack of humanity reinforced the Prime Minister's long-standing prejudices about the shortsightedness and selfishness of the mass of mankind. Many times in his life, Menzies had occasion to speak publicly on the subject of democracy. Usually he spoke at length in terms that were relatively uncontroversial. Just after the general election in 1940, he wrote a short foreword to a book on the life of Sir Littleton Groom. In his office at Victoria Barracks in Melbourne, in the midst of anxiety about the reconstruction and stability of his own government, he wrote in a way that clearly exposed his unhappiness with the Australian people:

It is a regrettable feature of our politics that the name 'politician' has come to be spoken, if not with contempt, at least with indifference, with a shrug. And yet, in a self-governing country, politics must be the greatest business. Indeed, politics, the art of government, is no mere business, since it deals not with the profit or loss of the conductor, but with the profit or loss of millions of others. It is a vocation, the highest civil vocation to which a man may be called. Burke's famous words are (as so often) perfectly in point: 'to bring the dispositions that are lovely in private life into the service and conduct of the Commonwealth'; that is the business of politics.

It is a common error to talk of democracy, the essence of which we are defending in this war, as if it were a great end achieved by our race during the long struggle of history. In reality, it is a means, not an end. The fact that all adult persons have an equal right to elect Parliament, to approve or reject policies, to grant or refuse mandates, is in itself an indifferent fact. How that right is exercised is the crucial, the dynamic fact. No matter how numerous the electors may be, their votes, if given idly, corruptly, selfishly or ignorantly. cannot be the sign of freedom and equality, but are merely an expression of slavery no less abject than that of a dictatorship. In other words, democracy is a good and a splendid thing only if it embodies a spirit of individual responsibility and social, not individual, advantage. At its best, it can

represent the enfranchisement of the human spirit, with all those
ideals of freedom and justice which flow from it. At its worst, it can
produce tyranny as well as any medieval or modern despotism; for
the injustice of a mob differs only mathematically from the injustice
of a single tyrant.

The price of a good democracy is thus seen to be eternal vigilance.
The hall-mark of a good democrat is equally clearly seen not to be
fluency, plausibility or cunning, but character, constancy, unselfishness
and a clear understanding that we are our brother's keeper, and that
we are bound to think more of our brother than of ourselves.

These, you may say, are counsels of perfection. True, they are.
None of us can hope to embody them completely in his own conduct.
But 'a man's reach should exceed his grasp, or what's a heaven for?'

Whatever the trials or torments of the coming years, we shall do
well to keep our faith clear. For a clear faith as to the cause and the
goal is the one thing that can really glorify war and convert it from a
brutal deflowering of humanity into a good and holy thing.

There was something implicity prophetic in Menzies' apprehension
of the injustice of the mob. His own time of trial had almost arrived—a
time of judgement but not necessarily of justice.

IV

THE
HUMILIATION
1941

THE RECORD of Menzies' wartime government is sometimes written as though it were an uninterrupted story of drift—a sorry failure to measure up to the level that events demanded. Its poor performance in the September 1940 general election—its majority vanished, leaving the UAP–Country Party coalition, which had been formed in March 1940, to rely on the votes of two Independents—demonstrated at least that the government was not completely in tune with public opinion. Attempts by UAP publicists to identify their government with the recently created Churchill administration in Britain were frustrated by lack of the essential Churchillian ingredient—the kind of man whom Menzies had described to Bruce in February 1940 as 'a menace' and 'a publicity seeker' who lacked judgement and stirred up hatreds. That there were achievements made by the Menzies Government, however, is not to be denied. In London on 11 March 1941, the Prime Minister himself summarised what had been done, so far as it could be publicly advertised, at a meeting of the study committees of the Empire Parliamentary Association at the House of Commons:

> We, as an integral part of one people found ourselves, as I imagine other British countries did at the beginning of this war, not very well

prepared for it. I became Prime Minister in April 1939. In that financial
year, ending in June, we spent on defence in Australia £14 000 000;
and strange as it may be, looking back on it, we rather thought we had
done pretty well. 'Why', we said, 'this is a record peace-time expenditure in the history of this country'; and there were a few people who
thought we were almost war-mongers for having spent so much. I will
remind you that we have just reached our seventh million of population,
and so we thought £14 000 000 was not bad. In this financial year, to
the well-concealed joy of the tax-payers of Australia, we are spending
just on £200 000 000 on the same purpose!

Now, Sir, on what principle have we laid out these sums and recruited
large forces, and set in train processes of manufacture for the purposes
of war? On three guiding principles. In the first place it is our responsibility to defend our own country. That is no small responsibility.
Australia and New Zealand share with Great Britain the extraordinary
dual responsibility of defending themselves against possible attack at
home and participating actively and extensively in operations abroad
. . . it has been necessary for us on this occasion, as it was not on the
last, to provide for our own defence in such force that we shall be able
to resist any probable or possible attack by any possible enemy. . . .

Our second responsibility . . . was to make the most effective
possible contribution to the joint Empire effort wherever and whenever
it might be required and pursuant to that we have been able to do
certain things that I will refer to in a moment.

Our third responsibility was to see that those forces we had provided
both at home and abroad were adequately equipped, not with museum
pieces but with modern equipment. That responsibility was perhaps
the most difficult of all to discharge. . . .

At the present time we have a Defence Force for Australia which is
built up on the basis of having at any given moment a quarter of a
million men, each of whom will have had at least ninety days consecu-
tive camp training; and this has revolutionized the position of our
internal defence. At an early stage of the war we re-introduced compulsory military training. We have no conscription for overseas, but
we have compulsion for training and local service, and accordingly
when we want to keep this force of ours up we can do it by bringing
in fresh drafts of trainees under the compulsory provisions of the
Defence Act. The importance of having a local Force is twofold. In
itself it affords us a real land defence of Australia, but in the second
place it is the best of all recruiting grounds for the Forces that are to
be organized and sent overseas. . . .

We have an Air Force in Australia. I suppose the number of pilots
that we had when war broke out was at that time regarded as a military
secret. It can be regarded now only as a matter of curiosity, because, as
I remember it, we were training in Australia to produce 420 front-line
pilots for the Royal Australian Air Force, and we had not reached that
objective when war broke out. But we have now contracted over an
agreed period, and I am happy to say we are well ahead of our contract

in point of performance, to train and produce under the Empire Air Training Scheme for service anywhere a total of 20 000 pilots, gunners and observers, and in the meantime we have largely extended the actual numbers of our local Air Force.

On the naval side, of course, you can never say that any Force is purely local. The Navy has great fluidity, as I am constantly being reminded, though I doubt on the whole whether it has as much fluidity as the Italian Navy! But we did after all establish the Royal Australian Navy, which was designed primarily to defend our trade routes. So that in these three particular ways we were attending to our own defence. Then we approached the problem of oversea Forces. On the naval side we placed many of the vessels of the Royal Australian Navy, a not very large Navy, at the disposition of the Royal Navy itself. I am sure there were political risks attaching to what we did at the time we did it, but I have some satisfaction now, looking back on it, in realizing that many units of our Navy have taken part in combats in the Atlantic, in the Mediterranean, and in the Red Sea, and I think it can be said with safety that not one ship we were able to send has not been concerned in some glorious and successful adventure.

On the Air side I have already mentioned in a very passing fashion the Empire Air Scheme. This scheme is, I believe, the greatest piece of Empire co-operation yet evolved in this war. When we were communicated with from here, and when we were told of the numbers that would be required, I must say that we sat in Cabinet and looked at each and said: 'The spirit must be willing, and therefore the answer is 'Yes',' but we really did not know how we were going to get those numbers. You see, in the days before this war began, we all of us used to operate a great deal by rule of thumb. Worthy men were to be heard in every corner who said to you: 'Ah, but there is a limit to the number of airmen a country can produce.' I remember saying: 'What is the limit?' and I was told that the limit was that you could produce one effective air-crew man out of every thousand of the population. And I remember questioning that with all the scepticism of the lawyer—for I used to be a lawyer—and being told that I did not understand these things, but that that was the fact.

So that when we were asked to produce 20 000 instead of 7000, which would have been our proportion on the alleged rule, we felt a little uneasy. The scheme is not very old yet, but its first-fruits are already to be seen walking in blue uniform in the streets of London. Before I left home I asked for the current figures up to December, and I found that out of this vast undertaking to be performed over a period of two or three years we already had actually in training 4000 men under the scheme, and we had on a waiting list placed to a reserve, fully examined and tested both physically and mentally and morally, and by whatever other examination an airman has to go through, 8000 men. . . .

On the Army side we have by progressive stages organized an Australian Imperial Force for service abroad on the basis of an Army Corps of four divisions, with corps troops and a great stream of reinforcements. Consequently this Expeditionary Force will be built up over a period of years to a very large total indeed.

In addition to that we have announced that we propose to organize and equip an Armoured Division, and no doubt in due course when an Armoured Division has come into existence it will be necessary to break up the Australian Expeditionary Force into two Army Corps so that the whole will constitute an Army and will be, I believe most confidently, a most powerful factor in the overseas struggle.

All these things involve in themselves a tremendous use of man-power, and the total of that man-power can perhaps be fully appreciated only if you realize what amazing demands are being made upon industrial man-power at the same time. There was a time when, if one came to London and fell in either at luncheon or dinner with a British manufacturer, one was not quite sure whether one would not be offered a convivial glass of hemlock, whether one's genial host would not say: 'You are a very agreeable fellow so far as I can judge but you know your country ought to be growing wool and wheat and butter and eggs'—I do not want to make your mouths water by running through a catalogue of these things—'If you will do this, and will leave the manufacturing to us, all will be for the best in the best of all possible worlds.'

I hope nobody here will take it amiss if I permit myself a little rapid backward glance at that kind of argument. Suppose we had done it, would our eggs and butter and meat and sugar and cheese be coming here to-day? Would your boards to-day be groaning under the weight of these commodities? Would my friend, Lord Woolton, have never reared his—I was going to say 'ugly head', but nobody can honestly say that, of course—above the horizon? You would still have had your problem of shipping, and we instead of being, as I confidently believe we shall be, a source of real strength to the Empire in this struggle, would have been in many respects a sheer liability. If we had been compelled to say to Great Britain at this time 'Come over and help us! Please let us have all these things that in obedience to economic theory we have never ventured to make,' what would your answer have been? You would have been put to some very grim choices. You might easily have been called upon to determine whether you should help Australia by abandoning some other vital interest elsewhere. Fortunately you have not been put to that choice. Fortunately Australia, rich in raw materials and rich in ingenuity and resource—(Why not? The stock does not deteriorate just because it goes to the other end of the world) —has been able for a term of years to attack the problem of production in a way that some people would have thought fantastic some time ago.

Let me say something to you about the munitions potential that has been developed in Australia, and which has, if I may use language I hope not excessive, excited the surprise and almost the wonder of the delegation sent out from this country to the Delhi Conference. We established years ago an iron and steel industry in Australia, and I have some satisfaction in knowing that since the war broke out 400 000 tons of Australian steel have come to Great Britain. I also have satisfaction

Getting ready for the enemy, Geoffrey Street assisting, 1940

in knowing that whereas in the last war we produced men, uniforms, rifles, and some supply of small arms ammunition, and at our busiest moment employed 2700 people in the manufacture of munitions, we shall by the middle of this year be employing 80 000 people directly on munitions and another 70 000 indirectly.

What are these people doing? If I had a schedule of production here —which I have not—I could give you lists of hundreds of various types of munitions that we are now able to manufacture. I could tell you the story of how we have been able, fortunately, to give large assistance on the munitions side to our sister Dominion, New Zealand, which is, as usual, behaving so magnificently in this fight. I should be able to tell you of assistance that we have been able to afford to British and Allied countries in the Far East. But I cannot go through that schedule. I merely want to say something in a general way about it. Rifles and small arms ammunition constituted the undertaking in the last war. In this war small arms ammunition is still of immense key importance. Anybody in the Air Force will have no hesitation in telling you that. We were able last year to send of our production, notwithstanding scanty reserves at that time, between 60 000 000 and 70 000 000 rounds of small arms ammunition to this country. Our production of small arms ammunition . . . is already twelve times what it was when I took office in April 1939. It will be twenty-four times by December of this year, and although I am, of course, not at liberty to mention particular quantities, I may tell you that I am not thinking merely in terms of proportion, but I am talking of very large production, of a production which in point of fact compares very favourably, having regard to population, with the present production in Great Britain.

This has been a source of strength to us. It means that we have ceased to be a liability to you. . . . We had never attempted until this war, or shortly before it, to manufacture modern weapons of offence except the rifle and the machine-gun. I am glad to say that the day before I left Australia we had completed all the slow and painful pangs of producing the Bren gun. . . . We shall in the course of this year be producing a 25-pounder, and we shall in the course of a few weeks be producing a 2-pound anti-tank gun. We are already in production of anti-aircraft artillery of the most modern type. All these things, mark you, are not being done by the process of assembling components in relation to which we rely upon other people; these things are being done from the basic metal, and I say, I hope with reasonable modesty, they represent a remarkable industrial achievement.

You may be interested to know just how this amazing expansion has been done—an expansion which has increased in something like a year or eighteen months to a production of munitions in Australia of twenty times what it was. I hasten to say it was not done by me. I do not know, but I sometimes suspect I am a very bad politician because I do not really think I do these things, though I had one wise contribution to make to them—only one. I went to the biggest industrialist in my country, Essington Lewis, the head of the Broken Hill Proprietary Steelworks, and I said to him, 'Will you come and help the country by becoming Director-General of Munitions with a charter as wide as the seas and as high as the sky?' and he said, 'Yes, I will.' I said, 'Can you gather about you all the best men in the industrial world in Australia?' and he said, 'Yes, I can. If am to have a clear and wide authority, then I can get other men to share it.'

He got together a Director of Machine Tools Production, a Director of Gun Ammunition, etc., eight of them. These nine men were without exception among the greatest industrial experts in the whole of Australia. They came in on this job, and they were given all the backing of the Government service and were told in effect to 'write their own tickets.' Harried chiefs of staff who had always said, 'I do not know what these politicians will do,'—you know how chiefs of staff look at these things—harried chiefs of staff were told, 'Throw away dull care and write down exactly what you really need for your Forces and the development of them that you can envisage over the next two or three years. They did so, and within six weeks of the creation of that new organization we had approved a programme of construction to cover a period of two years, subject to all the pluses that will go on to the programme of construction—not of £3 000 000 a year, which I suppose our munitions production was before the war, but of £120 000 000 in two years!

... Committees have been set up in every State of men who know the State, and men who know every workshop in the State, and their job has been to see that there is no scientific or industrial resource in the whole of their community that is not being directed adequately to the production of munitions. ...

I now turn from that, Sir, to the other phase of construction—aircraft production, and I am not sure that this is not really the most remarkable achievement that some of these men have been able to bring about. I remember being here in 1936 and having mild and courteous debates about the prospects of Australia manufacturing an aeroplane. This subject was discussed with an almost melancholy kindness by people who gave me to understand it was very valiant of us to endeavour to do this job, but, of course, it could not be done. There was a lot to be said for that, because when this war broke out we had never manufactured a motor-car engine in Australia in the whole of our history, and it might have been said with a good deal of force, 'If you cannot manufacture a 25-horse-power engine, how are you proposing to manufacture a 700 or 1200 horse-power engine?' But the task was essayed. We knew, as you know, that while you can get plenty of people in various parts of the world to build air-frames, it is a thing of a very different character to make air-engines.

America was short of engines, because of the terrific demands that were being made on her, and you were likely here to be short of engines. The problem of engine production was almost the key of the aircraft 'mystery'. At the present time—and the war is after all only eighteen months old—we are producing in Australia the whole of our requirements of elementary training craft, engines and all, and we shall be exporting them to other neighbouring British countries that require them, by the middle of the year. We have already produced some hundreds of a plane that we call the 'Wirraway', which is an adaptation of a North American model with a Pratt and Whitney single Wasp engine of 650 horse-power. The production of that is very good and very successful, and as I say, hundreds have already gone into service. You regard them here, under another form, the 'Harvard', as a trainer, but we of our necessity have been compelled to use them also as operational craft. It is not of a high order of performance as operational craft, but it is at any rate capable of dealing with all those sea-borne aircraft that may come along to trouble us. This was a great achievement. We have a magnificent works, and a splendidly trained staff.

Concurrently with all these things it has been necessary to establish engineering schools on a scale quite undreamt of in peace, and to put into training men for the highest precision work of fitting and turning, to the tune of thousands in each case. That has been done. ...

In the third place we will, I think, by the end of next month, have produced our own 'Beaufort' bomber, and here again we have had not only the problem of materials, the problem of air-frame construction, but also the problem of producing an engine. By the end of next month we shall have produced a Twin-Row Wasp engine of 1050 horse-power, the engine of the well-known Lockheed. I have sat behind many in the course of my flying career as a politician. If you take all these things, the elementary trainer, the 'Wirraway', and the 'Beaufort', and add them together, and you consider the technical and industrial problems involved, and in particular the production of engines for them, and if I cap all that by telling you that by the end of next month, certainly by May, our total production of aircraft will be 35 per cent of what your total production was when I was last in England, you will appreciate exactly what this means.

I do not tell you of these things because I want you to say 'What a good boy you are!' 'Isn't this marvellous. If you only keep that up, it will be good.' It will not be good enough just to keep that up. If there is one complete conviction I have about this war it is this—and it puts on one side all economic theories—that you cannot beat this enemy of ours with even 95 per cent of your effort. This notion one always had in the past that we could take on anybody with one hand tied behind our back has gone. Unless my country is doing just everything that human ingenuity and resolution and speed can do, then Australia is not pulling its weight, and that goes for every British country in the world.

I say to you, however, with some pride, that it would be idle to pretend I do not feel satisfaction in what has been done. It would be indeed idle for me, because for the first nine months of this war I personally had to submit to the most violent and ill-informed criticism in my own country because it was said nothing was being done. Nothing ever does appear to be done when you are digging the foundations.

At almost exactly the same time as Menzies was making this eloquent defence of his government's performance, an anonymous critic in the March 1941 issue of *The Australian Quarterly* summarised the thesis of a controversial book by four young Sydney economists, S.J. Butlin, T.K. Critchley, R.B. Macmillan, and A.H. Tange. The book, *Australia Foots the Bill*, argued that Australia's war effort was 'on a mean scale which reflects no credit to the country'. And it further contended that the nation's war effort, such as it was, was being financed by inflationary methods and that 'no real effort is being made to restrict private consumption'.

By this time, however, Menzies had left Australia with a small group of officials, to travel to England for consultations with the British Government. Two telegrams from the recently released papers of Stanley Bruce, Australia's High Commissioner in London, reveal the Prime Minister's concerns at the beginning of 1941:

3rd January, 1940

MOST SECRET. For your urgent consideration and reply. I am a good deal exercised about projected visit to Great Britain as political position here precarious and principal lieutenants in Cabinet not very experienced. However I feel strongly that much mutual benefit might result from visit provided I could be sure of prompt and sufficient opportunity for consultation with Churchill and chief Ministers.

Would be glad if you could frankly give me idea of value of visit and also ascertain from Churchill whether this is a convenient time for him. In particular I feel that clear definition where we stand in the Far East and reasonably long range policy of Middle East would enable me to plan Australian effort on man-power side more soundly. Also interested to give United Kingdom Government a clear picture of amazing munitions potential developed and developing here and to see how far greater joint use, could be arranged. But as always I will be much influenced by your own opinion.

Regards,
Menzies

5th January 1941

FOR PRIME MINISTER. PERSONAL HIMSELF. Your cablegram 24 has caused me much anxious thought. In my view decision dependent on weighing political position in Australia against results you could achieve here. On former at this distance I can offer little useful comment. On latter following is my appreciation. Prompt and sufficient opportunity for consultation with Chief Ministers would be forthcoming but this of limited value. As regards major policy as this increasingly centred in Prime Minister's hands and little influenced by other members of War Cabinet who frankly are not prepared to stand up to him my view is Prime Minister would endeavour treat you in much same way—most cordial welcome—utmost courtesy—invitation to attend meetings of War Cabinet and apparently every possible opportunity for consultation. When however you tried to pin him down to definite discussions of fundamental questions of major war policy I am inclined to think you would find him discursive and elusive necessitating your either (a) taking a line that would mean a considerable show down between you or (b) leaving with a sense of frustration.

(a) would be immaterial and in fact beneficial if your visit was of sufficient duration to enable you to sort position out and re-establish cordial relations. In the limited time at your disposal this might not be possible and to have to leave with your relations at all strained with the Prime Minister would be most unfortunate.

(b) would be imperative if there were any major lines of policy on which you felt United Kingdom Government was going wrong and with regard to which you had to take a strong line. While such a position has existed in the past, e.g. reinforcements for Middle East in August and September last and maximum co-operation in regard to Far East with United States of America based on complete frankness, developments over past few months have removed all the major issues on which you would have had to take a strong line.

At the moment everything is governed by what Hitler's next move is going to be—it is difficult to see how it can be other than on the grand scale—and until it becomes clearer I see no definite line we would want to press on the United Kingdom Government in the field of major policy.

With regard to other matters you would be dealing with two about which I have cabled you recently and which appear to me to be difficult politically for you to handle

(1) Reduction of Australian exports due to serious shipping position

(2) Suggestions in Board of Trade memorandum re-rationing and reduction of production for home consumption

While I would greatly desire your visit and feel strongly you would do most valuable service in your discussions with Ministers here I have given you the points I feel you must take into account in making your decision.

Bruce

Towards the gunfire: Noumea, January 1941

On their way to London, the Prime Minister and his party paused in the Middle East. Their visit coincided with one by the British politician and diarist Henry ('Chips') Channon:

5 February   *The Embassy, Cairo.*
This evening the Lampsons and I drove in some state to a cocktail party given on a Nile barge by the Australian General (Blamey) and Lady Blamey; and I was warmly greeted by Lady Wavell whom I now like enormously. She is a vague, motherly, lazy, humorous creature. The General calls her 'Queenie' because her name is Eugenie and she is said to be a God-daughter of the old Empress. . . . He, of course, is altogether more charming, more cultured, more silent—a very rare bird indeed.
   There was an impressive dinner party at the Embassy to meet Mr [Robert] Menzies, the Australian Prime Minister. He is jolly, rubicund, witty, only 46 with a rapier-like intelligence and gifts as a raconteur. . . .

9 February   *The Embassy, Cairo.*
To Air House to dine with Longmore who had a banquet which had begun by being a small dinner for me. I was between Tedder and Wavell, who was silent and bored at first. He only thaws gradually. I noticed that he focuses badly with his one eye and that he sometimes upsets things. . . . After dinner we listened to the Prime Minister's broadcast which was none too well received, particularly his references to the Middle East. Then Wavell, who knew what was coming, hid behind a doorway. As the Churchillian compliments to him were handed out that magnificent language seemed rather forced, almost comic. I was embarrassed as the only English politician present. When the broadcast ended Wavell came and sat down next to me and we had a long conversation and he was charming, almost affectionate to me. After an hour Menzies rose and the party broke up; General Wavell offering to drive me back to the Embassy but I refused politely as I was already going with the Prime Minister of Australia. . . .

10 February   *The Embassy, Cairo.*
Only a few more days. . . . It is decided; I am to fly home with Menzies and Donovan. I ought to be thrilled; instead I am bored by the prospect of such close proximity with the great. We leave on Thursday, probably. . . .

13 February   *The Embassy, Cairo.*
Accompanied by Madame Sirry, the gay alert wife of the Prime Minister, and Bob Menzies, I went shopping in the Mousky. We had two amusing hours together and I piloted them to the best shops. Menzies wanted to buy a present for his wife and at last decided upon an emerald brooch in the shape of a peacock. There was much Eastern haggling and at last I got it for him for £45. He was enchanted. I was called Excellency everywhere.

14 February, St Valentine's Day   *The Palace, Khartoum.*
About 12.30 we arrived at Khartoum. . . . We were whisked off to the
Palace and rested for two hours and then had tea on the lawn of the
Palace which was Kitchener's house and is huge, but there is no real
splendour. It is built on the actual site of Gordon's original house.

Thus ends my fabulous Egyptian visit.

16 February   *Guest House, El Fasher.*
We took off at 1.30, all the Sudanese Government being lined up to see
us off. Menzies is a sympathetic travelling companion, highly intelligent, but he looks much more than his 46 years. . . . He says he does
not intend to be blitzed by Winston, but he will be.

19 February   *Palace Hotel, Estoril, Lisbon.*
A dreadful day, really, overcrowded and exhausting. . . . We arrived
in Lisbon Bay before nine o'clock a.m., having dozed most of the way
from Lagos. . . . Everywhere else there had been officials and red
carpets, but here the Embassy had done nothing, and the Prime Minister of Australia was allowed to land like any ordinary traveller. Luckily
I had my laissez passer given me by the Portuguese Ambassador in
London: thanks to that our luggage was not examined. Menzies,
hungry, unshaved and affronted, was in a rage. I tried to calm him by
ringing up the Embassy but there was no reply. At last we got into a car,
Menzies and I, and drove to Estoril where no rooms had been reserved.
I made a row and procured one which we shared for a few hours . . .
whilst he bathed I slipped below and rang up Noel Charles and told
him of the situation. Later Menzies and I had breakfast together, and
Charles, sleek and apologetic, arrived. The Embassy obviously had
been caught napping. The Hotel is full of spies, impoverished grandees
and nondescript people, including Rothschilds down to their last two
millions. . . .

In the afternoon I went to Queluz. The Palace is a dream of pink
paradisical beauty, like a seraphim asleep. . . . The sophisticated
garden, the tired statues, the tiled canals, all too rococo and beautiful:
it makes the Trianon seem tawdry, even Bruchsal look rough. Aged
Infantas still inhabit the wings. I was in a daze from the heat, the pink-
ness, the faded splendour. . . .

Back to Estoril to bathe and drink cocktails with the Australian
Prime Minister, and drive him to the Embassy. . . .

I fear I am reluctant to return to beleaguered Britain.

20 February   *Belgrave Square.*
I was called at five in Estoril, not by the waiter as arranged but by the
loud complaint of the Duchess of Santona, next door, who was called
by mistake instead of me, and drove alone to the airport, as Menzies was
not yet up. A long wait for him, the luggage and the light. There was
some doubt about the weather, and whether we should get off. However
we did, before eight—and all the way back to England as I dozed over
'War and Peace' I wondered what disappointments, what problems,

what difficulties will I find awaiting me? No matter what happens—
and it may be much—I shall have had one of the happiest, most
successful and glamorous trips of my life. . . .

The excitement of Menzies' Australian entourage was touching to
see as they approached England for the first time. We came down at
Poole. . . . The Kangaroo party disappeared and I chartered a car for
£8 to drive me to London. England was cold and dark—blackout
again. . . . I heard the sirens as we approached London. . . .

What was Menzies to do in London? In his own account, based
on records kept at the time, but not written until a quarter of a century
later, he gave special attention to 'the problem of Japan' and 'the Greek
intervention'. Both subjects were deeply contentious in 1941 and have
remained controversial. They involved questions of the most fundamental significance for the defence of Australia. How real was the
likelihood of Japan entering the war? And to what extent could Australia
afford to divert her military resources to the existing European theatre
of war? In *Afternoon Light*, Menzies recalled:

On 26 February 1941, I attended a conference in Mr R.A. Butler's
room at the Foreign Office in London. 'Rab' was then a Minister under
Anthony Eden, who had gone to the Middle East, on an investigation
which led to the expedition into Greece.

Somewhat to my surprise, the chair was taken by Sir Alexander
Cadogan, the permanent head of the Foreign Office. Lord Cranborne . . . was present. I was accompanied by Bruce . . . and Shedden.

I at once raised the question of the tendencies and probabilities of
Japanese action.

Cadogan at once was quite frank about the matter. The Japanese had
engaged in a drive in which they had obtained a footing in Indo-China
and to some extent in Thailand, with the apparent object of by-passing
Singapore. They had their eyes on the Netherlands East Indies and,
he agreed, constituted a menace to Australia and New Zealand. Recent
indications had convinced the Foreign Office that Japan had some
arrangement with Germany for a simultaneous development of trouble
in Europe and the Far East. The United States knew of these indications. Japan had been informed of this knowledge and the general
feeling was that the developments had been postponed.

It became clear that the Foreign Office thought that the getting of
Japanese air-bases in Indo-China or the west coast of Thailand would
be dangerous. . . .

I put the view that the Japanese were opportunists, and might be
careful. But they could well get into a position where they could not
retreat without loss of face. Where should we draw the line? I conceded,
of course, that it would be difficult for Great Britain or the rest of us
to know whether we could nail our colours to the mast without knowing
the United States' attitude. But there was nothing more dangerous
than drift.

My main point was that diplomacy and military provision or action could not exist in water-tight compartments; and therefore the reinforcement of Singapore was the most important diplomatic move that could be made. I made special mention of the need for munitions and aircraft. Two or three squadrons of fighters sent to Singapore could have an effect out of all proportion to their intrinsic significance. If the Japanese were to establish themselves in the Netherlands East Indies the whole Australian defence policy and plans would have had to be recast.

These propositions were, I thought, generally accepted around the table, but there were obvious (and understandable) reservations on two points.

The first, of course, was that British and Commonwealth resources, in men and particularly in aircraft, were already fully stretched, and, at a time when German bombing raids occurred every night, a substantial diversion of fighter aircraft could have been regarded as taking a risk with an existing war in order to guard against a possible one.

The second was that a war in South-East Asia against Japan could not be willingly contemplated unless there was a near certainty of American intervention. Mr Butler felt that the immediate need was to make as solid a front as possible between ourselves, the United States, and the Dutch, and to extend that front to events in Thailand.

We thus had much common ground; it was clear that London understood the dangers of Japan, but equally clear that advance warnings to Japan would not be entertained in the absence of American support. I wrote down a note that night, which reads—'Drift seems to be the policy of the Foreign Office. Why should we allow an atmosphere of inevitability to drift into our relations with Japan? We need firmness, definition, and friendliness, and they are not impossible.'

Naturally, I kept coming back to this matter during the rest of my stay in England, but without material success.

One of the men who frequently saw Menzies in action in London was the Permanent Under-Secretary of State at the Foreign Office, Sir Alexander Cadogan. In a detailed daily diary, Cadogan wrote candidly of the key figures grappling with the major strategic issues: 'PM' (Churchill), 'R.A.B.' (R.A. Butler, the Parliamentary Under-Secretary at the Foreign Office), 'A.' (Anthony Eden, the Foreign Secretary), and Menzies:

Monday, 24 February
PM arrived just before 12, when he was due to see Jap, and Turk immediately after. He sent for me to ask what to say. I gave him the dope. . . . Had a talk with R.A.B., who is exercised as to the figure he will cut at his first attendance at the Cabinet this evening. He needn't bother! . . . Read Chiefs of Staff report endorsing proposals for a Balkan expedition to help Greece. On all moral and sentimental (and consequently American) grounds, one is driven to the grim conclusion. But

it *must*, in the end, be a failure. However, perhaps better to have failed in a decent project than never to have tried at all. A. has rather jumped us into this. But it is impressive that *Wavell*, and Dill endorse him. Cabinet at 5. Menzies there. He evidently doubtful, but the general sense was to go ahead with it. It's a nasty decision, but I *think*, on balance, I agree with it. PM evidently made up his mind.

PM seems to have seen the Greek this afternoon, and I got a message during Cabinet that an agency was putting out that Greek had said his country didn't want help until invaded. This of course a lie, but I suggested to PM that it might be useful to us to let it go, to camouflage our plans! He agreed.

Wednesday, 26 February
Had a meeting at 3.30 with R.A.B., Menzies, Bruce and Shedden— mainly about Far East. What irresponsible rubbish these Antipodeans talk!

Saturday, 1 March
Glad to find PM has sent a sobering telegram to our temperamental Secretary of State, saying 'You appear to have got nothing out of the Turks'. And that is true: he is going on a lemon-gathering expedition, and he has only got that ninny Dill, with him. (Wavell is in Cairo). I rang up No. 10 to make sure Wavell was being kept informed. This stunt trip is a most disastrous one. And A. seems quite gay about it. The only explanation I can conceive . . . is that A. expected the Turks to react strongly against our giving all our help to the *Greeks*. And of course the Turks *didn't*. They—quite rightly, don't expect to be at-tacked—yet. But that doesn't help the Greeks—or *us*. What the hell is A. going to say to Greeks and Yugoslavs? It's a diplomatic and strategic blunder of the first order. And what will Menzies say? (We shall have an interesting Cabinet on Monday!) Talked to O.S. and R.A.B., who share my amazement at A.'s Angora telegram. . . . BBC tonight announce signature of Axis Pact by Bulgaria and entry of German troops. A real answer to A.'s silly antics.

Monday, 3 March
I sent message to PM asking what I was to do at Cabinet about the Balkans. Cabinet haven't seen the telegrams and will be sure to ask. He authorised me to read A.'s raspberry from Ankara. Which I did, and left them all looking rather blue-nosed. (Menzies had already seen it). Everyone's reaction is the same—how *can* one account for the jaunty tone of a recital of *complete* failure? Germans have swarmed over Bulgaria, and there we are. I confess everything looks to me as black as black. Shipping situation very bad, and I don't see where we are to turn. I'm sure a forlorn hope in Balkans will only do us harm—in France and Spain. I *wish* we could have gone on into Tripoli and joined up with Weygand. Probably now too late (if *ever* it was possible) as Germans seem to have landed. Complete silence from A. since his raspberry telegram! . . .

A closer look at the war: Alexandria, January 1941

Thursday, 6 March
A. has evidently committed us up to the hilt. Telegram this morning gives text of agreement signed with Greeks. . . . Cabinet at 6. Awkward discussion. PM evidently thinks we can't go back on A. and Dill, and I don't think we can—though I would if I could see any better alternative! K. Wood, Alexander and J. Anderson evidently out for A.'s blood. Finally decided to defer decision till we get A.'s answer to telegram which PM sent him last night. Meanwhile Palairet telegraphs saying we can't now let Greeks down, and A.'s answer will be the same.

Friday, 7 March
Cabinet at 12, which practically decided to go ahead in Balkans. On a nice balance, I think this is right.

Saturday, 8 March
Had just go into bed, and trying to go to sleep when, at 12.30, Winston rang me up from Chequers about some telegrams from Belgrade which I hadn't seen. Nothing for it but to get up, dress and go to FO and ring him from there. Found messages from Prince P[aul] showing he was sending an officer to Athens to find out what help he could expect. This *may* be a good sign. So rang up Winston and told him I'd send a telegram to Athens urging that the utmost encouragement should be

given. (Have since been ticked off by A. for doing anything from here except through him!) So I needn't have been to all that trouble! But just as well to do it, as Winston talked about the FO being 'shut down'. Must see about this.

... Wonder whether Yugoslavia really will do anything! What a chance to give the bloody ice-creamers the final kick in the pants!

Monday, 10 March
Cabinet met in the Dollis Hill War Room. I left with R.A.B. at 11.30 and we arrived on time. Arrangements impressively good. PM not there—has slight bronchitis. I in a difficulty, as I didn't know this, and didn't know how much he'd want me to tell them. Gave them a hazy general impression (there isn't much definite news, as a matter of fact). Menzies then held forth for 40 mins. on Australian war effort. Very impressive, but no one but an Australian would have done it! However, he didn't do it badly.

Menzies was uncomfortable. The drift of policy concerned him. So too did Churchill's style of war government. The occasional interventions noted by Alexander Cadogan were not the only times when Menzies wanted to speak. He was too used to dominating his own colleagues to find Churchill's War Cabinet performances altogether agreeable. He was puzzled by the prolonged silences of others in attendance at meetings where high policy was being made. Many years later in his memoirs, *Full Circle*, Anthony Eden recalled how he had made it clear to Menzies why there was so little debate:

With Churchill: 'a dictator' surrounded by 'yes-men'

I remember that when I arrived back in London from Cairo and attended my first Cabinet, I found Menzies sitting next to me. He passed a note, 'This is the strangest Cabinet I ever sat in. Since you have been away I have only heard one voice. Do none of them ever speak up?' I explained to him afterwards how the technique worked. The War Cabinet did not wish to be immersed in the details of military operations. Whatever the Prime Minister had to say on these topics, which sometimes filled the greater part of our discussions, was not usually commented upon then, because it was the Defence Committee which handled those affairs.

The London visit was not all work. Chips Channon recorded a dinner he held on March 3:

> My dinner for the Prime Minister of Australia. Mr Menzies arrived on time and my dinner party was a huge success from the very start, one of the gayest and most riotous festivals I have ever arranged. There was a round table; too little to eat but much to drink, the three supreme ingredients of gaiety. Menzies told lengthy stories with great gusto and imitated me in the Mousky of Cairo, etc. He is immense, a raconteur . . . full of sense and charm. 'Shakes' Morrison came in for a drink afterwards and added his curious flavour to the banquet.

What Menzies did in his 'off-duty' moments was not, of course, made known to the citizens of Great Britain or of Australia. His public engagements were another matter. A contemporary account by the journalist, Tahu Hole, appeared in his book *Anzacs Into Battle* in January 1942:

> I fixed a picture of Mr Menzies in my mind as I saw him one afternoon at the Dorchester Hotel speaking to one of the most representative, critical audiences one could be asked to meet. The National Defence Public Interest Committee invited scores to lunch to hear him. Even outside, uninvited people gathered in the halls, listening. Perhaps he has never been seen or heard to better advantage. He was a picture of assurance.
>
> The catholicity of the audience was amazing. Stage personalities like Miss Irene Vanbrugh were there, industrialists like Lord Nuffield, smart in khaki; the readable, fabulous Fleet Street character, Hannen Swaffer, and strings of officials from the offices of various Governments, including the British Government.
>
> Said people after his lucid speech (he dwelt on Australia's war effort, urging the sky must be the limit if the Empire was to win reasonably quickly): 'Menzies is a great talker!'
>
> As a statesman, he was something new, different. To begin with, there was nothing impersonal about him. There was the different voice, distinctly Australian. His comparatively easy-going manner, the suggestion of the delight he could take in pouring phials of acid on

stuffed-shirts and mandarins. At the same time his intelligence was as plain as a pikestaff, and you watched him with a certain amount of caution, treated him with respect since you knew instinctively that he could bite pretty sharply. He was aggressively independent, a master of sarcasm and subtle insinuation. So they summed him up.

There, that day, stood a Dominion statesman who held, with almost pontifical elegance, a hard-headed, widely experienced crowd of people with no more difficulty than Lord Birkenhead held them in his heyday. Lady Eleanor Smith, Birkenhead's daughter, said to me long after Mr Menzies had left Britain: 'Yes, a lot of people say he reminds them of my father in the speed and pointedness of his speeches.'

There he stood easily, a solid, challenging, slightly ironical lump of Australia, dumped in the middle of London's West End, attracting admiration because of his obvious independence yet so wholly demonstrating that this independence sprang from a conviction that the Empire had never been more securely united and that, just as in a family circle, frankness was welcomed as a tonic.

The whole burden of his tale of Australia's determination to fight to the death if necessary was one of 'family'.

REACTIONS

He shone that day—glittered, in fact. This thick-set, greying, strong-haired, sharp-witted Prime Minister, given to enthusiasm but never to emotionalism who was head of a thrusting lovable seven million people, impressed London during his 1941 visit as he never impressed it before, and as perhaps has no other Australian-born Prime Minister. . . .

Broadly speaking, Mr Menzies' stay in Britain, from March to May, 1941, was a great success. . . .

So far as the man in the street is concerned, he saw Mr Menzies for only a few seconds on a newsreel. For the millions, he acquired most of his stature as the eloquent, sturdy embodiment of the fighting spirit of the Australian troops. Their heroic feats in North Africa held the headlines before he arrived. The echo of their deathless daring in Greece was ringing in every home after he left. Praise for their preparation to meet the worst Hitler can hurl against them in the next Middle Eastern battle was sounding before he had gone.

What did those in Britain think of him? Mr Menzies carried away a Press cutting book compiled for him by Australia House officials and a newspaper clipping agency who combed daily the Press of the United Kingdom and Eire for any line published about him. If it is studied with the essential amount of objectivity, it amounts to a fairly good mirror reflecting glimpses of the picture of him which a considerable section of the newspaper-reading public saw. There are about 900 clippings, long and short, and photographs.

Most of the clippings are reports of speeches: about 20 per cent are gossipy paragraphs noting his husky appearance ('He is like John Bull', one reader wrote to the *Daily Telegraph*), his tastes in literature, his audiences with the King, his handshakes with De Valera, his demonstrations of kindliness to persons less fortunate, his physical courage, his selection of one of Mr Churchill's earliest books ('The River War', published 42 years ago) to read *en route*, his quips with the groundsman at Old Trafford cricket ground, his voice ('He schools his ear to the cadence of words by reading verse', Lord Castlerosse wrote in the *Sunday Express*), his attendance at practically every meeting of the War Cabinet, his readiness to snub snobbish officials, his wise-cracks, his downright democratic manner.

Other clippings are from editorial columns. After he had flown to America, editorial references to him continued.

Only Cabinet Ministers like Lord Halifax or Mr Eden, or outstanding visiting personalities like Raymond Gram Swing or Wendell Willkie have addressed audiences so large and representative as one or two of those Mr Menzies faced.

'I think I have made only two worth-while speeches in London—speeches worth printing', he said to a friend before he left for New York in May. This is typical of his self-criticism.

What neither Hole nor any other newspaper correspondent reported was Menzies' candid views of Churchill and the War Cabinet. But among the Australian journalists in London was Colin Bednall, whose diary for Saturday 26 April 1941 contains a scribbled and barely punctuated account of an 'astonishing Press Conference with Menzies' who talked 'with despair' of:

> . . . shocking lack of guts and drive in War Cabinet. Cabinet meetings just gatherings to hear Churchill deliver his pep talk. All yes-men except Beaverbrook who so disgusted with meetings just doesn't attend stays at his office and gets on with his job. I ask if you went back to Manchester would you still talk of Churchill as 'bobby-dazzler' Menzies replies 'yes although he doesn't dazzle in every direction. Churchill is concerned with broadest strategy—the chess-board—airily dismisses or passes over any detailed problems such as propaganda supply etc. Needs a good lieutenant to take over Home Front. Somebody to stand up to him.' I asked about American belief Beaverbrook is responsible for fighting against single plane going to Greece or out of England, Menzies says that was true until 2/3 months ago since when they have been pouring out stuff to Middle East and elsewhere. Greek Expeditionary Force was well equipped. 'Beaverbrook's chief trouble is he is a newspaper man. Names like Spitfire and Hurricane and Typhoon are *news* so fighter stocks gone up and up while bombers struggled on.' Menzies extremely bitter and scornful of British chiefs of staff. Generals still talk of masses of men instead of tanks, etc. Just evade question if don't agree. Talks particularly sweepingly of 'Wavell's colossal blunder' in under-estimating German strength in Libya. Menzies prediction is Panzers quietly feeling way across desert and will suddenly pounce on Khartoum, But says despite all is confident about Egypt. . . .

Two days later, Bednall dined at the Savoy Hotel as Menzies' guest:

One of the most remarkable functions ever known guests Smith, Mitchell, Ross, Bednall, Tritton, Arthur, Brodsky, McAlpine, King, Tebbutt, Hole, Baume, McLaughlin, Maxwell and Douglas. Enthrallingly interesting and at times acutely embarrassing as Baume drunk hurls foulest threats and language at McAlpine, as King also very drunk tries to get ideas off his chest. Menzies has an idea to sell and everyone tickles his vanity. Now decided to come back to London—Finally has all [?] declaring will tell public of Australia that Menzies is wanted in London—as if it was their own idea. Menzies invites us all to say just what we think of War and how it is being run. Ross and Hole squib it. Smith and Tritton squib also at first but having heard others try have a go too. I get into it, can't get out. Trying to demonstrate how devastatingly conservative are English[?] that if UAP and ALP were to contest election in England, English so tragically conservative that UAP would get 90 p.c. vote!! Menzies repeats his condemnation of British government. Says very significant thing about his sense of values undergone complete change. Now really must social reconstruction after war. Only thing he is concerned about is that everyone should get poor with him. Tells us Dill that afternoon estimated about all but 10 000 shd get out of Greece . . . Menzies also said had tremendous respect for Duncan (Sir Andrew).

Unfortunately for Menzies, this exercise in self-promotion reached the ears of Churchill. Several of the journalists present sent full reports to their head offices. Irvine Douglas—who as Lyons' Press Secretary until August 1938 had watched dissension grow between Menzies and his chief—wrote a letter to the secretary of the Australian Associated Press that was circulated to the proprietors of Australian newspapers. According to Douglas, Menzies saw himself as an alternating brake and spur on the British Cabinet. The reports of Douglas and others were opened by British censors and their contents conveyed to Downing Street. Eventually, no doubt, they also provided intriguing reading for Keith Murdoch, Warwick Fairfax, and Frank Packer. While in London, the left-wing British journalist, Claud Cockburn, told readers of his 'insider' news magazine, *The Week*, enough about Menzies' opinion of Churchill to make ears burn in the Australian Prime Minister's camp.

Interspersed between press briefings, attendances at meetings of ministers and officials, and the whirl of gaiety of which Chips Channon gave such a vivid description, Menzies spoke publicly to a variety of audiences. The National Defence Public Interest Committee heard him on February 26; the Foreign Press Association on March 3. In the House of Commons on March 11 he spoke to the Study Committees of the Empire Parliamentary Association. On March 18 he addressed factory workers in Manchester. Three days later it was the turn of the

Coventry workers; then those in Bristol. There were speeches in Belfast, broadcasts to British and Australian audiences, and an Anzac Day luncheon. Notwithstanding his own deprecatory remarks about the quality of all but two of the addresses, the complete series was collected in a small book published by Longmans, Green and Co., called *To the People of Britain at War*. Five thousand copies had been sold by the end of July. In the introductory section, Menzies wrote lyrically of some of his recent experiences and memories:

When Messrs Longmans, Green asked me if I would care to publish my speeches made over the past few weeks in Great Britain, I hesitated. My speeches, though their form and argument naturally engage my attention in advance, are never prepared in point of language. They are addressed to my audiences and not in any sense to posterity, which I have always suspected will be completely indifferent to them. But there was, and is, one good reason for publication. It is that many people have told me that they have derived encouragement from what I have been able to say here on behalf of Australia. The great-hearted people of Britain are sustaining an ordeal for which history can afford no precedent. They are in their daily lives fighting not the Battle of Britain, but the Battle of the World. If any word of comradeship from their Australian kinsmen, who are, like them, in this war to the end, can serve to stay or fortify them, then let that word go out to them.

In the days of peace, it was an easy voyage, leisurely and almost dawdling, of 12 000 miles from Melbourne to London. With a little time to spare one might reckon upon at least a glimpse of the blue coast of the French Riviera and a day or two among the bright lights, the ordered beauty and the spontaneous gaiety of Paris. Arrived in England, one looked serenely in their turn for the crocuses, the primroses and the bluebells. In April there was talk of cricket in the air; I have myself in mid-April discoursed learnedly and anonymously with the grounds-men at Lord's. London had always its own charm of soft mists and the washed white brilliance of Portland stone in Wren's church towers, the sprawling leisure of the parks, the curve of Regent Street, the classical façade of Carlton House Terrace as it looked across the Mall, the sight along the river to where the dome of St. Paul's rose gloriously above the early morning fog. These are superb memories and they would be still—if one had the time to look—superb facts. But the times have changed.

Travelling by air, I flew 17 000 miles to get here, coming down each evening in places I had never expected to see, but always pressing on, the route changing to suit the sudden and changing circumstances of war. Never have I, or those travelling with me, had such an experience.

So I came to England across Africa, now standing on some ancient battlefield, now in the quaint market-place of some almost unknown native village; now sweltering in a morning of almost tropical heat and twenty-four hours later wrapping up against the cold of an Atlantic gale. Now why do I mention these things in this kaleidoscopic way?

Because the mention of each place casts up a picture in my mind? Yes, but that is not all. To me the most striking things about this air odyssey in time of war, were two in number.

First, wherever the aeroplane came down, we found some young or youngish Englishman waiting to receive and instruct us. Sometimes he was a Governor, sometimes a Commissioner, sometimes a Resident, sometimes (*mirabile dictu*) a Law Adviser. But whatever his description he always turned out to be fresh-faced, cultivated, alert, composed about his job and, though I suppose this to be mere coincidence, incredibly good-looking. The words of George Santayana frequently came into my mind:

> 'Never since the heroic days of Greece has the world had such a sweet, just, boyish master. It will be a black day for the human race when scientific black-guards, conspirators, churls, and fanatics manage to supplant him.'

Is there a moral in these observations? I think that there is, and I think that it is this. No nation can be found decadent which year by year can attract to its service young men of character and intelligence and humanity. I salute the British Colonial and other Oversea services. They have done much in many places in the world to cheer me and restore my faith in our future.

Second, I found great inspiration in Palestine, Egypt, and Libya, because I looked on the faces of my own people and found them good. That is not to say that I did not find every sort of nose and ear and eye and shape in the Australian Army. The tall, lean, hatchet-faced Australian is a composite, almost legendary type, not a common individual one. But what the Australian fighting men possess in common is not a face but a philosophy. I found it everywhere—in billets at Tobruk (where they cheerfully demanded beer!); in an old quarry at Benghazi; on a damp and grassy plain at Barce, where by a remarkable effort of intelligent anticipation Australian gumtrees had been planted years before. This Australian soldiers' philosophy is a simple one—as Christianity is. It has made them crusaders. . . .

And as I am writing of these men of Australia whose interests I seek to serve, and for whom my heart beats warmly at every thought of them, I must add something about their discipline. The alleged indiscipline of Australian soldiers has become famous. Each war adds to the legend, for a good story has a life of its own, and can never be held down to the facts. When I arrived in England, they told me a beautiful anecdote about the Australian soldiers who had been stationed at, shall we say, Oddcaster. Some of them had from time to time encountered the local police—playfully, of course—in what Melbourne people would call the Sydney manner, and helmets, if not heads, had been broken. As the time for the departure of the Australians came near, the Colonel of the battalion was delighted to receive a deputation from his men asking permission to present to the police, 'with whom they had had some difficulties, but whose work they appreciated', a souvenir for police headquarters. Just as there is joy in heaven over one sinner who repenteth, so there was joy at police headquarters. A date was fixed, the Superintendent was present; the Colonel was present; speeches were made—every Australian soldier carries a member of parliament's baton in his knapsack—and a splendid Australian boomerang, suitably inscribed, was handed over. As Mr Wodehouse would say, 'A good time was had by all'. Next day the curator of the local museum arrived breathlessly at the police station to complain that his only Australian exhibit was missing! This, I think, is a good story; but the belief it nourishes is essentially a false one. Australians are an informal people, with no hint of servility. But nobody has yet been heard to complain of their discipline in battle. At Bardia they advanced under fire so steadily, so implacably, that the Italians broke and surrendered. At Benghazi they found a fine modern town and they accepted its surrender at the Civic Centre with the honours of war and the calm of veterans. No shop was looted, no civilian molested. I found them passing their money across the bar of an Italian hotel to the Italian proprietor as if they were his guests and not his conquerors. What you must remember is that the Australian Army is a civilian army. It tears up its roots and goes to war reluctantly, but when it goes, it goes to fight. Its ranks are filled with all classes and all occupations. It is the perfect example of democracy in arms. If it pays minor attention to the fripperies of soldiering, its enemies will not be able to say that it neglects the essentials or that it lacks the knowledge, resource, *esprit de corps*, dash and cool courage which it is the object of true discipline and training to produce.

To think of them as I came to England was to be fortified with something of their own spirit, a spirit which in the speeches which appear in this volume it has been my task and privilege to interpret to the beleaguered but dauntless people of Great Britain.

Among those watching Menzies from afar, with a mixture of envy and admiration, was the most recent star recruit to the Labor ranks. In spite of the forcefulness of his public criticisms of the Menzies Government and of the Prime Minister himself, H.V. Evatt tried quietly behind the scenes to keep open a line of communication to Menzies. On 18 April 1941, Menzies received an unexpected cable from Sir Gilbert Dyett, Federal President of the Returned Soldiers' League:

18th April, 1941

RT HON R.G. MENZIES,
AUSTRALIA HOUSE,
LONDON.

DURING RECENT CONVERSATION BERT EVATT HE SPOKE APPRECIATIVELY YOUR WORK ENGLAND AND ASSURED ME YOUR PERSONAL POSITION SECURE STOP HIS SENTIMENTS OBVIOUSLY SINCERE STOP BEST WISHES CONTINUED SUCCESS AND KINDEST REGARDS.

DYETT.

The Prime Minister's reply to Dyett pointedly made no reference to Evatt:

26th April, 1941

SIR GILBERT DYETT,
FEDERAL PRESIDENT,
RETURNED SOLDIERS' LEAGUE,
MELBOURNE.

FOLLOWING FOR YOU FROM LONDON DATED TWENTY THIRD APRIL BEGINS
VERY GRATEFUL FOR YOUR TELEGRAM STOP I KNOW THAT YOU WILL PLAY
YOUR PART IN KEEPING UP PUBLIC MORALE AT THIS DIFFICULT TIME STOP
LOOK FORWARD TO BEING HOME SHORTLY MENZIES ENDS.

SECRETARY,
PRIME MINISTER'S DEPARTMENT.

Menzies' discontent in London made him a natural ally of the curious embryo coalition of critics of Churchill's dictatorial behaviour. Among the self-selected saviours of the nation was Lord Hankey, Chancellor of the Duchy of Lancaster in Churchill's Government, but previously a staunch supporter of Neville Chamberlain. Hankey's diary records the steps by which Menzies was drawn perilously close to the centre of a conspiracy to curb Churchill's power:

30th April
Shedden lunched with me to-day. He was at the Defence Ctee. last night with Menzies. His account tallied with my own experience at the War Cabinet on Monday—a monologue by one man—Churchill. Menzies had gone there to find out about [our] intentions if things went wrong in Libya, where the largest forces are from Australia and N.Z. Apparently Churchill burst out into one of his fervid orations as to how nothing would induce him to make plans or order preparations for such a contingency. If it leaked out, our army would be demoralised. They had to contest every inch and fight to the last and sacrifice their lives if necessary to defend Egypt and Palestine, and so forth. No-one else spoke a single word and Shedden gathered from Menzies that this was what happened every time he attended the War Cabinet. Menzies at first had fallen for Churchill, but gradually he had changed. He admitted now that it was dangerous to go to Chequers and spend an evening because Churchill was so persuasive. Shedden, with his incisive mind, has seen through the humbug of the present régime and is absolutely shocked. Australia has organised on my lines, and he says that, for all their inexperience, they have a [?] liver show than ours. At least they are not all 'Yes-men'. He has had a lot of trouble with Bridges, who will not give them the papers they want to take back to Australia—mainly about the Middle East, where Australia is supplying a large part of the forces. As to the Chiefs of Staff, they are a cipher—doped by Churchill's personality, as is Ismay. I am puzzled

what to [do]. All my friends, who were in Chamberlain's Government
have been scattered: Halifax at Washington; Sam Hoare at Madrid;
Chamberlain dead; Simon has become [a] cipher. I am trying to get
hold of Chatfield, but he is tied up in some trivial job about decorations
for ARP service and I cannot get hold of him. Salisbury still has his
'ginger group' (Fifth Column I used to call it a year ago) but unfortunately Cranborne, his eldest son, is S. of S. for Dominion affairs
and attends the War Cabinet, so if I went to him it would all leak. It
is hopeless to approach Churchill direct because he does not like me;
would not take my advice even if he did; and has deliberately smashed
the system to increase his own power. But letters in *The Times* and
the trend of questions in Parliament suggest that others are feeling
some anxiety.

1st May

Walking to the office this morning I was caught on the Horse Guards
Parade by General Kennedy, DMO, one of the best of the younger
generals. He at once tackled me about the Supreme Control of the
War; said he was very anxious about it; believed that we should lose
the war if it was not put right; I was the only man who could put it
right; Pug Ismay was completely bemused by Churchill. Kennedy
had been to Chequers last weekend, had discussed the war situation
with Churchill; had dissented from his views, and had returned home
very anxious and written to Churchill to say he had not altered his
views at all. He said Dill (CIGS) felt much the same as he did. This
gave me furiously to think. The next development was after a lunch
at Grosvenor House given by the Iron and Steel Federation at which
Menzies had made the principal speech. Menzies had arrived straight
from the War Cabinet, very cross and had made some acid remarks
at the outset of his speech about the complete ignoring of time by the
War Cabinet. After lunch I bade Menzies farewell. He leaves to-
morrow. And Adeline and I walked away down Park Lane. We heard
someone running and, lo and behold, it was Menzies himself. He
burst out at once about Churchill and his dictatorship and his War
Cabinet of 'Yes-men'. 'There is only one thing to be done' he said
'and that is to summon an Imperial War Cabinet and keep one of them
behind, like Smuts in the last war, not as a guest but as a full member'.
He was very much moved, and left us at the Dorchester.

On return to the office I recalled that now I have received complaints
from Generals Haining, Macready, Kennedy and have learned that
Dill is dissatisfied; that only yesterday P.J. Grigg, the very able
Secretary of the War Office, told me that in his view the situation was
very anxious and Churchill much too complaisant; that first Shedden
and then Menzies himself had poured contempt on the whole outfit;
and that all seemed to expect me to do something. At 4.45, therefore,
I went to see John Simon at the House of Lords, and under seal of
personal secrecy told him the whole story. He was very concerned.
We talked for nearly an hour. His final advice was as follows:—'the

best plan is to get Menzies to "bell the cat" before he leaves: he has become a great Imperial figure, has attended the War Cabinet and the Defence Committee for some weeks, has a big stake in the war, and is entitled to speak his mind; if he will not play, there is nothing for it but for you Hankey to see Winston yourself; you cannot ignore all this knowledge that has come to you; you can approach Churchill as a friend, pay a tribute to his powers of leadership, his ability to get the people to put up with leadership, and his powers over Parliament, recall your old friendship and repudiate any thoughts of intreague [sic] with the Press etc., and urge him to abandon the appearance of dictatorship and to use his political and military advisers properly.' But he advised me to wait until after the big debates in Parliament next week.

So I went back to the office, and after long delays managed to get Menzies on the telephone and asked him to tackle Churchill when he went to say good-bye. He said he had already decided to do so. I begged him to urge Churchill to drop his dictatorial methods and to use his military and political advisers properly. He promised to do so. I have returned home with an easier mind in spite of bad news that the outer defences of Tobruk have been broken through.

2nd May

Shedden came to say goodbye about tea-time. Menzies, it seems, got no change out of Churchill. In effect his answer (elicited from Shedden very confidentially) was 'You see the people by whom I am surrounded. They have no ideas, so the only thing to be done is to formulate my own ideas'! Of course they have none. He has got rid of all the people with ideas and deliberately surrounded himself with 'Yes-men', because he is rather intolerant of other people's ideas and wants to be Dictator. It leaves me in a difficult position. Checkmate in fact!

It *was* checkmate. But neither Hankey nor Menzies was prepared to give up. And Menzies took with him to Washington a very confidential letter from Hankey to the British Ambassador, Lord Halifax, who had been Chamberlain's Foreign Secretary. The letter conveyed Hankey's anxiety about the conduct of the war and his hope that the Australian Prime Minister might return to London as a member of the War Cabinet.

Menzies stayed in England much longer than he originally intended. When he left Australia in January, it was expected that he would visit Canada at the end of March. By mid-March he was scheduled to be in Canada on April 9. On March 24 the arrival was put off until April 21. On April 30 it was learned, finally and correctly, that he would come a week later—arriving in Ottawa on a Royal Canadian Air Force plane from New York—after a brief visit to President Roosevelt, and a whirlwind affair with the American press. The primary purpose of the journey to Canada was to establish personal contact with the Prime Minister, W.L. Mackenzie King. The Canadian Prime Minister's

own contemporary impressions of Menzies' breathless visit were
written in his diary on May 7 and 8. They were shrewd—the observations
of a man who saw himself as Menzies' equal, but was generous enough
to recognise his Australian counterpart's qualities. Mackenzie King
caught the lighter side, as well as the weighty political matters that were
discussed:

Wednesday, May 7, 1941

... Word came to me that Menzies would arrive sooner than expected
at the Uplands Airport. I had practically given up the thought of
going to meet him, when I read his interview in New York, saying
that, among other reasons for coming to Canada, was that he had not
met me. I immediately got up, dressed quickly, and drove to the
airport, arriving shortly before his plane from New York. He had
left London at the end of last week and had had very little rest on the
way over. Left New York early this morning.

Sir William Glasgow was the first to greet him on his arrival, and I
then followed, welcoming him cordially on behalf of Canada. We
started off together to review the Guard of Honour of the Air Force
and, later, a Guard of Honour of the Australian Air Force. Menzies
made a brief speech to the latter ...

At twenty to one, Menzies called on me at the office. We walked
together to the Chateau, where he spoke at a very large Canadian
Club luncheon, at which the GG was present. He drove back to
GH for a few minutes' rest. Was back to Parliament buildings at
three. In the meantime, I had discussed with the Speaker the arrangement that M. be given a seat on the floor of the House and an opportunity to address the Members. When he arrived, I took him in
to the Commons and moved the motion to adjourn its proceedings ...
He then spoke for some little time, making an excellent address, and
impression, as he had done at the Canadian Club. The Speaker made
a fine introduction. After shaking hands with the Members, I gave
the page boys a chance to shake his hand, and Tom Reid came with
his bagpipe and played Menzies and myself out of the Commons
chamber to the upper hall.

I took Menzies to my room, where he met members of the War
Cabinet. We discussed matters until nearly six. I then went with him
to his car, he taking a moving picture of myself from the steps. While
there, he thought of the pictures he had taken in England, and spoke
of using them after tonight's dinner. I promised to get lantern and
screen and told him to bring along the slides.

... Had dinner for about 60,—the GG being present, also the
Chief Justice. After the GG proposed the King's health, I then proposed Menzies. He replied and, later, we withdrew into the adjoining
room, where he showed coloured views of his journey from Australia,
through Africa, the Holy Land, his visit in England, etc. When concluded, we adjourned into an adjoining room for conversation.

It was almost midnight before we could get Menzies to leave. I felt sorry for the GG, who was thoroughly tired out, and really, in a way, treated with discourtesy by many of the guests leaving before he did. He was, however, nice about it all.

The last thing I heard was Menzies arranging for breakfast at Sir William Glasgow's to meet Malcolm MacDonald before he, Menzies, left for Toronto at eleven, to go on to Washington the same day.

It is quite true that Menzies took this city more or less by storm. He is a fine looking fellow, splendid presence, great vigour, and has a wonderful gift for speaking. He has endless confidence in himself, and does not mind putting himself very much into the limelight. He has qualities not unlike Bennett in his assertive ways, but not nearly so pompous, and much more of a gentleman. Reveals his Scotch Presbyterian origin in his thoughts and views generally. Has many of the qualities of a great leader, but I feel, while his sympathies are broad, he nevertheless is thinking pretty much of Menzies most of the time, and likes very much the environments of high society, palaces, etc., which will cost him, perhaps, dearly in the end.

I felt, as I looked at the pictures he threw on the screen, that when shown in Australia particularly, and seen by Labour audiences, they will cause many people to feel that he has not yet really understood the significance of this war, which is one against place and privilege. These beautiful estates, etc., in England, titled ladies with their

With MacKenzie King and Canadian cabinet, Ottawa, May 1941

shelters, privileged positions, etc., these are the things that the people are out to destroy. The one thing that seemed mostly in his mind, and which Churchill evidently had told him to discuss with me, was the desire for a conference of Prime Ministers—some kind of an Imperial Cabinet. His reasons for it were quite different from those which, I think, would actuate members of the British Government or *The Times*. He was quite outspoken in what he said about it all. What it really amounted to was that there was no British Cabinet, no War Cabinet—that Churchill was the whole show, and that those who were around him were 'yes men', and nothing else. He spoke, of course, in the greatest privacy at the War Committee, but said in effect, much as I have dictated.

First of all, he said there did not seem to be any Cabinet for general business of the country. Ministers were running things by themselves. That the War Cabinet was a curious combination, which he described, naming its members, pointing out that the Ministers of the Defence Departments attended, though not members of the Cabinet; that the Secretary of State for the Dominions did the same; that the Chiefs of Staff also attended, but that the meetings were held irregularly, indeed, seldom—once a week perhaps. That what happened was, when all together, Churchill reviewed the war situation, doing so in his eloquent manner. He did all the talking, and no one dared to say no to anything. If there was a matter to be discussed, it had been arranged before hand and those present were expected to be seen and not heard. He stressed that he himself was practically the only one who had ventured to question anything that was done. He gave as an example the conclusion that had been reached which had effected the disposition of the Australian Forces. He had read in the papers that this had been decided the afternoon before, but he had never been consulted. He immediately got in touch with Churchill and demanded an explanation, which he got in the form of an apology. He said that while he attended the War Cabinet, what his representation amounted to was that everyone was very polite, agreed to this and that, but went ahead and did as they pleased in the end.

He said Beaverbrook was the one man doing things, but had given up attending the War Committee, because it never accomplished anything.

He said he had visited Lloyd George, who had been equally critical and who had agreed that what was needed, and this was wholly what was in Menzies' mind, was the Dominions' point of view, when differing with that of the British, should be represented. There should be some one there who will be putting the Dominions' point of view always to the fore. It was evident that Menzies felt strongly about this; that he himself would like to be on such a Cabinet. I sensed the feeling that he would rather be on the War Cabinet in London than Prime Minister of Australia.

After he had put forward his views, I told him that I agreed very much with what he had said about what Dominion representation amounted to in London; that that was one of the reasons I wanted to avoid being on a War Cabinet; that there had been too much done for the sake of appearances and too little in the way of reality; that I felt, if there had been no League of Nations, we would have had no war. We would not have been relying on appearances and facing the real situation. He agreed to this. I pointed out that one had to consider the consequences of Prime Ministers leaving their Dominions, and asked him to imagine what the situation would be if Smuts, Fraser, himself, and myself were all in London with events developing as they are and being kept there for any time. He at once agreed that any meeting of any length of time was unthinkable. He finally came to the point of view that an occasional meeting might serve the purpose. I said the trouble as to that is that while the occasion lasted they would appear not to differ with your views but the moment you had gone the whole situation would slip back into the position it was before and, in the meantime, you would have incurred the responsibility without power. He admitted that this was true.

I then said I thought the more effective way was to have individual ministers go over and take up matters with their opposite members. His reply to that was he did not think you could get things done that way. Both Howe and Ralston took exception to that view and said they had been most successful in what they had accomplished.

Menzies spoke about a Council being needed to decide questions of strategy. I said to him to take the situation actually as it was. He had spoken about disposition of forces, etc., etc. I said if I were at a meeting of the Council, I could not offer advice on that matter without being not quite hypocritical, but an impostor, as that was something on which I would have to accept the views of the Chiefs of Staffs. I would have to have experts. I thought any Prime Minister, going to England, would have to bring these advisers with him. If they were in England, they would be out of Canada, where they would be most needed. Also, that even then I would be separated from my colleagues. I could not say what division might arise in the Cabinet or in the country while I was away. I believed my real service was helping to keep all united. If we failed in that, nothing else would much matter.

I spoke particularly of our relations with the US. and asked what service I could render in London comparable to that rendered here in relation with the US. I spoke about the Province of Quebec, the prairie Provinces, British Columbia, etc., and asked him to imagine war breaking out on the Pacific when I was in London, or on the Atlantic, with America in the war. Once there came the question of Atlantic command, I could say the word if I was here surrounded by my advisers on these matters, but would be absolutely out of every-thing in London. He then agreed no two Dominions had the same problems and that we in Canada had special problems. He then said that consultation was the thing we should aim at. I agreed as to that but said I thought we could do that more effectively through the machinery we already have. I could get a point of view across to Malcolm

MacDonald through his presence here that I could not get by myself in London. I could get it across with the authority of the Canadian Cabinet. Also, that communications to Churchill would be of record and valuable. I said now that he and I had come to know each other, we could combine in a message which would be more effective than anything we could do at a meeting called by Churchill to consider matters there.

I agreed that the moment might come when some great decisions were to be made, for example, as to peace and, after, peace proposals. I thought we should reserve absences from our own countries for those very special occasions. If we started going back and forth, influence would amount to little at the right time. I think he saw the force of what I said, as I saw the force of what he said. His point of view amounted to the need for a real Cabinet, which he thought the Dominion Prime Ministers could give and a lack of any confidence in the British Cabinet as constituted. He believed that Churchill was capable of mistakes.

When I spoke about one of the problems being anything happening to Churchill, he replied that the British attitude toward that was that it would not do to even discuss such a possibility. It could not possibly happen, though he, Menzies, felt it might happen any night. He said they did not yet face realities.

Tonight, as I looked at the pictures he showed of the different ministers in the present Cabinet, I confess I felt it was a terrible thing to think that the fate of the Empire is in the hands of the few men whom we saw portrayed there. I would feel infinitely more confidence in the group that I have around me in Ottawa from the point of view of judgment and wisdom than I do in the men at present in the British Administration. There is far too much thought of the role people are playing in history—far too much style of certain families and groups.

Menzies told me that Beaverbrook was not a well man; that one of his eyes was giving him much trouble; that he did not think we should take too seriously the appointment of Minister of State as Deputy Prime Minister.

The problem of government has got to be too great for those who are trying to carry it. I feel a deep concern as to the future.

Menzies was more hopeful about the Japanese situation than I expected to find him. Not too hopeful about the Middle East, or the Mediterranean. He was quite decided about this being a terrifically important time, and outspoken as to no certainty of victory thus far, and certainly no victory without US. co-operation, which he thinks should be much stronger and immediate. He may do a little harm in what he says in public on that aspect. Americans will strongly resent any word in the nature of coercion from him.

I confess I found him a most interesting man. He still has sufficient youth on his side to enable him to get through a great deal, and has real ability. I shall be surprised, however, if he does not find, when he gets back, that he has lost ground and that Labour has been gaining on him. He is too much the dictator to be a persuasive leader of the mass of the people. On the whole, however, I have come to like him very much.

I think he greatly enjoyed his visit to the Capital. Indeed, he was deeply moved by being invited to speak on the floor of the House, and I think he regarded that as great an honour as had been accorded him at any time. I felt I had gained a place in his confidence and that we would continue as real friends. He has many of Bruce's qualities, but I like him much better than Bruce. There is a certain arrogance, but there is also a very fine nature beneath it all . . .

Churchill was under no illusions about what Menzies wanted. The Secretary of State for Dominion Affairs, Lord Cranborne, briefed the British Prime Minister on 12 May 1941 about Menzies' suggestion of an imperial conference:

. . . The present proposal clearly emanates from Mr Menzies, and I have reason to know that he does not necessarily put it forward because he thinks that the time is ripe for a conference to consider all matters of Imperial interest, but for a quite different reason. He has come strongly to the conclusion, during his visit here, that there should be permanent representation of the Dominions on the War Cabinet by an outstanding Empire personality, preferably himself. He considers that the only way to achieve this result is by means of a resolution of an Imperial Conference. For that reason, he made it clear, before he left England, that he intended to press for such a Conference . . .

I am not personally opposed to the proposition, which appears to have a good deal to be said for it. But it seems to me that you should have the background, in case you have not already got it.

In a characteristically terse minute, Churchill noted: 'I have got it. WSC 14.5.41'. Although Churchill at first cabled Mackenzie King that a meeting of the Imperial Conference 'would be most desirable if it could be arranged', he does not appear to have been unduly distressed when both the Canadian and South African Prime Ministers indicated that a meeting in July or August would not be convenient for them.

However, Menzies was not easily rebuffed. Indeed his persistence—in the face of the undisguised reluctance of Mackenzie King, Smuts (the South African leader) and Fraser (the New Zealand Prime Minister) —suggests that his motives were deeper than the documents disclose. It seems clear that, while he was in England, Menzies had come to the conclusion that his own political future—at least as far as it could be foreseen—did not lie in Australia. The entreaties of Lord Hankey, tantalising hints of a welcome to the Conservative ranks in Parliament, and his own repeated attempts to secure support and acceptance for arrangements that would entail his presence in London, make it hard to come to any other conclusion. As late as 3 July 1941, Menzies told

Mackenzie King he 'would be prepared to run any political risk at home if by going to London for suggested conference I could contribute to what I feel is an essential change'. This over-eagerness to find a justification to return to Britain after he had come home to Australia, was to play a significant part in damaging his standing in the Australian Parliament. Yet it must be said that, for a man with a powerful analytical mind, a tongue to match it, youth, energy and ambition, the challenge of Westminster and Whitehall was an unbearable temptation. It was not simply that he had reached the summit of Australian public life—a position that could be retained or lost but never enhanced. It was also that he was truly a British patriot. To serve the Empire at its desperately threatened heart: that was the plain duty of any loyal Australian Briton who had the chance.

Even before he reached Sydney—by flying-boat after a nightmare journey across the Tasman—Menzies had learned of intrigues being conducted against him while he was away. He was met in New Zealand with messages and a personal briefing from a trusted member of his staff. The alleged conspirators included Harold Holt, Bill Hutchison, Sir Charles Marr, and Bill McCall. Exhausted, and obviously shaken by having flown through a terrible storm for eight hours from Auckland, the Prime Minister virtually ignored Arthur Fadden who had acted as Leader of the Government during his absence. Fadden, who had emerged as the petulant Cameron's successor when the top contenders for the Country Party leadership, Page and John McEwen, had deadlocked, recalled: 'He seemed about as happy as a sailor on a horse. After curt greetings he drove away from the Rose Bay flying boat base in the official car in which I had arrived.' The unfortunate Country Party Leader was forced to share a car back to the city with his colleague, Senator Foll, the Minister for Information. Two days later, on May 26, in a speech of great passion, Menzies spoke to a meeting of about 3000 people in Sydney Town Hall. When the speech was reprinted the following month, the Commonwealth Publicity Officer wrote that it bore 'the marks which grim war experience made upon Mr Menzies'. It also demonstrated the enormous psychological gulf which had opened up between the Prime Minister and the Australian people:

> I would be a very insensitive person if I did not appreciate this magnificent welcome home . . . I have been looking forward to getting home for four long months—ever since I left. These four months have taken me into very many strange places and they have taken me through some of the strangest experiences of my life and I believe that they may have brought me back to Australia with some experience, with some contact with people in the world, with some added wisdom and some increased sense of the gravity of our position that may enable me to serve you better in the future than I have in the past.
> Before I say something about these wanderings of mine I do want to say this, that my journey abroad, my collaboration with the British War Cabinet during a period of ten weeks, my visits to Canada and to

the United States of America would have been impossible but for the existence behind me in Australia of a loyal Cabinet and of loyal friends. Every now and then in London that great fighting leader Mr Winston Churchill, would put down a newspaper or a cable and look at me across the table and say, 'You know, my friend, this fellow Fadden of yours seems to be a pretty good one', and it always gave me the greatest pleasure in the world to be able to confirm that. I thank him publicly as I thank all of my colleagues in the Cabinet publicly for the way in which they have held the fort.

This is not a party meeting to-night, and it gives me real pleasure to be able to say that I also thank my friend the Leader of the Opposition. It is something that the cynics have never quite been able to understand that the Prime Minister and the Leader of the Opposition should be genuine and wholehearted personal friends. I am happy to know that it is so, and I have always hoped that that uninterrupted personal friendship might ultimately prove to be a symbol of all-round co-operation by all parties. . . .

Before I ever went away I had read what the cables could tell us, what the onlookers could tell us, and I thought occasionally: this is overdone; this just a little too picturesque an account of how people behave in war; but no account that I have ever read could possibly do justice to the magnificent people of the Mother Country.

I think the whole matter sums itself up in the best remark that I think has been made in Great Britain since the war began. His Majesty the King who, with Her Majesty the Queen, is to be seen in every stricken field in Britain, and who grows in vigor and force us she grows in charm, was visiting an area in which bombs had fallen from the sky, in which homes had been shattered, in which lives had been lost. As he moved around this area with words of encouragement and sympathy to the people, one of the onlookers, one of those who had been beaten out of his home, put his hand in a friendly manner on the King's shoulder as he went by and, in a casual Australian sort of manner, said 'Thank God for a good King'.

The King turned like a flash and made one of the greatest replies in history. He said, 'And thank God for a good people'.

A FIGHTING PRIME MINISTER

How fortunate we are in Australia that at the centre of this Empire of ours there should be fighting, not only for themselves, but for us, a great King and a great people, a great people led by a Prime Minister who is the embodiment of the fighting spirit of the race. How fortunate we are that at this crucial time in our history—because it is a crucial time: this is the year of Fate—there should be leading us at the centre of the Empire a great fighting Prime Minister who enjoys the loyalty of an entire Parliament, who enjoys the loyalty of an entire people, a people who have put on one side all those things which might divide them and have concentrated only with passion, with reality, with earnestness on those central and imperishable things that must for ever unite them.

Having said that, what shall we say of the people whom he leads? To almost everyone of us war is in its nature something remote, something we read about, something in the cables, something to give us a little spasm of pleasure when the news is good, a little spasm of pain when the news is bad, but all the same, something distant from us.

The war is not distant from anybody in Great Britain. I say this to you—and I speak of this at first hand—that there must be nobody, for example, in the City of London who sees the sun set and the darkness come down over the earth who can confidently say that he will ever see the sun rise again.

NIGHT IN LONDON

We never have that feeling here; but the people of Great Britain have it. Every inhabitant of London, every inhabitant of those great cities, knows that when the darkness comes he may, within an hour, hear this banshee howl of the air raid alarm, he may hear the bumble bee noise of the bombers overhead; he will see the flash of the anti-aircraft guns; he will see the lightning of their explosions in the skies.

I speak of these things because, in common with millions of people in Great Britain, I have seen them happen time and again. And he knows that at the mere whim of the tyrant that night the bombs may fall in his area and, if they do, his time may have come.

What feeling has that produced? Has it produced any dull feeling of despair?—not at all. Has it produced any blind and stupid fatalism? —not at all. Faith beats as high in the heart of men in Great Britain to-day as it ever did. You may speak wherever you like in these devastated cities to women dressed in new bought widow's weeds, and you will get only the one answer: 'Ah, well, it has been a bitter thing; it has been a bitter time; but they are not going to beat us this way'.

MORALE OF BRITISH PEOPLE

When I think of that, when I think of the spirit, of the morale of the British people, I am not talking of fine speeches made on platforms, I am not talking of resounding phrases, I am not talking about how the great look at these things—I am talking to you about how the common men and women of England look at these things.

This war has produced a new order of chivalry and its knights are to be found in the back streets and lanes of Great Britain.

In one week I saw eight or ten of the largest industrial cities of Great Britain. Round every one of them were vast factories pouring out aircraft, guns of all sorts, all sorts of materials of war, and in the centre of them, every one of them, were great ragged gaps where the bombs had fallen; street after street of ruined houses, block after block of cottages, of simple homes, blasted out of existence in a night. In every one of them death had been so widespread and the dead so unidentified that there had been community funerals, with hundreds of victims buried in a common grave. Can you imagine anything so eloquent of utter human anguish as that?

Yet, within two days, within a week, all these people who were left were back at their places, working in their factories, smiling at their work, and working harder than ever before, determined not to look for some compromise, but determined that so long as they had one ounce in them to resist this infamy should never happen in the world again.

SEVERITY OF RAIDS

I hope that nobody will believe that air raiding of civilian populations is a matter of little moment. The farther you are away from air raiding the more philosophic you are about it; but, I remember on more than one occasion when bombs had fallen, when streets of buildings were burning, seeing old men and women and men and women not so old being led along the streets, dazed and broken, with the whole of their lives in a material sense in ruins behind them, just being led on to a new life of which they could not even see the dim beginning, and I would have thought when I saw these things that this kind of wound was a wound that would take weeks or months to heal; but you could go back to that same place in a week's time and move round among the people who had suffered these cruelties and degradations and you would not hear from one human lip one hint of defeat, of despair, or even of discouragement.

Many times I thought of those 'wise' people who have been saying to us for years rather contemptuous things of the street-bred people. Their muscles were not the muscles of the new German race; they were not large and imposing people. But I say to you that in those people there burns the purest flame of courage that this world has ever seen . . .

LUCKY HERE

I spoke at one great aircraft factory to the manager of a shop which seemed to cover acres of floor space in which many hundreds of people were employed and there was a buzz of activity.

I said to the manager 'You have apparently been lucky here?'

'Well,' he said, 'I do not know what you mean by lucky. We have been bombed three times in this building'.

I said 'I see no signs of it'.

'Well,' he said, 'you just can't sit round when you are bombed. If they bomb the roof off we put it on again. If they bomb a hole in the wall, we plug up the hole in the wall. Not long ago they came along and put down the largest calibre of bombs almost slap into the middle of the shop and almost blew it to pieces and in three weeks we had increased our production 'by twenty per cent'.

Thus, I might talk of them forever. When I find myself started on this business of how these magnificent people, your kinsmen and mine, are standing up to this ordeal, I feel I could go on for ever; but, Sir, I do not want to go on for ever on that, because if there is one thing I come home feeling strongly it is not merely that we are fighting side by side with magnificent people and that we ourselves are magnificently represented by great soldiers, sailors and airmen.

I come back here completely convinced that we in Australia must do more than we have ever done before.

When I say we must do more than we have ever done I am not subscribing to the cheap remark that Australia has fallen down on the job. Australia has not fallen down on the job. It would sound very oddly in the ears of English-speaking people all over the world, who are superbly proud of what Australia has done, if we were to tell them that we had fallen down on the job or that we proposed to.

I believe that we in Australia have done well. I know somebody will say that that is mere complacency. I say this to you, and nobody can speak of it at closer hand than I can, that for over two years it has been my responsibility to direct this grim effort.

MIRACLES OF PRODUCTION

Australia has in two years in many ways almost worked miracles of production for war. But that does not mean we must fold our arms and say 'All is for the best'. I believe, on the contrary, that we must keep moving and keep driving until we are able to say that so far as it lies within our power we are doing as much and suffering as much and sacrificing as much for this war as the beleaguered people of the Mother Country.

How will we do it? I am not here to make dramatic political suggestions. The last thing I am here to do is to endeavour to make some cheap political capital. If I have talked to-night, or in the last couple of days, of political disunity it is not to say I am pointing my finger at one party or one man. I am not.

If we in Australia are to do what we ought to do in this war, then we must have a co-operation between all men. I say this to my friends of the Labour Party who have been so courteous as to come here to-night and be on this platform, I am not suggesting to any political party that it should extinguish itself or give up its identity. I am not suggesting to any political party that it should abandon any of its own ideas.

These are all healthy things and in normal times the clash of these political forces would bring political health and in the long run bring social and industrial progress. But we stand in the supreme crisis of our history.

THIS YEAR OF FATE

Is there anybody here to-night, is there anybody listening to me to-night, who does not realize clearly and vividly in his heart that with one turn of the wheel this power that we belong to might be extinguished forever? Does not everybody in Australia realise that we are fighting in a war which has gone on for the better part of two years, in which we have sustained defeat after defeat, in which we have found ourselves confronted by a foe who outnumbers us mechanically, who has more aircraft than we have, who has thousands more tanks than we have, who has six years of cruel preparation behind him? Don't we realize that if there is one year in the history of the British people that can be described as a year of Fate it is 1941.

I say, and speak of what I know, because I have gone right round the world. I have spoken to the rulers of most of our countries, sat in the War Cabinet day after day in Great Britain. I tell you I pray to God we shall go through 1941 to safety.

I do not underestimate the task we have. It has never occurred to me to think that we could ever know defeat; but it has occurred to me many times that we may court defeat unless we decide, every man jack of us, that this war is his business and nobody else's.

It is our great privilege to be governed under a system of Parliament. It is a characteristic of our parliamentary life that there should be parties and party debates. I am the last man to say cheap things about the party system or about party debates; but I say this, that at this solemn hour in our history, this fateful hour in our history, it is for us if we be intelligent men to make Parliament an instrument of war and not an instrument of dissension.

TRIBUTE TO MR CURTIN

I have never had any lack of understanding of the point of view honestly held and candidly expressed by my friend Mr Curtin. In my absence for four months I believe that I owe a great deal of stability to his understanding; but you will understand my utter astonishment coming back from the scenes I have witnessed, coming back here from this magnificent unity of purpose and of function and of organization that exists in Great Britain, to find that men sitting on the Opposition benches, men like Mr Curtin, Mr Forde, Dr Evatt, Mr Beasley and Mr Makin, those men who sit on the Advisory War Council, should have no executive function in the direction of the war and should be compelled to stand off and become the critics of an effort to which they might easily be powerful contributors.

Again, let me say this: this business of being a Prime Minister in time of war is no sinecure. This is no soft-seated job for which any-body might strive. In war there are great decisions to be taken, there are great crises to be faced, there are vast responsibilities to be assumed; and the man who has to lead his country in the taking of them occupies no post of ease; he occupies no easy post of cheap honour; and when he finds himself there, then he is entitled, as Winston Churchill is entitled in Great Britain, as Franklin Roosevelt is entitled in the United States of America, to say to his own people, 'Put your whispering away; let us have no more imitation friendship; let us have no more self-seeking; let us have no more petty intrigue. If you want to engage in these things, in future, engage in them when we have won this war.' . . .

OUR RESPONSIBILITY

This is going to be a long job. I want you to understand that in the Battle of 1941 we must for all essential purposes, particularly in the Middle East, depend upon our own strength, upon our own resources. We must draw drafts upon our own courage, our own resolution.

When I say that to you I do not say it to you—God forbid I should say it to you—in order to endeavour to paint a picture of horror; I do not. But if there is one thing I do believe it is that the day has gone by for any leader of a great and brave nation to feed it with pap.

The last thing I want to talk about is this: we in Australia still enjoy most of the pleasant things of life. It can scarcely be said by any ordinary citizen of this country that he finds his daily life mode changed from what it was two years ago. We must begin to change our lives; we must make up our minds that war of this magnitude against an enemy of this strength and power can only be won by completely organizing every bit of our energy for his defeat, and we cannot organize every bit of our energy so long as we have energy running to waste in Australia, so long as we are still spending money on non-essential imports, so long as we are expending money, capital and skill on non-essential production, so long as we are still spending financial resources on non-essential consumption. . . .

I do hope that we shall all throw aside all those things that trouble us, all those little things that divide us, and realize that we have one destiny to fight for, that we have a powerful foe to fight and that we can win only if we are as united in function, united in action as I know we are in spirit and belief. . . .

. . . every bomb I have heard fall, every life I have seen ruined, every experience that I have seen people go through in Great Britain, every memory I have of our own people and their magnificent work in this war-torn world, has left me more and more convinced that the time has gone by for the old fights in our country.

AUSTRALIANS—GO TO IT!

There is one fight only that matters to-day and I call on the whole of Australia to go to it.

One Australian who wanted to 'go to it' was H.V. Evatt. Although he was careful not to make his offer too blatant on paper, Evatt made it known to the Prime Minister that he would respond to a personal invitation to join the Government. On the day Menzies arrived back in Sydney, Evatt sent him a long confidential letter. This had evidently been discussed beforehand with Menzies' old friend, Ambrose Pratt, who wrote on May 22 that he was 'confident it will accomplish the intent'. Meanwhile, Evatt had also been making a point of contacting Menzies' father-in-law, Senator Leckie, in terms which may be inferred from Leckie's reply thanking Evatt for 'your kindly reference to the PM. He will be glad to know that any little political differences are not carried into private feelings.' A copy of the letter to Menzies, never previously published, remains in Evatt's papers:

Dear Prime Minister,   24.5.41.

I feel it my duty to express certain views to you before the result of the Boothby by-election is known. It seems scandalous (and it is certainly most trying) to conduct such a contest at a time like the present; but as I see it there is no halting place between a general political truce and an 'all-out' fight in every such by-election.

The people of this country are suffering from a deep sense of frustration. Lack of enthusiasm for the war effort is growing. Recruiting progresses slowly, contributions to war loans have to be fought for, and even the voluntary gifts to the various funds are falling off.

The campaign in Greece has created the feeling that our troops were inadequately supplied with mechanised support. No one has contended that it was wrong to go into Greece. But few are satisfied that proper precautions were taken to give some chance to the undertaking.

For reasons which need not be gone into, the Munitions Department and that of Supply are not working as satisfactorily as they should. While you were away there were scandals over footwear and bread shortages. Some little time ago the Minister for the Army presented a written report to the War Council dealing with equipment available in the case of a typical command. This was the Eastern Command. The report showed a desperate state of affairs and I hope you will read it at once. Following upon this the business heads directing the Munitions Dept. attended the War Council. The questioning showed 1. that some of the executives were plainly incompetent. 2. that some of them were unable to dissociate their business interests from those of the country. 3. that Lewis, (the director) did not regard himself as being in supreme control. 4. that no one was making it his business to synchronise supplies of munitions with the needs of the Army so that the Army could be supplied quickly with some of the munitions which might save Australia or the territories close to Australia. 5. that the priorities committee (merely determining an order of relative importance) provided no solution whatever of the problem of urgent supply.

There has been public controversy over this department and the 'cost-plus' system in relation to the target price together with the question of separating business control from government control have come in for keen discussion.

In my opinion the central feature of the present drift is the unstable parliamentary situation. While you were absent Ministers were unable even to adjourn the House except by consent which was seldom forthcoming. If I may say so with respect it is most unwise to suggest an era of great poverty after the present war. Men live by hope as well as by fear. It is also unfair to suggest that your opponents are the persons who are 'playing politics'. Your own colleagues have been playing exactly the same game in exactly the same way. Some of them talk about a National Government but it is the last thing they really want.

Frustration is apt to give way to despair and something must be done quickly by those in responsibility. You have a special opportunity because no one at the present time questions your right to the leadership of the nation. Some form of closer association between the parties for war purposes only must be obtained. Some time ago I felt that you did not really desire such an object to be achieved but I can hardly believe that you will not fight earnestly now to accomplish that aim. There is no tyranny like the tyranny of words and a National Government in the full sense is out of the question. But there are many possible alternatives between 1. a complete division of executive posts between the two parties and 2. continuance of the present system. The War Council has in some respects deserved well of the country. But it is intolerable to reach a position approaching decision only to find that the decision is not taken and the matter goes over for a another week or ten days. Something ought to be done to vest such a body or a smaller body with supreme executive power as in the case of New Zealand where too the procedure is not regarded as amounting to a National Government. If you want these things done in order to preserve this nation you should not make public challenges or offers. On the contrary you should act privately using your undoubted powers of persuasion in order to reach some agreement before it is publicly mentioned.

I cannot express in words how deeply I feel about the urgency of the present position. By themselves your Ministers cannot unite the nation and do the job. I am worried to distraction about the disillusionment and the defeatism which are evident in so many places. I am prepared to co-operate with you to the very limit of my power providing you on your part will go 'flat-out' to achieve the objective I suggest in one way or the other. My own purpose is to serve this country in the most suitable capacity for the period of this war and then to give up political life as a career. At present I am prevented from performing this service which the people wish me to give. There are others in the same position. You and you alone can resolve such difficulties and give stabilization to the parliamentary position without interfering with the rights of opposition or the separation of the two parties.

Yours sincerely,
H.V. Evatt

Menzies did not trust Evatt, and realised that a united all-party government was probably the only way to preserve his own influence. In order to make a national coalition more palatable to the Opposition, he was even prepared, as it soon emerged, to step down from the supreme position. But first he had to try to deal with his own supposed supporters. Jean Spender, wife of the Minister for the Army, recalled a grim encounter:

. . . At the time his political popularity was at an extremely low ebb; he was under a barrage of bitter criticism, not only from the Press and public, but from many so-called friends. After a somewhat stormy session in Parliament had ended, Percy and I left for Melbourne by train, as did the Menzies. In those days, with differing rail gauges, you had to change trains at Albury, on the Victoria and New South Wales border: a most uncomfortable and daunting procedure in the middle of a winter's night. On Albury station the four of us found ourselves lining up together for a cup of coffee. At that time I was still rather shy and somewhat in awe of the leader of our party, whom I both admired and liked. Just as I was taking my first sip of bad, but very hot coffee, the great man turned to me, looked down what seemed like the two feet or so between our heights, beetled his heavy eyebrows and declaimed, not too pleasantly, 'Give me the dagger, Lady Macbeth!'

I was utterly taken aback and gaped up at him wordlessly. Of course I guessed what was in his mind. Many members of the United Australia Party, seriously perturbed at Mr Menzies' lack of public popularity at that time, were wondering how they were going to fare under a leader of whom so few seemed to approve. A little ironical in view of the prestige that was to surround him in the future.

Be that as it may, because of wide discontent, talk of another leader was fairly common. In that connection the name of Spender had frequently been brought forward. We ourselves could not but be aware of this. Too many people had attempted to raise the matter. It was somewhat enbarrassing, for at no time had any such suggestion emanated from, or been encouraged by, my husband, as I was in the best position to know. On the contrary, for some time past at parties and so on in Sydney it had fallen to our lot to take up the cudgels in Mr Menzies' defence, even against some he considered, and still numbers among, his closest friends.

While Menzies was abroad, the malcontents at home had been busy. One of the men unavoidably at the centre of events in Canberra was Jean Spender's husband, Percy Spender, the Minister for the Army, and former Treasurer. After the ancient Billy Hughes, he was Menzies' senior lieutenant in the UAP. Any moves directed against Menzies would inevitably have to take account of Spender's position and attitude. Fortunately for the historian, Spender kept a diary, and subsequently wrote frank recollections of the closing weeks of the Menzies' Ministry. In Menzies' absence, Spender wrote, the knives had been sharpened:

. . . One could not be in Canberra for long without learning what was in the wind. The chant that the 'Big Fellow' was unpopular increased in volume. It was being said here and there, and more and more, that Menzies could not lead a Government, or win at the polls. The game of Cabinet-forming under a new leader became a favourite pastime. This or that Minister would be promoted, or receive some other portfolio; a place would be found for this or that person not then in the

Cabinet. So the carrot was dangled before the eyes of more than one. Menzies' best service to Australia, it was being constantly said, would be to represent her in the British War Cabinet. It was there that his great talents could be put to maximum use. It all sounded so smooth.

Fadden was put forward as the successor, not by chance, but deliberately by a small band of what I would call 'the operators'. Was not Fadden popular with the Press and the Opposition? He would, so it was gossiped, be a leader who would attract the support of the people. The Labor Opposition would give him a 'fair go'.

Under Fadden, it was said, we could all present a united front. Was he not doing a good job as Acting Prime Minister? (or so it was said). Fadden would give us stable government to give maximum impetus to the war effort.

To fan the flames there was another kind of criticism. Menzies' place was in Australia. He had been too long away. He was too fond of the dukes and the duchesses, and so on. Either he should remain in Australia, or remain in England. All this propaganda had its effect.

It had been said that the move to displace Menzies from the leadership began in his own party—the United Australia Party. Credence to this story seems to have been given by the public pronouncement of two of its members, McCall and Hutchinson (the 'two Bills') but, in fact, they were men of no great influence. It is true that McCall and one or two others had challenged Menzies' leadership as far back as August 1940, but this was a small, unimportant part of the picture.

It was true also that disaffection existed and grew in the UAP, but certain members of the Country Party played an important role in Menzies' deposition. Almost as soon as he went overseas there was a concerted move to replace him with Fadden—a move which every politician of sense in the Ministerial parties must have been aware of.

There had already been straws in the wind at the abortive discussions between Labor and the Government parties which took place the latter part of 1940, when Menzies had offered to serve in a National Government under another Prime Minister if he were not acceptable; Page of the Country Party had advanced the odd suggestion that a Prime Minister should be elected by Parliament itself.

The attempts by Menzies to form a National Government and the length to which he was willing to go to achieve one, rather gave aid and support to his political enemies, and there were a number of them, since they gave ground for arguing that Menzies alone was not capable of giving stable government to the nation.

Menzies could hardly have been unaware of this. Speaking in Parliament on 9 December 1940, replying to questions put to him by McCall, he wondered whether the latter's observations on the formation of a National Government 'are being made with the object of bringing one about, or to embarrass me as leader of the Government'.

Not only did those who sought and planned to dislodge Menzies come from within the UAP—and in my view from within the Country Party —there were of course more than a few Labor members who wanted the same thing. Fadden as Prime Minister would have been acceptable to them, if for no other reason than that this would diminish the stature of Menzies, and so lessen the authority and standing of his party and the Government. It is unlikely that they would not foresee, in that event, further dissension within the UAP. The Labor Party, hungry for power, would be only too happy to throw some wood on the fire. It could hardly have feared Fadden as a Prime Minister.

It had at times been put about that I was one of the chief conspirators. I have my full share of faults, but I don't play the game that way. I feel sure that Menzies was sold the story that I had worked against him during his absence. I recall that when finally Menzies stood down, he and his wife were walking from his room along the corridor leading to King's Hall. My wife and I were standing there, and made an approach to speak to him. He coldly refused to notice us. Did I feed some misgiving which I think he then had of me; some suspicion of political aspirations on my part, because at a Cabinet meeting held not long before his downfall I had said that stronger leadership from him was called for?

During Menzies' absence I was spoken to, as were others, by more than one member of the party, 'sounded out' is, perhaps, the right phrase. McCall was one. I made it quite plain where I stood. I said I knew what was afoot, and would have nothing to do with it. Menzies could not lead the party if the sniping and disloyalty did not cease. If he could not successfully lead the Government, Fadden, I said, certainly could not.

Some time before Menzies returned to Australia from England, Sir Sydney Snow, then high in UAP circles—I think he was president of the NSW branch—telephoned and asked me to see him urgently. We met in Sydney. He showed me what purported to be an official letter from Country Party Headquarters in New South Wales to a prominent member of the Federal Parliamentary Country Party. Sir Sydney said the letter had come through the post, addressed to him. He assumed it had been put accidentally in the wrong envelope, and had reached him by mistake.

The letter said, in effect, that Menzies would have to go if a coalition Government was to continue in office, and be replaced as leader by a Country Party man. My name was mentioned as the member of the UAP who would have to be 'side-tracked' if this was to be brought about.

Snow thought the letter was authentic, as it fitted in with what I had told him of happenings in Canberra, and with his own information. He thought I should inform Menzies before he returned to Australia, of the contents of the letter, of how it came into Snow's possession, and generally put him in the picture of what had been happening in his absence.

Menzies was already on his way home, but I wrote to reach him *en route*. To put it briefly, I told him how his political grave was being dug.

When he arrived he stayed briefly in Sydney before 'going into smoke' for a few days at a friend's place near Moss Vale, some 100 miles or so south of Sydney, preparing a major speech which he was to deliver at the Sydney Town Hall. He did not communicate with me.

The Town Hall meeting was a tremendous success.

After the meeting a reception for a small group of people was held by the Lord Mayor in his rooms. Menzies was surrounded by his admirers. He made no attempt to speak to me until he saw my wife and myself standing rather apart. We had been watching what was taking place with, perhaps, sardonic detachment, because one of the themes of the evening had been the loyalty his colleagues in Cabinet had given him during his absence! He broke off and strode over to us. Without ado he said: 'Well Percy, where is this grave you wrote about?' My reply was: 'It's been dug all right Bob: it is only waiting for you to be pushed into it.' He made some remark to the effect that I must have a vivid imagination, and strode away.

Within a couple of months he was no longer Prime Minister. Not once did he raise the subject of the letter again, or seek my opinion or advice. This struck me as rather odd. I have nothing to go upon, but I cannot fail to wonder whether one of the many whisperers in politics had been at him, and had cast me in the role of the pretender to the throne. This I do know: not for quite a time thereafter was the close relationship which previously had existed between Menzies and myself resumed. I was no longer his 'faithful Achates' as sometimes he had called me.

Menzies' disappearance into the blue—incommunicado—before he addressed the meeting at the Town Hall added fuel to the fire of criticism of him. England was at bay, her back to the wall. The Empire was in desperate straits. It was being said that Menzies was not facing up to the task of making the extensive administrative changes which he had foreshadowed with a view to a more intensive war effort. He was proceeding at too leisurely a pace. Couldn't fight a war on speeches—and so on.

Menzies indeed was in for a rude awakening. I think he found it impossible to believe, after the great reception he had received in England, and the high regard in which rightly he was held there, that his position as Prime Minister could be assailed.

Four weeks after his return to Australia he reconstructed the Cabinet, and outlined the administrative changes he proposed. The Cabinet reconstruction was not of any great significance beyond the establishment of a Ministry of War Organization of Industry and the appointment of three new Ministers—Spooner, and Abbott from New South Wales, and McDonald from Victoria, all newcomers to the Parliament (they had won their seats in the 1940 elections.)

The reorganisation of the Cabinet did nothing to diminish the dissension, discontent and personal animosities which abounded in the UAP—if anything it made them worse. Menzies' hold on the party was declining rapidly and the disarray of the Government soon became public knowledge.

. . . McCall of New South Wales, a crony of Billy Hughes (who had no particular love for Menzies) and Hutchinson of Victoria, carried their opposition to Menzies not only into the Party Room, but into the Press. Public utterances by them that Menzies should go received considerable publicity after the Cabinet reconstruction. A section of the Press was gunning for Menzies. Finally Hutchinson, three weeks after the reconstruction, publicly demanded that Menzies should go and Fadden, not a member of his own party, take his place.

By this time Menzies was well aware that there was discontent with his leadership not only among the rank and file of his party, but within the Cabinet itself.

At a Cabinet meeting he put himself, needlessly in my view, on the 'hot plate' by asking his colleagues their views of the campaign against him. He invited us to say frankly on what grounds, if any, it was thought he had failed, and what suggestions we had to make. It was a quixotic gesture, but a mistake.

What he should have done was either to speak privately to some key members of Cabinet, or failing that, to ask bluntly in Cabinet what Ministers were against his leadership—in short to call upon them to stand up and be counted. That, I believe, would have put an end to the rot. There were quite a number of us who would have stood beside him. As it was, some spoke strongly in his favour, others did criticise his leadership, but not in hostile terms. Hard things were certainly said, some of them by me.

It was my view that the war effort needed more drive, and he was the one who should supply it. His personal influence was needed to restore unity in the party. He had drifted away from the rank and file. Moreover, absence overseas, no matter how justified on general grounds, did not give to the people the leadership that could only be given by a Prime Minister actually in the country. It was up to him to remedy the situation.

Some Ministers were more critical than I, whereas others again claimed there was no ground for criticism at all. Among these was Eric Harrison, who was so emotionally disturbed by some of the things that were said, that he was near to tears.

It was a sad occasion—sad for Menzies, sad for many of his colleagues. However there was no suggestion that he should resign, although I am satisfied more than a few Ministers wanted just that, but were not prepared to say so before him. That could wait on events.

Menzies decided to take the criticism of himself by McCall, Hutchinson, Marr and others, to the Party. The UAP met alone, while the Country Party waited and watched. A number of members absented themselves from the party meeting, and only about two-thirds of the members were present.

Hutchinson was not there but McCall was, and he was more than just critical of Menzies. But McCall did not carry much weight in the party. Others, including at least one Minister, as I recall, spoke against Menzies, but in more restrained terms than McCall. There was, however, no attempt made to depose him from leadership. It was evident that a definite majority of those present were prepared to continue to support Menzies. The possibility of an early election raised its ugly head: and that always tends to restrain precipitate action.

Menzies handled himself much better than he had done at the Cabinet meeting, and he won the day handsomely. He was still in a position of strength, and he could have maintained it if, in his subsequent actions, he had shown some of the political sagacity for which he became so renowned later.

There was however one ominous suggestion put forward, supported by quite a few members. This was that if any change of leadership did take place, Menzies' successor should be chosen by a joint party meeting.

The suggestion was obviously designed to have a Country Party man elected as Menzies' successor. It was certain that members of the Country Party would vote almost to a man for one of their own, and that fewer than half the UAP votes would be needed to ensure his election—actually about twelve votes out of a total UAP membership of thirty-eight. With the support of a substantial majority of the UAP behind him it might have been expected that this would give Menzies a decent breathing space to enable him to repair his fences. But his troubles were not over. A section of the Press, including the *Sydney Morning Herald* came out against him, suggesting that his qualities could better be used in London, at the centre of things, rather than as Prime Minister.

I think that with a show of strength and vigour, and the use of a little political discernment, Menzies might have weathered the storm, had it not been for a decision taken by the full Cabinet early in August that he should go to England immediately because of dangerous developments in the Far East. The Japanese had landed in what was then called South Indo-China, and it seemed possible that they would invade Thailand. The Cabinet regarded it as essential that Australia's views and interests should be put before the British War Cabinet.

The proposal that Menzies should go did not come from him, although he very willingly adopted it. My recollection is that it first came from Earle Page—certainly he strongly supported it. The decision was immediately communicated or became known to the Press. This was unfortunate.

As it was, Forde (the Deputy Labor Leader), Beasley and Evatt attacked the proposal at a meeting of the Advisory War Council. Evatt was particularly caustic and personal, alleging that Menzies' proposed journey was simply a political ruse to save himself from being pushed out of the leadership.

Characterising the suggested trip as a 'political ruse' was going too far. But Menzies' willingness to leave a poisonous Australian scene for the global centrality of London was only thinly veiled in an 'urgent, confidential and personal' cypher telegram to Stanley Bruce on August 13:

13th August 1941

MOST IMMEDIATE. Urgent confidential and personal to Mr Bruce

Cabinet has asked me go to London again as it feels Far Eastern position will require important exchanges of policy and strategy. But, more than this increasingly convinced that our point of view must be pressed in British War Cabinet itself.

As you know I sent my views on Dominion representation to British War Cabinet to Mackenzie King and Smuts but neither of them is interested in it, Smuts going so far as to say in March that we Dominion Prime Ministers should mind our own business and leave Churchill to mind his. This completely overlooks the fact that many matters dealt with by British Cabinet and Foreign Secretary are our business as well as Britain's and that present Cabinet set up excludes us from a real voice at the right time. But I do not need to explain this matter to you. Your own cables to me have (mooted) it admirably.

I have informed my colleagues that I will put the question before Parliament as a Minister going to London must have backing.

There has been clammering here by a disgruntled and personally hostile section of the press that I should resign from Premiership and be sent to London as an ordinary Minister. I have pointed out to my colleagues that such a course would be in my opinion fatal, for I could scarcely hope to carry real authority or weight in British War Cabinet if I had in fact been just rejected in my own country. In any event great majority of Government members are completely loyal to me.

As matter will no doubt be discussed thoroughly during next week I would be personally most grateful if you could explore and advise me upon following questions. In getting answers it might be worth having a confidential chat with Beaverbrook as well as going through ordinary channels.

(1) If a Minister other than Prime Minister were sent to London would he be given a seat in the War Cabinet.

(2) If I went to London not as Prime Minister but as an ordinary Minister would I be given a seat in the War Cabinet.

(3) If I went as Prime Minister but after a month or two felt my indefinite absence from Australia was creating embarrassment here and then resigned Premiership what prospect would there be of my being asked or allowed to continue to sit in the British War Cabinet.

(4) What is your own opinion on the business generally.

I should add on my return to Australia Government stocks rose very high. There had apparently been almost complete satisfaction with my work abroad but during the past few weeks news print rationing has made (recalcitrant) newspapers bitter petty revolts among a few members have been encouraged and whole atmosphere has become murky though fundamentally I have more confidence in underlying sound sense of the people than have some of my colleagues.

At the same time if you will allow a personal note I believe I am more effective in London than here where at present a hail-fellow-well-met technique is preferred to either information or reason. If you could be admitted to British War Cabinet the whole question would be answered to my perfect satisfaction but have assumed this is not practicable owing to presence of other High Commissioners in London.

Menzies.

Preferring the Prime Minister's presence, if not his information and his reason, the Labor leaders baulked. What were their motives, Sir Percy Spender has asked:

Did they fear that with the Prime Minister in London on an important mission, their chances of gaining the Government benches might be adversely affected? This would appear to have been Evatt's view, for he is reported as having said that the whole proposal was designed 'to hinder effective opposition to the present Ministry during the intervening absence abroad of the head of the Ministry.'

Curtin was somewhat non-committal. He was not as hungry for office—if he were hungry at all—as Evatt and other of his Labor colleagues on the Council. Menzies' duty, said Curtin, should be discharged in Australia, yet he saw some merit in Menzies going to London for the limited purpose of securing Australian representation on the British War Cabinet on a matter which could (and in the end did) vitally affect Australia.

But Evatt and Forde—Evatt giving the lead—carried their opposition into the public arena. Menzies' readiness to go again to the scene of his former triumph a few months after his return to Australia was manna from heaven to Evatt who, in my opinion, was now the spearhead of the movement to dethrone Menzies and bring Labor to power.

The danger signals were now flying for all to see. The Government depended upon the uncertain vote of one independent—Coles. Yet Menzies went ahead. I don't know whether he sought the support of Coles before he brought the issue before Parliament, but knowing him I doubt it.

In this atmosphere Parliament met and Menzies rose to speak. First he reviewed the international situation, which was grim enough. The danger of Japan entering into the war was surely evident to all members of the Advisory War Council, though Evatt and others either refused to recognise it or were not prepared to accept it as likely.

Menzies then told the House of the proposal that he should go to London.

'Having regard to the balance of parties in Parliament,' he said, 'I have indicated that it would not be practicable for me to go abroad at present, except with the approval of all parties', and he suggested that party meetings should be held to discuss the proposal. He based his argument in favour of it largely upon the view that Curtin had expressed in the War Council, namely that he might go to London for the limited purpose Curtin had then suggested. This was indeed a slender reed to rely upon in the light of the opposition of Evatt and others at the Council meeting. Was there no one in the Government who could have efficiently presented Australia's request for representation on the British War Cabinet? No doubt Menzies thought not.

By the following day it was evident that Curtin had failed to hold his party. Labor was against Menzies going to London, although it agreed that arrangements should be made with the British Government for representation of Australia in the Imperial War Cabinet.

The party declared that the gravity of the war required that the Prime Minister should be in Australia 'to direct the administration in the organisation of a total war effort.'

Forde descended from the dignified manner in which Curtin had presented his Party's declaration to Parliament, and set the tone of the opposition by saying that the proposal was 'a most shameful exploitation of the international situation in order to extricate the Government from political difficulties, and enable it to unload, on the other side of the world, a man who it regards as an unpopular leader.' It was an idea which, in my opinion, had crossed the mind of more than one of Menzies's own Ministers.

On the same or the next day—21 or 22 August—Menzies, by letter, offered the Labor Party an all-party government in which he was willing to serve under Curtin, or any other person selected as Prime Minister. He suggested that the Coalition parties should have only half the Ministerial portfolios. I have no recollection of this letter having been discussed by Cabinet before it was despatched. It was briskly and brusquely rejected by the Labor Party.

Menzies had now allowed himself to be manoeuvred into an impossible position. It was not only the dissidents in his own party who were after his blood. Curtin, in his letter to Menzies rejecting the all-party government proposal, wrote:

'Such stability as the country now lacks as compared with what was the position prior to your return from London' (a strange reference, by innuendo, to Fadden) 'can have no other explanation than the dissensions which have emerged between your Government and certain of its nominal supporters.'

Curtin said that Menzies' offer of an all-party government indicated 'that he was not able, as Prime Minister to give stable Government.' Labor could provide that Government, and Menzies should return his Commission to the Governor-General and advise him of the purport of his (Curtin's) letter.

When the Cabinet met to consider Curtin's letter, it was immediately obvious that the Country Party Ministers, supported by a few UAP Ministers, sought to read into it what surely was not intended. Pointing out the contrast which the letter drew between the political position before Menzies' return from London, and the alleged instability in Government since his return, they argued that perhaps under another leader (a political idiot would have known who was in mind) Labor would be willing to make Parliament workable. Curtin, they said, did not want an election.

This was contested by most of the UAP Ministers. They said we should stand fast. Menzies' offer of a national Government, with the expression of his own willingness to stand down if necessary as Prime Minister was generous. We should return the ball to Labor's court and leave the next decision to them.

The discussion was inconclusive. . . . In result, however, the talk of another leader tended to weaken still further Menzies' position. He seemed more concerned with hearing the views of his colleagues than in giving the Cabinet a firm lead. He seemed very frayed and despondent after the torrid time he had been through. Fadden had little to say.

Only a firm lead by Menzies and a strong stand by him, could save the Government now. It was not forthcoming. Menzies had been through a shattering experience since his return from London. It was a devastating blow to his pride and self-esteem to endure, as he had, in the few weeks since the beginning of June, the insidious, hostile campaign against him, not only from Labor, but from within his own party. He was weary of the whole thing and about to throw in his hand.

Yet he could, in my view, still have saved the day if he had said to his Cabinet, 'We shall remain in Government. We will cast the burden upon the Labor Party to attempt to throw us from office. I shall in the meantime, continue as Prime Minister; let any Minister not willing to serve under me, stand up and say so, and he may surrender his portfolio.'

He could have said, as the leader of the majority party in the Coalition, 'I shall put the question of my leadership before my party. If it fails to confirm me in leadership, I will call upon it to elect another leader from our party to take my place, and recommend to the Governor-General that he be commissioned to form a new Government. If, on the other hand, I am confirmed in the leadership, I will expect loyal and undivided support from every member of the party. If they fail to give it to me, they cannot remain in the party.'

I believe this could possible have scotched further rebellion in the Party; the rebels would have been publicly isolated. And he would have stemmed the movement by the Country Party behind the scenes to have Fadden made Prime Minister.

Parliament adjourned on 28 August. Menzies immediately called the Cabinet together. The time had arrived for his departure. He said, in effect, that it appeared to him that he had lost the confidence of his Cabinet colleagues. This was denied by a number of his UAP colleagues, including myself. But there was however a chorus of silence from most of the Cabinet.

The Country Party then discreetly withdrew to leave Menzies alone with his UAP Ministers. He told us he had decided to resign. A number of us asked him to stand fast, but he had made up his mind. It was evident there was no fight left in him. It was a sorry thing to see a man of Menzies' stature pull down the flag and vacate the field to his enemies. The meeting was over in about an hour.

The humiliation was not yet over. Arthur Coles, who had been elected an independent MP for Henty in 1940, had pledged himself in writing to support Menzies after the Prime Minister returned from England:

> ...I was approached by a member of the government, Mr Eric Spooner, who asked me down to his office and he put the question to me, 'What would be your attitude if the Prime Minister resigned?' I said, 'Has Bob indicated that he's going to resign?' He said, 'No, not yet.' I said, 'That means you're going to force him within Cabinet?' 'Oh,' he said, 'I wouldn't put it that way but I've been asked by my colleagues to get your opinion.' 'Well,' I said, 'I'll give it to you. If you do this thing you will lose my support.' The result was Mr Menzies resigned. A party meeting (I had joined the party) was held with Mr Spender in the chair and before any discussion took place I left my seat and I stood close to the door with my elbow on a filing cabinet and I said, 'Mr Chairman, may I ask a question?' He said 'Yes.' I said, 'It has always been my opinion that a party elects its own leader. Now you've had the resignation of the leader without any reference to the party. I believe that it has been forced by his colleagues in the Cabinet. I want to know. May I move that I can nominate Mr Menzies to the leadership of the party so that the party can vote on the question?' Mr Spender ruled, 'No. Mr Menzies has resigned. We are here to elect a successor.' I said, 'In that case I resign from the party', and I walked out. Technically he was probably correct ...

On August 28 Menzies' last day as Prime Minister, Canada's Acting High Commissioner, E.B. Rogers, explained in a confidential cable to his superiors that Menzies' problems were to a large extent attributable to his own behaviour:

> Mr Menzies is a man of great personal charm and of outstanding intellectual capacity. Unfortunately, however, he lacks the qualities that a successful leader of a nation and a government must have. He has not been able to command the loyalty of his party and is unpopular with the people. He is tactless and he seems to have a flair for antagonising people by unnecessarily parading his intellectual superiority. He seems to exercise very poor judgment. His handling of the situation in the last few weeks can only be characterised as inept.

Menzies left with dignity. Wounds were, however, clearly visible when he returned to Melbourne and spoke extemporaneously to the Automobile Club on August 30:

Mr President,

I am not going to make a speech.

I am sincerely grateful for this demonstration of goodwill and under-standing on the part of an organisation that gave me such a warm welcome on my return from England a few short weeks ago. I would ask you, however, not to allow your sympathy for me to distract your minds from the grave issues Australia is facing today. It is true that the last two weeks have been something of a trial of endurance; but it is well known that the events that led to my displacement have been in train for a long time, and that my solution was inevitable, disappoint-ing as it may have been to my friends who could watch developments from the outside only.

My decision is the result of an attempt to take an objective view of the political predicament in which Australia finds itself. There are no interests, personal or party, which can be weighted for a moment against the graver issues of an uninterrupted war effort. You will, I know, believe me when I tell you that I could regard the turn of events with a light heart, as you too would, if the Australian people can be united for this great common purpose of keeping the Australian com-munity what we want it to be. So I say again, don't let your deter-mination be distracted by my political misfortunes. The work must go on. It has been my responsibility to carry on under difficulties greater than I believe those faced by any Prime Minister of Australia in the past. Two years of unremitting crisis have tried our system of government, perhaps tried it beyond its capacity: but economically and industrially as a people, we have done almost miraculous things. I take no credit for that: I have had great men—the very greatest and most disinterested patriots—always ready to carry the Government policy a stage further: and, despite all the talk about bottlenecks, they have never failed in anything the Government has asked them to do.

No, gentlemen, what has happened is for the good of this country if we can awaken the people to the real dangers facing the Common-wealth. They must be warned that they must be ready to accept real sacrifices; and that tolerating minor inconveniences will not be enough to save us. At this stage the government's policy may seem to the unthinking to call for too much sacrifice. I pray with all my faith that we shall not realise in twelve months' time that it is too little. Yet many sections are anxious to tone down the effort to something milder. Looking towards you respectfully, Mr President, I cannot refrain from saying that the interests of shareholders must not stay our hand if we are to win out. I am a motorist, but the interests of motorists cannot be allowed to hold us back. Neither must trade union aspirations, how-ever legitimate they may be in peace, retard us in war. Nor dividends, even more so. Nobody and no interest can be allowed to interfere for a moment with the essential requirements for the safety of this people. My political set-back is the merest trifle, unless it bespeaks unwilling-ness on the part of Parliament and people to face its grim facts.

As my friends you are entitled to know that there was no real alternative, and on my part, no hesitation as soon as all issues had been clarified. It has been a step forward to have them clarified even if my light has gone out. (Voice: Temporary eclipse, sir?) Thank you for that cheerful assurance. If I had fought against the facts of the situation as revealed under stress, I should have split the Government from top to bottom, possibly split it so that no possibility of further coalition of the two parties would have been possible. That would have been regarded by my own party, by Parliament, and by the people as a totally wrong thing. I saw that clearly, and knew as I always knew, that no personal interest or following could be allowed to stand in the way of stability. At the last it seemed better to keep the Government together at this critical moment than to go down fighting in a cause already lost for reasons I cannot discuss fully.

You see my fortune and misfortune is to have had to shape a war policy from the ground up. There was literally nothing to build on: we had to start in digging the very foundations, and I know better than anyone how my successor or successors will gain by the sound, well-planned policy we have hammered out and operated. I can tell you that without any shadow of doubt the output of munitions will be doubled within the next six months. I know that: and the crop we have sown and tended with such anxious labour will be harvested by others. But what does that matter, gentlemen? Not the slightest if we get on with the job! My only fear is that unless the people of this country—a great freedom-living people if ever there was one—unless they make themselves heard on the really important issues, we may not win this war as we want to win it. That's a serious thing to say, but I have said it with all the conviction that's in me since I came back, and it's wholly true. Don't let us forget that.

Well, Mr President, I said I was not going to make a speech and look what's happened. Before I close, let me say again, I'm not going to moan; I mean that—all of it. I've been a lucky man. For no special reasons I've had success beyond the average. I've had health, I've had friends, I've had supremely interesting work. I've poured myself into work but I've been very, very lucky. You see I have been Prime Minister at a great moment in Australian and Empire history. What luck for any man! And I can still make some contribution I hope because I've learned a lot in two years of war. My only desire, my one ambition, is to be allowed to serve in any capacity where I may help to keep this Commonwealth and its people safe. That's all I want to say except thanks again.

In London, the Australian political crisis was watched with some puzzlement. *The Economist* on September 6 reported:

... The question of the London visit, which precipitated the crisis, is still unsettled; it is not yet decided whether a visit will be made, whether Mr Menzies or another will be the visitor, or what the status of the visitor will be. What does seem certain, however, is that the

political situation is as unstable as before Evidently the most gifted
man in the Commonwealth Parliament, Mr Menzies lacked the common touch; and there can be no doubt that his inability to meet other
people, especially his colleagues, on their own ground was a source
of constant friction. But, even now, friction has not been eliminated.
The Labour Party remains angrily suspicious, and the Government's
position in Parliament has been made more precarious by the withdrawal of Mr A.W. Coles from the United Australia Party. He has
announced that he will sit as an Independent and that his future actions
will depend on the Government's. If he votes against the Government,
its slender majority will disappear. In the meantime, the Budget is
approaching, and it is probable that, if Mr Fadden falls, it will be over
this obstacle, which was only cleared last year by making tax concessions
to the Labour Party. That Mr Fadden realises this is shown by his
statement that his aim is 'to leave the public with every possible
fragment of spending power which can be spared from the war effort
—but not at the expense of the war effort.' This, of course, is starting
at the wrong end of the stick, as his aim should be to minimise non-
war spending in order to set free the greatest possible amount of
resources for the war. The statement contrasts badly with Mr Menzies'
broadcast in June, when he announced the complete overhauling of
civilian consumption, the concentration of civilian industries on a
limited number of essentials, the prohibition of strikes and lock-outs
and so on. It is up to Mr Fadden—and Australia—to prove that the
change of leadership does not mean that the Commonwealth's war
effort is to be slowed down.

Artie Fadden's reign was short. Arthur Coles owed him no allegiance; and the other independent, Alex Wilson (who was sedulously
wooed by Evatt), joined Coles to vote for a Labor no-confidence motion
on October 3. John Curtin formed a government, inaugurating what was
to be more than eight years of Labor rule. Menzies, having served
Fadden as Minister for Defence Co-ordination, now stepped back into
the political shadows. His party colleagues, while deposing him from
the premiership, had not bothered to remove him from the party leadership. Now, however, the political assassins completed their work.
Although the UAP was larger than the Country Party, the majority of
its members made it clear that they would not support Menzies as Leader
of the Opposition. With a mixture of dudgeon, relief, and despair,
Menzies proclaimed that a party unwilling to lead was not worth leading.
He resigned the leadership of the UAP but remained one of the Opposition representatives on the Advisory War Council. Two reports in
The Times, sent from Melbourne on October 8 and 10, and appearing in
London on October 9 and 11, may conclude this melancholy chapter:

At a joint meeting of the United Australia Party and the Country
Party Mr Fadden was unanimously elected Leader of the Opposition.
Mr Menzies did not compete for the post. At an earlier meeting of

the United Australia Party Mr Menzies resigned the leadership, which was filled by the election of Mr Hughes, who had a clear majority over Mr Spender and Mr Allan McDonald. Mr McLeay and Mr McBride were elected leader and deputy leader of the United Australia Party in the Senate.

The eclipse of Mr Menzies, who now sits on the Opposition cross-benches, constitutes one of the most extraordinary chapters in the history of Australian politics. Apparently Mr Menzies' friends canvassed the prospects of his election as Leader of the Opposition, but discovered that there was no hope of success; hence his withdrawal. Moreover, with Mr Menzies the predominating consideration continues to be the unity of the Opposition. Hostile newspapers, which have continued unrelentingly to pursue Mr Menzies since his deposition from the office of Prime Minster, have insistently advocated Mr Fadden's claims to the leadership, accusing Mr Menzies of dereliction of duty in refusing to go to London and also in omitting to speak for the government in the Budget debate.

Another argument was that a united opposition was impossible under Mr Menzies, owing to the hostility of certain members of the United Australia Party.

Mr Menzies has given me the following comment on my despatch to *The Times* on Wednesday, a summary of which was cabled back to Australia:—

I should be most unhappy if the virulent campaign of misinterpretation conducted against me by a section of the Australian Press caused any misunderstanding in the minds of my friends in Britain. *The Times* is reported here as quoting certain newspapers stating that I failed in my duty by not going to London, and not speaking in the Budget debate. I told the cabinet before resigning the Prime Ministership that in my opinion only a Dominion Prime Minister would sit in the British War Cabinet. Anybody else sent to England would therefore merely be duplicating unnecessarily the splendid work of Mr Bruce. Was this view wrong? On the contrary, I have the best reason to know that it is shared by the British Cabinet.

The significance of my not speaking in the Budget debate has been grossly exaggerated. It is not the practice, either in Australia or in Britain, for Ministers generally to speak on the Budget. I had prepared a speech, but the declarations of Mr Wilson and Mr Coles brought the debate to a stage at which no purpose could have been served by its prolongation. The great majority of Ministers, therefore, including myself, did not speak. My abstention would not in any event have surprised the government, for my financial views, particularly on the very extensive case of Central Bank Credit, were by no means identical with those of my colleagues. I had, as they well knew, remained in the government only for the sake of maintaining the greatest possible amount of political unity.

Throughout the personally distressing events of the last six weeks I have refrained from saying anything in my own justification, for personal controversies do not help to win the war. My self-denying ordinance will continue, but it is, I hope, permissible to say that my own small contribution to Australia's great effort in the war is something of which I do not think I have anything to be ashamed.

V

RESURRECTION
1941–1949

MENZIES' EJECTION from office had been a bitter blow. 'It was,' he said many years later, 'the stroke of doom; everything was at an end.' With pride battered, he plunged into doubt. While still Prime Minister, he had been willing to make gestures of self-effacement, to stand aside in the interest of national unity. Finally, he was brought down not by his assembled enemies, many as they were, but by his own hand. Arthur Coles, Percy Spender, and other close observers saw what they construed as something akin to a failure of nerve. Menzies himself, driven to reflect on the causes of his misfortune, was naturally more inclined to dwell upon the entangling filaments of 'partisanship, intrigue, and prejudice', than on the deficiencies of judgement and character that led him unwisely to struggle and surrender almost unaided by his colleagues.

In the political crisis of August 1941, Menzies resigned only after a long walk and talk with his wife, and a telephone consultation with his parents, brothers, and sister in Melbourne. It was a recurring pattern of family implication in major decisions—to stay in Melbourne in the First World War, to go to Canberra in 1934, and then to yield to his detractors in 1941.

When siren voices in Britain had intimated that a man of Menzies' talents would certainly cut a wide swathe in English politics, they had been all but irresistible. Now, rejected by his ungrateful countrymen, he looked again for opportunities of service overseas. After Pearl Harbour, as the shock and grief of Japan's advance began to shake Australians out of their earlier complacency, the former Prime Minister was unsettled and unsure about the future. Liberation from office gave him a chance to do something to replenish his personal finances. But, more important, he could take stock of his political fortunes. He was intelligent and sensitive enough to realise that his fate was inseparable from his own conduct and from the way in which those around him perceived and predicted his behaviour. He could and did resolve to try to cultivate his tolerance of human emotions, foibles, and faults. Nevertheless, his reputation was so low that he could not count on ever again being leader of a party, let alone Prime Minister. Was he to be another Stanley Bruce, self-exiled, placated with honours and appointments, always the ex-Prime Minister but never the coming man?

At the end of 1941, with Japan and the United States now in the war, a visiting British minister, Duff Cooper, threw out the suggestion that Menzies might become 'Commissioner General for the Far East'— a sort of chief co-ordinator of the imperial war effort in the south-west Pacific. The vision of maps and uniforms, decisions and drama, was entrancing. But the plan fell through. Three months later, in March 1942, there came a tentative offer from Curtin that he should replace Casey as Australian Minister in Washington when Casey moved to become member of the British Cabinet resident in the Middle East. Again the temptation was great. Taking a diplomatic assignment would have meant abandoning Australian politics, probably (it then seemed) for ever. Yet he was prepared to make that sacrifice. Spurned by his own people, perhaps he might find recognition if his undoubted ability and dedication were displayed on the world stage.

It was not to be. Ironically, his destiny was settled by Labor ministers, among them such resolute opportunists as H.V. Evatt, who reacted against the proposed appointment, not least because it turned out, as Menzies knew, to have been suggested by Winston Churchill. What Menzies did not know was that he had been considered for the Middle East post that Casey was offered. Anthony Eden told Stanley Bruce on 19 March 1942 that it had been decided that Menzies 'probably would not get on with the people in the Middle East being a somewhat difficult person'.

If his destiny lay in Australia, could Menzies restore his authority?

The journalist and historian, M.H. Ellis, recalled many years later in *The Bulletin* (22 March 1961):

> Only Archie Cameron, sitting in his shirtsleeves, with one brace hanging loose over his left shoulder and his elastic sides on a Government-owned table, divined the truth: 'Finished? He'll be back. The bloomin' big cow's only stepped off the road to clean the muck off his boots and cut himself a new waddy.' And then he summed up the reasons for the late (not much lamented) Prime Minister's failures:

'No newchum can drive a team of mixed bullocks bogged in blacksoil and panicking, when he doesn't speak their language. A big whip blooming well makes it worse.'

Not speaking the language of his colleagues was bad enough; but not speaking the language of the people was, in some ways, even worse. Experience on the back-benches was new and salutary. Returning to the camaraderie of the Bar, with the leisure for conviviality that was denied to a Prime Minister, was also helpful.

Apart from his membership of the Advisory War Council, Menzies played no direct part in the national war effort after the defeat of the Fadden Government. He had time for long walks—as gossip columnists and friends were quick to notice—and time to think. In a series of broadcasts from 2UE in Sydney, which were also heard in Victoria and Queensland, he reflected at weekly intervals during 1942 on a variety of topics. Although inevitably he had a lot to say about wartime issues—censorship, propaganda, the American alliance, sea-power, finance and so on—the dominant theme was an emerging political creed for the post-war period. Believing that the Labor Government 'scum—positive scum' as he described them to the United States' Consul in Melbourne in April 1942, were bent on using the war emergency to promote and implement socialist policies, he saw the need for a reinvigorated conservatism.

Never before had Menzies been so explicit, not just about the values that he felt ought to prevail in the community, but about the kinds of people whom he believed he represented, and whom he regarded as the backbone of the country. 'The forgotten people,' as he called them, were the middle class: 'those who are constantly in danger of being ground between the upper and the nether millstones of the false class war.' Embroidering this seductive appeal, he told his listeners that the real life of the nation was not to be found in great luxury hotels and the petty gossip of so-called fashionable suburbs—with which, no doubt, he was rather more familiar than most of his audience—or in 'the officialdom of organized masses'. It is to be found, he said,

> in the homes of people who are nameless and unadvertised, and, also, whatever their individual religious conviction or dogma, see in their children their greatest contribution to the immortality of their race. The home is the foundation of sanity and sobriety; it is the indispensable condition of continuity; its health determines the health of society as a whole.

The nameless, unadvertised people were not being offered many tangible benefits. Apart from those he called 'the weak, the sick, the unfortunate'—three categories in which few people willingly identified themselves—Menzies warned in July 1942 that most Australians after the war would be materially poorer than before. 'If human homes are to fulfil their destiny, then we must have frugality and saving for education and progress.' In one short talk on 22 May 1942, the words 'frugality' and 'frugal' appeared five times, as defining characteristics of the 'forgotten people'.

Astonishing as it might seem to those who think of Menzies as the prophet of the rampant materialism of the 1950s, the unambiguous evidence of his pronouncements to Australian journalists in London in 1941 and to the Australian people the following year is that he expected the post-war era to be one of privation rather than plenty. Accordingly, his message was addressed to those who hoped for better times but were by no means sure that they would come, and those who resented the growing burden of taxation and the selective disbursement of benefits. Parents of children at private schools were cheered by the affirmation on 19 February 1943 that church schools were unlikely to 'efficiently survive' without state assistance.

In a passage that revealed his own unhealed wounds, Menzies listed the maladies of Australian democracy: 'To discourage ambition, to envy success, to hate achieved superiority, to distrust independent thought, to sneer at and impute false motives to public service.' However much his motives were to be calumnied, he was ready by the end of 1942 to fight his way back. At a convention of federal and state parliamentarians in Canberra in November 1942, he demonstrated enough of his old ebullience to earn a rebuke from the Leader of the Labor Opposition in South Australia for indulging in 'clever satire', 'biting sarcasm', and 'ridicule approaching the bounds of personal abuse'.

The subject of the convention was a proposed alteration of the constitution to extend Commonwealth powers for purposes of post-war reconstruction. Agreement was eventually reached that the States should 'refer' to the Commonwealth power to deal with a wide range of economic, social, welfare, and industrial issues for five years after the war. But there was an eruption of protest and pressure from business and rural interests; and in a short time the scheme was sabotaged in every State but New South Wales and Queensland. Menzies told a group of Victorian employers that the proposed powers over employment, distribution, and prices were 'most dangerous' and 'sinister'. Billy Hughes, still good for a memorable phrase, had protested that the Attorney-General, Evatt, was trying to 'disembowel, to eviscerate, to emasculate the Constitution'. But, as Stanley Bruce learned from Percy Spender on November 26, Hughes's grip on the UAP leadership was weak:

> I asked whether anything was likely to happen and Spender stated with considerable confidence that there would probably be a change in the Leadership early in the New Year. When I asked him what form that change was likely to take he stated that he and Menzies had an arrangement that if the going was good for Menzies when the time came he, Spender, would support Menzies—if on the contrary the going was not good for Menzies, then he, Menzies, would support Spender.

That Menzies should have been reduced to what this implies gives one a very considerable shock.

On 1 July 1943, the British High Commissioner in Canberra, Sir Ronald Cross, wrote to the Labour Leader, Clement Attlee, a long description of the Curtin Government and its opponents. Cross, a former member of Neville Chamberlain's Ministry, was unflattering about the crumbling UAP and Country Party:

> ... The Opposition have been disunited and contemptibly feeble throughout the period of Curtin's Prime Ministership and are relying for their case mainly upon the mistakes and misdeeds of his Government. I must say it seems to me that they have plenty of good brickbats to throw, but the brickbats lose very much in value from being associated with Fadden as potential Prime Minister, with the octogenarian Billy Hughes and the discredited Menzies hovering in the background as the principal supporting figures.

Discredited he may have been. But Menzies' ambition was unquenched. He did not respect either Hughes or Fadden enough to stand permanently in their shadow. There was no one else in the non-Labor parties to whom he could defer. Menzies' impatience with Hughes had come to a head at the beginning of April 1943. With sixteen other dissident UAP members, he dissociated himself from the official leadership of the parliamentary party. Writing a signed column in his Melbourne afternoon newspaper, *The Herald*, Sir Keith Murdoch welcomed the group's protest against 'the existing stultifications'. But, as Murdoch said on April 5, Menzies' statement had one great flaw; it argued that until the war was over nothing else mattered. Yet in areas like agrarian policy, employment and housing, Murdoch contended that expectations of improvement could and should be created. 'Unhappily', he went on:

> ... many of those associated with Mr Menzies stand opposed to such activities, and he himself is allied to those who ask for unrestricted private enterprise and refuse any transfer of powers from State Parliaments to Canberra.
>
> The dissident UAP members are, in effect, the Right Wing of the party and they have so far put forward no Australian design other than that of the past.
>
> The bulk of Mr Menzies' support comes from Adelaide. Apart from war-winning, in which they are a splendid example, the main objective of those who at present rule the South Australian Liberal and Country League is to prevent the growth of a National Parliament at the expense of the local legislature.
>
> The breakaway of the 17 UAP men does not therefore solve any problem. It is a contribution, with a dangerous facet in that some of its members claim that three years in the wilderness are essential to the health of the non-labor forces. ...

The 'National Service Group' must explain themselves further. They must say what their design for Australia is, and how they propose the country shall be not only saved, but made strong.

In a vitriolic attack on the man who had sought to overthrow him, W.M. Hughes broadcast to the nation from the Sydney radio station 2UW on April 6:

The people looking to the National Parliament to set them an example of that unity without which we cannot win the war, have been treated, in these last few days, to a deplorable exhibition of intrigue and reckless disregard of national interests calculated to bring into well-merited contempt the institutions of democratic government.

Let me shortly state the facts. On Wednesday, March 24th, I received a requisition signed by certain members of the Parliamentary UAP requesting me to call a meeting of the Party for some undisclosed purpose.

At the meeting which was duly called the following morning, a resolution was moved that 'all offices be declared vacant'. The object of the motion was to remove me from the chair, and put Mr Menzies in my place. The question was discussed on this assumption. There was some plain speaking. Mr Menzies said that there must be unity, that the Leader must lead, and that those who would not follow should leave the Party.

I made my own position quite clear. I reminded members of the circumstances under which I had been elected. Mr Menzies had resigned, I had not sought the leadership, that it had been thrust upon me. A vote by secret ballot was taken and the motion was defeated by 24 votes to 15—since then Colonel White's vote has come in and the final figures show 25 for and 15 against me.

In all the circumstances, this was a decisive victory. My opponents had been intriguing for months—they had not struck sooner because they were not sure of success. This time they were confident of an overwhelming majority. The result of the ballot came as a rude shock. Victory and defeat are tests of men's character. How did these men react to this test? Instead of accepting the decision of the Party in good spirit and showing that they placed the interests of the Party and the country above their petty intrigues, they set to work to split the Party.

WOULD NOT ATTEND MEETINGS

A week from the day when the ballot confirmed my leadership, they handed me a letter signed by 17 members notifying me that it was their intention to form a National Service Group, but that although they remained within the Party they could not attend Party meetings under existing conditions.

The first thing to be said about this latest development of the intrigues of a reactionary clique is that it is a palpable sham—a smoke screen to cover the real purpose of these Party saboteurs.

A NEW ORDER!

They pretend that they are 'gravely anxious' about many vitally important matters, which they allege justified their action. But the real reason is that they failed to depose me and put Mr Menzies in my place. Had they succeeded we should not have heard a word about any of these things about which they pretend they are so 'gravely anxious'. On the other hand, the imperative need for unity and loyalty to the leader would have been shouted from the house tops. For a brief season the intriguers might have ceased to plot, but after a short breathing spell would most certainly have concentrated all their forces against Mr Fadden, for nothing short of leadership of the combined Parties will satisfy Mr Menzies—or them. They know by a sure instinct that he is the man for them, that in his capable hands the New Order will be reserved for the right kind of people—their kind.

I have said that the 'reasons' advanced by those who have cut themselves adrift from the Party are a mere smoke screen.

The grave developments to which the signatories draw attention are, so they would have us believe, the direct result of my leadership. If they do not mean that their attempts to depose me and elect Mr Menzies are pointless. What they say in effect is this—that the policy of the Party, and the action which should give effect to that policy, have been responsible for all those conditions that have given them such anxiety.

POLICY SHAPED BY UNITED PARTIES

It is difficult to find words to express my opinions on this irrelevant, illogical and petulant jumble. If the policy of the Party, or the action taken to implement it has been unsatisfactory, who is responsible? How has the policy been shaped?

From the day the Opposition Parties came together under Mr Fadden as Leader and myself as Deputy Leader all matters of policy and action in the Parliament have been decided by the Executive and by the Party at duly summoned meetings. Nothing has been done by Mr Fadden or by myself that has not been authorised by the executive and endorsed by the Party. The Party and the executive decided what we were to do or not to do. If then there is anything wrong the Party is responsible.

TEN NOT TO FACE ELECTION

Now take these 17 men who signed this letter—10 are Senators— only 2 of whom have to face the electors this year—and 7 members of the House of Representatives. Of the 17, ten are from South Australia. Without South Australia this National Service Group would never have been heard of. Without it Mr Menzies' supporters would be reduced to six in both Houses. The 17 signatories to this letter have helped to mould the policy in Party meetings, and they are as much responsible for it and for action in the House as other members.

WHO FRAMED THE POLICY?

We come now to the Executive, which includes the most prominent men in both Houses. No less than five of the signatories to this letter are members of the Executive—and Mr Menzies' name, like that of Abou Ben Adhem, leads all the rest, and along with him sit Senator McLeay, the Leader of the Opposition in the Senate, and Senator McBride the Deputy Leader. Mr Harrison is there, too. In framing the policy of the Party on all those matters which give the National Service Group such grave anxiety, these gentlemen took their part. In most cases, if not in all, the decisions were unanimous. Mr Menzies, Senator McLeay, Senator McBride and Mr Harrison, shaped the policy of the Party in the Executive, and urged the Party to accept it in subsequent meetings. Neither Mr Fadden nor myself have ever heard complaints, direct or by inference, of any lack of vigorous leadership in giving effect to the Party's policy.

PREFERENCE TO SOLDIERS

The signatories to this letter pretend to be deeply concerned over many things—over strikes, absenteeism, finance, disorganisation of food and manpower, the reluctance of the Government to grant men in the fighting services adequate preference, and lack of appreciation of Britain's war effort. . . .

But their affectation of concern is not only silly, but as a reason for deposing me, audacious for I not only led the demand in the second reading debate for preference of employment for returned men over the whole industrial field, but am responsible for preference to soldiers as it has existed since the last war.

That a group headed by Mr Menzies—whose record in the last war is, to say the least of it not very distinguished, should advance preference to soldiers as a reason for deposing me is an insult to the intelligence of the electors.

And they cap this by talk about inadequate appreciation of Britain's war effort: surely this is a charge that cannot be laid against me, for in this war as in the last, and in the intervening years, I have been in the forefront of those who recognised the greatness of Britain and all that we owed to her.

HAPPENINGS AT CANBERRA

On Saturday Mr Menzies spoke over the air; he was heard all over Australia. The title of his talk was 'Happenings at Canberra,' but beyond saying that '17 of us had decided to form a group—the National Service Group'—and that there would be no doubt some criticism of their action, he said nothing at all of those happenings at Canberra in which he had played so prominent a part, but at once launched an

John Curtin, the Duke of Gloucester, Arthur Fadden, Billy Hughes, Robert Menzies, March 1945

attack on the policy of the Labour Government. He covered the whole field with one wide sweep of condemnation. . . .

All those evils about which Mr Menzies spoke are not fungoid growths that have sprung up over night; they have been patent to all for many months—some of them existed when Mr Menzies was Prime Minister—and they certainly existed when a week or so ago the Party meeting called to depose me was held, yet at that meeting Mr Menzies, then confident of success, was heard above all the rest pointing out the need for an unbroken front by the Opposition against the Government. Unity was then of supreme importance. He is defeated, and within a week he forms this precious group and shatters that unity of action which he has so passionately advocated on very many occasions since war broke out. . . .

SELF-SEEKING AND WHISPERING

His speech, like the composite letter of the Group, is a palpable sham intended to distract the minds of the public from his humiliating failure to secure the Leadership and to create the impression in the public mind that this group of Party wreckers had been inspired to take action by altruistic motives in order to save the Commonwealth from some national disaster, overwhelming and imminent, due to the deplorable policy of the Government, and the ineptitude of the Opposition Leaders.

What miserable humbug all this is.

He deplores self-seeking, whispering campaigns, and petty intrigues; he passionately urges the need for unity, but is himself the great self-seeker, the man behind the scenes in every intrigue, the fountain head of every whispering campaign, the destroyer of unity.

REACTIONARY WRECKERS

He talks about one Army! He was Prime Minister for the first two years of the war, he could have merged the forces, but he did nothing. He is contemptuous about the miserable amendment of the Militia Bill—but when he had the power he did not even attempt to extend the area in which our Militia could be made available!

He expresses alarm at rising prices, about strikes, absenteeism, lack of food and manpower organisation—but when these great burning questions about which he professes to be so concerned are brought up for discussion in Parliament he is either absent or silent!

He deplores double and treble rates for overtime, but if men are getting double or treble rates it is because awards of Courts and Tribunals that he appointed or supported, have so determined. And Mr Menzies must accept his full share of responsibility for all that these Tribunals and Courts have done.

He talks about strikes on the water-front, but when the government orders the military forces to do the work—work that must be done, that no loyal citizen dares to leave undone—instead of supporting this action as both Mr Fadden and I have done, he forms this reactionary group of wreckers!

This Group is going to put everything right. Under Mr Menzies' inspiring leadership we should hear no more flabby talk about unity, or wishy-washy pap of trying to make the Parliament work.

This National Service Group is going to breathe life into the dead bones of the Opposition. They will do wonderful things. He did not tell us just how they would do them. Sooner or later, however, they will have to make an attempt to match their brave words with appropriate action.

'Appropriate action' had to wait. But there were more brave words in a broadcast by Menzies on April 10 explaining 'why we did it'. So clear and true was his utterance, his friend Lionel Lindsay assured him, 'that it was doomed to lying recrimination'.

Keith Murdoch returned to the theme of 'Political Confusion' in his *Herald* column on April 13:

To a surprising degree the immediate policies of the country are complicated by the McLeay–Menzies breakaways. It is urgent that the future be clarified.

Will the gap from which sulphuric fires and thunders now leap be widened, or will it be bridged?

Will the group proselytise and purge as it now intends, or will it agree that the government, which it lustily condemns, must be changed by combined efforts at the near-by elections?

.   .   .

The formation of the Group has been attended by the fumes and furies of seismic disturbances, and it is, in fact, a big boiling over.

A number of opposition members became so outraged by ineffective national policies that they could bear no more. They expressed their opinions by booting about some rather shoddy favored-class Government legislation in the senate. The Government accepted the booting quietly to get into recess.

But the Senate members, and some of those of the Representatives who felt the same way, turned and booted the opposition leaders, who, in truth, have been sinking principles for the sake of avoiding an election.

.   .   .

The rift between the National Service Group and the Faddenites and Hughesites is sharp and deep. Personal feelings are intense.

It is not yet a rift on policy. The Group includes men with views wide apart from the progressive men in the UAP. This break occurred, however, purely on a question of political tactics.

Men cannot govern the timing of the crises in their lives, but it was at least unfortunate that the issue arose immediately after the failure to put Mr Hughes out of the UAP leadership. This gives the Movement the appearance of a ruthless claim by Mr Menzies for leadership, and it is branded as such throughout New South Wales and Queensland.

It is true that Mr Menzies had been close in the councils of the McLeay men, but he did not initiate either move. That he is ambitious to take command is, I believe, true.

But the round robin initiating the attack on Mr Hughes was well on its way before he knew of it, and the collaboration of the breakaways had come to the point of decision before he knew of their fixation.

The position of Mr Menzies is, of course, a big subject with many complexities, but there is one point on which all should agree. Few men have paid more heavily in family rest and enjoyment, in fortune and in ease of mind than Mr Menzies for the country. Heavy earnings have been abandoned year by year, trains and aeroplanes have been his habitations, and his company has been not what he chose.

I point this out because it is one bit of justice to a man in some degree misunderstood, and also because it would be wrong to expect that Mr Menzies should not continue some part of his law work. This part, limited though he makes it, must preclude constant touch with the Canberra lobbies.

That, if all circumstances were clear, Mr Menzies would get a majority of votes in the party for leadership is, I believe, certain. His group contains 17. He needs four more to have a majority, and these four can be seen in a trice. But the leadership would split the party even more seriously than the Hughes leadership.

This is plainly a moment which comes in the history of all parties, when a leader with a fresh start should be chosen. It is no unusual thing in Parliamentary government for two strong men to stand aside in the country's interests for a third.

If Mr Hughes and Mr Menzies gave him loyalty, a new leader would bring to the UAP a chance to rise to the full stature of a great creative force. But where is he? It must be someone in parliamentary life, federal or state. Names come to the pen; there are several possibilities.

There were widespread repercussions from the war in the ether. And when spectators started suggesting that the warriors should leave the field to a new champion, it was time for a truce. In an obtrusively circumspect letter, Menzies told Hughes on April 28 that sections of the press were 'as usual' out to make mischief and damage him. Maintaining that he was a loyal and dutiful supporter of the UAP Leader, Menzies said that he did not propose to become a candidate for the party leadership. *But*, if at any time in the future the party, 'as a party', asked him to resume the leadership that would be a different matter. Provided that the 'real will' of the party was represented, he would feel obliged to respond. Of course, he had not, and would not engage in any sort of 'manoeuvre' to secure the leadership which he had, after all, 'relinquished quite voluntarily'. Hughes, with malicious understatement, replied on May 1 that he had noted Menzies' 'pregnant but ambiguous qualification'.

On the platform, as yet another general election approached, there was growing rowdiness. At St John's Hall, Darlinghurst, a piece of pig iron was hurled on to the platform, and the Fascist salute was given to the speaker who was almost continuously interrupted and booed. Menzies had expected a dirty campaign; and by going into the heart of E.J. Ward's East Sydney electorate he provoked the 'howling thugs', as Lionel Lindsay called them, into fulfilling his prophecy.

Warwick Fairfax, exercising proprietorial prerogative, contributed a political portrait of 'The Bewildering Mr Menzies' to *The Sydney Morning Herald* on 17 August 1943:

Mr Menzies is the Opposition's Hamlet. Prince or not, it cannot help revolving around him. Slain though he was by William Morris Laertes and his place taken by Fortinbras Fadden, his friends yet feel that the audience is not very interested in Fortinbras, that sooner or later he will be dragged back to the centre of the stage, wreathed in smiles and confusion, to receive their plaudits, and that he will appear again in the title role to-morrow night. All the well-known quotations characterise him perfectly.

His indecision—'To be or not to be.' His dislike of having to face great and dangerous issues—'The world is out of joint, O cursed spite that ever I was born to set it right'; where Mr Churchill would have said, 'Thank God that I was born to put it right.' His figure—'He's fat and scant of breath.'

Mr Menzies is acutely conscious of his central position and convinced he deserves it. He was as disconcerted and as furious at his fall in 1941, as Hamlet would have been had he been stabbed from behind the arras by Polonius in the Second Act, and deprived of all his speeches from that point to the end of the play. However, one notices, too, as the play runs its appointed course, the other characters, being immensely impressed by Hamlet at the start, take him less and less seriously. They grow increasingly doubtful that he will ever do anything but talk, and they can seldom understand what he is talking about. Anyone who attempted to place complete and absolute confidence in Mr Menzies was likely to become so bewildered that at least a partial withdrawal was necessary to avoid the fate of Ophelia. However, this observer admits freely that, after exhaustive conversations with the other characters, he almost longs for the tantalising entertainment of the postures and declamations of Hamlet.

How, exactly, is Mr Menzies brilliant? Firstly, in his mastery of that English language which stands unrivalled, except by ancient Greek, as a perfect and flexible expression of human thought and feeling. In recent Australian history, he, almost alone, reminds one of the golden age of English politics, when a great statesman was almost always an orator. Why then does he not move the nation? The answer is that occasionally he can and does. When he forgets political manoeuvring, when he drops the self-conscious backcloth of the interests and the personality of Mr Menzies, and the supreme question whether they will get adequate recognition, when he speaks from the bottom of his heart of something that has impressed and moved him, he does move the nation. He moved it on his return from England, as he had moved his hearers in Britain and America, and as maybe he could move them again.

Mr Menzies is both a liberal and a democrat. In times when all political parties are more anxious to look after the interests of those supporting them than to maintain liberty and democracy in doing so, this is important. Unlike so many of his colleagues, Mr Menzies knows his jurisprudence, his history, his political philosophy, and is aware that liberty and democracy in this country are not commodities of which there is an illimitable supply available, like water from the bathroom tap, but are much more like a barrister's income, which needs un-remitting skill and hard work to be maintained. Mr Menzies likes talking on this subject. He means what he says, and there is no one in Australia better fitted to expound it.

Although Mr Menzies as a social reformer will never set the Thames on fire, this is not so much a matter of capitalistic prejudice as of temperament. Though he has allowed himself to be carried along on the capitalist band-waggon, that was a matter of convenience rather than of conviction. Mr Menzies is a professional man, with no particular aptitude for, or interest in, commercial matters, and his favourite pastime is definitely not hob-nobbing with men like 'Gunboat' Smith or Essington Lewis. He is free from the vindictive prejudice against everything that issues from Labour or unionism, which one finds at times in high places among the people he often associates with. He gets on well with Labour men in the House, and during his term of office had a particular respect and admiration for Mr Curtin. The only really spiteful and intemperate remarks this observer has heard Mr Menzies make, or has heard of him making, have been against non-Labour persons or interests whom he felt to have thwarted him.

In short, it is not at all difficult to get Mr Menzies's ear for any progressive scheme of social reform. It will be remembered that he resigned from the Lyons Government in 1939 upon its refusal to implement national insurance. If any Cabinet of his possessed one or two men with the driving force and zeal of the true reformer and the capacity to put their schemes into a workable and practicable form, the voice of Mr Menzies would be very far from being an obstacle.

Considering his travel and his opportunities for observation in the years between 1935 and the beginning of the war, Mr Menzies's views upon world affairs were, in some ways, not so impressive. He was free, it is true, from the narrow isolationism and little Australianism of the then Labour Party, but both his views and his actions on defence and foreign policy lacked strength and conviction. This observer, who was also abroad and who in 1934 caught a glimpse of Austria's struggle for freedom under little Dollfuss, and her appeals for help as the German python crept towards her, remembers well a year later trying to persuade Mr Menzies that the Abyssinian problem must be looked at in the perspective that the real menace to peace came not from Italy but from Germany. He met with an incredulous smile. Later on, when the 'Herald' attacked Chamberlain's foreign policy and supported Eden's resignation, it was met with withering scorn and indignation by some of the most conservative circles in Sydney and Melbourne, who, because it urged immediate preparation for an almost inevitable war, branded it as a paper full of scares and warmongering. Mr Menzies was not on the side of the 'Herald' either then or up till the outbreak of war, and in those critical days of 1940 he could find strangely little enthusiasm for the advent to power of Mr Churchill.

Despite this, however (and let him who is without sin among us cast the first stone), Mr Menzies does possess, more than almost any of our political leaders, that breadth of views and vision which realises that the greatest Australian is he who recognises the interests of other countries than his own, and Australia's obligations towards them. It is undeniable that his war-time visits to Great Britain and the United States were a success, and not just the type of success arising from polite agreement with the views of his host. So much so, indeed, that there was bewilderment in both these countries at his fall, and not a little feeling that Australia was an ungrateful country incapable of recognising one of her own great men.

It is to Mr Menzies as a man that we must turn to throw light on the often disconcerting difference between promise and performance. Temperament and inclination are not things that their owner can wave aside at will, and candour compels us to admit that Mr Menzies is a lover of ease and comfort, both physical and mental. To give them up in order to perform great deeds needs an effort which he does indeed make, but which is neither so continuous nor so successful as is needed by the truly great. He is a 'bon viveur', a lover of good wine, good food, good company, and good conversation. His greatest recreation is a dinner party, particularly a mixed one, at which all of these are present. He is a brilliant and amusing talker, and his wit and felicity of expression show that his oratorical gifts flow naturally, and are not the results of painstaking study. He is interested in events and the part people play in them, particularly as they affect himself. Unfortunately he is very little interested in other people as individuals and human beings.

The problem of how an indecisive man can make himself decisive is somewhat beyond this observer. To the decisive temperament, the greater and the more baffling a problem is, the more eager is he to drop everything else and to fight it until somehow he gets through. It was the frequent habit of Mr Menzies, with that distaste for mental discomfort which led him to push the threat of war away from him, to discuss it for a while, to leave it for further consideration, to make a decision eventually, and quite frequently to alter that decision when made. It is tendencies of this sort that rob his assurances and statements of so much of their value.

There is one sort of determination, however, that Mr Menzies does not lack. He is ready to go and face his adversaries wherever or whoever they are, and put his case before them. There are not many Prime Ministers who have addressed mass meetings on the coalfields in the middle of a strike; there are not many UAP leaders who have carried the fight into the electorate of a man like Mr Ward, where they know well enough that gangsters and toughs will be organised to meet them.

With a candour which is necessary in discussing a public man with claims to greatness, one must record that Mr Menzies is an unbelievably self-centred person. From this fact spring the faults which have led him to most of his worst mistakes. His personal vanity, his reluctance to give unstinted praise to, or express confidence in, anyone else in the world from Roosevelt and Churchill downwards, his unwillingness to have close to him men whose ability even remotely approaches his own, his general judgment of men which is far from good, are all reflections of this. It was depressing to see him taking advice from those far beneath him in ability and judgment, and his choice of associates was often really deplorable. These are hard words to say of any man, but there is every indication that had he been continuously successful these faults would have grown worse. Only his fall, which he took with such intense and bitter vindictiveness, could possibly have given him a hope of overcoming them.

From that fall has already emerged a Mr Menzies less jaunty and self-assertive, more wary and better able to dissemble, but with an

absolute determination that this shall not be the last of Mr Menzies.
It is inevitable that he should have gone through the purgatory of being
disillusioned, first about political life, and secondly about himself. If he
can purge his system of the bitterness which that disillusionment brings,
he will most assuredly emerge a greater man.

Whatever might have prompted Warwick Fairfax's wounding
portraiture—and there were some who discounted his views because of
alleged personal offence or clash of interest—his opinions were widely
shared. Not that Menzies was without allies in the Press. Frank Packer
of Consolidated Press was a loyal supporter who used his newspapers
to advance Menzies' interests. R.S. Whitington in his biography of
Sir Frank, quotes Packer's advice to Don Whitington, the head of his
Canberra bureau from 1941 to 1944: 'I don't care what you say about
the other politicians, but I have a terrific respect for Menzies'. Normally,
neither Packer nor the editors of his principal paper, the Sydney *Daily
Telegraph*, gave instructions to their political writers. But the 1943
general election was an exception. Don Whitington was called to Sydney
and installed at Usher's Hotel in Castlereagh Street:

> The next morning Packer asked him to call at the *Telegraph* for a
> conference with himself and the editor, Lou McBride.
> 'What do you think about this election? Who's going to win?' Packer
> asked.
> 'Labor are a stone dead certainty. They've been in office for two
> years and haven't put a foot wrong. The UAP are divided,' Don replied.
> Then Packer said, 'Well, I don't think you want to be too enthusiastic.
> I want whoever accompanies Curtin to write some criticism of him.'
> 'As far as I'm concerned I'll criticize Curtin or anyone else if I think
> it's warranted, but from my observations over the past two years, Curtin
> is by far the outstanding man we have and I wouldn't be disposed to do
> anything just for the sake of knocking him,' Whitington replied.
> 'Well.' said Packer, 'we've been thinking about this and we think it
> might be better to keep you in Sydney to supervise and advise on the
> whole operation and we'll send someone else on tour with Curtin.'
> Don says he spent the next month at Usher's Hotel in Castlereagh
> Street at the office's expense doing very little. He says Packer was so
> convinced that Curtin would be defeated that he organized a victory
> dinner for Menzies. Those attending it from the *Telegraph*, about ten
> or twelve all told, returned to the office between 10 and 10.30 p.m. and
> took one look at the board showing the voting figures. Said Colonel
> Travers, Consolidated's General-Manager, to Don, 'Well, you were the
> only one who told us what was going to happen.'

The best first-hand account of these events is in the memoirs of
Sir Percy Spender, *Politics and a Man*. Spender's diary, which is quoted
in his book, is the only available contemporary eye-witness document
that records the daily manoeuvrings on the opposition benches during
Labor's wartime government:

When the Prime Minister announced that elections would be held—perhaps somewhat earlier than Menzies and his political henchmen had expected—Menzies' thrust for leadership of the UAP became more noticeable. This issue was one that would have to be determined immediately after the elections, as would, also, the question whether the two parties, in power or in opposition, were to be led jointly by Fadden. I have little doubt the Country Party's aim was that Fadden should become Prime Minister if we were successful at the polls, or leader of the Opposition if we were not.

But Menzies saw things differently in 1943 than he had done in 1941, when he had abdicated in favour of Fadden. The reasons are, I think, fairly transparent.

A few days after Curtin's announcement that general elections would be held, a joint Opposition party meeting was called for the morning of 1 July. . . .

My diary note speaks for itself:

'1 July. House met a 2 p.m. In morning a meeting of joint Opposition parties. The National Service Group attended. Everything is, however, not so united as may appear on the surface. Francis (Q) (who had in 1941 been a busy advocate of Fadden for Prime Ministership) and Jolly (Q) with Eric Spooner, NSW (all UAP members) foreshadowed a motion of confidence in Fadden and Hughes as leaders. Menzies told Francis that, if it were persisted in, fifteen members at least would walk out of the room. So it was dropped.'

On Sunday evening, 18 July Fadden called at my home in Sydney and asked me to read through his draft policy speech. He said he would welcome any suggestions I cared to make.

What could one do to a speech that, as a policy pronouncement, I found unimpressive? It had, obviously, already been settled with his advisers, whoever they were, and approved by the joint Opposition Executive, of which neither I nor Menzies were any longer members. Among his proposals was a scheme for post-war credits to be provided out of existing taxation. I was critical of it, and suggested it be omitted. But Fadden, whose brain child I expect it was, was adamant. He said that it having been approved by the Joint Executive, he could not go back on it. There was little I could do with the speech, other than to suggest certain alterations and additions. . . .

He delivered it in Brisbane on 22 July. He seemed quite sanguine that the Government would be defeated. I think he saw himself as Prime Minister once again, in alliance with Hughes as leader of the UAP. He was not then too friendly with the 'Big Fellow', as he often used to call Menzies. What had occurred at the joint Party meeting of 1 July would hardly incline him to be so disposed. Had victory come to us at the polls, it might have been difficult for Menzies to shift Hughes, despite the National Service group—his solid core of support.

Post-war credits had, off and on, been talked about in Opposition circles, but it was, I thought, mostly just talk. Menzies publicly criticised the concept, and this brought forth an angry blast from

Fadden. He declared, so that all the world—or the Australian people
—would know how he felt, that it was a 'stab in the back, another
betrayal in the series for which Mr Menzies has become notorious'
(*Sunday Sun and Guardian*, 25 July 1943).

When told of Fadden's outburst, Menzies is reported to have said,
in part, 'The public should know that this proposal about retrospective
refunds became known to me for the first time when I listened in to the
policy speech the next morning. I at once sent a telegram to Mr Fadden
telling him that I could not support the proposal.

'Last night, in my opening meeting in Kooyong, I prefaced my
speech by stating that on this matter, I could not accept the Opposition
policy.'

As might be expected, the dispute between Menzies and Fadden
received full publicity. . . .

Fadden fought the election campaign with courage, but I am bound
to say unimpressively.

As for Hughes, the less said the better. . . .

Election day, 21 August, proved a debacle for us. In NSW only
four UAP members survived. . . .

In a House of 64 members, the total UAP and Country Party
mustered only 23, of which number the UAP, with decimated ranks,
totalled 12.

It was now evident that Menzies, even if Hughes ran for leadership
of the UAP, would be almost impossible to defeat. Some of Hughes'
old supporters had not been re-elected, while more than one who had
retained their seats were deserting him. One Queensland Senator who
had shown little affection for Menzies, and who had been a consistent
and stalwart Hughes' supporter was, within two weeks after the
elections talking of 'pitching Billy Hughes out'.

A UAP meeting was called for 22 September. It had become common
gossip that Hughes had decided to stand down from the leadership. He
was making a virtue of necessity. The tide was against him, and Menzies,
with his National Service Group in the Senate and in the House, was
riding that tide. The voting power of this group had not been greatly
weakened by the elections, as a number of them were in the Senate.
Although Labor succeeded in winning a majority of eight in the Senate,
old members not re-elected would hold their seats until July of 1944.
Indeed, with the losses the UAP had suffered, the strength of the Group
was relatively greater within the Party than before. Of the UAP
members in the House, six were Victorians of whom all but one
(Hutchinson) were Menzies men, with the possible exception of White
(Victoria) who, from 1938, had seen himself as a prospective leader.
Harrison of New South Wales remained a stalwart supporter of
Menzies, as, I would think, was also Stewart (Sir Frederick).

I arrived in Canberra early on the morning of 22 September, convinced that Menzies had the numbers to elect him against any opposition. Apart from the National Service Group he needed only a few
votes to accomplish this.

I had a private talk with Menzies that morning. We were in full agreement that the Joint Opposition arrangement had to end. We should revert to our separate and independent party entity.

The question of leadership naturally arose. I told Menzies that his election was a certainty, but that nevertheless I intended to submit my own name, *pro forma*. I was informed that White would also submit himself, and that it would be odd if I, who had been elected with by far the greatest majority of any of the four UAP members in NSW, and who had borne the brunt of the electoral campaign in that State failed to submit mine. Hughes had already informed me that he was not a candidate for any office.

I told Menzies that I was not a serious contender for leadership. I considered, however, that it was politically wise to put myself forward. I said that I had not sought, and would not seek a vote in support of myself for the leadership, but would support him. I was, however, a contender for the Deputy Leadership (which in the previous Parliament had been left unfilled). My view was that the Deputy Leader should come from NSW, and I believed my claims were indisputable. That both the leader and his deputy would be Victorians would be politically unwise. The only members other than from Victoria and New South Wales were Cameron of South Australia and Guy of Tasmania, neither of whom could be elected.

Menzies is always inclined to play his cards close to his chest, but when I left him, after what was a cordial talk, it was with the impression that he would support me for the Deputy Leadership and use his influence in my favour. He certainly said nothing which suggested he would not.

There was, however, an unpleasant surprise ahead of me, of which I had not the slightest prior warning.

The party meeting was to take place in the afternoon. I became aware of a good deal of corridor talk, of the putting together of heads, and of small coteries of two or three who suddenly fell silent as I approached. That was par for the course, just as are the comings and goings, and special affability of members canvassing for votes for the support of a 'ticket'. I knew that much of this atmosphere had to do with Menzies' bid for leadership. What I didn't know was that a 'deal' was in the making, and a ticket being canvassed on which my name did not appear.

The first business the party dealt with was its association with the Country Party. The concept of a joint Opposition was put an end to. The election of the leader of the party was next decided. Hughes was not a candidate. Bob won easily. I voted for Menzies as I had promised.

In this book *The Measure of the Years*, p. 14, he states that the party 'unanimously requested me to resume the leadership'. This is a slight exaggeration: Menzies' memory is I think at fault. There was no unanimous request. There was a ballot for leadership—what is called an exhaustive ballot. Where there is only one candidate he, of course is declared elected without more ado. Where there are two or more, a successful candidate must receive an absolute majority of the votes cast. If there are more than two candidates, and none receives an absolute majority, the candidate who receives the least votes is eliminated, and the process continues until one candidate does. There were, if I remember correctly, three candidates on this occasion, and more than one ballot.

We then proceeded to the election of a deputy leader. There were two—or three—who immediately offered themselves for election—myself, Holt and Hutchinson (both from Victoria). To my amazement Hughes, who had remained silent, suddenly announced he was also a candidate. . . .

Following this—to me—shock announcement by Hughes, received by appropriate favourable murmurings in the party, Holt and Hutchinson, to whom Hughes' candidature must also have come as a surprise, withdrew their names. This left me out on a limb.

I immediately concluded, and I think rightly, that Hughes had prior knowledge of the fact that the majority of the party members would support him. Their attitude was 'let us not rock the boat by dumping the old man; the safest political solution is to make Menzies Number One, and Hughes Number Two. Spender and Holt have plenty of time, etc. etc.' . . .

After Holt and Hutchinson's withdrawal, there was, in my judgment, no alternative for me but to withdraw my own candidature and wait my time. I realized Menzies' influence would not be coming my way. He must have known before the meeting a little of what was in the wind. Hughes 'walked in'.

With Menzies now at the head of the principal non-Labor Party, Australian politics was about to enter a new phase. Over the next twenty years, the Labor Party was to have a succession of leaders: Curtin, Chifley, Evatt, and Calwell. Opposing them all was one massive figure. The stature of any leader is always measured in part against the alternatives. Thoughtful observers realised by 1943 that they must assess the party leaders in relation to their promise for peace, as well as for their performance in war. The Canberra correspondent of *The Times* provided English readers with a penetrating analysis of the Australian political scene on 6 October 1943:

Each side in the new Commonwealth Parliament is fittingly led by its most commanding personality. The Opposition has taken a decisive step towards rehabilitation by the election of Mr Menzies to its leadership. It has thereby not only done what it could to repair a great wrong —the ousting of Mr Menzies from the Prime Ministership in 1941— but has also placed at its head its most incisive intellect. Throughout his relegation to the back benches Mr Menzies has disdained to court restoration to favour by refraining from telling Australians unpalatable truths about their national shortcomings or about the sacrifices they must make to win a secure place in the post-war order. Now he is impressing on his followers the need for recasting the Opposition's political ideas. There is plenty of room outside Socialist philosophy, he rightly says, for a vigorous liberal programme giving proper protection and security to the wage-earner and a proper incentive to private enterprise.

. . . Labour's unprecedented triumph presents it with an unparalleled opportunity for a fundamental stocktaking. What the party most needs is a considerable influx, both in and out of Parliament, of men whose horizon is not bounded by the limits of the trade union movement. Mr Curtin and Dr Evatt, its two outstanding leaders at this moment, are men of this type; but for years the trade union machine which has dominated the party has jealously excluded men of higher education with those ideas about social planning of which the Labour Party is sorely in need. Neither the Labour Party nor the non-Labour parties have done much to ascertain the facts on which all thought of planning must be based, and there has been a sad dearth in Labour circles of that constructive thinking which in the party's early days produced Australia's early social legislation and her system of industrial arbitration.

Labour must learn, too, to allow its leaders to lead. It is still loth to profit from the lessons of those great crises in its history which lost it Mr Hughes and Mr Lyons. Yet Labour must learn not merely to respect and respond to, but positively to encourage an able and imaginative direction. Its policy at present is too much a policy of literalism—of applying the brake to prevent the party platform from being carried to its logical fulfilment, as in the Militia Service controversy, merely because that fulfilment is not explicitly laid down in black and white. This hampering attitude is profoundly discouraging to any self-respecting leader. Above all Labour needs to mark how much it has owed in its greatest triumphs to the support of those whose backing Dr Evatt shrewdly acknowledged after the recent election—the "small" business and professional people and primary producers. Such people are not interested in a Socialistic Utopia and do not conceive themselves as giving Labour a mandate for such in putting it in office. But they are intensely interested in social security for all and a fair deal for the underdog.

If Labour thus needs to reconsider its future what is to be said of the Opposition? First that its abysmal failure at the polls is largely explained by 24 years in office interrupted only for two years by Mr Scullin's ill-fated regime of 1929–31. That is a condition of things unconducive to the health of any party or of any parliamentary system, to which it is essential that both sides should share the experience of office. For 13 of those years Labour provided its opponents with their leadership—Mr Hughes (1917–23) and Mr Lyons (1932–39).

LITTLE FRESH BLOOD

The United Australia Party, especially, was hopelessly enervated by this protracted term of office. It had found little fresh blood with which to renew its strength, and such vigour as it retained was dissipated by internal strife. The Country Party is frankly sectional. It is in politics to protect the interests of the man on the land. But the United Australia Party claims to be as broadly based as the English Conservative Party. Conservative would be its name were it not that in Australian politics, owing to the eagerness of all parties to be regarded as 'advanced,' that word has come to be used almost as a term of reproach. Its present somewhat meaningless title is typical of the vagueness of its thinking. It has tended increasingly to depend for re-election on Labour's sins and shortcomings.

Like Labour, the UAP needs to relate its platform to realities. It is at present little better than a series of pious aspirations. Crucial tenets which are the party's *raison d'être*, such as the maintenance of private enterprise, are too apologetically expounded. Of social philosophy the party is almost destitute. Before the war it toyed with national insurance, but despite Mr Menzies's protest it did nothing effectual, and in the recent campaign it missed a golden opportunity to propound a contributory alternative to Labour's non-contributory scheme of social services. Towards finance, currency, and banking, its attitude has been too negative and reactionary, too much opposed to all liberal and reformist policies. In office the party's political leaders too often lacked the courage and power of decision to give effect to their principles. The failure to enact a provision for compulsory military service beyond Australia is a case in point. Labour, despite its faults arising from lack of administrative experience, has shown a superior resourcefulness and resolution.

PUBLIC RESPONSIBILITY

There are certain shortcomings common to all political parties because they are characteristically Australian. These help to explain some of the peculiar phenomena of Australian public life. All parties suffer from that Australian disrespect for personal pre-eminence which makes their leaders the butt for all sorts of ill-informed and irresponsible criticism, often couched in the most vulgar terms. Many a discerning visitor to Australia deplores the refusal of the average Australian to admit that there are any great Australians in public life, and his lack of gratitude for a first-rate public service. The lot of a public man in Australia is singularly thankless. Perhaps that is why the tradition of public service has such shallow roots. Too few men of worldly experience and good education offer themselves for election to Parliament. Too many prefer to pull the strings behind the scenes.

All parties suffer from the lack of disinterested attachment to principle and disinterested concern for the quality of the life of the whole nation. Each tends to shape its course too much in accordance with policy and sectional interest. Great political ideals are at a discount and platforms are based more or less frankly on the material concerns of relatively few people. One disastrous result is that Australian politics run too closely along class lines. It is this fact that invests political controversy with a bitterness that shocks visitors and fosters a growing class consciousness that troubles all far-seeing Australians.

The British economist and journalist Walter Layton, visiting Australia early in 1944 in a British press delegation, formed the impression that the Labor Party under John Curtin would be in office for a long time. After hearing Layton's report on Australian political prospects, Cecil King, the editorial director of the *Daily Mirror* and *Sunday Pictorial*, recorded in his diary on 5 February 1944: 'Menzies is apparently completely bust.' Other British observers also concluded that Menzies had no future in Australian politics. When Captain Alan Hillgarth, Chief of the Intelligence Staff of the Royal Navy's Eastern Fleet, submitted his report on a visit to Australia from 6 to 28 March 1944 he wrote of what he saw in Canberra:

> I met many politicians of all three parties, including Mr Fadden, Country Party leader and Sir Earle Page (CP), Dame Enid Lyons, (UAP) and Mr Makin (Navy Minister), Mr Forde (Army Minister and Deputy Prime Minister) and Dr Evatt (Minister for External Affairs and Attorney General). Of these only Dr Evatt and Dame Enid Lyons could hope to hold down their jobs anywhere else. Indeed, the standard of intelligence in Australian politicians generally, seems to be low—Australians themselves agree about that.
>
> A particularly virulent brawl had just taken place in the House. I had the best account of this and of the political set-up generally from Dame Enid Lyons, a woman of great character and charm. . . . No party has an outstanding leader. Mr Menzies is—in the words even of his followers—finished, Mr Fadden is a nonentity and Mr Curtin is too honest for his extremists.

On 30 May 1944, Sir Robert Dalton, the United Kingdom Trade Commissioner in Australia, described the 'hopelessness' of the Opposition to Stanley Bruce. Menzies, he said, was quite discredited and there was no hope of his coming to power again. If Menzies were to regain power, and to hold it, he needed a party that was more than a 'fortuitous conflux of incongruities'. Moreover, he wanted to be emancipated from the thraldom of the controlling financial interests of the UAP—the men, like Ernest Willis and Sir Robert Knox, who had so restricted Lyons' freedom of manoeuvre. There is nothing in Menzies' record, either before or after the war, to suggest that he had any particular animus against economic 'interests'. What he did object to was the appearance and reality of *any* fettering of his own authority. He had a sort of political fastidiousness—an understandable disinclination to dance at any outsider's bidding. When his friend and business partner, Staniforth Ricketson, had offered, on behalf of unnamed associates, to assist him with funds for election expenses in 1932, he declined to compromise his independence. And throughout his life he made no secret of his contempt for those whose political influence could be bought.

Menzies wanted power. He believed that he could govern better than any of his contemporaries. He ought to be Prime Minister again. And things that impeded the consummation of that ambition could not be tolerated. He had identified his future political base. But how were 'the forgotten people' to be turned into a winning electoral combination? As he confided to a meeting in Ivanhoe, Victoria; 'It is true, lamentably true, that appeals to passion, to hate, to fear, to self-interest, are more effective than appeals to cold reason.' Happily, as *The Argus* reported on 3 June 1944, there was, he believed 'a core, a residue of righteousness, a body of reasoned and reasonable opinion which, although it may be not large numerically, gains strength by its very integrity, and so comes to exercise an influence out of proportion to its numbers.'

Could the 'residue of righteousness' be mobilised? The existing anti-Labor forces were bewilderingly divided. There were Institutes of Public Affairs in New South Wales and Victoria. The Australian Constitutional League was active in Victoria, Tasmania, and Western Australia. In New South Wales, the Democratic Party and the Liberal Democratic Party competed for support. There was a Nationalist Party, a National Party of Western Australia and a United Australia Organisation in Victoria, not to mention the Australian Women's National League and the Queensland Women's Electoral League. Victorian voters were also courted by the Services and Citizens Party; and, if they lived in Menzies' own constituency, they could join The Kooyong Citizens' Association.

As early as November 1941, Menzies had supported abortive moves by T.T. Hollway to reconstruct the Victorian section of the UAP. In September 1943, when he became Leader of the Opposition, he spoke of 'far-reaching ideas on reorganisation which I will discuss with the appropriate people.' Prominent New South Wales political leaders were among the first to try to unify the United Australia Organisation with other groups. The Institutes of Public Affairs, financed by big business and acting sometimes (and most effectively) behind the scenes, initiated discussions aimed at uniting the anti-socialist forces. As leader of the proposed new party, there was only one conceivable candidate. However much they might have pined for a new prophet to proclaim capitalism, the tough-minded manufacturers and financiers who had the inclination, the time, and the resources to control conservative political organisations, were agreed that Menzies, for all his faults, must be their man.

Four secret meetings between June and September 1944 prepared the ground for the amalgamation in Victoria of the United Australia Organisation, the Services and Citizens Party, and the Young Nationalists. Meanwhile public transport and newspaper strikes hardened community attitudes; and the temporarily orchestrated anti-Labor forces, under Menzies' baton, defeated a referendum in which the Labor Government sought fourteen new federal powers ostensibly for the purpose of post-war reconstruction.

Seizing a propitious moment, when the referendum campaign had shown widespread distrust of government control and interference in business and private life, Menzies wrote to various organisations inviting them to a conference to consider 'the establishment of a nationwide political movement'.

The time seems opportune for an effort to secure unity of action and organisation among those political groups which stand for a liberal, progressive policy and are opposed to Socialism with its bureaucratic administration and restriction of personal freedom.

The Australian Labour Party has an efficient Commonwealthwide organisation. To resist effectively those aspects of Labour policy to which we are opposed and to gain the public support enabling governments sympathetic to our views to be formed we must match Labour's organisation with an Australian organisation of our own. This organisation should possess an Australian policy and have the closest contact with its Parliamentary leaders and representatives.

I therefore invite you to be present at a conference to be held at Canberra on October 13th, 14th and 16th.

I sincerely hope that you will participate in a full and frank discussion. You will be entirely free to make your own decisions and will not, of course, be bound by any majority of other persons.

It is possible that a further conference will be found necessary after our first discussion has taken place, but my colleagues and I believe it to be most desirable that those of us who share the same broad political beliefs should first see if a basis can be found for unity.

A successful outcome to such discussion might quickly and completely alter the current of Australian politics.

E.K. White, President of the Liberal Democratic Party, summed up the feelings of most of the recipients of this invitation when he wrote in a private memorandum:

.... The multiplicity of names and varied machinery controlling non-Labour politics are inherent weaknesses causing disunity, waste and ineffectiveness, and the ground lost to Labour can only be recovered with a better organisation than that of the Labour Party.

The Conference will prove futile if it accepts ineffectual agreement for more co-operation between existing organisations under their present names and controls.

The conference met on October 13, and Menzies delivered the opening speech at 3.00 p.m.:

This Conference has been convened in an endeavour to produce unity of organisation among those who do not support Socialism as the solution of Australia's political and economic problems.

It will be noted at once that the Country Party is not here. The reason for this is that the Country Party has already had an Interstate Conference at which a high degree of unity was achieved and has a right to expect that those of us who espouse the general liberal cause should become equally united so that we may be in a position to discuss co-operation or alliance, or even full organic unity.

The present position of what I will call liberal political organisation in Australia, particularly on the men's side, is far from satisfactory, and all its implications should at once be considered quite frankly.

In New South Wales there are in the field of active political organisation the Democratic Party and the Liberal Democratic Party. The Democratic Party itself represents the merger of the United Australia Organisation and the Commonwealth Party.

Without going into the merits of local controversies I am prepared to assume that the emergence of the Liberal Democrats was due to a feeling of dissatisfaction with the point of view and organisational character of the then United Australia Organisation.

It is just as clear that there must be thousands of people in New South Wales impatient of Socialism and apprehensive of continued Labour rule who still find insufficient stimulus in either the Democrats or the Liberal Democrats.

When I say these things I engage in no criticism of individuals I merely point out that a spirit of political revival is not always best expressed by endeavouring to put new wine into old bottles.

Before leaving New South Wales, I should add that while at present, and for a long time to come, national politics must be of overwhelming importance, the queer position exists that the two United Australia Party Members of the Federal Parliament have no United Australia Organisation behind them at all, but must look for support to the Democrats or the Liberal Democrats or to some special local organisation of their own or to all three.

In Queensland, Federal United Australia Party Members also have no United Australia Organisation in the electorates. In the normal course they look to the Country National Organisation for support. Yet, as a result of a decision which I do not presume to discuss, the Country National Organisation at the last State Elections did not run any candidates at all and is therefore for most purposes a not very large organisation with no State Parliamentary representation.

Much more active in the State political field, though not in the Federal, has been the new body—the Queensland's People's Party—which has brought into the political arena some men of marked ability and energy. I regret that that Party has not felt able to be represented at this Conference, though I have the assurance of its good wishes for a successful outcome. But surely in Queensland we need something more adequate than two quite separate organisations, neither of which undertakes to cover the whole political area. In that State the Queensland Women's Electoral League has done good work, but in the light of the facts that I have mentioned it will be seen that that work has been done under difficulties.

In Victoria, the organisations of long standing are the Australian Women's National League, the United Australia Organisation, and the Young Nationalist Organisation, now the National Party. As between the latter two there have been some sharp differences of opinion. As between the public and both of them it is quite clear to any thoughtful observer that there has from time to time been a feeling

of dissatisfaction and a warm desire to see some revived and comprehensive movement that will attract the attention of people not previously
engaged in political work, and particularly of those who matter most
to the future, namely, the young men and women. The feeling of
discontent to which I have referred gave rise some time ago to two
new movements—the Services and Citizens' Party, which is well
represented here to-day, and the Middle Class Organisation, which is
not represented, preferring to maintain a non-political character.

South Australia has, by reason of the broad basis of its organisation,
managed to avoid any local split, and does cover both town and country
interests.

Western Australia has adhered to the name 'Nationalist', while in
Tasmania both names, 'Nationalist' and 'United Australia', are to be
found in the title of the organisation. Yet in both the men's organisations and the Australian Women's National League in Tasmania the
constant political visitor like myself is always struck by the want of
cohesion which exists between the Southern centres of the Island and
the Northern centres.

The picture thus presented is one of many thousands of people all
desperately anxious to travel in the same political direction but divided
into various sects and bodies with no Federal structure, with no central
executive, with no co-ordinated means of publicity or propaganda, and,
above all, with no clearly accepted political doctrine or faith to serve
as a banner under which all may fight.

COMMON ORGANISATION IMPERATIVE

In the Parliament at Canberra, as you will have noticed from reading
the reports of the recent Session, we have achieved, through mutual
loyalty and support, a high degree of effectiveness in debate, though
the numbers are against us. But more and more we have been driven
to believe that if our Parliamentary battles are to lead to electoral
success a common organisation outside Parliament is absolutely
imperative.

The Labour Party, though its policy and administration are repugnant to us, is not something which exists under a different name
and with a different set-up in each State. It is the Australian Labour
Party. Its membership depends upon common considerations all over
the Continent. It has State branches and local branches. It has State
executives and a Federal executive. It has all over Australia a system
of journals so effective that it has been my experience that the same
point of view in almost the same words will be produced by a Labour
supporter in Bunbury as by one in Rockhampton.

The result of this unanimity and cohesion on the organisational side
has been that the disunities which exist in Labour circles are usually
below the surface, are not advertised, and so have nothing like the
public effect that is produced by the well-advertised minor differences
of opinion that may exist in our own ranks.

When I consider the structure of the Australian Labour Party and realise that the political warfare to which we have been committed for a long time past by no choice of our own is a struggle between political armies, I am driven to wonder how we could ever imagine that a concerted force under one command and with one staff is to be defeated by divided units under separate commands, and with no general staff.

PRESENT DEFECTS

Let me sum up what I believe to be the defects in our present establishment:—

First—we have no Federal organisation, which means that we have no Federal secretariat, and therefore no true nexus between the Federal Parliamentary Party and those who are to do the political work in the field.

Second—we have, apart from periodical election policies, no comprehensive statement of our political objectives. I will return to the all-important matter at a later stage.

Third—we have no means for bringing about a periodical revision of our policies by a process of consultation between those in Parliament and those out of Parliament.

Fourth—we have many names, but our name in the Federal Parliament—UAP—has ceased to possess any intrinsic significance.

Fifth—we have no properly organised means of conveying our views by print and broadcast to the public.

Sixth—we have for the most part no constant political organisation in the electorates, particularly in key electorates, except such as is carried out in their spare time by a relatively small band of devoted and enthusiastic men and women.

Seventh—we have no sufficient means for assuring to young men and women a place not only in our work but in our counsels.

Eighth—on the financial side we lean too heavily upon individual donations and have no adequate rank and file finance, which ought to be the monetary basis of any true democratic organisation.

I am not optimistic enough to suppose that all of these matters can be brought to finality in one conference, the members of which are in many cases not authorised to bind their organisations. But at least I hope that two things can be done:—

The first is that we should declare our common belief that one organisation, Australian-wide in character, should be set up. The second is that we should express our common adherence to the broad outlines of a liberal and progressive faith which will have in it the foundation upon which a new generation can really hope to build a new Australia.

When I refer to 'one' organisation, do let me emphasise that I am not merely proposing that existing bodies should by a process of negotiation and compromise go into some form of uneasy partnership. The truth is, and I want to say it quite plainly, that too many of the people whom we want to see interested in politics from our viewpoint have either no interest in the existing organisations or in many cases an actual hostility to them.

It is not practical to expect such people to sink their ideas and join up with some body which fails to satisfy them. The real hope—and it is a great hope—is that a new movement should be brought into existence, that existing organisations should so far as practicable go out of existence in its favour, that all persons joining the new movement should do so on an equal footing, and that through branch executives, State Councils, State executives and a Federal executive, all democratically chosen, every joining member should feel that he or she has an effective chance of influencing both policy and organisation.

In a word, a new movement must come into existence unhandicapped by vested political or personal interests of any kind.

I am not so foolish as to believe that it is a reflection upon any of us that we have for years been prepared to devote our time to politics while most people have ignored them, and I therefore believe many of those active and prominent in a new movement will inevitably be drawn from the ranks of those who have worked so hard in the past.

But what we must look for, and it is a matter of desperate importance to our country, is a true revival of liberal thought which will work for social justice and security, for national power and national progress, and for the full development of the individual citizen, though not through the dull and deadening process of Socialism.

POLITICAL FAITH

Let me now turn with more particularity to the question of our political faith.

We have, partly by our own fault and partly by some extremely clever propaganda by the Labour Party, been put into the position of appearing to resist political and economic progress. In other words, on far too many questions we have found our role to be simply that of the man who says 'No'.

Once this atmosphere is created it is quite simple for us to be branded as reactionaries, and indeed if we are not careful the very unsoundness of so many of Labour's political proposals may accustom us so much to the role of critic that we become unduly satisfied with the existing state of affairs.

There is no room in Australia for a party of reaction. There is no useful place for a policy of negation.

In my opinion we need to direct our minds to two matters: First, what do we desire to achieve for the Australian people in the future?

Second, how do we propose to go about it?

Those are the fundamental ingredients of every real political programme.

FOR A REMODELLED AUSTRALIA

Let me set out our ultimate objectives as I see them.

What state of affairs would we like to have existing in a remodelled Australia after this war?

We would like to have a country safe from external aggression and living in the closest communion with its sister nations of the British Empire, playing its part in a world security order which maintains the necessary force to defend the peace; a country:—

in which all who have risked their lives in its service enjoy honour and security;

in which constant employment at good wages is available to all willing and able to work;

in which the unavoidable minimum of unemployment arising from sickness or change of occupation is provided against by adequate pecuniary unemployment benefits;

in which the farmer and the farmer's wife and children, as well as the city dweller, enjoy stability and the amenities of life;

in which employer and employee have a sense of common interest and duty, and share as co-operators in all advances of prosperity;

in which living standards rise steadily as physical resources expand and ingenuity grows;

in which there is free thought and free speech and free association for all except the enemies of freedom;

in which no consideration of wealth or privilege will determine the education of either child or man, who shall each be fully trained in his own powers;

in which values will have been so corrected that the greatest rewards go to those who perform the truest services to the people;

in which all families are enabled to live in attractive and comfortable homes at a reasonable cost;

in which citizens are free to choose their own way of living and of life;

in which Parliament controls the Executive and the Law controls all;

in which public health services and preventive medicine have been extended and medical treatment is within the reach of all;

in which scientific research improves the standard and skill of production, both primary and secondary;

in which the population is growing, but shortage of population is made up for by the initiative, resource and courage of the citizens;

in which National defence is a matter of universal duty and in which the notion of getting something for nothing has become discredited and the idea of a dole abhorrent to humane thought, but all citizens having regard to their capacity and needs are both contributors to and beneficiaries of organised social life and service.

That brings me to the last question:—

How do we propose to get these things?

By looking primarily to the authoritative action of Government or by looking primarily to the encouragement of individual skill and initiative?

As to this, I believe that we can have no hesitation.

Without attempting to discuss detail, and confining ourselves to broad principles, we can see that the realisation of the objectives referred to above will depend upon certain matters.

We must aim at the fullest development of individual capacity.

The principle of such reward, sometimes sneered at as exhibiting the profit motive, is the dynamic force of social progress and is of the essence of what we call private or individual enterprise.

Again, we must aim at the growing exploitation of our natural resources. Governments do not provide enterprise; they provide control.

No sensible person can doubt that the revival of private enterprise is essential to post-war recovery and progress. Yet our opponents constantly criticise and handicap what even they must admit is the major instrument available to our hands.

There cannot be rising living standards if all we propose to do is to redistribute what we now have. We must produce more and produce it more cheaply if we are to survive and grow.

Excessive attention to monetary problems has obscured the truth that the cost and quality of production is still of major importance. The reducing of costs and the raising of quality have been achieved by private enterprise and not by public authority.

When we turn to the urgent problem of housing we must be frankly appalled at the idea of Government Departments building scores of thousands of homes for us because that would mean a drab uniformity of types, expensive work, and an undue burden of cost upon the householder.

Man does not want to be regimented into a home. To restore architects and builders to their rightful place will mean quality, variety, and the cheapness which results from competition.

Concentration upon Government action and the payment of social benefits entirely out of the public Treasury means the discouragement of thrift. Without thrift there can be no independence and without independent citizens there can be no independent nation. Thrift during this war has filled our war loans. Do we propose to abandon it after the war, and if we do, where are our new benefits to come from?

Thrift and independence must therefore be positively encouraged by our political policies. This involves a complete overhaul of our taxation system in order to help people with family responsibilities.

It involves the conversion and extension of our social services on a contributory insurance basis and it involves the use of the Central Bank and of Government economic policies not to create short-term political advantages but to produce stability not only of employment but of currencies.

We sometimes forget that nothing so destroys thrift and cripples independence as fluctuating monetary values, affecting as they do insurances, pensions, superannuations, and all future provisions.

Again, our monetary and other economic policies must be devised to encourage investment, for upon the active investment of private funds the achievement of our social objectives will largely depend.

Public works may, and should, be used either to provide the foundation for investment and development or to supplement private activities at times when there has been some recession in business activity.

But I hope that we shall not be so misguided as to treat large public works' policies as good things just because in the short run they appear to create a large number of short-term jobs and put a good deal of money into circulation.

We recognise that in the post-war economy there will be room for much more thought and planning than ever before. But if a planned economy means a perpetuation of Government controls, then it will unquestionably lead to a totalitarian system.

As we know, authority tends to feed upon itself.

Certain temporary Government controls no doubt will be needed, but in the long run the function of Government should be to guide and encourage industry to do its own planning in the light of its own expert knowledge and experience.

In a vision of the future, therefore, I see the individual and his encouragement and recognition as the prime motive force for the building of a better world.

Socialism means high costs, inefficiency, the constant intrusion of political considerations, the damping down of enterprise, the over-lordship of routine.

None of these elements can produce progress, and without progress security will turn out to be a delusion.

It thus appears that private enterprise and the State are both engaged in a task in which the people will prosper best if the individual and the State each perform his or its proper function.

As I see them, the true economic functions of the State are as indicated in a recent publication of the Institute of Public Affairs of Victoria, called 'Looking Forward'. I quote from p. 29 of the booklet:—

'In general terms, the economic responsibilities of the State should be regarded as fourfold:—

First, to assist in preventing the periodic recurrence of largescale unemployment;

Second, to secure to all responsible citizens (through social legislation) at least a decent and reasonable minimum of economic security and material well-being;

Third, to impose a framework of law which will give the utmost encouragement to the enterprise, resourcefulness and efficiency of individuals and groups, and which will lead to the greatest possible output of the goods and services which the community needs;

Fourth, to conserve, in the long-range interests of the community, those natural resources fundamental to the life and future prosperity of the nation.

In this conception of the future activities of the State, the State and private enterprise are regarded as partners in the common purpose of improving the material conditions of the community. The tendency, prevalent in discussions of post-war economic policy, to emphasise or imply a fundamental divergence of interest between the State and industry is wholly disastrous and misleading. From plans of State action designed to secure full employment and social security, private enterprise stands vastly to gain. Conversely, in its objective of providing better living standards and security for all, the State will be greatly aided by a vigorous, healthy and enlightened private enterprise.'

Following Menzies' speech the proceedings were held in camera. Committees were formed to consider the name and objectives of the proposed new organisation, and the structure and constitution that it should have. On October 16 the committees reported, and it was unanimously decided to adopt the name Liberal Party of Australia, except in South Australia. It was further resolved:

We will strive to have a country—
1. safe from external aggression and living in the closest communion with its sister nations of the British Empire, playing its part in a world security order which maintains the necessary force to defend the peace;
2. in which national defence is a matter of universal duty, and in which the spirit of patriotism is fostered and all Australians united in the common service of their country;
3. in which an intelligent, free and liberal Australian democracy shall be maintained by—
   (a) Parliament controlling the Executive and the Law controlling all;
   (b) freedom of speech, religion and association;
   (c) freedom of citizens to choose their own way of living and of life, subject to the rights of others;
   (d) protecting the people against exploitation;
   (e) looking primarily to the encouragement of individual initiative and enterprise as the dynamic force of reconstruction and progress;
4. in which all men and women who have been members of the fighting services and their dependants shall enjoy honour and security, preference and generous repatriation benefits;
5. in which the primary industries are promoted and stabilised new and adequate markets developed, the lot of the country man and his wife and children improved, rural amenities increased, and decentralisation of industries encouraged;
6. in which constant employment at good wages is available to all willing and able to work;
7. in which employer and employee have a sense of common interest and duty, and share as co-operators in all advances to prosperity, and in which living standards rise steadily as physical resources expand and ingenuity grows;

8. in which social provision is made in relation to superannuation, sickness, unemployment and widowhood on a contributory basis, free from a means test, and in which adequate medical services are within the reach of all;

9. in which there is a revised and expanded system of child and adult education, designed to develop the spirit of true citizenship, and in which no consideration of wealth or privilege shall be a determining factor.

10. in which family life is recognised as fundamental to the well-being of society, and in which every family is enabled to live in a comfortable home at reasonable cost, and with adequate community amenities.

These decisions were communicated to the press and Menzies issued a statement explaining what would happen next, concluding that the new movement had not been established upon any 'negative ideas'. Menzies was confident, he said, that 'a great and powerful body of Australian public opinion which for some time has felt itself dissipated by internal differences will become vocal and effective'. In the mythology and iconography of the Liberal Party of Australia, the role of Menzies as founder is a central symbol. That he was the single most important person in the creation of the Liberal Party is unquestionable. That he had more influence on the initial philosophy and structure of the party than any other individual is indisputable. Above all, the crucial difference between the Liberal Party and the United Australia Party, and its satellite fragments, was that the new organisation was to be a genuine party

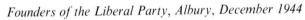

Founders of the Liberal Party, Albury, December 1944

machine. It was not to be a phantom creature manipulated by invisible interests, and moribund between elections. It would have a mass membership and an income—estimated by one of Menzies' associates as £100 000 a year—which would guarantee its independence from sectional pressures.

Some of Menzies' finest speeches were given to gatherings of his own supporters and political associates. His approach was more relaxed, his wit more pointed, when he was surrounded by a congenial audience. In talking to party gatherings, especially when he felt a genuine need to revive their spirits or to confront dissatisfied elements within their ranks, he seemed to discover a slightly more vigorous and homely style. These were people to whom he really could speak directly, rather than the heterogeneous microcosm of the electorate that he was likely to encounter at public meetings. A good example of this point is the speech he gave on 17 October 1945 to the First Annual General Convention of the New South Wales division of the Liberal Party of Australia. Here is the authentic Menzies, untrammelled by the cautious qualifications imposed on official spokesmen on foreign affairs or the economy:

> In the first place I want to express my own acknowledgment and the acknowledgment of those who serve with me in Parliament for the splendid work being done outside Parliament, and I make special reference to the work done by the President, Mr Spooner in the last ten months. At any rate I do not think there is a man in Australia who

has devoted more time, more energy and more patience to the work of bringing the Liberal Party to full existence in this State than Mr Spooner.

Time after time when I myself have had to encounter the various difficulties that arise in the formation of a party I have marvelled at that slow patience of his, that capacity for seeing the other man's point of view. On the Parliamentary side I hope you will allow me to express my profound sense of indebtedness to my Deputy Leader, Mr Eric Harrison. You know it is much easier to conduct parliamentary debates at a distance than on the spot.

I received letters from people to say 'Why don't you get rid of this Government?' But I want to tell you that for a dozen men in a Party in opposition to be called on for a session which began in February and ended only about a week ago to keep up to date with matters of legislation, and to be prepared to speak about Bill after Bill, week after week, is a colossal task. I myself have been in one Parliament or another for 17 years. I do not think that whatever is said about me, and I assure you I know it, it can be said about me that I have taken an inactive part in the politics of this country for 17 years. This session at Canberra that has just concluded is the heaviest session I have ever gone through in any capacity in Parliament, and yet if I came out of a coma at three in the morning during the Committee Stage of a Bill the one thing I felt certain about was that Eric Harrison, as fresh as a daisy, would be walking into the Government with horse, foot and artillery. You will then appreciate a first class fighting deputy just as I appreciated it . . . The Party has undoubtedly, as an organisation, made marvellous headway in the last twelve months. It has had its disappointments, it is still far too handicapped by dubious supporters. It is still far too crippled by the half wit who is to be found in every gathering of our party, who is always explaining how much better he would be than the Leader of the Party, than the man the Party has, but these handicaps exist in all movements and parties. The truth is that we set ourselves almost a year ago a most tremendous task, and that task was to produce one Liberal Party in every state of Australia, one party on an Australia-wide basis, and we have succeeded in doing it. . . .

Our task is to bring to the service of the people in Parliament the best Parliament that this country can produce, a parliament of the best, the most upright, the ablest and most diligent people this country can produce, and our greatest task of all is to induce into the service of the people, men of such fibre as will enable them to give great service to the people. It is the search for candidates which is our greatest undertaking. We will have good organisation as long as there are thousands of people who are prepared to carry it on in fine or in rainy weather, but our permanence for political good in Australia will rest primarily upon the calibre of the people we send into the Parliaments of the Commonwealth and the States. . .

The greatest problem at this moment in Australia is one you do not need to be told about, in fact it is the problem of industrial lawlessness and anarchy . . .

When I hear a Prime Minister of Australia say that an industrial dispute in NSW is a State matter, I shudder at such a want of comprehension. I say to you people in NSW, this must never be forgotten. You are the key State in Australia, and no major dispute could sweep your State which does not silence the factories in other States, and consequently it seems to me a dreadful thing to hear this matter described as a purely local one.

There are two things at present producing the immediate symptoms. The first is our trouble on the coalfields. So much has been said that one can add nothing, but what we do know is that through this war, and now into the peace, the Australian coal miner is denying to the Australian people the most vital element in Australia's reconstruction, and when I say the Australian coal miner I do not mean to convey to you that the average coal miner is an irresponsible fellow or that the majority of the coal miners are inconsiderate or hostile to the welfare of their country, but I say that if Australian Trade Unionism is to justify its position of power in this country, then its first task is to discipline its own minority who would set industry by the ears. I have little respect for the courage of the majority of the coal miners. Because some beardless youth has decided he won't work a strike is called and the entire industry is thrown into idleness. Loyalty is a great thing, and has meant a lot in building up strength over the years, but there comes a point when loyalty to some rule must give way to the country as a whole. Trade Unions must realise this and carry in to its own ranks the disciplining of irresponsible minorities. . . . When we begin to think a little more clearly we will begin to discuss our standard of living, but in terms of real things, what you have on the table, what clothing you have to wear, what kind of a home you have and what security you have for the future. Because that is so true we have in this country a series of laws which are designed to stabilise the purchasing power of wages and salaries.

It would be a popular thing for the Government to take away wage pegging, rationing and price control tomorrow, but by tomorrow evening prices would have been allowed to run. Let us take over wage pegging, rationing and price control, and there is not one increase in pay that we will secure in the next three months that will not be more than wiped out by the increase in prices. . . . No government can complain of anarchy if that Government is prepared to see its laws treated with contempt. The law must be observed and enforced to the letter, or it must be changed by the people who made it. There is a good deal of talk about discipline. When one refers to industrial discipline one is accused of being a fascist. Discipline is regarded only as the prerogative of dictatorship. The most powerful of all discipline is the discipline that a proud people will impose upon itself. There can be no greater discipline than the discipline of the law in a democratic country in which all people take a hand in the making of the law, and when we are the rulers as well as the ruled, what can be our answer to discipline?

I want everybody here today never to lose sight of the fact that there is no scheme of social security, there is no policy of full employment, there is nothing in the future than can succeed for more than a year without a true sense of discipline.

There was a time when Mr Justice Higgins, who was one of the great constructive founders of Arbitration in Australia could write a book about Arbitration and call it a new process for law and order.

Those were the days when to every Trade Union Leader the door of the Arbitration Court was the door to a world of new hope and progress and honest advantage and in those days it was understood perfectly that you could never have the protection of this new law unless it had the authority of law and today we have reached a stage when every militant trade union in Australia will go to Court, it will take what it can get from the Court and it will go on strike for the balance, and when it is discussed by any of us the immediate reply will be 'You want to take away the right to strike'. How can you maintain a system of compulsory Industrial Arbitration and have side by side with it a perfect right to go their own way if the decision does not suit them. Whatever opinion may be at this moment the time will come in Australia when we become sufficiently aware of this truth to determine that in the industrial field there shall be no delay in technicalities and that every party to a dispute will be bound to go there to settle his argument, just as we insist now that neighbours are to go to the court and not resort to brickbats across the back fence.

Menzies then turned to what he called the 'external crisis', which had been 'resting very heavily on my chest for at least a year':

The external crisis concerns the British Empire. There may have been a time when all reference to the British Empire appeared some form of jingoism. I hope we have become sufficiently aware of this today to know that the continued existence of the British Empire is vital to the peace and the future of the world. Before this war Great Britain was a richer country, a stronger country, a country more equipped with strength and power, and with a mercantile marine on the seas. In the 19th century Great Britain of her own strength, pre-siding over the entire family of nations was the greatest power in the world. It may very well be that the comparative peacefulness of the 19th century was due to that fact. In this century Great Britain has now on two occasions in enormous wars exhausted herself, has gone on two occasions almost to her knees, and has come back from her knees to save the world. And now that this has been done the time has come when a gentleman named Laski in England can say that Great Britain is a second-rate power. It is because of those conditions Professor Laski is right, and that I want to talk to you about this matter. The very argument used by those in charge of Australian Foreign Policy—I refer to the waterside workers—the very arguments used for throwing the Dutch out of the East Indies are the arguments which will be used to throw the British out of Malaya, to throw the British out of Burma, India, for throwing the Australians out of New Guinea. This is a genius we have for thinking that an argument applying to one set of people cannot apply to another. I tell you we are looking at this moment at a position which is designed to surround Australia on the North by a series of Communist Republics. Under these circumstances I would have thought that from the best possible motives Australia might like some friends. Our foreign policy is to select them almost entirely from the Latin American republics. It is perfectly true that if the British Empire remains together it is one of the great powers and able to play a great part in the world. Is it not equally true then that if the process of breaking up the British Empire proceeds so that Great Britain finally in five or ten years time speaks for herself and herself only we will no longer be a first class power. We won't solve that by running away from it, or by imagining that the middle of the 20th century contains conditions exactly the same as those of the 19th century.

Take Great Britain. In this war she, with a population smaller than that of any of her European rivals, had enormous power, for what reason? First of all, I agree, because of the character and spirit of her people, secondly because she was the greatest mercantile marine power in the world. . . . Thirdly, she had enormous overseas investments, the product of her expansion of the 19th century, with thousands and millions in total investments in the markets of the Far East, Australia and all over the world. She was the greatest Naval power in the world. She was for some generations the greatest manufacturing and industrial nation in the world, but today she is certainly not the greatest manufacturing or industrial nation of the world. Today her mercantile marine tonnage has been decimated by ruthless sinkings during the war. Overseas investments have gone before Lend-Lease, gone for dollars to pay for help in this war. The result of all this is that if the inhabitant of Great Britain is to maintain the standard of living he had before the war he must export millions of pounds worth of goods more than he did before the war. If ever people all over the world should be devoted to the building up of the very heart of their nationhood this is the time. If ever there was a time when there ought to be a conference held between the British Nations of the world it is now, and at it Australian commercial policy, agricultural policy, import and export policy should be considered in the light of how Great Britain is to continue to be a strong centre of a strong empire. Yet Australia under its present administration does nothing about these things. We turn occasionally to spare a word of admiration for these magnificent people. We drop a retrospective tear over the pains and trials of these magnificent people, but when we have done that we say to them, 'Of course, we cannot send you more food because, on examination, we find that you are no worse off for food than we are'.

The tragedy is that it has come to be a sign of good Australianism to be against every other country. I am sick of having demands for help by these people answered by the statement to the effect that in this way we in Australia have pulled our weight. Let us get over this lying and boasting. Let us get back to this, that the existence of this country depends absolutely upon the maintenance of the complete cohesion and the strength of the British Empire, and there can be no strong British Empire if there is a country in the centre of it with nothing but her glory to live on. The answer always is 'Yes, we have heard that kind of thing before, but it all comes right in the end. Therefore there always will be a British Empire'. Unless those who understand these matters are prepared to act upon them, to concentrate every effort upon them, the British Empire will have fallen from its place in the world. Every time there is an International Conference, Australia's contribution is to conduct public quarrels with the British Government and enlist the aid of voters from Bolivia, Ecuador and Liberia in order to secure the majority of votes against the greatest country in the world. Not a very intelligent contribution for Australia to be making. It does not represent the real views of 90% of the people of Australia. I say to you, let us pipe down a little in the advice we are always so ready to offer about strange countries in this world and concentrate upon our own task, on the re-integration of this great British family of nations. Establish in every capital of every dominion and in London itself Secretariats from all the dominions, so that at all times the British Empire countries are in touch with each other on matters of mutual concern, and so that in any future time of trial as in the past, the house will stand together. It is not a matter of vague honour and glory, but a matter of existence itself. Every ambition we have for Australia, every hope for the future of our children and those after them is bound up in the existence of a free British community in this country, and if we are to be free and British we must awake at once to the danger of disintegration which confronts us.

Late in 1941, the first Australian public opinion polls, using techniques developed by the Gallup organisation in the United States, were published by Roy Morgan. Over the next twenty-five years Australian Gallup Polls asked a number of questions that revealed public attitudes towards Menzies. As can be seen from the polls reported at intervals through this book, the level of approval and support for Menzies as party leader and Prime Minister fluctuated significantly. A particularly fascinating series of questions was asked about voters' preferences for party leaders. In July 1946, with a general election only two months away, Roy Morgan reported a survey of the relative standing of the most prominent Labor, Liberal and Country Party federal politicians. Although the commentary did not say so, it was notable that Menzies was the first choice of less than half of the prospective non-Labor voters. And he was substantially less popular with Liberal and Country Party supporters than Chifley was with Labor voters.

'Chifley for Labor' and 'Menzies for Liberal-Country' are the popular party slogans, according to a nation-wide survey of electors by the Australian Gallup Poll in June.

In its latest survey of political sentiment, the Gallup Poll asked people how they were likely to vote in September, and then asked them to select their party leaders from lists of five Labor men and five Liberal-Country men.

People who intend to vote Liberal or Country Party made these selections for leader:—

Menzies . .　44 per cent.
Casey . . . .　34　,,　　,,
Fadden. . .　10　,,　　,,
Earle Page　5　,,　　,,
Spender . .　3　,,　　,,
No answer　4　,,　　,,

Second preferences of people who are voting Liberal or Country show:—

(1) A straight-out contest between Menzies and Casey would go to Menzies, with a majority of about 5 to 4.
(2) If Casey had not been in the vote, Menzies would have received 63 per cent., against Fadden 15 per cent., Earle Page 9 per cent., and Spender 7 per cent., with 6 per cent. undecided.
(3) Without Menzies, Casey would have led with 56 per cent., against Fadden 24 per cent., Earle Page 8 per cent., and Spender 5 per cent., with 7 per cent. undecided.

In the election of September 1946, the Liberal Party won more seats than the UAP had done in 1943. But the anti-Labor forces remained heavily outnumbered. For Menzies, the 1946 general election was a setback. Charles Meeking, who travelled throughout the campaign as the Leader of the Opposition's Press Secretary, recalls that his chief was astonished by his defeat. Temporarily blinded by local enthusiasm encountered wherever he spoke, Menzies had apparently become convinced that there was a groundswell of support for his new party.

On 30 September 1946, two days after the election, a special correspondent of *The Herald* asked 'What Will Menzies Do?':

Over recent months Mr Menzies has hinted to friends that he might not continue leading the party if it were not victorious at the election or had not made substantial gains.

The party faces considerable difficulty.

During the campaign Mr Menzies exerted a personal effort which probably constitutes an all-time record. Almost certainly he covered a greater area and addressed more party meetings in so short a while than any other leader in Federal history. He put forward a policy which was balanced and constructive, as well as specific and detailed, and his policy speech was considered by many to be the finest speech of

its kind he had ever made. But the impact of this effort, following
nearly three years of indefatigable work in organising the Liberal Party,
has been negligible so far as it can be measured on the tally boards.

There is a wide feeling that this can only be explained by the fact
that in its personalities, the Liberal Party still lacks electoral appeal.

Most members of the Labor Party claim that for election-winning
purposes, Mr Menzies is their greatest individual asset.

Throughout his campaign, for instance, Mr Chifley played heavily
on Mr Menzies, and usually concluded his addresses with a declaration
that 'the alternative to a vote for Labor was a vote for a Menzies
Government'.

There has been evidence lately that Mr Menzies's public standing
has increased; but the election result hardly suggests that it has increased to the point where he is again a popular public leader.

But there are two factors which may induce the Liberals to retain
Mr Menzies as Opposition Leader, for the present at least—
1. He certainly deserves the gratitude of the party for his years of hard
    work for it, and on the more practical side
2. The Parliamentary Liberal Party remains so bankrupt of outstanding
    personnel that no big figure is available to succeed Mr Menzies.

Moreover, sectional cross-currents would probably be so strong
that there would be no unanimous support for any other member of
the Party if Mr Menzies decided to step down.

Menzies did not retire. When Parliament reassembled there was
no challenge to his leadership. But the return of the Labor Party demonstrated that the electors still had to be convinced that a government
under Menzies would be something desirably different from the discredited UAP—Country Party coalition which had been swept from
office in 1941 and trounced in the 1943 election. Within a month, on
30 October 1946, *The Border Morning Mail* announced that 'Mr
Menzies Looks to Bright Horizon'. In three related stories from the
meeting of the Federal Council of the Liberal Party in Canberra, the
Albury paper reported Menzies' optimistic speech to delegates and
their vote of confidence in him. More ominously, the *Mail* (like many
other papers around the country) told its readers of the Liberal Party's
newly expressed wish to unite with the Country Party—a dream of
strength through amalgamation that was to prove as elusive in the 1940s
and 1950s as it had done in the previous decades:

HIS FAITH IN THE LIBERAL PARTY

The Liberal Party could look back on the Federal elections with
great satisfaction, because it had achieved three things, declared the
Parliamentary Leader of the party (Mr Menzies) today.

They were:
(1) The party had produced for the first time in the history of
     Australia one Liberal Party all over Australia.

(2) It had been enabled to present to the people in a coherent form the Liberal platform; and

(3) The party had arrested the progress of the Labor Party, and had made some tactical gains.

Mr Menzies, who was speaking at the first annual meeting of the Federal Council of the Liberal Party, after an address of welcome by the president (Mr Malcolm T. Ritichie), said some people might think the progress made electorally was disappointing.

That might be so to some extent, but the party had a most formidable task, and had been in full blooded existence for only more than a year.

'One point I emphasise.' said Mr Menzies, 'We are now living in the post-war world which requires post-war ideas, and it is to our credit that we produced for the people a truly post-war policy. Although the people did not accept that policy to the extent of turning the Government out, we emphasised post-war thinking and progressive ideas, while Labor dwelt rather heavily and sluggishly on the past.

'This policy is going to produce its results, because its soundness and progressiveness will ultimately find a response in the majority of the people of Australia.'

Mr Menzies said the progress of the Labor party took some arresting, and the Liberals made tactical gains to a degree that it had attracted younger people to the services of the Liberal party.

He said Communism had seized the imagination of young men and women, but the Communist Party was not looking for results tomorrow morning.

The Liberal Party gospel, which was not mad, but sane, was not confused, but clear and straight; it was not destructive, but calculated to build a real nation, could gain more support among the younger generations than the Communist gospel.

Liberalism was desperately needed in the world, Mr Menzies said.

The party must face the local political task of organising the party and formulating a policy, but the greater task was a crusade in favor of basic liberal principles.

LIBERALS WANT FUSION WITH CP

The Federal Council of the Liberal Party of Australia decided tonight that negotiations should be entered into with the Country Party to amalgamate both parties with a view to furthering their mutual political interests.

This decision, which was unanimous, was made after a thorough debate by delegates from the six States.

Approaches are to be made to the Country Party, it is understood, as soon as possible.

In January negotiations were conducted with the Country Party for a certain amalgamation of interests which resulted in agreement being reached for joint Senate teams in the Federal elections and an exchange of preferences in the electorates where both Liberal and Country Party candidates were sitting.

The things he has said stamp Mr. Menzies as Labour's Best Frozen Asset.

The Liberal Leader as portrayed on the cover of a Labor pamphlet written in 1948 by Arthur Calwell

In its recommendations to the Federal Council the Liberal Party Federal Executive, which met yesterday, said the present trend of political thought and action demonstrated that there was an urgent need for the union of the two non-Socialist parties in the interests of Australia.

There were no fundamental differences in the political views of both parties.

Each was concerned with the primary industries and country development on the one hand, and with secondary industries and city development on the other.

Both would work for a balanced national economy and development.

The secretary of the NSW branch of the Country Party (Mr Munro) declined tonight to comment. He could not indicate whether or not the party's Federal executive would meet soon to consider the position.

CONFIDENCE IN MR MENZIES' LEADERSHIP

A vote of confidence in the leadership of Mr Menzies was carried by the Federal Council of the Liberal Party tonight. Council placed on record its 'deep appreciation and admiration of his outstanding and inspiring work which Mr Menzies had performed in bringing into being the Liberal Party of Australia two years ago; for his invaluable energy and drive within the party, and for his outstanding leadership in the campaign itself. It was clear that Mr Menzies had gained in prestige and power during the campaign.'

Menzies had certainly gained in prestige and power. But he was not everywhere admired, still less obeyed, even within his own party. From a document leaked to a very senior Labor minister, we may see a glimpse of Menzies' difficulties with state Liberal leaders. In a post-mortem on the failure of Liberal publicity in the election, Menzies urged a more unified national effort:

It is not proposed that all advertising of a political kind to appear in Australia should be written by one person sitting in Canberra. It is proposed that the control of the general substance, the points being made in advertising, should be controlled from the centre so that we would be playing one tune.

That is very important. If someone says Labor advertising was better than ours, I agree. It was cleverly written, and it was adapted to meet Mr Playford's point to various localities. Potato men wrote advertisements to potato growers and butter men to dairy men, but all these advertisements proceeded from one factory. We have this parochial idea that it is only people on the spot who can run advertising. This meant that you could read one advertisement in one State that was completely cancelled by an advertisement for our Party in another State. And most of them were pretty dull.

If we are going to match the Labor Party, let us face up to the fact that the Labor Party had a clever set of advertising tradesmen at work in the centre. They produced uniform quality. It is a great strength to the Party to have the one team approach everywhere. These local problems are alright, but the great themes of election campaigns must be approached in the same way all over the place. You get every Labor man in Australia, every Communist in Australia playing in the same orchestra. But for us, it is bits and pieces far too frequently.

There is a second aspect. What are we going to do about a central publicity staff if we say, 'You can draft what you like but it may go into the waste-paper basket because real control of publicity is in our State and not in the centre'? Do you suppose you will get a first class man to keep on doing that thankless job? This job calls for top-notchers. You must give the man a chance to know he is doing something really important, working on lines that will affect our general propaganda all over Australia. I am critical of a great deal of our publicity, but I have a great admiration of the work done at our Federal headquarters. People like Mr White, for example, are doing good jobs, but if I were in his place I would feel frustrated all the time. He produces something which someone does not like and nothing is done.

But I am not allowed to put my brains in soak with the Federal Secretariat of the organisation and determine what are the particular arguments to be put by suitable advertisements. If you are going to have Federal contact with publicity merely trial and error, you will have a secretariat not worth anything.

There is a very strong feeling regarding local advertisements. We know what our local people want, but you people decide often that we do not. Labor has to apply its arguments to as large an audience as ours. The whole Labor propaganda was centrally organised in this election. It licked ours. It was always consistent, and in addition it was extremely plausibly and cleverly written. And it was topical. You opened the paper and there was an intriguing advertisement which hinged on something that had happened only a few days before. Although centrally controlled it had flexibility. It was at the nerve centre, not at the extremity. Our advertisements gave us the impression that each was, say, number five in a long schedule, and that in a fortnight's time, whatever happened in the election campaign, the next one in the series would be published. They were as dead as a doornail. The Labor Party showed us how to do it.

It is no use telling me that a high degree of central control of Federal advertising will not permit of flexibility. The Labor Party did it, and the Labor Party's advertising had more flexibility than ours ever dreamt of. South Australia protests. Very well, but advertisements in Tasmania, Victoria, New South Wales, Queensland and West Australia can have that applied to them.

At this point, the South Australian Premier, Thomas Playford, insisted: 'They all have to be passed by the local Director'. Menzies, who many years later was to write in a foreword to Playford's biography that his 'immense physical strength and his intellectual virility made him an almost terrifying negotiator', continued unabashed:

Yes. We did not exclude the possibility of review by local people. All we say is that the great work of organising and planning the publicity campaign should be done from the nerve centre of this organisation. That does not exclude the work of local men who are in the organisation. They should censor the advertisements to the extent of saying which week they should appear. The question is where will things be determined, where will the original impulse come from? Unless we had a Federal set up on publicity we will never catch up with the Labor Party on this matter.

The Labor Party's advertising always had a bite in it. They have no mealy-mouthed ideas of the kind we suffer from. They say to themselves, 'How do you knock him over?' They reply, 'by saying he is a stinker'. Then they say it, and say it so forcibly that people think he is. They always attack. It is these attacking advertisements that are read.

We do not do any attacking of these people. People read that Labor were the saviours of the country, that the sceptre of power fell from our trembling hands when Japan came into the war. For some reason we decide we will be as pure as snow on this matter. There is no attack, there is just talk in [a] rather common-place manner. You don't win a campaign without delivering a few stout blows with the claymore. We tend to die of anaemia, we think it is a genteel campaign in which we take all the rape and give none. We accept everything they say, and reply with some remarks about taxation or something of the sort.

We have to make up our minds in these three years that in our publicity we don't pull our punches. We fight, and we fight these people. These people are fighters. They are unscrupulous. There is no need for us to be unscrupulous, we can fight a clean fight and knock these boys out of the ring. The whole case for the Liberal Party and its Federal organisation is exactly the same as for Federal direction of publicity matter and propaganda.

In broadcasting we are babes in the wood. It suits a broadcasting company to say an announcer will give a few scatters. Some poop gets up and reads a stilted statement in an affected voice. It is all too silly. The average person will not listen to a dreary talk from the studio, when he hears the pages being turned over. But a lot of people will listen to a well-selected meeting, when they feel they are present in the hall. They hear the off-stage noises. If it is a good meeting it is listened to for an hour, when a studio broadcast will not be listened to for five minutes.

If we woke up to this business of broadcasting we would realise it is a great modern weapon. When the leader of the Party, for example is on the air at Geelong when addressing a meeting there he should also have a hook-up throughout all the western district broadcasting stations. He would address an audience of thousands instead of hundreds. But if we use wireless as the stations would like us to use it, filling in little gaps and using studio broadcasts, we will spend a lot of money and do no good with it.

I am referring only to Federal publicity, and the States must always have the right to reject advertisements. In South Australia I saw some local pamphlets which were extremely well done. With the Federal set up they would go to Federal headquarters for general distribution and effective use all over Australia. If we operate as six islands we will get no co-ordination.

Although he was fully alive to the value of appropriate publicity, Menzies' contempt for most of the working press was never a secret.

He himself was well aware of what journalists thought of him. Charles Meeking, who became his Press Secretary in 1944, received a copy of *The Home Book of Quotations* when he transferred to the Liberal Party headquarters in 1948. On the flyleaf of the book, his Chief had written a mock dialogue:

ANY DAY 1944–1947

C.J.M. (brightly):	Good morning! May I suggest a press conference?
R.G.M.	You may, but I won't have one.
C.J.M. (wistfully):	The boys would like one.
R.G.M.	Curse the boys.
C.J.M. (doggedly):	Well, then, what about a written statement on a burning topic?
R.G.M.	There are no burning topics.
C.J.M. (perspiringly):	It would be good if you could consent to be photographed while shaving! The Sydney readers . . .
R.G.M.	'Out, damned spot'
C.J.M. (faintly):	Well, what can I arrange?
R.G.M.	To close the door behind you!
C.J.M. (despairingly):	Hell, what a job!

Though Labor's propaganda barrage against Menzies was always fierce, his personal relations with both John Curtin and Ben Chifley were friendly and relaxed. The Western Australian journalist, Victor Courtney, often spoke to the Labor Leaders 'off the record'. In his memoirs, *All I May Tell*, he recalled:

> . . . Menzies, as Leader of the Opposition, came on a trip to Perth during the war. One of those receiving him at the aerodrome made the remark that Curtin was sick.
> 'Shick, you mean,' interrupted another party 'yes' man.
> Menzies turned on him like a tiger. 'That's a foul lie!' he said, 'and you can tell the person who told you that I said so. John Curtin is a sick man, and he has never taken a drink since he has been Prime Minister.'
> It was a fine act of political sportsmanship which I will always remember of Menzies, and was typical of the understanding between the two. For Curtin, though Menzies's political adversary, was a keen personal friend of the Liberal leader.
> I asked him on one occasion what he thought of Menzies—off the record.
> 'The chief thing I can say about Bob,' said Curtin, 'is that he's a fool. Not in the way you think,' he added, noting my raised eyebrows.
> 'I mean he is a fool because he is undergoing all the abuse and all the accusations of self-interest that a politician has to suffer when he

need be working only three months of the year at his profession and making three times what he is ever likely to get as Prime Minister. If Bob has a fault it is that he does not suffer fools gladly. And I am afraid that you have to learn to do that in this job.'

Strangely enough as his war-burdens mounted, Curtin himself was to find that he fell victim to the same weakness because at the height of his war worries he developed an ever increasing impatience with those who did not see as clearly or think as quickly as he did.

Yet it is difficult to imagine any other person as Prime Minister in the dark days of the war.

... The last time I saw Chifley was a few weeks before his death when he came to Perth as Leader of the Opposition and invited me over for a chat. He looked well and relaxed and in no way a man so close to the Shadows. The thing he seemed most worried about was not losing the Prime Ministership but the abandonment of price fixing.

'Costs are going to go sky high,' he said, 'and the thing that the other side are now hailing as a great achievement will be the chief worry of Treasurers later on.'

Which time has proved a fairly accurate prophesy.

I asked Chifley off the record what he thought of Menzies apart from politics.

'Bob's alright,' he said with his characteristic smile, 'I would call him a Liberal with a small 'l'.'

And I don't think the Prime Minister could value any tribute from his political opponent more than this.

On another occasion Chifley is said to have remarked that the only thing wrong with Menzies was that he was in the wrong party. Chifley's relaxed attitude to Menzies was reflected in his parliamentary style. Harold Holt remembered:

He had a dry sense of humour which found a perhaps somewhat mischievous but certainly very effective expression in the way in which he used to handle the then Leader of the Opposition ... Sir Robert would present a most formidable unanswerable argument, compelling in its logic, and the more compelling this argument the more homespun and disarming Ben Chifley's answer would be. He would come to the table, sitting down and looking round the House for a while to gauge its temper, and at length he would rise and say, 'There's no doubt about the Leader of the Opposition. He can make a wonderful case in a most brilliant and logical way; but if only he had *our* case to put, what a superb piece of advocacy we should get from him then!' And by the time Ben had finished, after going off on one or two byways of his own, the general impression (not merely in the House, but perhaps more importantly among the listeners beyond the House) was, 'Here's a very reasonable charming sincere earnest man, and he's the man we want for Prime Minister.'

Menzies' position as Liberal leader is sometimes regarded as having been unassailable from the moment that the party was created. His ascendancy in the later 1950s was so complete that memories of earlier, less dominant, days were effaced. Yet, early in 1947 the New South Wales Liberals froze him out of the State election campaign. The Queensland Liberals did the same. The New South Wales state Opposition Leader, Vernon Treatt, wrote to Menzies on 26 February 1947: 'We feel it would be better, tactically, to confine this election to State issues and State personalities.' Menzies cleverly enquired in his reply: 'I suppose I may take it that this ruling applies to Federal members—including New South Wales Federal members?' But Treatt rejoined: 'We do not envisage that New South Wales Federal members will not speak during the campaign, particularly in their own electorates.' On March 6, Menzies commented drily to Matt Calman, campaign director for Kevin Ellis, Liberal candidate for Coogee: 'We now know exactly where we stand.' It was not just in New South Wales, however, that Menzies was under attack. At the annual state council meeting of the Victorian Liberal Party on 17 April 1947, the Nhill branch moved for a change of leader. J.L. Gregory of Nhill stated that 165 out of 172 of his members were opposed to the present leader. Some respondents said Menzies was 'too conceited', others that he was 'too up in the clouds'. The Nhill motion was thrown out by the council. But momentary unanimity in rejecting public criticism was not a guarantee of eternal loyalty. And the leader's standing continued to be in doubt.

As late as the middle of 1947, Menzies and the Liberal Party were failing to make significant gains in public support. The Gallup Poll suggested that if an election had been held in July 1947, Labor would have been returned with a similar majority to the one gained in 1946. Two other polls at the same time revealed both that Menzies himself was failing to improve his personal popularity and that the party's image was still very fuzzy in the minds of the electorate:

Labor, Liberal Difference
Discussed By Electors

More than ever before, elections are being fought on a party basis, yet, when Gallup Poll interviewers asked nearly 2000 men and women what they thought was the main difference between the Labor and Liberal Parties, one person in three could not describe it.

The question 'In your own words, what would you say is the main difference between the Labor Party and the Liberal Party?' brought different reactions from supporters of the two parties.

Nearly half of the Labor Party supporters interviewed said something like: 'Labor is best for the workers.' Ten per cent. said there was no difference between Labor and Liberal, and an equal number gave various answers, leaving 31 per cent. without opinions. Very few mentioned that they thought Labor meant Socialism.

LABOR VOTERS SAY:

Labor for the workers .. ..49 p.c.
Various answers .. ..10 p.c.
No difference between Labor and Liberal .. ..10 p.c.
Cannot answer .. .. 31 p.c.

Most of the Independent voters with opinions on the subject think there is no difference between the two major parties:—

INDEPENDENT VOTERS SAY:

Labor for workers, Liberal for capitalists .. ..15 p.c.
Various answers .. ..12 p.c.
No difference between Labor and Liberal .. ..42 p.c.
Cannot answer .. .. 31 p.c.

Liberal-Country supporters have a wide range of ideas as to what is the difference between their party and the Labor Party.

LIBERAL-COUNTRY VOTERS

Liberal for employers, Labor for employes .. .. .. 13 p.c.
Labor means union control .. .. 11 p.c.
Labor means Socialism .. .. 6 p.c.
Liberals have broader outlook .. .. 7 p.c.
Liberals better administrators .. .. 5 p.c.
Various answers .. .. 18 p.c.
No difference between Labor and Liberal .. .. .. 10 p.c.
Cannot answer .. .. 30 p.c.

100 p.c.

Bigger Vote For Liberals
If Menzies Not Leader?

If a Federal election had been held in July, with someone other than Mr Menzies as leader of the Liberal Party, it is possible that a Liberal-Country Party Government would have been returned to power.

This possibility was revealed when Gallup Poll interviewers asked a nation-wide sample of voters for their opinions about the leadership of the two major parties.

People interviewed were first asked which party they would probably vote for if an election were held now.

The result ... shows no change in party support since the last Federal election a year ago.

Those who said they would vote Labor or Independent were then asked: 'Would you vote Liberal or Country Party if Mr Menzies were not leader of the Opposition?'

On the other hand, Liberal and Country Party voters were asked: 'Would you vote Labor if Mr Chifley were not leader?'

Answers of Labor voters divide as follow:—

10 per cent. said they WOULD vote Liberal or Country
    Party if Mr Menzies were not leader.

8 per cent. said PERHAPS they would vote Liberal or Country
  Party, and
82 per cent. said they would NOT vote Liberal or Country Party
  whether Mr Menzies were leader or not.

These Labor voters account for 53 per cent. of the electorate. Supporters of Independent candidates comprise another 3 per cent. of the electorate, and almost half of them said they would change to Liberal or Country Party if Mr Menzies were not leader.

Liberal and Country Party supporters, who represent 44 per cent. of the electorate, answered:—

3 per cent. said they WOULD vote Labor if Mr Chifley were not
  leader.
5 per cent. said PERHAPS they would vote Labor, and
92 per cent. said they would NOT vote Labor.

Combined answers of Labor-Independent and Liberal-Country voters give the following result, with percentages stated in respect to the total electorate. (Figures in the earlier tables have been converted to the basis of 56 Labor and Independent voters to every 44 Liberal and Country voters, as at the last Federal election):—

Of Labor and Independent Voters 6 per cent. would vote Liberal-
  CP if Menzies not leader,
  4 per cent. might vote Liberal-CP,
  46 per cent. would not change.
Of Liberal-Country Voters
  1 per cent. would vote Labor if Chifley not leader.
  2 per cent. might vote Labor,
  41 per cent. would not change.

From the above figures, it seems that if an election had been held in July, and Mr Menzies had been replaced by another good leader, the Liberal and Country Parties might have polled nearly 50 per cent. of the first preference votes. Judging by the 1937 and 1940 elections, that would have resulted in a small majority of the seats going to Liberal and Country Party candidates.

These polls could scarcely have been comforting to Menzies. Paradoxically, though they served to reveal a moment of opportunity for his most popular rival within the Liberal Party, a time when a bid for leadership by R.G. Casey might have been successful, the polls must have been galling to Casey as well. For Casey, recently elected Federal President of the Liberal Party, was not a member of Parliament. He had been out of Australia between 1940 and 1946; and he did not regain a seat in the House of Representatives until the general election in 1949. Menzies was thus secure. Casey could not challenge him from outside Parliament. In a few months there was a dramatic shift in popular feeling. On Saturday August 16, the Labor Cabinet decided to seek power to nationalise the private banks. And, in an astonishingly casual announcement, the news was disclosed to an unprepared nation in a 42-word statement released to the press without any explanation

Struth!

CYRIL DILLON

CHIFLEY IN A STEW?

or briefing. For the Opposition, this was a heaven-sent issue. In mid-September, 63 per cent of electors said they would vote against nationalisation in a referendum. By the end of October there were still only 28 per cent of voters in favour; and the Gallup Poll showed that 'the Chifley Government would be fortunate to escape defeat if an election were held now.'

Meanwhile, strangely, Menzies' popularity as measured by the Gallup Poll was slipping. By November he was the first choice as leader of only 41 per cent of Liberal and Country Party supporters. Casey had moved up to 40 per cent; and, although he too was a Victorian, he was more popular than Menzies in both New South Wales and South Australia. In view of the size of the sample and the normal margins of error involved, it would be fair to say that the two men were virtually on level pegging.

Historians have usually traced the turning point in the Liberal Party's fortunes to the bank nationalisation controversy. They have also tended to assume that Menzies' image was also enhanced by the same issue. But it seems clear from the limited evidence of the opinion polls that, at least in the short term, Menzies did not personally benefit from the overwhelming surge of anti-Labor sentiment. It took a different issue—a renewed development of anti-communist attitudes—to give Menzies a boost. Just before Easter in 1948, interviewers found 84 per cent of people in favour of fighting communism. Over the next twelve months opinions polarised over a wider range of problems, and the key emerging issues were industrial relations and the threat of communism in Australia. The Gallup enquiries show how the increasing salience of these divisive issues worked to Menzies' advantage:

January 1949

Chifley, Menzies, First Choice As Leaders

Mr Chifley is accepted as leader of the Labor Party even more widely than ever before, and Mr Menzies is now undoubted choice as leader for Liberal-CP, the Gallup Poll finds.

People interviewed were handed a list of 10 leading Parliamentarians, 5 Labor and 5 Liberal-CP, and asked:—
Which of these men are your first and second choice for leader in Federal Parliament?
It was the third time in four years the Gallup Poll had asked the question and comparison shows that, among Labor Party voters, support for Mr Chifley has risen from 55 per cent. to 78 per cent.:—

LABOR 1st PREFERENCES

	1946 p.c.	1947 p.c.	1949 p.c.
Chifley	55	62	78
Evatt	31	23	16
Ward	5	9	2

Calwell.............................	—	I	2
Dedman............................	2	' I	2
Forde..............................	4	—	—
No Answer	3	4	—

Second preferences disclose that, without Chifley, Evatt would be supported by 68 per cent. of Labor voters, compared with 10 per cent. for Calwell, 9 per cent. for Dedman. 9 per cent. for Ward and 4 per cent. undecided

LIBERAL-COUNTRY LEADER

Answers of Liberal-CP voters show that Mr Menzies now has a clear majority over other non-Labor Leaders. (In the latest survey Mr Harrison's name was substituted for Mr Spender):—

LIBERAL-CP 1st PREFERENCE

	1946 p.c.	1947 p.c.	1949 p.c.
Menzies...........................	44	41	53
Casey	34	40	27
Fadden............................	10	10	10
Earle Page	5	4	5
Harrison	—	—	3
Spender...........................	3	2	—
No Answer	4	3	2

Second preferences of Liberal-CP voters disclose:—
- In a straight-out contest between Menzies and Casey, the result would be:—Menzies, 60 p.c.; Casey, 32 p.c.; and undecided, 8 per cent.
- If Casey had not been in the vote, Menzies would have been selected by 70 per cent.
- Without Menzies, Casey would be supported by the majority (54 p.c.) of Liberal-CP people, compared with Fadden 24 p.c., Earle Page 10 p.c., Harrison 7 p.c. and undecided 5 p.c.

May–June 1949

'Put The Brake On Socialism' say most Australians

Most of us are approaching this year's Federal election in a far more conservative (and less socialistic) frame of mind than in 1946.

The Australian Gallup Poll has found a big swing to the 'Right' among people of all ages.

Electors in a full range of circumstances throughout the six States, were interviewed in May, and asked:—

During the next few years, do you want our Government to go to the left or to the right—that is, to be more socialistic or less socialistic?

Altogether nearly 2000 people were interviewed and answers of every 100 of them divide:—

54 are 'rightists'; they want less socialism.

14 are 'leftists'; they want more socialism.

16 spontaneously answered 'no change'; and

16 have no opinion on the subject.

Proportions of Rightists and Leftists among women are almost the same as among men.

In all age groups, from the 'twenties' to the 'sixty and over', there are at least 54 per cent. of Rightists and not more than 15 per cent. of Leftists.

This is a remarkable change compared with a similar Australian Gallup Poll a few months before the last Federal election. The following figures show that opposition to socialism has almost doubled:—

	1946 p.c.	1949 p.c.
Want to 'go right'	28	54
Want to 'go left'	27	14
Want no change	30	16
No opinion	15	16

POLITICAL ANGLE

People interviewed were asked how they intended to vote at this year's Federal election. Separate counts of Labor and of Liberal-CP voters on the question of socialism demonstrate the stupidity of claiming that a vote for a particular political party necessarily implies agreement with all of its policy.

As shown in the finding above, 43 per cent. now plan to vote Labor, 39 per cent. Liberal-CP, and 2 per cent. Independents. The other 16 per cent. are still undecided.

● Of every 100 Labor Party supporters, only 24 want MORE socialism, as against 31 who want LESS of it. (In 1946 only 14 per cent. answered 'less.')

On the other hand, the Liberal and CP policy of opposing socialism is approved by overwhelming majorities of supporters of those parties —as well as by the preponderance of Labor voters!

'UNDECIDED' GO RIGHT

It is important to note a strong rightist tendency among the 16 per cent. still undecided on the election. They answered: Less socialism, 47 per cent.; More socialism, 10 per cent.; No change, 11 per cent.; and No opinion, 32 per cent.

Gallup Poll interviewers always ask people to give reasons for their opinions. The general attitude on this question of socialism is portrayed by three comments:—

'They've gone far enough already,'

'Private ownership creates incentive,' and

'Socialism might lead to communism.'

Party Prospects Same As In 1946

Election prospects of the Federal Labor Party continue to recover from the setback caused by announcement of bank nationalisation in 1947.

Division of electors' support between Labor and Liberal-CP is now almost the same as at a comparable stage before the last Federal election in 1946.

One of the difficulties in presenting the leader of the Opposition to his followers and potential supporters was that he himself was volatile. His moods could oscillate violently. The benign, avuncular figure so familiar to television audiences of the 1950s and 1960s was only one of his personalities, temporarily ascendant. When he was still the prophet of a reborn Liberalism, with an uncertain political future, Warren Denning described him privately as 'the Mona Lisa of Australian public life'. In late 1947 or early 1948, Denning tried to sketch Menzies' character while drafting a chapter for a book which was never published:

It is indubitably true that Mr Menzies liked the nice and easy things of life. Memories of him that recur, are his careful choice of precisely the right cigar; his connoisseurship of wines, and impatience with those of inferior quality; his nice tastes in food; his exquisite feeling for good art, in which, though, he tended towards form rather than meaning; his dislike of the hard routine work of Parliament, where he preferred to reserve himself for what he liked to think was the devastating and unanswerable speech, leaving his henchmen—often bewildered henchmen, secretly angry at his indifference—to clear up the debris, round off the odds and ends of debate.

He liked nice furniture, pleasant surroundings, the right setting for himself; he responded to these influences as less emotionally sensitive men respond to heat or cold, sun or rain. He needed flattery, hated criticism, refused to have able men, as lesser suns, around him.

It has been said that he came into politics after his due time; that his true political epoch was the House of Commons of a century or more ago, when a Prime Minister's success and survival depended so much less on 'party', so much more on gathering a personal circle around himself. But even then Mr Menzies may not have lasted; the contradictions of his nature would have defeated him.

On the score of the nice and easy things, though, it is fair to point out that had he surrendered wholly to this part of his nature, he may never have gone into, or remained in, politics; he could have made ten thousand pounds a year at the bar without the slightest difficulty, far more than he ever could make, or has made, in Parliament.

He remained on amid the comparative financial sacrifices of public life—even at times when his private finances were far from reassuring, and real anxiety beset him—because hidden away among all the other facets of him, there was a note of desire to serve and even sacrifice—the most elusive, but the finest, quality in his complex character, so far as his public life was concerned.

Mr Menzies was a person of many and unpredictable moods. Those who felt them most were the people who came into daily contact with him—his secretaries, advisers, colleagues, journalists, and the like.

My contact with him was as a Parliamentary journalist, in the course of frequent, almost daily, press interviews. One day he would be genial, friendly, warm, entirely human, with an abundance of the charm which in this mood was so entirely part of him.

Next day, he would be the cold, aloof, remote statesman, far beyond the ordinary folk of this world—disdainful, contemptuous, lost in his own psychological Shangri-la. Another day, he would be the petulant man who has all the world against him; no friends; no sincerity around him; nothing to rely upon; nobody to trust—a figure of tragic frustration, one single spark of divine consciousness in the midst of a universal stupidity.

Yet another day, he would welcome us with a wickedly malicious gleam in his eye. Then would come the subtle, super-refined leg-pulling, the calculated quotations from Latin to those among us whom he knew were unacquainted with the Latin; the turn of a phrase upon a classical image which he thought, and hoped, may be beyond our range of knowledge. And when he scored—as he often did; we admitted it without rancour, but without much in the way of loving kindness towards him either—the sardonic joy was written widely across his face.

Next, a few hours later, he could again become the good companion, almost the comrade of the road, ready to do a good turn, or help with a friendly or informative word. Some of us admired him, some really liked him, some of us quite candidly disliked him. But none of us ever really got his measure.

As with us, so with others. He would sit at his desk for hours looking into space; what he saw mirrored in eternity was something between his God and himself, for nobody else ever knew.

Urgent decisions were waiting; the challenge of dire events was at his elbows; yet in these moods he retreated from the world into some icy fastness of the philosophical mind. Nothing could be got from him; never a man of action in any dynamic sense, in these moods he allowed reality to rush past him, so that he could never catch up with it.

The essential difficulty in interpreting Mr Menzies as a personality, is that there were several natures within the one man, natures which were contradictory and sometimes mutually-cancelling. Out of this came the lack of a continuity of purpose, or even of thought, which contributed much to his Prime Ministerial difficulties. The very brilliance of his mind was in some ways his enemy, leaping as it did with piercing insight but disconcerting unpredictability from crag to crag, without realising that crags only exist because of the valleys in between.

There was first of all, the Mr Menzies of high attainment and ripe legend. To this Mr Menzies belongs his redoubtable scholastic triumphs; his eminence at the Bar; his standing as a constitutionalist; his recognition as a fine speaker in all the formal phases of his career; his leadership of government and opposition; his hypothecations of the liberal conception of social life.

Then there was the Bohemian Mr Menzies, the liker of good as against elevated talk, of good wine, good food; the Mr Menzies who did not resent being admired by attractive women; the artist in good manners, in charm, in the elegant style; the Mr Menzies who inspired the thoughts that he belonged in spirit to a more exquisite century and setting. This was not the first Mr Menzies relaxing; had it been on that level, the second Mr Menzies may have done the first Mr Menzies no harm. But it was really another nature, at war with the conventional stature of the first.

Somewhere else there was a Peter Pan Mr Menzies, the faint suggestion of an adolescent not grown up. From this Mr Menzies there came the bitter criticism of the people who did not understand him, would not work with him, were not loyal to him. In this nature he was entirely egoistic, seeing himself as the sun in a universe of pallid moons, never quite realising there were others, though maybe of a lesser intellectual fibre, who could nevertheless claim a foothold in a man's world, having dignity, rights, duties, sensitivities, and dreams of their own.

Finally, there was a curious little pucklike Mr Menzies, an elfin creature of mischief and malice, never able to resist sticking pins in the world's pants, always under temptation to twist the noses of pompous people, or to dance on the prides, the pretensions, and the illusions of nearly everybody who crossed his path.

All these different natures of Mr Menzies combined in the person of a massive-headed, quick-eyed, wide-shouldered, tall, burly, and slightly corpulent man, who had on his hands the well-nigh impossible task of reconciling them within the personality of one individual who had committed himself to high, responsible, and public paths.

It would not have been so difficult had these lesser natures refrained from interfering with the substantial Mr Menzies at inconvenient and dangerous times. But they would not. Just when the Prime Minister was in the midst of a delicate negotiation upon which his government's, and perhaps his own, reputation depended, along came the elf to suggest a little subtle, but not always-unseen, mimicry of the other negotiating party. Just when an issue arose in the party-room which needed handling by a matured and disciplined mind, up would come the adolescent, tormented by a frustrated ego. Just when friendship, loyalty, and respect, from rank-and-filers in the party were most desirable, there Puck would be to mock some dull follow upon whom, nevertheless, the essential Mr Menzies depended for political survival.

The upshot of all this inward conflict—which must have been as disturbing to Mr Menzies himself as it was to those who experienced the effects of it—was that Mr Menzies made enemies among many of the rank-and-filers in the UAP who, a year or two before, had gladly supported his bid for leadership. They may have been dull, straight-laced, earth-bound souls while the eagle soared above; but they were, nevertheless, the material out of which Parliamentary parties are made, so that whether by intention or omission, arousing their dislike was no formula for a long and tranquil period in leadership, war or no war.

These were precisely the men whom the genial, charming, gracious after-dinner speaker could not reach. Intellectually they were out of the world which Mr Menzies inhabited. But they had power, and when he had made enemies of them, they had all the hatred to impel the use of the power they had. Mr Menzies was brought down, finally, not by one big issue, but because his lesser but fatal natures, pursuing their irrational and unpredictable careers, undermined the otherwise solid structure of character and ability which belonged to the essential Mr Menzies.

He was always a difficult man to work with; his changing moods, his readiness to put urgent issues to one side, demanded strong nerves and iron patience in those who served him. He often tended to under-rate the abilities of his officers or his colleagues. He was a nightmare to his publicity man. At one time he would demand the evidence that the publicity man could shower him with publicity; but then he would withhold the essential information with which good publicity could be gained. This was not entirely to his discredit; he was too good an artist to be interested in fake, while he rarely sought publicity for publicity's sake; yet it did not make him the less difficult, for he would not proceed to the logical end of his attitude by doing away with a publicity depart-ment.

In many ways he was an admirable Parliamentarian, yet he tended to use Parliament rather as a dramatist uses the stage, for definite and explicit purposes, rather than in the truer Parliamentary sense of patient and painstaking routine work studded with occasional flashes of brilliance and controversy. Sometimes I wondered whether Mr Menzies ever really grasped the essential difference between Parliament and a court of law; in Parliament, after a speech of outstanding quality, there was often the queer feeling that eminent King's Counsel was gathering his robes, picking up his brief, bowing to the bench, and sweeping out to leave the judge to make up his mind.

Mr Menzies had 'presence', which gave him dignity without effort. He had a deep dramatic instinct, which taught him to seize the right moments for speaking in the House, the technique of dealing with interjectors, the rapier-like retort, cutting and sometimes cruel, the self-possession and self-awareness of the born actor. Perhaps his spirit half-belonged to the theatre; perhaps he would have found his truest self-expression there.

He had a beautifully modulated voice, full of power, music and charm. It may have lacked the passionate overtones of the truly great orator, but it was a perfect instrument for the mind behind it. Irony, wit, all the pastel shades of meaning, a genius for the right word, a fine constancy in holding the thread of an intricate line of argument, were all at his immediate command.

His one weakness in this field was that he seemed to speak from the head rather than the heart; a coldly-logical mind, rather than a vital and suffering spirit, so often seemed the source of his power. But within the wide octaves of its range, the Menzies voice could sooth, charm, embitter, castigate, destroy, ridicule. It could express a deep complexity of thought with a calm, onsweeping majesty which clothed all his speeches in a melodic beauty, common alike to the gay after-dinner address or the weighty pronouncement on a grave issue. This voice, with the superb capacity for controlled expression which went with it, were the outstanding public qualities in the first Australian Prime Minister of the second world war. Without it, he may have been a lesser man—or a greater! Part of the irony surrounding Mr Menzies was his enslavement to his own voice.

The Liberal Party's publicity machine worked hard at humanising their leader's image.

The columnist, David McNicoll, noted in the *Daily Telegraph* on 28 October 1949 that Labor MPs to whom he had spoken believed that the Liberals would have a far better chance in the forthcoming general election if Menzies were not their leader. McNicoll went on:

> But close political observers say that Mr Menzies is no longer an incubus to the Liberals. They say that the 1949 model Menzies—which has abandoned its shiny duco for rough paint, its antelope upholstery for slightly battered fabric, its purring Rolls Royce engine for more homely T-model Ford mechanism—is a vehicle which has started to appeal to the electors and has even won over thousands of the most vocal detractors.

A Liberal Party pamphlet produced for the 1949 election provided answers to the question 'HOW WELL DO YOU KNOW THIS MAN?'. He was 'a man of the people' who had 'made his own way in life'. A man of 'simple tastes', he 'has the typical Australian's love of sport'. And he was 'a fighter' pledged now to ban the Communist Party.'

From 1947 onwards, Menzies' strategy of attacking the Labor Party's 'socialist' policies was increasingly successful. The Gallup Poll analysis in October 1949 identified socialism as the chief issue of the election due on December 10, and 66 per cent of people were said to be opposed to more nationalisation of industry, including 46 per cent of Labor voters. A week before the election there were still 57 per cent opposing nationalisation, including a quarter of the confessed Labor voters. In interpreting voting intentions, Roy Morgan concluded that only 'a big and unexpected event, such as Labor discarding socialism, can now have much effect on the result of the Federal election'. What would people be deciding on December 10?

The polling day issue of *The Australian Women's Weekly* included a feature page on the policies of the Liberal and Labor Parties. Oddly, it was not the Prime Minister, Chifley, who presented Labor's case, but his deputy, Evatt:

LIBERAL: INCREASED PRODUCTION
By the Right Hon. R.G. MENZIES

Through economics and public finance have been commonly regarded as the special reserve of men, the people who have paid the greatest price for the false economic and financial doctrines of the past few years have been our wives.

Consider the matter of working hours, Is it not true that as men have worked shorter hours women have worked longer, and that as men have gained more leisure their wives have enjoyed less?

It is true that such problems as these cannot be completely solved by Act of Parliament. But it is indeed high time that attention was paid to those matters of interest to women.

In the joint Opposition policy speech I emphasised our determination, in co-operation with the States, to facilitate the training and provision of domestic workers so that the present burden on so many thousands of wives and mothers can be lightened.

Our plans for reducing the inflated cost of living were also stressed. This is probably the most worrying problem confronting the housewife to-day; the problem of getting a little more value out of the Labor-Socialist £.

Statisticians conservatively allow that the pound of 1939 is now worth only 12/2 in 'buying' power. But the average Australian housewife know only too well that it would be nearer to the mark to say it is worth only 10/-.

Prices can be reduced only if increased production of essential goods and commodities is achieved. We believe that increased production will be achieved as soon as workers realise that they will benefit directly by their additional effort. Under Labor-Socialist government, they have no such realisation or prospect.

Under the new non-Socialist Government, keen patriotic productive effort will be rewarded by incentive payments and profit-sharing.

But there is another angle. While encouraging production to the full, our Government will hold itself ready to pay price subsidies in appropriate cases; particularly in respect of items affecting the cost of living of basic wage earners.

Further, we have pledged ourselves not only to steady reduction in rates of taxation, but to a review of indirect taxation which so seriously affects cost of living and of housing.

Increased tax allowances for medical, dental, and similar expenses is another objective we will attain, together with increased allowances for educational costs.

I fear that the present Government has approached the vital problem of public health by looking for votes rather than for public welfare. At present it is at war with the medical profession.

We are utterly opposed to the Socialistic idea that medical service should become salaried government service, with all its implications, penalising skill and experience and destroying the vital personal relationship between doctor and patient.

We will increase the value of Social Services: and I wish to make it very clear where we stand on the question of child endowment. If the basic wage, whether increased in amount or not, remains on the same foundation as at present, we will give some extra help to families by providing an endowment of 5/- per week for the first child under 16 years, the second and subsequent children continuing to be endowed, as at present, at 10/- per week. If the foundation of the basic wage is altered and its amount is calculated by reference to the needs of a married couple without children, then we shall, of course, provide endowment for the first child on the 10/- rate.

LABOR: A PLANNED SECURITY
By the Right Hon. H.V. EVATT

The women of Australia are deeply concerned with two forms of security, at home, the safety of the family bread-winner in his job; abroad, the continuance of peace, to preserve the lives of sons, husbands, and sweethearts.

These two securities are the dearest concerns of the Labor Party.

The Prime Minister, in his policy speech, has told you that the protection of the community from want, unemployment, and insecurity, is our great objective.

On women, the heaviest burdens of unemployment fall. Many have the bitterest memories of the depression of the 'thirties, when the men of the family were out of work, and despair entered the bravest hearts.

The Labor Party will never accept the defeatist theory so often put forward that depressions are inescapable, that they spread out of repercussions from abroad, that once recession begins in the financial centres of the world it must lay its paralysis on industry in every corner of the world.

We believe that wise forethought and vigorous measures can cushion any shock to Australia's economy.

It is our resolve that Australian women shall never again have to spin out a dole in an attempt to put adequate meals on the family table and shoes on the children's feet, to face the shame of eviction for unpaid rent. Ours is no empty resolution. It is based on a practical programme.

A vast industrial and development programme has been drawn up. Should any overseas slump begin to show its effect here, these undertakings will immediately take up any slack of employment. Nobody will be left without work.

While everybody works, everybody buys. The money goes round to the grocer and the landlord; secondary industries which have expanded so much during the past ten years can keep on producing goods which consumers can keep on buying. By these means, this country can—and will—be protected against unemployment.

None of these works would be undertaken just to provide jobs. They are the schools, hospitals, houses, roads, and irrigation the country needs now, but for which it lacks the necessary manpower and materials. No country in the world has such a weapon against depression.

As a last word on employment—we reject with contempt the theory that a percentage of unemployment, small enough not to affect trade too badly, is essential to discipline the worker, who, such theorists say, works best when the fear of dismissal hangs over him.

We say the fear of unemployment is a nightmare thing that saps men's initiative, cows their spirit, and fouls the very air of freedom that is every Briton's heritage.

The Labor Party knows that, without peace abroad, its finest schemes for welfare at home are futile. In all the councils of the nations in which the Government has shared, it has looked for international understanding and settlement and lasting peace.

It will continue to do so, to save Australian manhood from the hours of war and Australian womanhood from the heartbreak war brings.

We, the Labor Party, have one fundamental principle—the betterment of the people. We aim to make Australia great by making it a better place for all Australians.

It was to be 23 years before a Labor government again had a chance to pursue this vision.

VI

THE MENZIES ERA?
1949–1966

THE 1949 ELECTION was a runaway success for the Liberal-Country Party alliance and a personal triumph for Menzies. He had come back on his own terms. The new House of Representatives—now enlarged from 74 to 121 members—had a 27-seat anti-Labor majority. But Labor managed to retain its Senate majority, as only half of the Senate seats were due to be contested. Though there were a few new faces and one or two old faces had gone, notably Billy Hughes, the new government had a familiar look about it. Arthur Fadden was Treasurer. Eric Harrison, a plain-spoken and loyal Menzies supporter, was Deputy Leader of the Liberal Party and held a variety of portfolios until he went to London as High Commissioner in 1956. Other senior posts were filled by Harold Holt, Percy Spender, Richard Casey, Philip McBride, and John McEwen. 'In power again', a writer for the popular magazine, *People*, reported on 22 November 1950, 'the Bob Menzies of 1950 shows just a few small traces of the rather condescending, superior Prime Minister of 1939'. The report went on:

At the recent Premiers' Conference his usual charm was not so much in evidence, and in his everyday dealings with Government officials, the Press and the humble citizenry he is a trifle less patient than he was as Leader of the Opposition. He has, of course, incalculably greater tasks and responsibilities than he had then, and less time to devote to the small things that loom important in the lives of many of his visitors. While they talk on and on, he cannot continue working or snatch a well-earned 'forty winks,' and sometimes the look of weary, resigned boredom that spreads over his mobile face makes his petitioners flush and go away more or less hostile.

In party and departmental circles he has become known as 'the boss,' and when he walks along the lobbies followed by buzzing respectful groups of advisers and helpers, he looks exactly that. There has been a noticeable smartening of dress on the higher levels of the Civil Service, in which it was thought hardly tactful to look too much like an elegant model from *The Tailor and Cutter* in the days when Prime Minister Chifley dressed as plainly as possible, and External Affairs Minister Evatt wore those deplorable hats and the knot of his tie away from centre. The new smoothness does not, however, herald the establishment of a cocktail-sipping, lazy-daisy, afternoon tea party hierarchy on the public payroll—everyone has to work very hard, indeed, and the Prime Minister himself is much too busy to care what they wear as long as they appear to wash and shave occasionally.

He and Mrs Menzies, who is a small greying, attractive woman with a flashing, whole-hearted smile, have, of course, re-opened the Prime Minister's Lodge, which was out of use during the Chifley regime. Their constant companions are a large, likable, but intensely self-satisfied white cat, and a fat, one-eyed dog of mottled ancestry, who does not belong to them, but who has 'adopted' the Lodge. The dog objects strongly to motor-cars and makes futile attempts to bite their front tyres off as soon as their engines start. Another acquisition is an English butler whose striped pants and silent service impress some visitors nearly out of their skins. An older helper is Stafford, the Prime Minister's driver, of whom Mrs Menzies says, warmly, 'He's a real friend.'

When Mr McKell was appointed Governor-General of the Commonwealth, Menzies expressed severe disapproval. But in contrast with his ever-loyal Deputy Leader of the Liberal Party, Eric Harrison, he has maintained the most cordial relations with Yarralumla and its occupant, and has let political bygones be bygones. The actions and statements of Deputy Leader Harrison and Speaker Archie Cameron must have embarrassed Menzies, and his expression has occasionally seemed to show inner disapproval of some of the more impetuous actions of Mr Cameron when in control of the House. But he refuses to get excited over such things, and nowadays it is difficult to the point of impossibility to trap him into saying anything that might create a breach in his ranks or widen a very narrow one. The smile with which he sidesteps 'curly' questions shows complete awareness of what his interrogator is trying to do, and sometimes a shade of appreciative amusement if the attempt has been a clever one. In the middle of 1949 there was astonishment on both sides of the House when Acting-

Speaker Clark suspended Menzies, following interruption of a speech by then Immigration Minister Arthur Augustus Calwell. Opportunity was rapidly created for readjustment of a situation in which one of the most courteous men ever to enter the House faced suspension, but it was not taken. The polished and polite *Ming* became the first Opposition Leader to be suspended since the fate overtook Sir Joseph Cook, in 1914.

A MODEL FOR YOUNG MEN

Though the value that is still leaking out of the pound is, perhaps, his main political worry, he is acutely aware that our currency and all our institutions could disappear out of the world altogether through unpreparedness in certain vital matters. A belief that he repeats from time to time he recently summed up admirably in the words, 'Righteous weakness will never prevent war being waged by unrighteous strength.'

His strong and pleasant radio personality was, ironically, detected and appreciated by most of his fellow-countrymen through listening to the parliamentary broadcasts begun by Labor, and the Prime Minister has been quick to realise the value of the medium in persuading the people to co-operate with the Government in the tasks ahead. However busy he may be with other matters he prepares each radio script he uses, so that not only the voice but every thought and turn of phrase shall be wholly his own.

On the personal level, as most of his parliamentary opponents have discovered, he is a man of wit, humor, and breadth of mind, whom it is extremely difficult to dislike.

Whether he will go down in history as a great Australian, or as a clever man who found the forces of his time too strong for him remains to be seen, but whatever happens it is certain that his complex and fascinating personality will be remembered and talked about as long as any of his contemporaries survive, and that in the fields of oratory and parliamentary behavior, at least, he will long be regarded as a model by many young men.

It was true that Menzies served as a model for some aspiring Liberal parliamentarians. But lacking his command of language and gesture, and not realising how much of his effect depended on a balance of fulfilled and frustrated audience expectations, his backbench emulators could not reproduce the essence of his style. Curiously, unlike Harold Macmillan in Britain, Menzies largely escaped the attention of radio and television satirists and impressionists. Perhaps this was simply a reflection of the chronic Australian dearth of that sort of comic talent. The Mavis Bramston Show was a brave exception. Managements were timid and politically hypersensitive. But it is tempting to conclude that somehow Menzies had managed to transcend satire. And, by consciously projecting an avuncular, and increasingly apolitical image, he had diminished the salience of politics in Australian life. Certainly, the longer he remained in office the more he seemed inclined to self-parody—a sure indication of his political security, if not necessarily of personal tranquillity.

With Menzies' return to power in 1949, there began what was later to be called 'the Menzies era'. Some of Australia's most discerning political journalists have wrestled with the problem of explaining Menzies' dominance. How could the man who had been so decisively defeated and discredited—a man who had seemed quite out of touch with the mood of the electorate—return to power and retain office for sixteen years? Donald Horne pungently expressed a widely held view when he wrote unflatteringly of Menzies, in 1964 as 'The Great Survivor'. Horne's portrait in his best-selling book, *The Lucky Country*, was severe. He was disappointed, as were many Australians, that Menzies failed to make better use of his talents and the opportunities presented by his prolonged ascendancy:

> It is a feature of Menzies's long rule that little of what he does seems to matter much. His great talent is to preside over events and look as if he knows what they are all about. His few active interventions have been mainly failures. He is a determined survivor—and even here he has been helped by the split in the Labor Party. It is a feature of his rule that most of the things in which he seemed to believe when he regained office in 1949 did not happen. His general posture in 1949 was one of 'free enterprise', support of British policies, anti-Communism, an interest in defence.* In his period of rule he has adopted many of the mechanisms of planning, if in a piecemeal way; the American alliance has been strengthened and the British connexion weakened; externally he has followed policies opposed to the expansion of Communist regimes in Asia, but, after a false start, (when he seemed to be making political capital out of it) there was less practical concern with domestic Communists than there was under Chifley; the proportion of national income spent on defence declined during most of his rule.
>
> The positive characteristics of his 'Age'—the spread of affluence, the considerable relaxation in social styles, the increase in national self assurance, the continued migration programme, the beginning of an interest in Asia and the growing tolerance of Asians resident in Australia, the demands of technology, the increasing power of overseas investment in Australia, are none of them the kind of thing that Menzies has 'stood for' and some of them are the opposite of what he said he hoped for before he came to power. When even Menzies appeared to be losing belief in the British connexion (at the time of the Common Market crisis) it is doubtful if he believed in anything anymore—except in himself. His attitude has been largely nostalgic; he has regretted much of what he saw of Australia in the 1960s. However he was stayed in power.

---

* His promise to develop the North in 1949 was so unfulfilled that he was able to make a similar promise in 1963 – and again do nothing about it. The North is like that.

He seems to believe that only he can run Australia. There was a period in the late forties and early fifties when Menzies seemed to believe in what he was doing, and it may be that at that stage, in his defence of 'liberalism', he was really saying what he thought. But for the most part ordinary Australians have held him in little regard: his elevation to the Order of the Thistle was treated as ludicrous; he is widely considered old-fashioned and has always been considered insincere. In personal image, where Menzies has scored has been against the even greater decrepitude in image of his opponent, Arthur Calwell. Time and again one hears young Australians say that they have no regard for Menzies but that Calwell with his ancient Labor rhetoric seems even more antediluvian—some relic of Early Man.

In judging statesmen one can take a reasonable view and judge a man by the possible, by the extent to which he associates himself with the likely and perhaps guides it, reforms where he can, crystallizes ideas and images, galvanizes the bureaucracy and seizes events and

With Speaker Sam Rayburn in the U.S. House of Representatives, 1 August 1950

incidents to make policy out of them. By this modest views of statecraft
one can say that since 1949 Menzies has seen few of the potentialities of
the age; that his reactions have usually been those of an old-fashioned
man guided by the vanishing standards of an earlier, more rural
community. In some ways at times he has seemed to reflect not even
the standards of his own generation, but of the one before him. Perhaps
when he was a young man making his way in the world those he admired
most were the Australian politicians who cherished the English
connexion. These were the real provincials: Melbourne gentlemen
who adopted what they took to be the standards of the far distant
metropolis. Throughout his career Menzies has stressed 'loyalty', by
which he does not seem to mean loyalty to Australia but to the British
connexion, and to the Monarch (when he was not referring to loyalty
to himself). He seems always to have associated himself with 'loyalty'
and the Labor Party with 'disloyalty'; even when the Curtin Government was defending Australia against the Japanese, in some of his
speeches Menzies seemed to be doubting its 'loyalty', by which he
meant not its conduct of a war to save the Australian nation, but its
attitude to the United Kingdom. If this interpretation is true it means
that throughout a period in which Australia has been in need of orientation towards Asia and towards technology it has been governed by
a man who has deeply absorbed the provincial standards of Melbourne
at the beginning of the century.

A complementary interpretation was offered by the veteran political
journalist, Don Whitington, when he wrote a preface to the revised
edition of his book, *The House Will Divide*, published in 1969:

In the golden years of the fifties, when Menzies had become a father-
figure to many Australians, especially New Australians, it was too
often forgotten that his successes were attributable only partly to his
own talents and political genius. Curtin's earlier dominance in the
Labor Party and Chifley's inability to fill the gap left by Curtin's
death; the resurgence of the extreme right wing of Labor once the
wartime emergency had ceased; the fear of the Catholic Action movement that the militant and ascendant Left that had emerged during
the war might supplant and destroy it in the Labor Party, and the
temperamental inadequacy of Evatt when confronted with these and
other major problems in the fifties, all contributed to the ultimate
triumph of the non-Labor forces that resulted in their unbroken
twenty odd years of power in the period that will be known to history
as the Menzies Era.

It was the Menzies Era because of Menzies' genius for capitalising
on the mistakes of his opponents and for heeding a public opinion
which once he scorned to recognise. Neither Menzies nor any of his
Governments produced great national policies or achievements that
will be remembered. In that sense, he was not an initiator. He was

content to build on the foundations pegged out and in some cases begun by Labor after the war . . .

For a man who for the first forty-five years of his life had displayed no apparent understanding of or sympathy with the wishes or sentiments of the masses, he displayed an extraordinary prescience, an almost clairvoyant knowledge of the thoughts and wishes of Australians and New Australians . . .

Quite cynically, he set out to give the public what it wanted. Cynically, too, and ruthlessly, he took advantage of every mistake his opponents made and every misfortune that befell them. Thus, with Labor's indecisions and divisions at the time of the Communist Party Dissolution Act, he precipitated a double disolution on a banking bill but used Communism as the real issue at the subsequent election. Again, in 1954 and 1955, Menzies precipitated elections in order to capitalise fully on the Petrov Royal Commission—another Communist scare that proved to be more shadow than substance.

For an Australian public obsessed more and more with making money and making a prisoner of prosperity before it fled; for New Australians who had known a generation of terror and persecution and poverty in Europe, Menzies represented the safe way, the Devil it knew. The mere mention of Communism, or any -ism at all, was enough to send the average voter, especially the New Australian voter, in a mad stampede to the Menzies corner.

Menzies set out also deliberately and systematically to destroy the men in Opposition he regarded as dangers to his own security, and was aided in this by the stubborn and intransigent attitudes of Labor leaders like Evatt, Ward and Calwell when it became obvious that Labor's bowyang days were past, and that a new-look younger generation would require a new-look Labor Party before it would be wooed from the Menzies mesmerism.

In those early years of the fifties, when wool prices soared to unprecedented heights and a hungry world was clamoring for the raw materials Australia could produce; when the political turmoil of Europe and Britain induced investors and speculators to turn thankfully to what appeared to be a prosperous and peaceful Australia, the Australian public developed an insistent, almost a greedy and certainly a selfish demand for comfort, well being, affluence.

It was a wish for more than security, which would have been venial. It was a wish that reflected the vulgar and almost avaricious hunger for riches of a voting public suddenly aware it possessed one of the wealthiest countries in the world, a country of huge untapped resources of water and power, minerals and oil, primary products and pulsating secondary industries.

Foreign policies and political philosophies were neglected or ignored in a rush of materialism. Men worked in two occupations at once; women put their children in creches and nurseries and went to work themselves. There came a craze for home ownership, for two cars to a family, for refrigerators and dish washing machines and electric

Press conference, Australia House, Tokyo, 14 August 1950 (Alan Whicker in striped suit; cousin, Harry C. Menzies, without jacket; Earnest Hoberecht, UPA correspondent, with bow tie)

kitchens, for television and transistor radios, for private swimming pools and for dining out at continental-type restaurants; for the American way of life with a dash of the Continent.

Wages soared, there was some inflation, hire purchase borrowings rocketed skywards, there were booms on the stock exchanges, and some busts and bankruptcies. The whole emphasis of living was on more and more luxury, more and more affluence, more and more selfish disregard of the pockets of poverty that still endured; an ever increasing desire to be soothed, tranquillised and protected from an unhappy world that was becoming clamant beyond the borders.

Over it all Menzies the dilettante, the Sybarite who loved luxury and leisure but scorned money, reigned supreme, paternal, aloof, distant now that his own position was assured, confident rather than arrogant, a father-figure to which a materialistic and irresponsible public was happy to delegate almost, but not quite, absolute power.

After his accession to power in Canberra, Menzies' personal popularity with Liberal and Country Party voters rose significantly. By March 1951 he was the first-choice leader of 75 per cent of non-Labor voters. Casey's following had slumped to 18 per cent; and Arthur Fadden, the Treasurer and Country Party leader—taking the odium for unpopular economy measures—had lost more than half of his support, a drop from 10 to 4 per cent. But even at this time Menzies was still not as strongly supported within his own camp as Ben Chifley was in his. Chifley's support was nine times greater (83 per cent) than his nearest rival, Evatt (9 per cent).

Some of the 1949 election promises were easier to fulfil than others. Bowsers could be filled with petrol even if value could not be put back into the pound. As for the disruption and alleged danger posed by Australia's communists—who numbered, it was said, not so many less than the number of Bolsheviks who had seized power in Russia in 1917—that too posed a major problem for the Government. The Communist Party Dissolution Act was struck down by the High Court in March 1951. In the general election campaign which followed in April and May, Ben Chifley (who had suffered a heart attack a few months earlier) dissected the Government's record. The previous Labor Government, he said, had *done* more against communism than Menzies who had been pushed into trying to ban the Communist Party by his Country Party allies. Menzies' real motive, Chifley claimed, was to fight the Senate, where Labor retained a majority. Whatever his motive, the Prime Minister did capture the Senate and proceeded to seek powers by referendum to suppress the 'active Communist conspiracy'. He failed.

Looking back after his retirement, Menzies told the Australian Broadcasting Commission's Peter Couchman that the one mistake he had made over the treatment of communism was being too candid in the referendum campaign and admitting that he was attempting to validate controversial clauses of his original legislation. 'If we had asked for power to deal with communists in a slightly different fashion the people would have voted for it.' Perhaps.

By the end of 1951, the Government could not have been pleased to learn that, while nearly two-thirds of the electorate still felt that something ought to be done to curb the influence of communists in Australia, communism was no longer a salient issue. It seemed that, unless there were disruptive strikes, and powerful anti-communist propaganda, the attention of the people was fixed on other issues.

Menzies must keep down living costs

The cost of living is THE problem the Government must solve this year, most people told the Gallup Poll in December.

Altogether 1500 people were asked what they thought was the biggest problem the Federal Government would have to tackle in 1952. Every 100 divide:—

48 said cost of living
8 said war, defence
7 said housing

5 said Communists
5 said trade recession
4 said production
3 said taxation
2 said financing public works
2 said food scarcities
7 gave other answers
9 could not answer.

Those who referred to the cost of living comprised 51 out of every
100 Labor voters and 47-in-the-100 of Liberal-CP voters.

Most who said production, Communists or defence was the chief
problem were Liberal-CP voters.

Most who referred to housing and trade recession were Labor voters.

An amazing change in public thinking is disclosed by the following
comparison between the most frequent answers listed above and
answers in a similar survey in May, 1950:

	1950 p.c.	1952 p.c.
Living costs	10	48
War, defence	—	8
Housing	14	7
Communists	45	5

So severe was the recession that even those in the business community who most trusted the Prime Minister became alarmed. The
President of the Building Industry Congress of New South Wales wrote
personally to Menzies on 28 February 1952 to warn him of the changing
mood in the building industry:

A little while ago it would have been possible to divide our Executive
into two schools of thought:
(1) Give Menzies a Go
(2) The Economists are getting out of hand

The pro-Menzies group was heartened by your own public and
private assurances that you recognise the building industry as key
to a stable economy—'the barometer of prosperity'—demanding
every possible encouragement. We believed that you aimed to assist
essential industries by making it easier for them to get labour as
released from non-essential undertakings.

Another sound argument in favour of your policy was that men
would 'stay put' in vital jobs when they couldn't walk down the street
and get a start elsewhere; they would also be inclined to work a bit
harder and so justify their retention. Our people did, in fact, make
out a remarkable case for the Menzies policy until the time came when
stark realities put an end to all the theorising. We had interim arguments
with State authorities whose political tactics had complicated the

issue. Our public statements were designed to assist you as you no doubt observed.

My own feeling is that your 'credit machine' is itself out of control. On the one hand we have your assurance that the Government does not intend to hurt or restrict this key industry and on the other irrefutable evidence that our basic industries *are* being grievously hurt and that the building rate is dropping daily. . . .

No doubt you will consult your advisers on this question to gain confirmation of the fact the there *is* a grave crisis in this industry. I do not presume to suggest a remedy as I believe your original plan must have included provision for relief to essential industries if and when required. Please believe that the time has arrived and our position is desperate.

In conclusion, may I say that most of us have every confidence in your ability to put things right; we feel, too, that you will waste no time about it.

How did the Government react to business pressure? Stewart Cockburn, Menzies' Press Secretary at the time, said in *The Bulletin* on 24 March 1954:

Again and again in the past two years pressure-groups in industry, in commerce and in the trade-unions have all-but beaten Menzies.

Some members of his own Cabinet would tend to panic in the face of strong public statements by these interests, prominently featured in the Press, and heavily backed by the Press itself, editorially, or in the treatment of material in the news-pages. Again and again Menzies has stiffened his colleagues to resistance in what he believed was the proper cause.

Of course, he had staunch and loyal allies, as well as waverers, inside the Cabinet. But the dissidents had no want of opportunity to express their views. For his control of Cabinet proceedings is said to be loose enough to permit every Minister, if he wishes, to air his particular views on any subject under discussion at some length.

This is commendable in terms of free speech. And it anticipates any complaint by Ministers that their Prime Minister is a 'dictator' in Cabinet. On the other hand, it slows the rate of decisions; and Cabinet, in the last few years, has too often risen with its agenda-paper far from clean.

Chifley, I have heard it said by senior public servants, was a more ruthless master of his Cabinet than Menzies, particularly during the last year or two of Labor rule. This, however, made for greater Cabinet efficiency, even if decisions too often bore the stamp of one man alone.

Like the late Lord Balfour, Prime Minister of Great Britain at the beginning of this century, Menzies is said to be masterly in his exposition inside Cabinet of the advantages and disadvantages of any proposed course of action. He can listen to a colleague's long exposition of a problem, seize upon the good and bad points in it, and produce a summary which is of utmost value in leading to a conclusion.

On the other hand, it is said that his drive is not always as strong in Cabinet as it could be. And his many successful efforts to avoid conflict within the Executive are frequently made at the cost of speedy decision.

Yet who knows whether this weakness, if weakness it be, is not a product of the exigencies of coalition government.

For the Liberal–CP coalition has been kept indissolubly united on the Cabinet- and Parliamentary-level since 1949 not by the bludgeon but by prodigies of skill and tact and delicate judgment which in themselves perhaps constitute the supreme tribute to Menzies's final mastery of the art of true leadership.

Prodigies of skill, and delicate judgement were not Menzies' only resources. The bludgeon did not have to be used to be effective. The power and authority of a Prime Minister, however unpopular he might be, are immense. The kind of discontent in Sydney that might once have threatened Menzies' position could be treated with disdain by a Prime Minister. Subterranean moves to promote Sir Percy Spender were futile. Rumours that Menzies might be persuaded to retire could be dismissed with unconcealed contempt. Stewart Cockburn reported Menzies' remarks to a private meeting of Liberals:

'The other day,' he said, . . . 'I picked up an eminent journal published in this city [it was Lang's 'Century'] which explained with loving care that this was my golden moment. I could become Governor-General or I could become Chief Justice.

'Gentlemen, the best answer I can give to you at this private meeting —because otherwise I like to keep the Press guessing—is:

'So much do I believe that this task [of defeating inflation and putting the principles of Liberalism back into Australia's economic and social life] remains to be done, and that it is my duty to do it, and to succeed, or to fail and take the rap, that wild horses wouldn't induce me to take either of those posts. "He that setteth his hand to the plough and looketh back" is not fit for the Kingdom of Heaven. And I haven't set my hand to the plough, as I set it in 1943, to take it away again because there are a few ruts and stones and obstacles in the furrows. . . . I believe that what we as a Government are doing is right. And so far as I am concerned I am going to see it through.'

Long before this speech, however, I knew his mind very well on the subject of candidature for the next appointment as Governor-General. As far back as August, 1952, when the speculation in regard to himself had barely started, he said to me in his office one night:

'A whispering campaign has begun with the object of having me transferred to the office of the Governor-General, or of Chief Justice.

'Now, the reasonable, thinking man knows without being told that, if I wished to do so, I could perhaps become Governor-General on the retirement of Sir William McKell; or, if I wanted to do so, that

At Hatfield House, home of Lord
Salisbury, Coronation Year: an ad-
justment to Heather Menzies' camera

Going 'home'—near the Gaur hydro-
electric scheme, July 1955

I could become Chief Justice when Sir John Latham's retirement
becomes effective next April.

'I have no wish or intention in respect to either position. So when
he sees in due course that I have not become either Governor-General
or Chief Justice the reasonable man will say: "Evidently he did not
wish for such appointments." The stupid or the malicious man will
say, however: "We frightened him out of taking them."'

The Prime Minister paused, then turned to me and smiled.

'One of the mistakes that people make in this life,' he said, 'is in
paying too much attention to the stupid and to the malicious.... It
is only the sensible and reasonable person who should be taken
seriously.'

Menzies, of course, had no thought of retiring. Who, after all,
would replace him? He did not have a very high opinion of his associates
and subordinates, as the new editor of *The Sydney Morning Herald*,
J.D. Pringle, learned in Canberra on 24 September 1952:

... McMahon, the young and ambitious Minister for the Navy
and Air, gave us a dinner at which several Ministers were present,
but before that Menzies saw us privately and then took us down to the
dinner where I sat next to him. The Prime Minister was in rather a

depressed mood, partly because of the present difficulties of the Government and partly because of the violent attacks by *The Herald* on the Treasurer, Sir Arthur Fadden, but he soon thawed and was both friendly and charming. He is an impressive man, still handsome though too fat, with an obvious but easy intellectual brilliance that makes him outstanding in this country. I found myself quickly talking to him as I would have done, say, at [*The Times'*] Tuesday lunch in London. He was very bitter—and very amusing—about the lot of a Prime Minister in Australia—badgered by the press, always expected to hob nob with every politician, and hampered by inefficient advisers and staffs. He said that a matter never came up to Truman until it had all been cut and dried so that he had only to make a simple choice between A and B and then put it in his Out tray where it was taken away and put into force. Here, he said, a Prime Minister was expected to think of the idea, draft the report, persuade his cabinet, bully his party, push it through Parliament and act as chief publicity officer in the country. Even after that he still had to see that it was carried out —the most difficult of the lot. Menzies did not add, what is usually said, that this is just where he commonly fails.

If it was still correct to say, early in the 1950s, that Menzies was often unsuccessful as a propagandist, it was probably also true to attribute something of this failure to his lingering platform inhibitions. Stewart Cockburn noted:

His internal emotions when speaking in public are frequently intense, and his efforts at self-control tremendous. Occasionally his self-control fails. When that happens, he suffers not a little for having 'worn his heart on his sleeve'.

A comparatively recent occasion on which, however, Menzies did abandon much of his usual self-control was at a political meeting at the Rivoli Hall, Hurstville, Sydney, in February 1953, when he was speaking in support of a candidate at the N.S. Wales State elections.

One of the Labor party's principal prongs of attack in this campaign was the alleged injustice of the Commonwealth Government's attitude to N.S. Wales demands for millions of pounds more money for public works. Menzies was so angry at the repetition of what he regarded as grossly dishonest allegations made for political purposes that he 'let himself go,' and his audience was emotionally stirred as I had seldom seen one of his audiences stirred before.

Another occasion on which, plainly moved, he communicated his own emotion to his audience was at the Ashfield Town Hall, Sydney, on April 17, 1953, during the course of the Senate campaign.

His audience was predominantly Liberal, and he found it responsive. He had had a bad day—up at 5.45 a.m. in Brisbane; an early flight to Sydney; interviews during the morning; a snack for lunch soon after midday; a meeting at the Assembly Hall at 1 p.m. at which he spoke for an hour; interviews and a 'miniature Cabinet' meeting in the afternoon; the news that the Government candidates had drawn the worst position on the ballot-paper in the vital State of Queensland; and, to cap it all, the announcement that the basic wage had again risen more than he had hoped—3s. in Sydney, 7s. in Hobart—on the eve of a crucial election.

He was in the heart of the capital where he has always commanded least personal support in Australia. He was tired. He had been subjected all day to colleagues' forebodings of disastrous defeat. And at the meeting in Ashfield he said something which convinced me—though he would probably never admit it—that in his heart he had conceded the Senate a lost cause.

An interjector had charged him with 'wasting his time', and the jibe touched a vital nerve in his sensibilities.

'Sir,' he retorted, 'believe me, you don't waste your time, *even if you waste your life*, in politics.'

It was a moment of agony impossible to describe. And he went on:

'For 25 years, with such intelligence and energy as I possess, I have devoted myself to the service of my people and of my country. I don't think anyone has seriously impugned my honesty. I don't think anyone has seriously said: "This man has some indirect motive". I may on occasions have been wrong. But I have not believed myself wrong. And I tell you quite frankly—whichever way votes may come and go I shall go on doing what I think is right and good for the people of Australia.'

What was 'right and good' for the people of Australia? For some of the people it was taking an unequivocal stand in the great world ideological conflict of the post-war era, and fighting communist North Koreans and Chinese in Korea.

For others it was fighting communists at home. This domestic activity had the double attraction of amplifying the Government's commitment to the 'free world' side in the cold war, and of identifying a scapegoat for the vicissitudes of the economy. On 18 March 1953, in the eighth of a series of broadcasts entitled 'Man to Man—Australia Today' (a title that twenty years later would have been assailed as the epitome of male chauvinism), Menzies spoke on the subject of industrial peace and communism. It was just a little over a year before he was to announce the explosive news of the defection and revelations of the third secretary at the Soviet embassy, Vladimir Petrov:

Good Evening, Ladies and Gentlemen:

Occasionally I hear suggestions that the Commonwealth Government has forgotten about the Communists and the Communist menace. Perhaps the best way to deal with suggestions so wide of the truth would be to put a few questions and give a few answers.

Question: Why doesn't the Government outlaw the Communist Party instead of letting it go about its work under the protection of the law?

Answer: We endeavoured to outlaw it under the Communist Party Dissolution Act. The High Court said we had no Constitutional power to do so. We then promoted a referendum to alter the Constitution to give us the power. The people refused it. So we can't pass an Act making Communism illegal.

Question: Why doesn't the Government proceed under the Crimes Act to secure an order against the Communist Party?

Answer: Because we could not offer proof under the technical rules of the law without exposing the whole of our Security Organisation, its members and its sources of information to the Communists. And we are not going to do that.

I can assure you that we know what they are doing, we have the fullest sources of information, but we are not going to tell the Communists how we know.

Question: Does this mean that nothing can be done to hinder the work of the Communists and that they may just run free?

Answer: Not at all. Look what we have done through the secret ballot! We passed a law, hotly opposed by Dr Evatt and his supporters, to provide for ballots to be conducted by the Arbitration Court. This procedure, designed to help anti-communist groups in the unions, has been used many times and many Communists have been democratically swept out of office.

Question: Has this helped to secure industrial peace and therefore increase production?

Answer: It certainly has. In 1951, when there was such a demand for labour that there were more jobs than men and industrial troubles might well have been common, less time was lost through industrial stoppages than for 10 years. Do you remember our opponents' prophecy at the 1951 election that there would be a 'national upsurge of industrial unrest' if the Menzies Government were re-elected? Well, last year's record of industrial peace was the best since the war. It prompted the Chief Concilation Commissioner to say only a few months ago that 'at present the country is freer of industrial disturbances than for many years past'.

The astonishing increase achieved in national production is directly related to industrial peace, to continuity of work, and to the reduction of the power of the Communists. It is the overwhelming reason why gas rationing, power rationing, black-outs and interruptions of work which were taken as common-place three years ago have ended.

Question: Apart from the Secret Ballot, has the Government exercised its limited power firmly and promptly?

Answer: We certainly have. In 1950, for instance, the Communist-led Waterside Workers' Federation adopted what has been called in Communist jargon 'the rolling strike'. That is a strike aimed at tying up individual ships in successive individual ports in order to cripple our overseas trade. When the 'rolling strike' first manifested itself in Queensland we acted quickly. Twice, we proclaimed the anti-strike industrial provisions of the Crimes Act. Each time, work was resumed immediately. Again in 1951, a dispute occurred in the coalfield over incentive payments to coal miners. The last thing that the Communist wants is production incentives for, on behalf of his foreign principals, he wants to keep production in the democratic countries down. Successful contempt proceedings were instituted in the Arbitration Court against three miners' leaders, two of them Communists. We also raided certain Communist officials' offices to secure evidence of their plans. We used the Army for loading operations in Melbourne and the Air Force for loading at Geelong. Volunteer labour loaded sugar for New Zealand in Mackay and various de-registration proceedings were initiated in the Arbitration Court. It is fair to say that by such action consistent pressure has been kept up against the Communists and their authority in the trades unions substantially diminished.

Question: As the Communists have constantly argued in favour of direct action that the Arbitration machinery was too slow, what has the Government done about that?

Answer: We have acted to remove legitimate dissatisfaction with the Arbitration system. We have appointed addional judges to the Arbitration Court to speed up the settlement of major disputes. When our predecessors appointed a great number of Conciliation Commissioners and provided that their decisions should not be

Sartorial smargasbord: Fadden, Townley, Holt, and Harrison, with their chief

subject to appeal, I correctly prophesied that the unions themselves
would soon complain. Indeed, they did complain. Last year, we
amended the Act to provide for a restricted form of appeal. Matters
of great principle are now determined by the Court itself. Our
amendments, strongly opposed by the present Opposition, are
proving very helpful to the trades union movement.

Apart from all this, we have positively, constantly and constructively
sought to build up good industrial relation. Within the limits imposed
upon us, we have, particularly through my colleague, Mr Holt, the
Minister for Labour, continually sought industrial and trade union co-
operation; and I am happy to say that the trades union movement has
co-operated splendidly on a great many issues. We have emphasized
that the prosperity of employer and employee is indivisible and that
rising standards of living depend upon a genuine co-operation in
increased productive effort. The measure of our success is that there is
now less evidence than for many years of the kind of blind warfare
which in earlier days so damaged the real prosperity of both Australian
industries and Australian workers.

True, you will still hear some people exaggerating unemployment
because they believe that an unemployment scare will harm my
Government. It is a treacherous sort of scare, because nothing harms
employment and prosperity more than unfounded fears of the future.
While all unemployment is unhappy, and I have the deepest sympathy
for any willing worker who finds himself temporarily unable to get a
job, recent real unemployment in Australia has been quite small and
is now being rapidly reduced. Barring a nation-wide drought or other
unforeseen disaster it can, I think, be taken as certain that such unemployment as we have had will continue to diminish and that with the
growing solidity of the Australian economy, production and business
should become increasingly active in the months ahead.

My colleagues and I, as political people, do not resent criticism.
Criticism of a Government may be good, but if it simply tries to create
a groundless fear about the future it goes far beyond damaging the
Government. It becomes a self-inflicted wound upon the well-being of
the entire community.

As always in these quiet talks to you about our problems, I invite
you, my friends, to discard the heated views of violent partisans, and
soberly consider the supreme interests of our country and of our children. For we are not dealing only with today; we have a great responsibility for tomorrow.

Menzies spoke often and spoke well. He reached millions over the
radio, thousands at public meetings, and hundreds—often strategically
placed business and community leaders—at more intimate and informal
meetings. On 10 April 1954, he took 'a representative gathering' of
Melbourne businessmen into his confidence—or so they no doubt felt—
and told them something of his political philosophy:

Political people like myself read all kinds of things. If I get a chance I like to read Ngaio Marsh's last detective story. But failing that, and failing that means, probably, occasionally for a period of three months, it is my great fortune or misfortune to read blue books, to read Treasury Reports, to read the last statistics, to read the Cabinet Papers, and although they are very important, every now and then every man who has great responsibilities in his own country ought to be lifted up out of the particular into the general. He ought every now and then to be given the opportunity of saying: 'Well, that's right, I think I'm right, I've made this decision and that decision and that decision, but now let me take two or three days to consider how all that fits into the pattern of what I regard as my own philosophy.' That I think is tremendously important.

What we need in Australia, what is needed in all free countries, is a body of men who don't set themselves up to say that the government is always right or that the government is always wrong, because, speaking as one with a fairly long experience in these fields, I know, nobody better, that a government is not always right, that if a government can feel that it is right most of the time, and what's much more important, always feel that it was honest about what it did, even if it turned out to be wrong, that is as much as any mortal man in public affairs may aspire to.

And if we have a general philosophy on these matters then we can test things by it. If we feel that any government, even a government that we like in the broad, is wrong judged by that yardstick, then we will say so, and I don't think that any intelligent political man objects to that.

A philosophic line, a body of principle, and if I may say so, gentlemen, our great danger in Australia and we are nearer to it at this moment than we perhaps ever were before, is that we should abandon political principle in favour of a series of purely ad captandum arguments. 'That's worth some votes, that ought to bring somebody in.' Look, of all the menaces in the political world, that is the worst. If you stand on a basis of principle you may go wrong but you will never go far wrong. You may go wrong according to the current political judgement, but in the long run somebody will be heard to say: 'That was right.' I know that we are all human and most of us, I suppose, like to feel that we will be given credit in six months or twelve months or two years, for something that was right. I don't want to appear to be a self-righteous person—I hope I'm not. But if I did something today which I thought was dead right for this country and they threw me out, like that, I'd rather like to think that in 30 years time, when I've been dead and buried, the fellows who wrote the records would say: 'That was right.' You see, political principle, a genuine philosophy, a genuine body of doctrine in your own mind, not an academic body of doctrine but that warm instructive feeling that decent men have that that's right. That's the most important thing in public affairs.

The greatest problem in politics is I suppose assumed to be the problem
of whether you win a by-election or lose it, or whether you win a general
election or lose it, and if that's the greatest problem in politics then
let me tell you that politics is just not worth while. Because in Australia
we have a general election for the Lower House every three years and
when we're two years old, under the present circumstances, there will
be a Senate election and a year later there will be a general election for
the Lower House, and in the meantime, there have been six State
elections and in the meantime, there have been by-elections. I don't
think anybody in Australia has yet fully realised how utterly inconsistent
with good government this plenitude of elections can be. If we're going
to have good government in Australia it's high time that we had parliaments that lasted for five years. It's high time that we put people into
offie and said to them: 'You have five years in which to give effect to
your policy.' But so far as I'm concerned I've been in Parliament, and I
don't apologise for it, for 25 years, and in that time I must have fought
13 or 14 elections. This is monstrous! It's terrible! Just as you're about
to get people to understand that this is the thing that ought to be done
over the next five years somebody says: 'Wait a moment, there's an
election in six months time or twelve months time and people won't
like it.'

Well, that creates great difficulties. But might I try, gentlemen, to say
something to you about the classical choice that confronts us. We can
politically have principles with no sense of expediency or we can have
expediency with no sense of principles. That's what some people say.
I'm putting it inaccurately but I'm putting it in a stark form. There are
those who say to us: 'Principle without expediency'; and there are
others who say: 'Expediency without principle'. This is a masterpiece of
modern thinking. It's the perfect, false dichotomy that you're presented
with all round the world. You're either in favour of A or you're in favour
of B. It's hardly ever true. It is not true to say that if you have principle
you can never consider expediency. It's damnably untrue to say that if
you bow a little to expediency then you must abandon principle. A very
much greater authority than myself, or anyone else in this room, said:
'All things are just, but all things are not expedient.' What we have to
discover is how to pursue principle, how to pursue what is just. And
when we accommodate ourselves to the expediency of current events
let us regard it as a mere side-current which doesn't blow us off our
course but from which we can always return to what we think to be right.

That I believe, Mr Chairman, is the greatest problem of politics. And
one of the great troubles about politics is that those who, for their sins,
like myself, are in the middle of it, living with it, sleeping with it, year
by year, sometimes feel disposed to say, when we read the words of
some critic: 'If only he knew about these matters.' You see, I'm not
asking to be free of criticism, and nobody thrives more on it than I do.
I welcome criticism, I welcome complaint, I welcome grievance. But I
would have a very poor opinion of myself, if, having set my course by

a star and being aside by some temporary storm, I then decided to retrace my course. When you are blown aside by a storm, well, you must recognise it and, to that extent, you go with the storm, but always at the end you must take your bearings and resume your course. That's the hardest thing in public life, and because that's the hardest thing in public life, because that's the hardest thing in public administration, it's terribly important that people like myself, who have devoted their years to political affairs, should know that there are men, honest, upright, able, experienced men who, from time to time, sit down and say: 'That is our body of principle.' And say why it is, and collect the facts, and make objective judgements. And the whole thing is that, with all the rough weather and the cross currents and so on, politics is not worth being in if when you leave it you find that what you think is good for your country is further astern than when you went into it.

Never forget that the leader of a party, and a fortiori, the leader of a government, frequently is over-ruled. Time after time I have submitted views that have been over-ruled. What am I to do? Am I to break up the Cabinet every time I'm in a minority? Am I to convert steady government in Australia into a sort of French government system in which governments flicker and flow week by week, month by month? Of course not! When I find that the overwhelming view of the Cabinet is that something should be done, then, unless it is a matter of principle on which no man ought to forswear himself, I accept it and I go into the House and I put it, and I go on to the platform and I'll fight anybody about it. This is practical politics. And unless we had that kind of thing we would have such uncertainty of policy and administration that this country would be as unstable as, I am unhappy to say, France is and in the case of France with such disastrous results in the world.

Please remember that, gentlemen, you can't always have your own way in this life. But what helps me a great deal is not to have a man who arrests me and bashes my ear about some interest of his and throws out a broad hint that unless the government decides his way he's against it. I've no time for that and I'd like to say to everybody that I'm utterly unmoved by it. But what I do like to think is that in this great city, with all its sanity and balance and responsibility, a responsible man, a leading man here, can say to me: 'So and so' and if I say: 'I'm sorry I can't do that', he will not at once go away and become an enemy and whisper in dark corners. But he will go away, and say: 'Well, after all I can't have that. What do I really believe in? What do I stand for?'

Sir, I'm sorry to have spoken so long and I'm sorry to have become like a man delivering a sermon. But this is one of those rare opportunities. Gentlemen, I invite you to consider that basic matter. If it's all expediency, if it's all what will win votes next week or next month, you don't need me. There are much better phonograph records than myself. All you need is a few humble, obedient time-servers and if those are what you want, you'll get them. There is something about Divine Providence which is magnificent. We get in the longrun what we want and if we want time-servers, and if we want vote-catchers, if we want short-term 'pleasers', let them have them.

But you know, if politics were really a matter of occupying a job, how many of us would be in it? Did anybody suppose that a man like myself who loves the law, and the practice of the law, and the whole philosophy of the law, would go into this turbulent stream, for a job? A job! Of course not! And what I ask you to realise is that people like myself— and I'm not the only one—go into this life because they have beliefs, because they have a faith, because they believe there is something that matters for their own country. And if they believe that, then don't be beguiled by this false choice expediency or principle. Remember always that a great deal of principle and, occasionally, a little expediency, is much better than impracticable principle and a million times greater than unprincipled expediency.

One of the most controversial episodes of 1955 was the imprisonment by the House of Representatives of Raymond Fitzpatrick, a Bankstown building contractor, and the Sydney journalist, Frank Browne. The Prime Minister incurred great odium from civil liberties advocates for using the power of parliament to punish two men for what many observers believed to be matters that involved no breach of parliamentary privilege. Frank Green, as Clerk of the House of Representatives, was an anxious participant in these events:

In April 1955 the *Bankstown Observer*, a free advertising newspaper circulated in Bankstown, owned by Raymond Fitzpatrick and edited by Frank Browne, published an article under the caption 'MHR and Immigration Racket', which the Labor Party member for Reid, Charles Albert Morgan, a Bankstown solicitor, claimed was defamation of himself. He brought the matter before the House as one of privilege. After Browne had written two articles on Morgan's 'immigration racket', Morgan brought the matter before the House as one of privilege, and the House referred it to the Committee of Privileges for a report. The allegations against Morgan were in respect of matters connected with his legal practice before he entered Parliament. In any case, whether he was, or was not at that time a Member of Parliament, the test of privilege as laid down in *May's Parliamentary Practice* is that the allegations have to be a libel on the member in respect of his conduct inside the four walls of the Chamber of the House, or in a Committee of the House. May says:
'To constitute a breach of privilege, a libel upon a member must concern the character or conduct of the member in that capacity, and the conduct or language on which the libel is based must be actions performed, or words uttered in the actual transaction of the business of the House.'
Usually the Clerk of the House advises the Committee of Privileges whether in his opinion privilege is involved. In this case I had no

hesitation in advising the Committee, in writing, that it would be absurd if parliamentary privilege protected a member against allegations in respect of his actions outside the Chamber of the House; it was not a matter of privilege; and the civil courts were open to him.

I had hoped that my advice would have influenced the Committee to end the matter by reporting to the House that no matter of privilege was involved, but the Committee decided to invite Morgan to give evidence. This evidence has never been published. He also tendered copies of the *Bankstown Observer*, from which it appeared that the whole matter was a local clash between two factions which were making allegations of corruption against each other. There was nothing new in any of these allegations; those against Morgan had been made in the House by a Minister of the Menzies government in 1941, and those against Fitzpatrick had been aired by Morgan whenever he got a chance to make his charges under the protection of parliamentary privilege.

After hearing Morgan the Committee decided to take the matter further, and accordingly reported to the House asking for authority to consider further articles in the *Bankstown Observer*. When the request came before the House a motion was moved by a private member that the Committee's request be agreed to, but the government members refused to agree to this course, and Sir Eric John Harrison, Leader of the House, moved the adjournment of the debate on which the House was divided, the government parties voting for the adjournment. After the division had been taken I was informed that the Prime Minister desired to see the evidence. I thereupon assumed that I had no need to concern myself further with the matter, for the Prime Minister would be unable, in my opinion, to find any breach of privilege, and would probably inform the Committee of his opinion. However, my judgement was wrong; four days later the adjourned debate was resumed and the Committee was given permission to proceed to search for a breach.

At that stage I confided to some of my colleagues that I was very disturbed. I told them I could find no case of a breach of privilege, but there was something in the background I could not understand, as if somebody was conspiring and using the Committee to get at somebody else. I went to certain members on both sides of the House and said: 'Tell me, what is behind all this?' None of them knew; it was obviously over the heads of the back-benchers, who would be instructed how they were to vote in due course. As a last resort, I went up to the Press Gallery and talked to two senior men who generally knew what was going on. I learned from them that both Prime Minister Menzies, and Arthur Calwell, the Deputy Leader of the Opposition, were against Browne, who had earned their dislike by using his news-sheet *Things I Hear* to their detriment. Apparently Browne had been a Liberal Party candidate for the Barton seat held by Evatt, and when he failed to win the seat Menzies had been unpleasant to him, with the result that, whenever he had an opportunity, Browne ridiculed Menzies in his journal. They showed me a very recent copy of *Things I Hear* in which the following appeared:

Not Eligible

'In his desire to hog the limelight on all possible occasions, Prime Minister Menzies leaves himself open for a riposte. This week, trying to get a little reflected glory out of the Test-match, he said that if he got to Valhalla he wanted to find a cricketer on either side of him.

'Tut, tut, Bob. Your knowledge of Norse mythology can't be as bad as all that. Valhalla is a *Warriors* paradise. You tore up your admission ticket way back in 1914.

'Incidentally, the blurb about him being "a natural for Television" seemed to misfire. That is, unless they want him to play Dorian Gray.'

After reading this I saw the light—Menzies was after revenge. However, in the hope that reason might prevail, I prepared a further and more detailed opinion in which were set out some House of Commons cases in which successive Speakers had refused to allow matters of privilege to be raised in respect of allegations against members of improper conduct and even of criminal offences in their professional and business activities. I also addressed a memorandum to the Chairman of the Committee stating that, in my opinion, the Committee should report to the House without delay that no breach of privilege was involved.

The Committee disregarded my advice and summoned Fitzpatrick and Browne to appear before them. They came, accompanied by a barrister and a solicitor. The Committee met, and rejected a request by these two men that their legal advisers be allowed to appear with them. However, they went before the Committee as willing witnesses. They were not warned that anything they said might be used against them. The members of the Committee included a Queen's Counsel, Percy Ernest Joske, who asked Fitzpatrick if he published this matter to intimidate Morgan in the course of his public duties, to which Fitzpatrick replied: 'That was our idea.' It is very doubtful whether Fitzpatrick knew the meaning of the word 'intimidate'. Outside his business activities, he appeared to be an ignorant man. He apparently thought he was merely hitting back at a man who was consistently hitting at him from behind parliamentary privilege. To the few questions put to him by Joske, which are published in the Report, he replied: 'Yes.' He gave the impression that he did not fully understand the questions and to save trouble took the easy course of saying 'Yes' and agreeing with everybody. If ever a man under examination by a barrister needed legal representation, that man was Raymond Fitzpatrick. He had asked for legal representation; it had been refused him; so out of his own mouth this man who had come as a willing witness was convicted without being charged of a breach of privilege in attempting to intimidate a Member of Parliament.

However, the Committee reported to the House that a breach of privilege had occurred in that an attempt had been made through newspaper articles to influence and intimidate a member. The Prime Minister then moved that the Report be agreed to; this motion was carried, after debate.

The House then ordered that Fitzpatrick and Browne appear before the Bar of the House at 10 a.m. next morning. The House then adjourned. Later that night I learned that the decision was not to be left to the House; Cabinet had already decided that the two men were to go to gaol; the government coalition parties would endorse this decision of Cabinet, and they had a majority in the House. I felt that this final action would shake the Australian people when they realized that citizens had been deprived of their liberty without benefit of the normal safeguards and processes of law.

I went to Parliament House next morning pondering over what might be done to avert what I considered disgraceful proceedings. About half past nine two well-known barristers from Sydney, John W. Shand and A.F. Mason, came to my room; they asked if they could appear for Browne and Fitzpatrick at the Bar. I told them that only one man—Menzies—could decide that. Parliament would have probably allowed it, but the Prime Minister had taken control of the matter, and Parliament had to do as he ordered. They then asked if they could see the Prime Minister before the House met. I left them and went to the Prime Minister's room, waiting there until he arrived a few minutes before ten o'clock. I asked him to see Shand and Mason before the House met. He said he would let me know in a few moments. He could see that I deplored the whole business, but I was anxious for them to meet for I believed that in such a meeting might be the only chance of finding a way out of the mess. I waited for five minutes, and then Menzies came out and said: 'No, I won't see them; I know all their arguments.' By the time I returned to my room the assembly bells were ringing and Shand and Mason had robed in anticipation. I told them of Menzies' reply to their request, and then walked along the corridor entering the Chamber as the bells stopped.

The scene in the House that morning is something I would like to forget. I prefer to think of the House in its great moments in the past when it reflected the mind and the will of the Australian people. Fitzpatrick was brought in, told that he had been found guilty of a serious breach of privilege, and asked if he had anything to say in extenuation. He asked permission for his counsel to speak for him. He was told that he could speak in person, but not through his counsel. He was abject, and faltered this:

'I would like to apologise to the House for what I did. When the article was published in the newspaper I had no idea it was against parliamentary privilege. I have apologised.'

He was then ordered to withdraw, and Browne was brought in. Browne obviously knew that whether he apologised or not it would make no difference to his sentence, which had already been decided elsewhere, so he expressed no regret but stated his opinion about what was happening to him and why; at least he displayed courage and his speech 'from the dock' was most impressive.

When Browne withdrew, the Prime Minister then moved motions declaring Fitzpatrick and Browne guilty, and committing them to police custody for three months.

Incidents like this, combined with an ever-growing and readily recited litany of past sins, began to create doubts in the minds even of those who admired Menzies most. In the 1955 election campaign Menzies' tactics were not universally approved even by traditional supporters of his government. From Coff's Harbour, a life-long Country Party voter wrote to the leader of the Labor Party on 2 December 1955:

> Please permit me to express my appreciation of the manner in which you have placed before the electors of Australia the progressive and constructive policy of the Australian Labor Party.
>
> Personally, I have never voted Labor in my life-having always given support to the Country Party.
>
> But as an Australian—who believes in British fair play—I felt that I had to write to you and express my utter disgust at the low-down tactics adopted by Menzies & Co. who seem to have thrown all decency to the winds and launched on a campaign of—no policy—but of lies and slander on you and your party. There is no doubt about it—they have certainly thrown everything that we call British to the winds and adopted the corrupt American tactics of 'Smear & Smudge.'
>
> Menzies repudiated the opinion of a Democratic people—when

At 10 Downing St, 26 May 1952.
'I never in my life saw anything like him before or since.'

Menzies on Churchill, 1967

Australia told him in no uncertain terms at the referendum to—in effect—'shut up about the Communists and get on with the business of the Country.' He replied to that vote by a greater campaign of abuse than ever and branded everyone 'Red' that differed with him.

Never in the history of Australia has a Prime Minister dragged politics to such an 'all-time-low'. Our Sovereign Independence—given to us by the Mother Country—was secretly sold by Menzies to a foreign power—American.

Menzies will go down in history as 'the Prime Minister who was a menace to everything British.'

To you Doctor, I wish you a great victory in your own electorate and an overwhelming victory for your Party throughout Australia—because I feel certain that it is the only way by which Australia can regain her self respect and by which she can again take her place as a Sovereign Independent State within the British Commonwealth of Nations and regain the dignity and respect of the Nations of the World.

Good Luck To You And Your Party.

Menzies had climbed near to the peak of his ascendancy in October 1954 when the Gallup Poll found that he was the first choice for leader of 87 per cent of Liberal and Country Party voters. His nearest rival, Casey, was down to 7 per cent. And the next five—Fadden, Holt, McEwen, Harrison, and Page—managed only 6 per cent between them. Menzies' dominance was even more pronounced in April 1955 when 90 per cent plumped for him rather than 'someone else'. At the same time, Dr Evatt could only manage 51 per cent support among Labor voters. Menzies was still at 90 per cent in July 1955; and even half of the Labor supporters interviewed in July admitted that the Menzies Government was 'handling things fairly well'. In mid 1956, Roy Morgan gave this retrospective summary of the fortunes of the Menzies coalition:

History of Menzies Government

1949: LCP, supported by 50 p.c. of the electors, displaced the Chifley Labor Government. The chief issue was bank nationalisation, but Gallup Polls in 1949 suggested that the coal strike was probably the deciding factor.

1950: Gallup Polls showed that LCP was supported by 54 to 57 p.c. of the electors until Labor ceased opposing the anti-Red Bill. LCP support then fell to the 1949 level of 50 p.c.

1951: LCP won the double dissolution with 50.5 p.c. of the votes. After the 'horror budget,' however, Gallup Polls showed that Labor support rose to 54 p.c.

1952: In the second half of 1952, import and credit restrictions caused Labor support in Gallup Polls to leap still higher to 60 p.c. LCP lost two seats at by-elections.

1953: A vigorous campaign by Mr Menzies kept the Labor vote at the Senate election down to 54 p.c., and LCP retained a bare working majority in the Senate. Gallup Polls showed that Labor support fell from 54 p.c. to 52 p.c. after the 1953 budget.

1954: Labor offered to abolish the means test for pensions, but received only 51 p.c. of the first preference votes at the House of Representatives election. LCP, with 48 p.c. of the votes, retained control of the House, with a reduced majority of only seven seats. After the 1954 budget and the Petrov inquiry, LCP support again rose to 52 p.c. in Gallup Polls.

1955: When sectarianism divided Labor's ranks, LCP support leapt to the record level of 56 p.c., but reverted to 52 p.c. after the budget. A Gallup Poll shortly before the December election showed a further drop in the LCP vote to 50 p.c. LCP won the election on December 10 with only 49 p.c. of the first preference votes, allowing for uncontested seats.

1956: Gallup Poll findings since the election have shown that LCP support has risen to 53 p.c. The situation seems similar to early 1950.

1956 was the year of Menzies' greatest splash in the international headlines, a moment on the world stage to be seized and savoured. He explained how it happened to Kenneth Harris on British television:

MENZIES: I had been over here on an errand as Prime Minister and was on my way home, rather overdue, going through America, when the news came of Nasser's so-called nationalisation of the Canal which to me was the confiscation of the Canal. And indications that there would be a conference in London. Well I rang up my people in Australia and they agreed that I ought to go back and attend it, because the Suez Canal is a great waterway from the point of view of Australia. So I went back and Mr Casey . . . he came over because he was the External Affairs Minister. I'd suggested that he should come and we had the conference . . . I arrived back into London I remember reading the papers that morning—reading to my horror that it was the common view that Nasser had a perfect right to do what he did. . . . And I went that day to have lunch with Anthony Eden and Selwyn Lloyd at Number Ten and told them that I was flatly opposed to these views and in my opinion this was a gross breach of international law, a great international contract with the mark of an international convention on it. It was monstrous to say that it was a legal exercise of power and they said, 'would you say so?'. I said I'd be delighted to say so. So I went out to Lime Grove and said so and gave my reasons and then we had the con-

Right: 'No collusion': with Anthony Eden, 27 June 1956, at 10 Downing St

ference and at the conference, Foster Dulles was the chief propounder of the proposals that ultimately went to Nasser and I was there and I made a speech, being called on and this attracted some interest, some attention. Ultimately we had eighteen nations out of 22 agreeing on a series of propositions and I went home to the hotel and went to bed. And about half past two in the morning, the telephone rang and I was literally hoiked out to go up to the American Embassy to see, not only the then Ambassador, Winthrop Aldrich, but also Eden and Lloyd and Foster Dulles and one or two others and I said 'What's all this about?' and they said 'We've decided that there ought to be a Committee to see Nasser' and Anthony said 'I want you to be a member of it'. And Dulles said 'No, your quite wrong, I want him to be chairman of it. Want him to be our spokesman. I didn't say yes. I didn't want to say yes. It was a hopeless proposition, you know, really, wasn't it. Here was Nasser the man in possession. However I got in touch with my colleagues in Australia and next day they said that they thought I ought to do it. So I said alright, that's how I became involved in it. After that of course, we had a lot of meetings and we went down and we had long discussions. Pretty fruitless ones as the result has shown.

HARRIS: Looking back on it . . . who was to blame for them ultimately being fruitless?

MENZIES: I think that after the British and the French had intervened with arms at the Canal, the whole matter might have ended up very satisfactorily with the overthrow of Nasser, if it hadn't been for the United Nations' intervention. And there wouldn't have been an effective United Nations intervention but for the attitude of the United States of America.

HARRIS: You blame the United States then?

MENZIES: And therefore, I don't want to blame the entire country, but I think that by this time my old friend Foster Dulles got a few wrong ideas in his mind.

HARRIS: Such as?

MENZIES: Such as that Great Britain and France were wrong to use force when negotiation had failed. This seemed to me to be a hopeless proposition. You're not to use force, you're to negotiate and negotiations failed. You're not to use force—no Foster said you must go to the United Nations. . . .

President Nasser's close friend, the editor Mohamed Hassanein Heikal, was well-informed about Menzies' mission to Cairo:

Dulles was asked to lead this mission but refused, and it was headed instead by Robert Menzies, the Australian Prime Minister. It was composed of the Foreign Ministers of Iran (as an Asian nation), Ethiopia (as an African nation), and Sweden (as a European nation) and Deputy Under Secretary of State Loy Henderson representing the United States.

They arrived in Cairo on the second of September and stayed at the Semiramis Hotel overlooking the Nile. Twice during the following day they met the President and explained to him what had happened at the London conference and gave him their mandate. They told him they had come to explain the declaration of the eighteen powers. They stressed the importance of the Canal to the maritime nations and expressed the hope that an agreement could be reached.

The President gave a dinner for the mission on September 5 at the Manial Palace, which before the revolution had been the palace of King Farouk's uncle, Crown Prince Mohammed Ali. It is surrounded by a marvelous group of old trees, and at dinner Menzies talked ecstatically about these trees, saying how beautiful they were. He exercised all his charm and amused the President.

Menzies asked Nasser: 'Have you ever met Churchill?' Nasser replied: 'No, but I admired him.'

'Have you ever heard him talking?' asked Menzies, and again Nasser said: 'No.'

'Do you know,' said Menzies, 'I have the reputation for being the best imitator of Churchill.'

'No man should undertake a public task without either a guarantee or reasonable probability of success, if he desires to avoid obloquy.'
Retrospective comment on mission to Nasser, 1956

And throughout the dinner Menzies kept whispering in Nasser's ear and everyone thought that they were talking important business about Suez when in fact Menzies was imitating Churchill's speech. He also imitated Bernard Shaw and General Jan Smuts. He was not talking seriously, but he set himself out to charm Nasser, and the President, indeed, found him very likable.

They had their third set of talks the following day, Thursday, September 6. Menzies pressed the arguments for an international administration to run the Canal. But Nasser refused on the grounds that this would be a new form of imperialism. Menzies asked how this could happen.

Nasser explained that if, after nationalizing the Canal, he then brought in an international administration, that administration would need protection and that protection would have to come from outside. And, once again, Egypt would be subject to occupation by foreign troops.

Menzies would not accept this argument and insisted that an international administration would solve all the problems. Nasser's reply was: 'You think that an international administration would end the trouble, but I think that an international administration would be the beginning of trouble.'

Menzies leaned forward over the desk, his thick eyebrows bristling, and growled: 'Mr President, your refusal of an international administration will be the beginning of trouble.'

Nasser immediately closed the files on the desk in front of him and said: 'You are threatening me. Very well, I am finished. There will be no more discussions. It is all over.'

Menzies grew red. The Ethiopian Foreign Minister tried to calm the situation. He said that Mr Menzies had expressed himself badly but it was not meant as a threat. Speaking for his country, an African country, he had not come to threaten, and he had not come to impose a solution on Egypt that Egypt would not like. The Swedish Foreign Minister also tried to ease the atmosphere, and Loy Henderson too argued that what Menzies had said was not meant as a threat. Menzies himself, by now terribly embarrassed, apologized: 'I'm sorry, I did not mean to convey a threat to you.'

But the President would not be mollified. He was angry: 'To tell me that my refusal to accept an international administration will be the beginning of real trouble *is* a threat and I will not negotiate under threat.'

That was the end for the Menzies mission. It was an abject failure. It was doomed anyway, doomed by its originator Dulles who, at a press conference in Washington on August 28, had told the world that 'the Suez Canal is not a primary concern to the United States.' He thus rendered Menzies powerless and President Eisenhower added to Menzies' discomfiture at another press conference on September 4, soon after Menzies had arrived in Cairo. 'We are committed,' said Eisenhower, 'to a peaceful settlement of this dispute, nothing else.'

When Nasser heard of this, he said: 'That man puzzles me; which side is he on?'

After Menzies had returned to Melbourne, he wrote to the British Prime Minister, Anthony Eden, with his own version of what had happened in Egypt:

You have about as difficult a task over Suez as mortal man ever had. I am sorry that we have not been able to get it solved for you in Cairo. Our report and, in particular, our *aide-mémoire* to Nasser will give a pretty fair picture of the arguments that we were using and of those we encountered. There are some aspects of this matter, however, which no committee could officially mention but which I would like to put down for your personal assistance.

Egypt is not only a dictatorship but it has all the earmarks of a police state. The tapping of telephone lines, the installation of microphones, the creation of a vast body of security police—all these things are accepted as commonplace.

I was told that Nasser was a man of great personal charm who might beguile me into believing something foreign to my own thought. This is not so. He is in some ways quite a likeable fellow but so far from being charming he is rather *gauche*, with some irritating mannerisms, such as rolling his eyes up to the ceiling when he is talking to you and producing a quick, quite evanescent grin when he can think of nothing else to do. I would say that he was a man of considerable but immature intelligence. He lacks training or experience in many of the things he is dealing with and is, therefore, awkward with them. He will occasionally use rather blustering expressions, but drops them very quickly if he finds them challenged in a good-humoured way. His logic does not travel very far; that is to say, he will produce a perfectly accurate major premise and sometimes an accurate minor premise, but his deduction will be astonishing. I will give you a powerful example of this which I think you might usefully have in mind. I will put it in the form of a substantially verbatim account of one passage in one of the arguments which I had with him.

NASSER: You say in your proposals that you are 'concerned by the grave situation regarding the Suez Canal'. I agree that there is. But who created it? We didn't create it, for all we did was to nationalize the Suez Canal Company and this was a matter which we had a perfect legal right to do. Therefore that action of ours could not have created the grave situation. It was the subsequent threats of Great Britain and France which created the grave situation.

MENZIES: But don't you see that the critical atmosphere in the world began at the very moment that you nationalized? It was that announcement which brought me back from America to the United Kingdom. It was that announcement which took Dulles from the United States to London. It was that announcement which brought

the representatives of twenty-two nations to London. What you
are overlooking is that the actual thing you did was to repudiate (and
I use that expression because plain language will be appreciated) a
concession which had twelve years to run.

NASSER: But how could anybody complain about that, if it was within
our power?

MENZIES: I don't concede it was within your power. In fact I think it
was not. But can't you see that if your attitude is that merely because
it was within your power you can repudiate a contract binding upon
you, this, in one hit, destroys the confidence that the world has in
your contractual word?

NASSER: I don't understand this. The concession would have expired
in twelve years anyhow and then I suppose the same uproar would
have occurred, if you are right.

MENZIES: Not at all. If you had not interfered with the concession, I
have no doubt that the company itself would have quite soon begun
negotiations with you for some future organization for the canal.
But those negotiations would have been conducted in an atmosphere
which was not one of crisis, and sensible and fair conclusions might
well have been arrived at without the heated exchanges on such
matters as 'sovereignty'.

NASSER: But this ignores the fact that we had the right to do what we
did, and if we have the right to do something we can't understand
how people can take exception to it.

This will explain the kind of logical mess which exists in his mind.
It is just as if one said that, as the Parliament of the United Kingdom
has power to pass any laws it thinks fit to pass, nobody should ever be
at liberty to complain about its law, to resent it, to seek to alter it.

With frightful reiteration he kept coming back to the slogans. Our
proposal was 'collective colonialism' which we were seeking to enforce;
he constantly came back to 'sovereignty'; to our desire for the 'domination' of the canal; to our proposed 'seizure' of the canal. I exhausted
my energy and almost wore out my patience in explaining to him that
he was surely under-estimating his own significance as the political
head of Egypt. What we were seeking was *an agreement*; and any
scheme for the actual control and management of the operations of
the canal, while leaving Egypt's sovereign rights untouched, was the
kind of working arrangement which was an exercise of sovereignty
and not a derogation from it, and could be described as 'domination'
or 'seizure' only if he made his agreement under actual duress.

I pointed out that many countries in the world had willingly granted
concessions to foreign enterprises to explore and develop national
resources, and that so far from thinking that these represented foreign
domination, the nations granting such concessions granted them
willingly because they were convinced that their own resources and
position would be thereby strengthened. To this he replied that he
saw no analogy, because the grantees of these concessions remain

entirely subject to national law (and, therefore, no doubt could have their concessions revoked at will).

The subsequent Anglo-French-Israeli military intervention at Suez was a disaster. Menzies denied foreknowledge of collusive plans to invade the Canal zone. But he defended the British action uncompromisingly.

While the Australian press, and, to a lesser extent, the Australian people, paid heed to the Prime Minister's utterances on grave international issues, it is difficult to believe that in Washington any antipodean posturing and preaching was of much moment. *The New York Times* carried brief reports of Menzies' statements. No doubt diplomatic cables conveyed fuller texts and interpretations. But there was little that could be known or said in Melbourne or Canberra that would be of concern to President Eisenhower or the ailing John Foster Dulles. Warnings about the dangers of Soviet communism could be at best irrelevant to a United States President who had already told his advisers: '... if these fellows start something we may have to hit 'em—and, if necessary, with *everything* in the bucket.' The memoirs of presidential confidantes like Emmet John Hughes and Sherman Adams reveal no evidence that Australian comments in late 1956 were of the slightest interest to American leaders. Some expert commentators, however, took the view that Menzies' enthusiastic support for Anthony Eden was both inept and injurious to Australia's interests. The opinion of Sir Alan Watt, a career diplomat of long experience, who had been Secretary of the Department of External Affairs 1950–1954, was forthrightly critical. In his book *The Evolution of Australian Foreign Policy 1938–1965*, Watt explained how Menzies dominated Australian foreign policy and was responsible for a rigidity of outlook and a widening gap between the Government's stance and public opinion. Then, in a persuasive analysis of the Suez episode he expressed a stern judgement that has subsequently prevailed:

If one looks at the Australian domestic scene during the ten-year period 1955–65, Menzies bestrides it like a colossus. Within his own political party, few approached him in ability and none could compete against his determined opposition. He personally has been predominantly responsible for Government success in every federal election since 1949. Only one man in his cabinet, namely, McEwen, Minister for Trade and Industry and Leader of the Country Party, was tough and skilful enough on occasion to advocate publicly policies which were not always quite in line with cabinet views as announced by relevant ministers—for instance, regarding the amount and kind of overseas investment in Australia and the sale to overseas interests of unprocessed raw material like iron ore. Whenever Menzies was abroad and McEwen was Acting Prime Minister, one quickly became conscious that McEwen was no mere stop-gap. Yet one felt that he respected Menzies and was prepared to work with him, while taking all necessary steps to ensure that Country Party interests did not suffer in the process . . .

Menzies' speeches and comments on the Suez Canal issue make painful reading today. As late as 8 July 1957 the Prime Minister roundly declared that he was 'utterly unrepentant about anything that was done or said over this great issue on our side'. No Australian should minimise his courage in pursuing a policy which was extremely unpopular internationally and strongly questioned within Australia, or fail to respect his intense loyalty to Britain in a situation of great strain and difficulty, even to the extent of refusing to criticise Eden's failure to consult with Australia before the ultimatum to Egypt was issued. In the result, however, British policy failed, despite Eden's half-hearted and *ex post facto* attempt—later echoed by Menzies—to justify it on the ground that Franco-British action against Egypt was necessary in order to galvanise the United Nations into sending a United Nations force into the Canal Zone. Australian support for British policy was, therefore, not only ineffective, but damaging to vital Australian international relations with other countries . . .

One is forced to the conclusion that his emotional attachment to Great Britain (where, incidentally, public opinion was seriously split over the Suez issue), his intellectual distrust of paper constitutions and international organisations such as the United Nations, and his instinctive leaning towards 'great and powerful friends' clouded his judgement.

Although Suez was seen as a fiasco for Menzies by many commentators and academic critics, the public at large seems at first to have been relatively unconcerned. When asked at the end of September 1956 to say what they thought the government was doing particularly well or particularly badly, most people responded by referring to a range of economic issues—finance, the cost of living, wages, inflation, pensions, overseas trade or unemployment. Those who expressed any opinion at all on Suez cancelled each other out—5 per cent thought it had been handled well, and the same proportion thought the opposite. On the general performance of the Government, 47 per cent thought it was doing 'fairly well', 34 per cent said 'not well', and 19 per cent, most of whom were said to be women, had no opinion. One-fifth of those who expressed dissatisfaction said they had voted Liberal or Country Party at the last election.

By December 1956, when people had had time to see the Suez drama unfold, there was a clear majority (61 per cent) that thought the British and French intervention was justified. By this time the Government was comfortably popular, and Menzies himself had a personal popularity rating of 77 per cent of Liberal and Country Party voters. Meanwhile, only 57 per cent of Labor voters chose Evatt, and a significant 38 per cent of them were unable to choose anyone.

On 3 April 1957 the Prime Minister broke the record for a single term in office. This was his 2663rd continuous day—one day better than W.M. Hughes achieved from 27 October 1915 to 9 February 1923. If Menzies' earlier period as Prime Minister were included, his tally was 3519 days. The government parties presented him with a celebration cake with the message in icing: 'May you take the cake for many years to come'. Following an exhausting tour of Japan, Thailand, the Philippines and New Guinea in April 1957, Menzies became ill and was confined to bed with a chest infection. The Queen cabled: 'My husband and I send our best wishes for your rapid recovery'. The Commander-in-Chief of the US Pacific Fleet, Admiral Stump, sent an encouraging box of cigars. 'On medical advice', it was announced, the Prime Minister sailed instead of flying to the Commonwealth Prime Ministers' Conference, leaving Fremantle on the *Arcadia* on May 27. Seven weeks later he had his tonsils removed at University College Hospital, London.

With or without tonsils, Menzies' platform mastery was legendary by the late 1950s. He was clearly in command of his subjects and his audiences to an extent that has rarely, if ever, been rivalled in Australian history. Shrewd parliamentary tacticians could hobble his performances by listening in silence, denying him the opportunity to make crushing ripostes. But out on the hustings there were sure to be noisy opponents who made big targets. Menzies thrived on interjections. Nevertheless, he could be ruffled by persistent heckling, as this report in *The Times*, 14 November 1958, shows:

LESSON ON THE HANDLING OF HECKLERS

MR MENZIES USES THE ROWDIES
From our Special Correspondent
Melbourne, Nov. 13.

A Menzies meeting is worth recording. This one is in the constituency of Maribyrnong, Victoria, which was a Labour seat until the Democratic Labour Party's first and second preference votes put in a Liberal, Colonel Stokes, in 1955. The candidate is talking. Dame Pattie Menzies, always with her husband on the platform, seems to be listening. Mr Menzies could be asleep: his eyes are shut. Then a heckler shouts, and the Prime Minister looks up and shakes with laughter, longing to get busy himself.

The candidate ends his speech. The mayor introduces Mr Menzies, and immediately there is a shattering tumult of boos and cheers. As it stills a voice is heard: 'Better have a drink, Bob. You're going to need one!' Delighted, and with all the aplomb of a great actor, Mr Menzies pours himself a glass of water. There are three uniformed policemen in the hall, which holds perhaps 400 and is full.

RADIO AUDIENCE

He starts to speak and his voice is drowned in boos, but the listening thousands on the radio can hear him shout, no more than a few inches from the microphone. 'To-night the comrades are very ill at ease— (pause)—because of the Hursey judgement.' A man, not 15 ft. away

In Burnie, Tasmania, 5 July 1961, with Liberal supporters

abuses the Prime Minister, who confides to the radio audience: 'It is an organized attempt to prevent me being heard.' The Mayor gets up to call for order. Mr Menzies waves him back to his seat: 'Don't bother.' He knows how to use this demonstration. He pauses, allowing the din to get across the air into every home with a wireless tuned in. Then he says: 'This is the kind of thing that can happen when the Labour Party gets frightened and the Communist Party gets truculent.'

Three men have already been removed by the police. The *crescendo* is becoming *diminuendo*, and it is now possible to hear within the hall something of what the Prime Minister is saying. 'One thing the noise merchants never understand is that a Government can pay people nothing which they haven't earned. That Yahoo there (pointing) thinks he's going to get something for nothing: but then it's race week.'

The police begin to remove a fourth man, who raises his right arm towards the Prime Minister, shouts 'Heil Hitler!', and has his photograph taken. It looks prearranged. Mr Menzies grins. 'Excellent! They give good marks for that in the *Tribune*.' He passes to unemployment, 'that poor old horse which has been put out on the track a lot in the last nine years—and never had a gallop.'

GETTING TIRED

So far Mr Menzies has been tough but good tempered. But he is getting tired of the persistent heckling of a man who has come back

The Communist menace in Kooyong: the Communist Party's Ralph Gibson,
with the successful candidate at the declaration of the 1963 General Election
poll

after being removed once and now stands by the door within 10 ft.
of the platform and 3 ft of a policeman. Mr Menzies turns from the
microphone: 'Do I understand the police approve of this kind of thing?'
He is testy now, but the policeman does not move. Nor, for that matter,
does the heckler.

In 1955 the Australian Labor Party was torn apart by internal feuding.
'The Split' as it came to be known reflected and accentuated a deep
ideological cleavage within the Labor ranks. A powerful anti-communist
faction, supported and strongly influenced by Roman Catholics, both
laity and clergy, crystallised into a new party, the Demcratic Labor
Party. The DLP became an auxiliary of the conservative forces, con-
tributing through the preferential voting system to the enhancement
of the coalition majority in the House of Representatives in the elections
of 1955 and 1958. Thus uplifted, the Prime Minister himself enjoyed
an extraordinary personal ascendancy in Cabinet, in Parliament, and
in the country at large.

Many former ministers have paid tribute to Menzies' leadership of
his Cabinet. Sir Paul Hasluck, in his account of his service as Minister
for Territories, with general responsibility to Papua and New Guinea,
was critical of the absence of Cabinet discussion of his portfolio's
concerns:

In these circumstances I sought mental reinforcement by an occasional discussion with the Prime Minister outside Cabinet. From about 1958 or 1959, I think, Menzies, following his visit to the Territory in 1957, began to respect, more than he had done originally, whatever qualities I had and to appreciate more fully both the intricacies and the value of doing the right thing in Papua and New Guinea. I myself, as I came closer to Menzies, was learning to value his great qualities more highly.

A lot of silly comments and many untrue statements have been made about Menzies by persons who never had the advantage of working close to him. He had a far better mind than anyone else in and around government in Australia during the quarter of a century in which I was close to affairs. He knew more, he could see a point more quickly and more exactly, he could think clearly and reach a conclusion reasonably and accurately after hearing the facts and arguments. Some foolish persons have referred to Menzies as a great speaker, as though that summed up his talents. They should recognize that Menzies expressed himself well because he knew what he wanted to say. When, at length, aided by the pressure of changing political events, I found the opportunity to engage his interest, I found that Menzies could understand what I was trying to do and why I was trying to do it far better than anyone else and he gave me the only real intellectual stimulus and encouragement on the rightness of our policy that I had from the Government during my most difficult years with the portfolio of Territories.

Another Cabinet colleague, Sir Howard Beale, has repudiated the charge that Menzies acted like a 'one-man band'. In *The Sydney Morning Herald*, 27 December 1971, Beale analysed what he called the 'Menzies Myth':

> All I can say is that during the years from 1949 to 1958 when I was in his Cabinet, and the years before that when I was with him in Opposition, Menzies did no such thing. There were many strong and able personalities in the party in those days—men like McEwen, Casey, Fadden, Holt, Larry Anthony, McBride, Spender, Spooner, Hasluck and others—and it is quite grotesque to suggest that they could have been over-ridden or dictated to, or indeed that Menzies would have tried to do so.
>
> The extraordinary statement in one newspaper article that 'the thinkers—the Barwicks, the Caseys, and the Spenders—were smartly removed as potential threats' is just silly. Casey stayed in Menzies' Cabinet for many years before retiring and later becoming Governor-General; Spender went of his own free will to render distinguished service in Washington; Barwick went voluntarily to the illustrious post of Chief Justice of Australia.
>
> This myth about domination, autocracy and dictatorship may derive partly from the high manner which Menzies sometimes adopted

in public, but mostly I think it comes from abysmal ignorance of how the Cabinet and party system worked in those days.

During our years in Opposition we met, with Menzies presiding, to discuss and decide our plans of campaign in and out of the House. There were a few who, because of inexperience or for other reasons, did not contribute much, but for the most part we were active and articulate individually, and hard-headed and united as a group.

The triumph of 1949 was due in no small measure to the sustained and vigorous attacks which we made upon the Government, both as individuals and as a coalition party.

After we gained Government in 1949, matters requiring Cabinet decision came to us usually in the form of closely reasoned, written submissions prepared by the minister concerned, or by his department and approved by him. As such submissions were mostly circulated beforehand, they were seen and examined by the Prime Minister, or by his department, which provided him with comments to assist him.

Sometimes, too, a minister would consult the Prime Minister beforehand about a matter he wished to bring to Cabinet. In these circumstances, the Prime Minister was in a good position to know before Cabinet met what the problem was and to marshal his own views.

But Menzies rarely tried to impose those views upon his colleagues. In important matters there was a full discussion in which all who wished to speak had a chance to do so. The only complaint I had of the way he conducted these meetings was that he sometimes let them go on too long, with too many ministers speaking too often.

Because Cabinet meetings were secret or were supposed to be,

With bust by Victor Greenhalgh, wartime camouflage expert, April 1965

ministers were able to speak freely, putting their thoughts across the table, making tentative suggestions, withdrawing them in the face of difficulties, expressing doubts as well as convictions, modifying views to meet those of others or to conform with what was practicable. Out of all this a consensus usually emerged.

Unless it were a submission brought forward by himself, Menzies would often refrain from offering his opinions until later in our discussions; then, having heard what others had to say, he would sum up the issues and indicate his own views. We did not normally take votes, but at the end of a discussion we mostly knew what the unanimous or majority view was, and this became the collective and individual responsibility of us all.

I would say that most Cabinet decisions went the way Menzies thought they should. This was natural enough, because a decision reached by this sort of discussion by a group of men trying to do the right thing usually ends up as a right decision.

But he sometimes found himself in a minority, despite his own skilfully expressed arguments; on such an occasion I have seen him put his hands on the table—the great oval table made from the teak decks of the first HMAS Australia—and say wryly: 'Well, gentlemen, I do not agree with you, but that is your decision.'

There were rare occasions, as I recall, when he might seek to have reviewed a decision which was made in his absence or one with which he strongly disagreed. This was a right every minister had if he felt deeply enough about the issue involved. In Menzies' case it was especially justified because, as Prime Minister, he carried the ultimate responsibility for Cabinet decision and action.

Not all Cabinet meetings were sweetness and light, for we (and he) were subject to the usual irritabilities due to exhaustion, frustration, or other frailties of the flesh. Nevertheless, the atmosphere around the long table was almost always genial and courteous, and sometimes even brotherly. This simply could not have been so under & Prime Minister who was a dictator or an autocrat.

In the party room things ran somewhat differently; most of the matters discussed there had already been looked at by Cabinet, so that the Prime Minister spoke for the Cabinet as well as for himself. Although the Prime Minister had a natural advantage over the rest of the party members by reason of his greater knowledge and his powers of exposition, those holding different views were able to express them freely, and we usually ended up with a decision which was either unanimous or overwhelmingly one way.

Occasionally the strongly held views of private members would prevail over that of the Prime Minister and Cabinet, in which case Cabinet would act accordingly—the early banking legislation is a case which comes to mind.

Sir Robert was not always an easy man to work with; he had his idiosyncrasies, as all men do. Nevertheless ... I remember him, not as a juggernaut, dictator, or autocrat, but as a man who, greatly strengthened by the loyalty and ability of his colleagues, gave stylish leadership based on experience, eloquence and personality.

If that constitutes 'domination' then the country could do with some more of it.

Probably the best comment on such rosy recollections is provided by Menzies' own account of a project dear to his heart, the development of Canberra. When he came to Canberra in 1934, Menzies thought of it, as did many of its inhabitants, as a place of exile. He made up his mind that it should become a 'worthy capital'. As Prime Minister, after 1949, he encouraged Canberra's growth and sponsored the creation of the National Capital Development Commission in 1957. His pet scheme was the central feature of Walker Burley Griffin's original plan for the city, an artificial lake. There were technical objections about mud flats, erosion, and mosquitoes, and understandable resistance from the Canberra Golf Club, whose course was to be submerged. But Menzies pressed on and at last included in the annual estimates a sum of about one million pounds for the construction of the lake and its surroundings. He went on one of his frequent trips to England, happy that his 'dream had been given shape'. However, when he returned he discovered that the item for expenditure on the lake had been deleted from the Budget by the Treasury:

> At the very first meeting after my return, and when I had completed a survey of the matters which had been discussed abroad, I turned to the Treasurer, who was my good friend and ultimate successor, the late Harold Holt, and said, with what I hoped was a disarming smile, 'Am I rightly informed that when I was away the Treasury struck out this item of one million for the initial work on the lake?' The reply was yes, and that Cabinet had agreed. I then said, 'Well, can I take it that by unanimous consent of ministers the item is now struck in?' A lot of laughter ran around the Cabinet room; there were some matters on which they reasonably thought that the old man should be humoured; and . . . men were on the job next morning.

Malcolm Fraser was a backbench member of the parliamentary Liberal Party for eleven years from 1955 onwards. Looking back as Prime Minister on the days when he was in his late 20s and early 30s, he recalled that Menzies was a good party manager. 'He knew what was happening in the party room . . . He always gave me the impression that if a viewpoint . . . was worth contemplation he'd consider it.' Of course, there were some men who made a nuisance of themselves. As Fraser put it, Menzies 'had a few people who would go around always saying precisely what they thought about everything regardless of the cohesion and unity of the party'. Menzies did not 'appreciate them very much'.

Proud men are unlikely to brand themselves as ineffectual or subservient. Memories lapse; humiliations are rarely advertised. And few of the Prime Minister's colleagues were aware of what he really thought of them. This makes all the more valuable an article by H.B.S. (Joe) Gullett published in *The Observer* (Sydney) on 3 May 1958. Gullett, the son of Sir Henry Gullett (who had been a member of Menzies' War Cabinet until his death in an aircrash in August 1940), met Menzies in 1935. He entered Parliament in 1946 and was Government Chief Whip from 1950 to 1955, when he retired from politics. He had observed Menzies at close quarters, in opposition and in power. He knew, and was prepared to be honest about, the way Menzies treated his ministers and party supporters:

With a docile Cabinet most unwilling to cross swords with him, the government of Australia is dependent upon the Prime Minister to an extraordinary degree ... Menzies has handled his parliamentary supporters with remarkable shrewdness, not to say artfulness. Proposed Government action or legislation is normally outlined by the Minister concerned at a Joint Party Meeting. The time for discussion is restricted and the time for thought much more so. Cabinet members are always united, having decided on their view beforehand and, like Labour Caucus, they are bound to support in the Party the majority decision of Cabinet, whatever their personal views.

The opinions of private members are listened to with politeness. The Minister with a great store of information at his fingertips, answers their queries. If this does not suffice he will volunteer—the soul of reasonableness—to meet them afterwards. 'But, of course, gentlemen, you understand time is pressing. We do regard this as a somewhat urgent measure. Naturally your views will be given the fullest consideration. ....' The gentlemen usually go quietly. No vote is ever taken.

Occasionally a member gets obstinate and digs his toes in. He is dealt with in various ways. If he is known to be in the mood to make trouble he may not be called to speak at all, or called at a time when members are beginning to look to the dining-room. Or a member may speak, for example, about War Service Homes. Before others have a chance to back him up someone will be called who is known to wish to talk about whale meat or the Argentine ant. There are more ways of destroying a discussion than stopping it. The Prime Minister is a masterful exponent of the old-boy technique. 'Don't think I do not appreciate your difficulties.' 'There is much substance in what you say.' 'We must consider it.' 'I am grateful to Geoff for reminding us of this.' 'Thank you.' 'Later perhaps.' And so on. If all this fails there are more drastic measures. A troublesome member like Wentworth can soon find himself isolated: 'He is disloyal ... He gives information to the Press ... He has been heard to say this and that.' One way and another the party does pretty much as it is told. When it is led to water it drinks or it goes thirsty.

The late W.M. Hughes once told me he considered the Prime Minister one of the greatest Parliamentarians and probably the greatest debater who ever lived. But under his leadership the prestige, authority and usefulness of parliament have so greatly declined that we have now reached a stage when only an ageing handful of members has ever seen a parliament work as it should, or appreciates its true functions.

The Prime Minister must accept a good deal of responsibility for this state of affairs. For although as Leader of the Opposition he made such a great use of the forum of parliament, as Prime Minister, Menzies has treated the parliament with little respect. To begin with, he and his Cabinet hardly ever attend debates. The general thing is for one bored Minister to sit dejectedly at the table while debates are going on or to bring in a file of papers and attend to them without the least sign of paying attention to the speakers.

Little by little the impression grows on the members that parliament does not matter and they bother about it less and less. But Menzies is not by any means entirely to blame. The members themselves all too often arrive tired out by travel and an exacting weekend in the electorate. They have done no homework on the matters before the House and are inclined to put up with whatever their leaders have advanced. Finally, they are mostly—the Liberals at any rate—ex-officers of the fighting services, men accustomed to obey and to whom loyalty is a cardinal virtue. It is not easy for them to disagree with their leader and for his part the Prime Minister makes it quite plain that the disagreement cannot be a small one. More than once he has threatened to resign if government policies were not accepted absolutely.

In general the PM is friendly but aloof from his followers, even though he gives them great loyalty in their adversities. He does not eat or drink with them and is seen little in the House. When he does speak it is generally to talk to the listening radio audience rather than to address members. They just happen to be there. He has largely replaced Parliamentary advisers with greatly trusted lieutenants from the Public Service, like Sir Allen Brown, and if he wishes for a report on a certain subject he almost always appoints advisers outside the ranks of Parliamentarians.

His selection of Ministers is extraordinary in that he almost always puts a man in the job he knows least about. Thus Davidson, a soldier, is Postmaster-General; Cramer, a most capable businessman and estate agent, Minister for the Army; and Fairhall, an ideal Postmaster-General with his radio station background is made Minister for the Interior. McMahon, a good administrator but city to the seat of his camel hair coat, is Minister for Primary Production; and Hugh Roberton, a farmer, is in charge of Social Services. We don't know the motives, but we do know the results. They could be better.

He has many friends and he is very loyal to them. But he has no really close or complete friends outside his own family. Rather are his friends in separate compartments. To each of them he reveals a different side of his character and different interests. No single person has his absolute confidence and he keeps his colleagues guessing about his real intentions. Different ones know his views on different matters but no one knows them all.

Above: with General Douglas Mac-Arthur, Haneda Airport, Tokyo, 14 August 1950

Left: with Dr Hendrik Voerwoerd of South Africa, leaving Lancaster House, London, after a session of the Commonwealth Prime Ministers' Conference, 15 March 1961

Right: with Jawaharlal Nehru, 1950

Below: as Minister for External Affairs, at the 15th regular session of the U.N. General Assembly, accompanied by Sir Garfield Barwick, September 1960

Robert Kennedy, a member of Menzies' staff for three years until early 1961, testified:

> To be invited to the Lodge is an honor; to be invited to dinner is to walk with the mighty. Few people receive the accolade, because the Prime Minister is not a gregarious soul . . .
>
> He dines out only when he has to, or on rare occasions because he wants to. He holds a dinner party at the Lodge usually only when he has to, although he can be (and always is) the most charming and perfect of hosts, with a rare nose for a good wine and the world's most delicate hand with a Martini. Only one member of Cabinet can qualify as a regular diner at the Lodge: the amiable and earthily-amusing Athol Townley who, more than anybody else in Australia, has made a fine art of knowing how far to go with the Prime Minister—who is so perfect an actor, so accomplished a listener, that many fall into the trap of going beyond the bounds of what the Prime Minister considers a reasonable thing. Many a promising political career has foundered on this rock.

Athol Townley, Minister for Defence 1958–1963, could well have shared with Menzies a joke or two about the gullibility of the electorate. Australians shivered periodically at communist bogeys but were sufficiently comforted by the apparent promise of American protection to be more pleased than alarmed at frugality of spending on defence for most of Menzies' reign. The people noticed but soon forgot their Prime Minister's foray into the United Nations General Assembly in October 1961 when the Indian Prime Minister, Pandit Nehru, described Menzies' proposal of a four-power summit meeting as 'negative, untenable and verging on absurdity'. Why, in any case, should Australians be concerned about what Menzies called 'the debating society in New York'? There was still, after all, the Commonwealth—a smaller debating society in which the old dominions were not yet overwhelmed by clamouring neutral or third world blocs.

As early as 1948, when he decided not to publish a completed but prematurely out-dated book, Menzies was conscious of the Commonwealth changing in ways that he found regrettable. Scarcely had he become an elder statesman when he was branded as an international anachronism, a custodian of irrelevant traditions and loyalties. Thus, left-wing critics throughout the 1960s attacked Menzies as an ally and defender of the South African Government. In fact, he was not an advocate of apartheid, much as he seemed to enjoy opportunities to avoid condemning South African racial policies. When the Commonwealth Prime Ministers turned against the South African regime, however, he did insist that the internal affairs of member countries were not the proper concern of the Commonwealth. In view of the stand which he took, and his sensitivity about Australia's immigration policy, it is curious that originally he should have himself floated the idea in February 1960 that there should be a discussion of South Africa at a

Prime Ministers' Conference. A Canberra-based journalist wrote privately on 1 March 1960, four weeks after Menzies had taken over the External Affairs Department following Casey's retirement:

We went to a dinner the other night, given by the South African High Commissioner, Hamilton, who was senior external affairs officer in London in 1947. Menzies was there and, over the brandy, he was quite interesting—there were only half-a-dozen men present. Hamilton said what a tremendous effect Macmillan had had in the Union and he described the ferment in the political parties there as a result. Verwoerd was a much more reasonable man than the previous PM and he thought he would decide to go to London. Menzies was obviously interested and then said he would like to be the man to raise at the Commonwealth Prime Ministers' conference the whole issue of South Africa, which had been dodged for too long on these occasions. He thought it was about time the PMs faced this one and had a good open talk about it. He didn't believe it would cause any great harm at all; and it might do some good. But Verwoerd ought to be warned in advance and made to understand the friendly spirit of everyone else. He would like to take Verwoerd aside before the conference and get him in the right mood.

Of course, I don't know if Menzies will go through with this and it depends, anyway, on Verwoerd going to London. But Menzies is fascinated by the possibility of doing something big and useful for the Commonwealth, and this kind of broad problem appeals to him.

As for his assumption of the External Affairs portfolio, I think the significance of this can be overstressed. On the whole, the great decisions in Australia's foreign affairs during Casey's long term were cabinet decisions, heavily influenced by Menzies' strong views and personality but, apart from Suez, it is hard to think of a time when Casey did not approve of the decisions.

There had never been a time since 1949 when Menzies was not closely in touch with foreign policy. His government's record could never be assessed fairly without examining the implications of the Colombo Plan of 1950, the ANZUS and SEATO pacts, and the development of relations with Japan, as well as the military involvements in Korea, Malaysia, and South Vietnam. When he retired, Menzies said: 'If I was asked which was the best single step that has been taken in the time of my Government, I think I would say the ANZUS treaty.' This regional security pact was negotiated by Percy Spender. The United Kingdom was excluded; but, as Menzies carefully put it, the treaty made the United States from 1951 'not perhaps technically, but in substance, our ally'. Substantially, if not in every technicality, Australian defence and foreign policy became increasingly infused with American perceptions and interests. Socialists were predictably outraged by blatant subservience to American 'imperialism'. Among Liberal supporters, there was probably more indifference than rejoicing at the strengthened American connection, although effusive pro-American

Home again: press conference after world tour, July 1965

rhetoric by Menzies' successors offended royalist and nationalist as well
as Labor sensibilities. It was all very well to have 'great and powerful
friends' but going 'all the way with LBJ' was another matter.

As far as Australia's defence policy was concerned, a very senior
admiral expressed an age-old service complaint in April 1960. 'The
Prime Minister and the Minister for Defence', he wrote privately,
preferred 'to get their professional advice watered down and commented
upon by numerous non-service advisers.' Oft-repeated but misleading
statements to the contrary only compounded a sin that a Chief of Staff
described as 'really wicked'. It was a commonplace of contemporary
criticism that Australia's defence spending ran down during the 1950s.
'Viewed from any angle', *The Sydney Morning Herald's* anonymous
commentator wrote on 21 January 1966, 'the three year, £1221 million
defence program announced shortly before the Senate campaign [in
November 1964], was no more than a resolution to make some repara-
tion for more than a decade of culpable neglect.'

Until official documents and eye-witness testimonies are available, it is impossible to be certain about the motives and reasoning of
Menzies and his colleagues and defence advisers. It can be observed,
however, that limited expenditure on military equipment and personnel
permitted greater priority to be given to economic development. On
Menzies' concern for the economy, Dr H.C. Coombs has said that 'most
of the time he would rather somebody else worried about it'. And it is
undeniable that Menzies seemed comparatively ill at ease with economic
issues. He leaned heavily on advice from public servants and a select
group of business and financial magnates. Dr Coombs, as head of the
Commonwealth Bank, found that 'if you felt there was a really serious
problem facing the economy and one which in your judgement the
Prime Minister should be concerned with, then he would listen, and
when he turned his mind to these matters, as with so many, he was
exceedingly percipient'. Whether by design or inattention, however, he
tolerated the distortions and inequities of inflation for too long. But
before the inevitable recession came, at the end of 1960, he and the

economy over which he presided were to earn the accolade of a *Time* cover story.

Australia's economic boom was not news to American investors, though as the tone of the *Time* story on 4 April 1960 reveals, even Menzies' frequent overseas' journeys had not succeeded in removing the impression that Australia was 'rawest and least favored by nature of the English-speaking countries'. In 'Out of the Dreaming', F. Hubbard and S. Karnow summarised in classic 'Timese' the state of the nation in 1960, and neatly encapsulated the popular view of Menzies' contribution to Australian prosperity:

> The speed with which Australia is coming of age astonishes Australians themselves and bemuses even the ruddy, self-assured man who has presided over the process. 'When I was a boy,' says Prime Minister the Right Honorable Robert Menzies, 'there was a distinctly colonial flavor to Australia. Now we are developing an outlook peculiar to Australia. We are becoming more significant.' . . .
>
> Today, after a decade of unabashed wooing of free enterprise by Menzies and his government, Australia (pop. 10.2 million) is the biggest industrial nation in the southern hemisphere, boasts an industrial output three times as great as Brazil's (pop. 64 million). Australia's gross national product has rocketed from $5 billion in 1949 to $13.8 billion. Aided by a bold immigration scheme that has brought 1 500 000 Europeans into the country since 1947, Australia is no longer a backwater, but confident of its dynamism and independence. 'Nowadays,' says a senior Australian diplomat, 'we can talk to anybody in the world without any sense of innate inferiority.'
>
> **Ming the Merciless.** The man most responsible for this change is one of the least typical of Australians. In a nation where distrust of 'the bosses' is an article of faith, Robert Gordon Menzies, 65, avows his concern for assuring 'the rights of the top dog.' Where nobody wants to appear to 'have tickets on himself,' *i.e.*, seem superior, Menzies once coldly rebuffed a parliamentary complaint that he suffered from a superiority complex: 'Considering the company I keep in this place, that is hardly surprising.' And where ordinary Australians flavor the Queen's English with racy Australian slang and delight in plain speaking, Menzies cherishes his reputation for classic eloquence. (Years ago, after delivering a speech in London with a fever of 103°, he turned to the Duke of Gloucester to ask: 'Sir, what did I say?' Replied His Royal Highness: 'My dear boy, I don't know, but it was damned good.')
>
> In tribute to Menzies' occasional superciliousness and permanent political cunning, Australians nicknamed him 'Ming'—partly a play on the Scottish pronunciation of Menzies as 'Mingis,'* but partly after a singularly repulsive comic-strip character called Ming the Merciless. In moments of passion, rival politicians have variously

---

* Menzies himself pronounces it as spelled.

described him as 'a back-stabber,' 'a stubborn mule,' 'a tool of the interests' and 'unfit to lead a flock of homing pigeons.' But the noisiest of opponents would concede that Menzies is far and away the most able man in Australian politics. Thanks to talent and talent alone, he has been Prime Minister for $12\frac{1}{2}$ years ...

Riding the Escalator. Menzies ... set out to make Australia an attractive place for private enterprise. To overseas capital, the new government offered such lures as no capital-gains tax, guarantees that both profits and capital itself could be easily repatriated. And when inflation threatened to get out of hand in 1950, Menzies responded with a 'horror budget' that increased the income tax by 10%, increased the sales tax, cut imports by 50%, and raised the price of tobacco and liquor.

Attracted by the opportunities, foreign capital has come pouring into Australia. British investment in Australia—still the largest—has increased from $484 million to $1.7 billion since Menzies took office; US investment, growing more than twice as fast as Britain's, is expected to reach $1 billion by the end of this year. Australians themselves are reinvesting 25% of their national income...

Menzies has not let sentimental allegiance to Britain blind him to the fact that 'empire defense' is a thing of the past. In 1952, despite Britain's unconcealed irritation at being excluded, Menzies led Australia into the ANZUS pact with the US. And he makes no bones about expecting ever closer relations with the US. Says he: 'We don't expect America to pull our chestnuts out of the fire ... But the US has developed responsibility marching along with power. We will be the beneficiary.'

No less important, Menzies and Casey between them have impressed upon Australia's diplomats and upon Australia's people the awareness that Australia's future is inextricably Asia's. 'To you Americans, 'says Menzies, 'it's the Far East. To us, it's the Near North.' Courageously defying his fellow countrymen's deep-rooted fear and dislike of Japan, Menzies three years ago began a campaign of *rapprochement* that culminated in a visit to Australia by Japanese Premier Nobusuke Kishi. Today, Tokyo, New Delhi and Djakarta are regarded by Australian diplomats as more important posts than Paris or Rome. And through the Colombo Plan, Australia has given technical and university training to 10 000 Asian students.

Doing the Dishes. Part of Australia's new international visibility comes from Menzies' fondness for the role of travelling statesman. He never fails to attend Commonwealth Prime Ministers' meetings ('I make a few statesmanlike remarks ... The eminent gentlemen of the Civil Service, who have already written the ultimate communique, say, "Yes, that was a good point"'). And in the past five years he has made three voyages to the US, two swings into Asia, and side excursions into Canada and Europe. But at home, despite the prestige he has won for Australia abroad, he remains respected rather than loved.

Among the Australians who love Menzies least are the newsmen assigned to cover him, whom he treats as contemptuously as if they were members of Parliament. When Australia's rough-and-tumble House is in session, Menzies sits alone at a center table, smiling gently at a remark that pleases him, casting a dark, withering glance at back-benchers who step out of line. So deadly are his ripostes ('The con-ducted tour of the Honorable Member's mind would have been more instructive if it had not taken place in gathering darkness') that Laborite backbenchers were cautioned not to needle him . . .

At Canberra's modest, stucco Lodge, official residence of Australia's Prime Ministers, Menzies rises late (about 8), does not set off for his office till 9 or 9:30. Once there, he plows rapidly through corre-spondence, with the aid of an occasional Grosvenor Club cigar. After dinner, which is normally preceded by two Menzies-mixed martinis, he goes back to the office until midnight or 1 a.m.

Keeping up this pace seven days a week leaves Menzies no time for cricket, golf and tennis, which he used to play, though he is such a cricket fan that he will stay up all night to listen to the Test Matches on short wave, or adjourn a Cabinet meeting to see them. He could easily earn $100 000 a year at law, but as Prime Minister his pay and allowances come to only $30 000. In near-servantless Australia, it is not uncommon for Pattie Menzies—who became a Dame Grand Cross of the British Empire in 1954—to play hostess at Sunday lunch to a returned Aus-tralian diplomat, then head out to the kitchen to wash the dishes with the visitor's wife.

The Qualitative Influence. For all its progress—and Menzies' confidence—Australia is not without growing pains. Wages and prices have risen so sharply that a month ago, Menzies felt obliged to relax import quotas sharply, hoping thereby to make Australia's marginal businesses more efficiently competitive. Politically, Australians worry about the chaotic state of their nearest Asian neighbor, Indonesia. And there is the perennial problem of the 'White Australia Policy'—which is not a policy but a practice whereby immigration officers class all colored people as 'undesirable immigrants.' Most Australians want the country to remain essentially white, but if Australia hopes to play any role in Asia, it will undoubtedly have to take in at least token numbers of Asian immigrants.

Menzies himself continues to proclaim: 'If I were a young man, with all the world in front of me, I would want to be in Australia at the beginning of what will be its most wonderful period of development.' And he insists that Australia can one day exert 'great qualitative if not quantitative' influence in Asia. Says he: 'We can offer intelligent resistance to Communism. We can, after generating our own capital requirements, be in a position to invest in Asia. There is certainly the possibility of Asian leadership before us. But we are not going to become leaders merely by proclaiming ourselves leaders.'

Menzies celebrated his 67th birthday in December 1960. In Feb-ruary 1960, 39 per cent of voters had said that they thought he should

A despondent Treasurer: Harold Holt, 3 May 1961

retire, and 30 per cent of Liberal and Country Party supporters shared this view. The Prime Minister's glamour had faded. The Government could not control the economy. Despite the weakness and continuing division in Labor ranks, Menzies came closest to losing power in the general election of December 1961. He survived with a majority of two (one after the Speaker was elected). The Liberal Party itself polled only one-third of the total votes cast in 1961. More people voted for the DLP than for the Country Party, which won seventeen seats. DLP preferences went overwhelmingly to the Government. But, ironically, it was the preferences of 93 Communist Party voters in Moreton, Queensland which, after prolonged counting, assured the Government of victory.

Meanwhile there was a menacing cloud on the 'Near North' horizon. Not long after the 1961 election a Canberra observer noted in a private letter:

I had a talk yesterday (January 3) to Brigadier Suadi, the Indonesian ambassador, who told me that he did not think Indonesia would have to fight for West New Guinea. He is close to General Nasution, the C-in-C, and appears to be no extremist and perhaps representative of army opinion generally.

Australia is in some difficulty, having insisted for years on the principle of self-determination. Now if the Dutch 'get out from under' Australia, largely in the person of Menzies, will find herself among the debris—it's a bit like the situation after South Africa left the Commonwealth, when Menzies found himself left high and dry by Macmillan (to change the metaphor). In fact many people blame Menzies for always insisting on making Australia's opinion—or his own—painfully plain, when there is really no need for a small, exposed country to put everything so firmly on record.

Menzies was very chastened for a few days after the election results and behaved quite pleasantly, for a change, at his first press conference in Melbourne. But in Canberra just before Christmas he was appallingly rude and back in his old form with the parliamentary press gallery. However the papers let him get away with it, although The Age is now publishing verbatim reports of his press conference, which do let the public know how poisonous he can be. If he has not learned his lesson, and it seems he hasn't, then he may not last beyond this year as Prime Minister. His government might fall or his party might contrive to get rid of him ... Everything, unhappily, points to a decline in the man. But all this may still be too premature.

On January 28, the Indonesian story was becoming quite extraordinary:

Four statements have now been made by the government within the past four weeks, each one a masterpiece in diplomatic double-talk and each one pretty unnecessary, because by now both the Dutch and the Indonesians must know very well that the Australians will *do* nothing. This week Barwick, the Minister for External Affairs, actually called together some newspaper editors and asked them to prepare public opinion for the obvious fact that the Australian government would have to accept very graciously the success of Indonesia's diplomatic offensive for West New Guinea. The Melbourne Herald immediately published the guts of this in a story beginning: 'The *Herald* understands that ... ', implying that it was officially inspired ...

Barwick had been authorised by cabinet to peddle this line, because Menzies is afraid that a too obvious acquiescence might cause right-wingers in his party, like Kent Hughes, to cross the floor when parliament meets on February 20 and perhaps bring the government down. So when the *Herald* story appeared, he thought Barwick must have gone too far or that the source of the story had become too obvious, and he directed Barwick very firmly to make yet another official statement, denying that Australian policy had changed and describing the story as purely 'speculative' . . .

Over the next few weeks there were fresh rumours that Menzies' days as Prime Minister were numbered. The Australian correspondent of *The Times* recorded in a memorandum of 2 March 1962:

W.C. Wentworth, a Liberal backbencher who is probably the most brilliant man in the party, told me yesterday that Menzies had never been more unpopular among Liberals and Country Party members. He thought the Prime Minister would have retired by the end of the year, having been (if necessary) edged out by his colleagues. Wentworth has clashed with Menzies often and his views must therefore be suspect; but he has always been utterly honest in expressing his views and has nothing to gain in the way of office if Menzies should go. I think he may be correct, because Menzies nearly lost the elections and he must take the blame for failure as well as success.

I also had an hour today with Sir Garfield Barwick, the new Minister for External Affairs, who is also still Attorney-General. The popular idea is that Menzies still dominates External Affairs and his Minister. I don't think this is true. Barwick is a tough little man and he told me that he had got Menzies to modify his attitude to Indonesia, as projected in the various statements put out in January. When pressed, he agreed that Menzies had made errors of judgment internationally in the last few years and went on to describe him as essentially 'European' in his thinking and out of sympathy with Asia. This isn't, of course, a new idea, but it seems significant if his Minister for External Affairs says it and makes it known that he himself is not like this . . . Barwick could succeed Menzies as PM (Wentworth told me that Holt would never get the succession now), although McEwen is now favourite to succeed, despite the fact that he is only the leader of the minority party in the coalition.

Both Menzies and his government recovered popularity in 1962 and 1963. Just before his 69th birthday, the Prime Minister was shown to have a dominating 79 per cent support in the coalition parties compared with 2 per cent for John McEwen and 1 per cent for Harold Holt. His lieutenants were so much in his shadow, that more than half of the government supporters polled in November 1960 had no idea who they would want as Menzies' successor; 21 per cent wanted Holt, 19 per cent were for the Country Party leader, McEwen, with Barwick trailing as an 'also-ran' with 3 per cent. As the months wore on, uncertainty increased. By August 1964, 65 per cent of Liberal and Country Party voters couldn't make up their mind on a successor. And, of those who knew who they wanted, more seemed to want McEwen (15 per cent) than Holt (12 per cent). By then Paul Hasluck had replaced Barwick at the head of the tail.

Speculation about the succession became rampant in the early 1960s, and evidence emerged of a struggle between McEwen and Holt. There seems little doubt that Menzies himself, much as he valued his partnership with McEwen, wanted Holt to succeed as Prime Minister. The succession issue became intertwined with the rivalry between the powerful Commonwealth Treasury and McEwen's Department of Trade, principally over Australia's response to the proposed British entry into the Common Market. H.G. Gelber, in a study published not long after Menzies' retirement, explained how McEwen's position finally was undermined:

During the discussions on the 1962 budget, . . . Mr Holt blocked Mr McEwen's attempt to secure more concessions to taxpayers. The Treasurer not only stressed balance of payments and cost stability considerations, but added that rural spokesmen had been particularly worried about this. It was a clear hint that if Mr McEwen, in his attempts to broaden the basis of Country Party support, went too far in wooing secondary industry, he would lay himself open to having his primary political support, among his own farmers, undermined by the Liberals. Yet if he ceased to woo industry, his claim to the Prime Ministership would be weakened. All this was apt to reinforce the long-standing Country Party suspicion about Liberal intentions, a sense of weakness also reflected in the discussions on electoral boundary reform at about this time. There were also specific local difficulties.

The two streams of opinion finally clashed at the end of July in an incident which led to the resignation of a Liberal Minister. The affair began, a fortnight after Mr Menzies' own reassuring remarks in mid-July, when the Minister for Air and Minister Assisting the Treasurer, Mr L.H.E. Bury, said that the possible damage British entry might cause to Australia had been much exaggerated. He declared, with unusual frankness, that the British application had given 'a severe emotional shock to the older generation', but that its potential effects upon Australia had been overstressed. 'Worry about the effects of Britain entering the Common Market, looked at from the viewpoint of Australia as a whole, seems to me very far-fetched'. The overwhelming majority of Australians would not notice any change or be materially affected. For the business community as a whole to be worried would be absurd. The rural industries which would be affected constituted, in the aggregate, only a minor element in the Australian economic scene. Only one-fifth of the country's exports were going to Britain; only a minor part of this fifth would be affected. Even in the unlikely event of this fraction disappearing entirely, the main fabric of the Australian economy would hardly be impaired. As it was, there was a transitional period during which to adjust and even after that, commodity exports to Europe and Britain would not come to an abrupt stop . . .

It was embarrassingly obvious that these views differed widely from the official position and in particular from the attitude of Mr McEwen. The Minister for Trade reacted strongly, saying he was 'shocked that

With the Cabinet: a farewell photograph, December 1965

a Ministerial colleague should publicly undercut the strength of Australia's negotiating position by declaring that Australia had little to fear from British entry, apparently irrespective of terms'. Some of his Country Party supporters reacted more strongly still. Mr Menzies himself showed some hesitation, but after conferring with Mr McEwen and Mr Bury, and following Mr Bury's refusal to recant, decided to ask for his resignation. In a friendly exchange with Mr Bury he stressed his unfeigned regret at being compelled to such a move. At the same time, he explained that Cabinet solidarity was supremely important in a series of negotiations which had been repeatedly declared to be the most important in our time . . .

Mr Bury not only made no attempt to modify his position, but he repeated his views both in the House and on later occasions. His reply to the Prime Minister was to say that while he supported the Government's stand in general, he differed on perspective and emphasis. To the House, he explained that the EEC issue was likely to be a crucial turning point in world history and the matter needed to be lifted out of 'petty, parochial politics'. He insisted that the overall effect of British entry on the Australian economy as a whole was likely to be minor 'and, in years to come, could well be beneficial' . . . Both Mr McEwen and some of his party colleagues left the chamber before Mr Bury began. When he finished, several of his fellow Liberals congratulated him, and several others—W.C. Wentworth, A.J. Forbes, Malcolm Fraser— either defended him outright or spoke along similar if milder lines. Most significant, perhaps, was the fact that Mr Menzies continued to be notably friendly towards the fallen Minister. There were indications that many, possibly even a majority, of Liberal backbenchers were now in favour of British entry and Mr Menzies seems to have made no

effort to rebuke the dissidents, even those who had supported Mr Bury in debate. Outside the House, too, Mr Bury was far from alone. It was generally assumed, surely with justice, that his views tallied closely with prevailing opinion in his own Department, the Treasury. An elder statesman of the Liberal Party, Lord Casey, agreed with him that Australia would not be greatly affected in the short term. Some economists took a similar view . . .

What is not in doubt is that the incident put an abrupt end to Mr McEwen's hopes of succeeding Mr Menzies. The Minister of Trade, in fact, suffered a much greater political setback than Mr Bury. As a result, there has been some speculation that the whole affair might have been engineered by Mr Menzies himself. There is no evidence for this. But once an incident of this kind arose, Mr Menzies would naturally make use of it to further his own purposes within the coalition. Much of the argument here revolves around the question whether Mr Menzies was or was not pushed by Mr McEwen into demanding Mr Bury's resignation. Mr Menzies subsequently maintained he was not. Mr McEwen not merely agreed but later claimed he had advised Mr Menzies against dismissal. Yet the impression remained in Canberra that such pressure had been applied. There was the obvious contrast between Mr Menzies' own initial hesitation and the strong Country Party reaction. Yet Mr McEwen's primary concern was probably to force the Prime Minister to re-commit himself to Mr McEwen's position on the EEC problem at a time when Mr Menzies seemed to be weakening. It is much less likely that he wished to force Mr Bury's resignation. In any case, Ministerial resignation is not so strong a convention in Australia that Mr Bury's departure was necessarily inevitable if the Prime Minister wished to keep him.

Much more intriguing possibilities are opened up if we accept the denials by Mr Menzies and Mr McEwen that any such direct pressure was exercised. Admittedly, Mr Bury's resignation may have been useful from the point of view of Mr Menzies' position at the forthcoming Prime Ministers' conference in London. But a politician of Mr Menzies' calibre must also have been aware of the probable internal repercussions of his actions. And his initial hesitation, followed by a resignation coupled with clear evidence of continued Prime Ministerial friendliness towards Mr Bury, was almost certain to confirm Liberal back-bench suspicions that Country Party pressure had been applied. Nothing could be better calculated to wean Liberal affection and respect away from Mr McEwen. Once this impression had taken root, moreover, any subsequent denials by Mr Menzies would naturally be treated by all concerned as a laudable instance of the Prime Minister backing up his Deputy and coalition partner. Mr Menzies would be in the splendid position of being able to tell the truth, knowing that no one would believe it.

The world was not waiting for new Australian leadership. In the month of Leslie Bury's resignation, the nation farewelled thirty Army 'instructors' en route to South Vietnam. The Government's publicity did not at first admit it, but the Australians did more than instruct. They fought, as did thousands of young Australians, many of them conscripted, who followed them. No issue since conscription for overseas service in 1916—1917 had divided the Australian people as the lingering and loathsome Vietnam conflict was to do. Detached and defiant, Menzies was to comment in retirement: 'The morals of a war don't depend upon whether the victory is quick or slow.' Equally coolly, the Prime Minister had despatched Australian troops to Malaysia, explaining that Australia had 'come to the assistance of Great Britain in Malaysia's defence'. Thus Australian infantry battalions found themselves participants in 'confrontation' on the Sarawak front in February 1965.

At home, the snap election of November 1963—the first campaign to exploit television—was notable for promises to introduce a home saving grant scheme for young married couples, an increase in medical benefits, and Commonwealth funding for independent schools. A system of grants for science facilities, and secondary scholarships tenable at any school, state or private, entailed direct financial support for all schools, including those run by the churches. The State Grants (Science Laboratories and Technical Training) Bill, introduced in May 1964 was described by the ALP leader, Arthur Calwell, as 'conceived in chicanery, born in duplicity and nurtured on deceit'. As late as May 1963, Menzies had gone on record in official correspondence as believing that the States were 'quite jealous of their education power and are making good use of it at present'. Six months before announcing the Federal Government's intention to make financial aid available to all Australian secondary schools, the Prime Minister had told a correspondent that

'I do not think our Commonwealth Constitution would mean much if the Commonwealth used its strength to intervene in such a case'.

There had been accumulating pressures of many kinds, from the States, educationists, businessmen, and politicians, to persuade the Commonwealth to enter the education field directly, instead of simply allocating substantial untied funds to the States. But only when the Labor Party was in disarray over the issue, and there was a unique opportunity to appeal to Roman Catholic (as well as other religious) voters, did Menzies at last abandon long-cherished conviction and risk reviving dormant sectarianism.

Federal aid for schools was, of course, long overdue. The Commonwealth had the power; and it should much earlier have recognised the responsibility, as it had with universities. Menzies' initiative in tertiary education in the late 1950s saved the universities, hitherto reliant on inadequate State funding, from financial disaster. In the ten years from 1955 the number of university students rose from 31 000 to 83 000. For almost fifty years after Menzies himself became a university student, the city of Melbourne had only one university. By the time Menzies reached his seventieth year, a third was already contemplated. Sydney was similarly endowed, and Adelaide was not far behind. Affluence made the expansion of higher education possible. Industry thought it needed more qualified men and women. Family aspirations for enhanced status and larger incomes, and even isolated outbreaks of individual intellectual curiosity, ensured the flow of prospective undergraduates.

Menzies knew perfectly well that a rapidly expanding university sector had dangers. In his Wallace Wurth Memorial Lecture on 28 August 1964, he warned:

> ... before we become too rhapsodical about the increase in numbers and the rights of people to have university training, we should face up to the problem that the greatest task, and in a sense the most difficult one, is to find the necessary trained and competent staff.

But it was not his problem.

Menzies' seventieth birthday prompted a fresh spate of tributes and assessments of his achievements and current position. One man who had watched his career since the 1920s was the political correspondent, E.H. Cox. In his 'Capital Talk' column in *The Herald* on 19 December 1964, Cox contributed a crisp and observant portrait of 'Sir Robert— 'King' of all he surveys':

> Five Prime Ministers of Britain have passed out of No. 10 Downing Street since December, 1949, and a sixth is precariously installed.
>
> Sir Robert has not come quite unmarked through the period.
>
> He seems a little heavier, moves a little slower, and in unguarded moments walks with a slight stoop.
>
> His one physical relaxation—long evening walks alone around Canberra—has been abandoned.

... he is not so sure or as deft as he once was in his dealings with interjectors at noisy public meetings, and he is sometimes a little short-tempered, when once he was uniformly suave in the House of Representatives.

But the qualities that have changed with time are less remarkable than those left unchanged.

He is still the silver-tongued orator of the House of Representatives, can still weave verbal spells when he wants to, and he is still the clearest expositionist Canberra has ever seen.

Keen observers notice occasionally slurred words where he once spoke with clearcut precision, but you have to listen carefully for them.

His personal way of life has not changed. He seldom appears before the gentleman's hour of 10.30 a.m., but still works far into the night.

His zest for good company, good food and good cigars is still un-dimmed. He still dominates every gathering at which he is either host or guest.

His control of his party and his cabinet is at its peak. Only 'Black Jack' McEwen dares to challenge his considered judgments, in a unique role as counterweight to the Menzies legend in Canberra and moderator to the Menzies authority.

Most of the backbenchers he brought to Canberra in 1949 have passed on. To a newer generation of Liberal members he is a strange blend between an ogre and a symbol of the innate superiority of Liberalism as they see it.

Australia has changed much more under Sir Robert than he himself has changed.

Our gross national product has risen from £2 200 million to £8 000 million. Population is up from 8.1 million to about 11.1 million.

Federal expenditures have quadrupled from a budget of £544 million when he took office to nearly £2 200 million now.

He failed dismally in his famous promise to put value back into the Australian pound. The Menzies pound is worth less in living costs than the ten shilling note he inherited from Mr Chifley.

But the average national wage has increased nearly three times. Except for the elderly on fixed incomes, Australians are better off now than 15 years ago.

Old political boundary lines based on class and status are fading.

Australia is moving from a traditional British prewar Australia closer to America. Unconsciously, Sir Robert has contributed to this.

Will Sir Robert remain in the Prime Minister's suite in Canberra?

Some predict he will stand aside before the Federal election late in 1966. There are even suggestions that he will move into Government House in midwinter next year when Lord De L'Isle moves out.

But nobody—probably not even Sir Robert himself—knows what he will really do.

He is as unchallengeably in the box seat in Parliament as he is in the Parliamentary Liberal Party, and can decide for himself when he is ready to decide.

The final press conference, 21 January 1966

Exactly when he decided to go was a secret, well-kept from even his chosen successor. After a few days of speculation, the announcement came on Thursday, 20 January 1966. 'Young Harold' Holt at last came into his inheritance. Three weeks later, at a meeting of the Liberal Party's Kooyong electorate committee, the local member, the Rt Hon. Sir Robert Menzies, KT, CH, QC, MP, disclosed that his resignation from parliament would be in the hands of the speaker of the House of Representative in a few days. Because of a Victorian electricity workers' strike, the meeting at the Kew Civic Centre had been lit by two portable gas lamps and a pair of candles. The last goodbyes in the foyer were in almost total darkness.

For the Melbourne *Sun*, the story of Menzies' dim farewell to the constituency he had represented for thirty-one years was not front-page news. A brawl at Pentridge gaol involving the long-incarcerated murderer, John O'Meally, took the headlines, and no fewer than three cricket stories jostled the newly retired Prime Minister over to page two. Young Australian batsman, Doug Walters, had been forced to cover his arms with a borrowed jacket in order to be served lunch at the Tavern at Melbourne Cricket Ground. The England Captain, Mike Smith, had a virus infection and was 'in doubt' for the fifth Test. And Wally Grout, Australia's first choice wicketkeeper since 1957, had announced that he would retire after the forthcoming Test.

Menzies had played his last Test. A public life of nearly forty years was over. There would be more entries in the Menzies press-cutting books—trips overseas, appearances at cricket and Australian Rules football matches, birthday tributes at eighty, an emotional meeting with the Queen during the Centenary Test, and the conferment of a knighthood in the Order of Australia. Articles and lectures, reviews and extracts from his memoirs (two volumes that revealed more by inadvertence than by design)—were to come. And even occasional interventions in current politics, as his successors came and went.

More than a decade of visible retirement could not fail to soften attitudes and erase memories of sins committed, and good deeds undone. But when Menzies died on 15 May 1978 there was a new generation of adult Australians too young to have anything more than fragmentary impressions of his career. Among those old enough to remember, there were few who exhibited grief. Newspapers, and radio and television stations attempted to portray a nation in mourning. But the nation manifestly was not mourning. The young columnist of *The Canberra Times*, Ian Warden, found the people of Melbourne on the day of Menzies' funeral to be 'nostalgic rather than grief-stricken'. The fact is that Menzies, unlike Winston Churchill, never captured the affection of the majority of his countrymen. There were of course many who had admired, respected, and even loved him. But the eulogies of 1978, suggesting that he had held a transcendent place in the hearts of millions of Australians, were hollow and unconvincing. He had been essentially a partisan, a man too often enticed by the struggle for short-term party advantage. The tributes of most of his surviving colleagues and political inheritors were embarrassing in their vacuous excess. Labor's leaders seemed at a loss for words that could not be construed as hypocritical. Those who were not afraid to be honest admitted that his 'greatness' was in winning elections, a much envied talent. Editorial writers and commentators, dusting down predictable phrases about 'the end of an era', showed much less candour than their predecessors had permitted themselves in 1966. 'His failures were few, but they were mighty', said *The Australian* in 1966. He did not, it contended, give the kind of leadership that a young country needed. The Menzies era, *The Sydney Morning Herald* pronounced, was 'dignified, prosperous sedate'. But ideas had not been welcomed, debate was not encouraged. *The Age* fell back on hallowed euphemism and evasion:

> Sir Robert's place in history is secure. The peaks and valleys of his career will be measured in the longer term. Yet the sum of all his efforts reflects a matchless political skill and a sure sense of direction in national affairs.

At 'The Lodge,' Canberra, after retirement

Apart from his own achievement on becoming what *The Age* called 'a symbol of political success', it was far from clear which 'direction in national affairs' Menzies had intended. His first volume of 'memories', *Afternoon Light*, was virtually silent on his period as Prime Minister after 1949. His 'series of vignettes of people and events as I knew them' dealt mainly with Britain, the Commonwealth, and international relationships. The second volume, *The Measure of the Years*, devoted more pages to recollections of left-handed batsmen than to problems of social welfare. The forty-three unrevealing pages on 'The Petrov Spy Case' were by far the longest chapter in a section called 'Some High-lights of a Long Term of Office'.

In chronicling his years as Prime Minister, Menzies did give details of reforms in the structure of banking, of the introduction of a health insurance scheme, of free medical treatment and prescriptions for pensioners, of housing for aged persons, and the rationalisation of airline services. The growth of Canberra, financial support for young home buyers, and educational developments were also described.

But critics looked in vain for a vision apart from a noble dream of imperial unity. Some, even among Menzies' friends and allies, thought they had found it in an ideology of materialism. Australia had become a showcase of regulated private enterprise. This view was never better distilled than by Menzies' appointed biographer, Frances McNicoll,

in *The Sydney Morning Herald* on 20 December 1977. Lady McNicoll
suggested that the recent electoral victory of the Fraser Government
should be a source of great joy to Sir Robert on his 83rd birthday:

> ... he ought perhaps to feel particularly gratified because, I believe,
> the Australian people were thinking not so much about such matters
> as the merits or demerits of leaders or of this or that tax, but about their
> general desire to see a return to the conditions that prevailed during the
> long rule of Sir Robert Menzies.
>
> Wasn't it a vote for the remarkable security and stability of that era,
> when not only Australians but the whole world felt that there was no
> limit to the rising prosperity of Australia?
>
> Wasn't it a vote for spending your own money and being able to
> start up a little business and feeling it worthwhile to put aside money
> for old age?
>
> Wasn't it also a vote for thinking sometimes about Australia and not
> exclusively for one's own immediate gain? ...
>
> A few months ago an opinion poll found that Australians, when
> asked who was the greatest living Australian, most frequently named
> Sir Robert Menzies. That was a remarkable result for a man who has
> been out of public life for 12 years.
>
> It was the more remarkable because great efforts have been made
> by Opposition sympathisers to belittle Sir Robert's achievement, and
> to paint for those too young to remember it a distorted picture of his
> time.
>
> The result of that poll should have been a warning to political
> commentators of how deeply Australians value the principles which
> Sir Robert represented.

It had taken skill to steer down the turbulent mainstream of prosperity. But Menzies had preached throughout his life the rejection of greed,
the superiority of thrift, and the obligations of citizenship. He could
surely take little comfort in the assurance that, as *The Canberra Times*
had put it in January 1966, most Australians were 'in a crude motor-
car-refrigerator-and-washing-machine way' better off than in 1949.

Was this to be the Menzies' legacy? All over Australia there were
buildings named after him; and university campuses dotted with colleges
and libraries bearing his name or decorated with plaques recording that
he opened them. These were the chosen memorials. But larger aspects of
the national life testified to his presence. Of these, the big cities of Sydney
and Melbourne eloquently proclaimed the values of a government that
closed its eyes to poverty when affluence was more obtrusive, passively
presided over years of urban sprawl, the neglect of community hygiene
and recreation facilities, and the maldistribution of hospitals and other
health and welfare services. Epitomising the mentality of the 1950s was

Right: Commonwealth Man, May 1971

'Dear Bob' receives the collected works of Winston Churchill, February 1974

the speculative overdevelopment of the central business districts. When the Sydney harbour skyline was altered by the erection of the AMP building it was fitting that it should be opened in February 1962 by a Prime Minister who was entranced by its 'dramatic significance' and who could praise it as 'a towering symbol of a constructive contribution to Australian national and individual life'. Ignoring the spectacularly intrusive architecture and the massive diversion of resources that such buildings entailed, Menzies concluded glowingly: 'It's not always that we can see in some great work attractiveness, impressiveness, utility and at the same time a symbolism that really stirs the heart and quickens the imagination.'

The irony of Menzies' life was that what ensured his political triumphs was the betrayal of his own values. There is no denying his appeal for millions of Australians. Most people were not looking for moral leadership. They wanted security and prosperity, and they did not want to feel guilty about striving for, and achieving, their personal goals. Menzies could give them reassurance. By perpetuating harmony with the Country Party he maintained the exclusion of Labor from power during his political lifetime, and guaranteed the dominance of the classes and interests that had sustained him in office.

Not long after his retirement Menzies consented to be interviewed at length for Australian television. Peter Couchman asked him about the so-called 'Menzies Era':

COUCHMAN: I wonder what sort of a person or what sort of a leader do you think you were during those sixteen years?

MENZIES: Well I think I was an industrious man. I think I had a reasonable amount of intelligence—I've never claimed to be a genius but I've always hoped to be intelligent. I was persistent—the things I believed in I battled for. I maintained the closest relations with my party members and every year or perhaps more than once a year I went around Australia addressing meetings, meeting people, getting to know what they were like. I think on the whole I ended up by being pretty well understood by the electors. They didn't understand me well enough to kick me out. They voted for me but still I was pretty well understood by the electors and I think I pretty well understood them. A Prime Minister's position is not a thing of glorification. I've known people in my life who, becoming ministers, blew out their bags and were almost in a sense saying 'look at me, I'm a minister of the Crown, I'm very important.' Not too many of those but some. In my experience a Prime Minister who's doing his work, who's working as I did for seventy hours a week and for fifty two weeks a year has no time to look at himself in the shaving mirror and say what a wonderful fellow you are. He's much more concerned with the problem that has to be dealt with that day. Of course he has enough self confidence to believe that he can deal with that problem. You must have some belief in yourself and therefore I don't think I ever regarded a problem as insoluble you see. But at the same time if he's standing aside from the problem and saying what a good boy are you—he'll never do any good and he'll never get anywhere. I think that the glory in the office of Prime Minister is a matter well left to one's descendants.

COUCHMAN: History's been critical of you as you've said yourself and you're quite aware of this.

MENZIES: You mean SOME historians.

COUCHMAN: Some historians. But at the same time I think practically everyone acknowledges that you are, if not the greatest, one of the greatest Prime Ministers that Australia's had since Federation. Is it important to you now that you be remembered? I mean do you care whether you go down in history as being one of Australia's great Prime Ministers or ...

MENZIES: Well look, apart from the comparisons and superlatives, of course I'm a human being. I would like to be remembered and I would like to be remembered in connection with various aspects of the national life. I'd like my descendants to have some pride in me. Of course, it'd be a mere pretence if I said I didn't. Every man wants recognition but a man whose only ambition is to be praised will in my opinion get nowhere. You must take praise, blame, love, hatred all in your stride, the main thing is that you should be doing your best. Your best may not be as great as somebody else's best but you must do your best, that's all. And when you've done your best and you retire then I think you can sit down by your fireside and enjoy the greatest thing that comes to old age, self respect.

Sources and acknowledgments

The source of each of the principal documents, publications, and oral reminiscences quoted in the book is identified in the text. I shall be happy to provide precise archival and other references to any reader who cares to contact me at the Research School of Social Sciences, Australian National University, P.O. Box 4, A.C.T. 2600.

In addition to those whose special help is recorded in the introduction, I also am very grateful to the reference staff of the Menzies Library at the Australian National University and to the following people and institutions:

For personal recollections:

Sir Alistair Adam, Miss Maud N. Adam, T.M.S. Argyle, Sir Howard Beale, Miss Dorothy Blair, Professor J.W. Burton, Sir Arthur Coles, Miss Hazel Craig, Sir William Dunk, J.Q. Ewens, the late Hattil Foll, The Rt Hon. J. Malcolm Fraser, Lady Harrison, Sir Laurence Hartnett, Loy W. Henderson, Dr Julie Hickford, F.T. Hill, K.R. Ingram, F.H. Keenlyside, W.J. Kilpatrick, Mrs Phyllis Lade, S.H. Landau, Miss Eileen Lenihan, Dr S.C. Leslie, Professor Brian Lewis, Sir Cecil Looker, Dame Enid Lyons, The Rt Hon. Sir John McEwen, Mrs A. McInnes, J.M. McMillan, Sir Chester and Lady Manifold, Charles Meeking, Dr Ronald Mendelsohn, Colin Moodie, Judge J.H. Moore, Geoffrey Nathan, Judge J.G. Norris, J.E. Oldham, J.D. Pringle, Sir Richard Randall, G. Warwick Smith, Sir Percy Spender, G. Steeper, Alfred Stirling, Mrs L.E.B. Stretton, Corbett Tritton, Sir Murray Tyrrell, Sir Keith Waller, Lady White, E.G. Whitlam, Sir Keith Wilson, J.R. Willoughby, Geoffrey Yeend.

For information from records in their keeping, or permission to see and quote unpublished papers:

Australian Archives (Attorney-General's, Defence, Defence Co-ordination, External Affairs, Industry, Prime Minister's, and Treasury Department Papers; Bruce MSS); Lady Barry (Sir John Barry MSS); Mrs Colin Bednall (Colin Bednall MSS); W.M. Calman (M. Calman MSS); Churchill College, Cambridge (Hankey MSS); Mrs E.J. Denning (Warren Denning MSS); F.H. Eggleston (Sir Frederic Eggleston MSS); The Flinders University of South Australia (H.V. Evatt MSS); Stewart Harris (Harris MSS); Lady Heydon (Sir Peter Heydon MSS); The Liberal Party of Australia; The Liberal Party of Australia (N.S.W. Division); Peter Lindsay (Sir Lionel Lindsay MSS); Dame Enid Lyons (Joseph Lyons MSS); Sir Brian Massy-Greene (Sir Walter Massy-Greene correspondence); University of Melbourne Archives; Mitchell Library; Dame Elisabeth Murdoch (Sir Keith Murdoch MSS); National Library of Australia (Lord Bruce MSS, Warren Denning MSS, Sir Frederic Eggleston MSS, Sir Robert Garran MSS, Sir Henry Gullett

MSS, W.M. Hughes MSS, Sir John Latham MSS, Joseph Lyons MSS, Sir Earle Page MSS, Sir George Pearce MSS, Sir Malcolm Ritchie MSS; and transcripts of interviews with Sir Arthur Coles, Irvine Douglas, Sir John Gorton, Sir Peter Heydon, Norman Makin, and Sir Thomas Playford); Presbyterian Church of Victoria; Public Archives, Canada; Public Record Office (London); Public Record Office (Victoria); Reserve Bank of Australia; The State Library of Victoria (J.P. Jones MSS, Sir Lionel Lindsay MSS, Sir James McGregor MSS, J.P. Stevenson MSS, Syme MSS); Mrs R.G. Thatcher (W. Thatcher correspondence); Waterside Workers' Federation of Australia; Wesley College (Melbourne); Lady White (Sir Thomas White MSS); Sir Ernest White (White MSS)

For guidance in archival collections, or access to unpublished research

Dr Peter Aimer; Joseph Aron; Dean Ashenden; Professor Weston Bate; Professor Robert Bothwell; Ms Cecily Close; Dr P.G. Edwards; H.J. Gibbney; Professor J.L. Granatstein; Dr P.R. Hart; John Hilvert; Michael E. Kino; C.J. Lloyd; Rev. A.M. McMaster; Humphrey McQueen; David Potts; Ms Catherine Santamaria; Professor Boris Schedvin; Dr Don Smart; Ms Jenny Stokes; Frank Strahan, John Thompson; Dr Peter Tiver; Margaret Vines; Dr David Walker; R.W. Watts; Thomas Webber; Ms Joy Wheatley; Peter Wilkie

For permission to quote from published works and television programmes

Australian Broadcasting Commission; Australian Department of Foreign Affairs (*Documents on Australian Foreign Policy 1937–49*); *Australian Journal of Politics and History*; Australian Labor Party (Victorian and New South Wales Branches); Australian Press Services; *Australian Women's Weekly*; Sir Howard Beale; *The Bulletin*; British Broadcasting Corporation; Cambridge University Press; Cassell Ltd; Paul Channon M.P.; Stewart Cockburn; *Daily Telegraph* (Sydney); Lady Dean; Mrs J.J. Dedman; John Fairfax Ltd; Sir Warwick Fairfax; Professor H.G. Gelber; Mohamed Hassanein Heikal; Hodder and Stoughton Ltd; Donald Horne; The Institution of Engineers, Australia; Jeparit Chamber of Commerce; The Law Book Company Ltd; The Liberal Party of Australia; The Liberal Party of Australia, New South Wales Division; Longman Cheshire Pty Ltd; *Melbourne University Magazine*; Oxford University Press Australia; Roy Morgan Research Centre; *Pacific Affairs*; Penguin Books Australia; Ruskin Press; *The Times*; The Victorian Bar; Sir Alan Watt; Wesley College (Melbourne)

For assistance in locating and reproducing illustrations, or for permission to use them

The Advocate (Burnie); *The Age*; T.M.S. Argyle; Associated Press Ltd; Australian Information Service; Australian National University Photographic Services; Australian War Memorial; Dr Irving Buzzard; Central

Highlands Regional Library Service (Ballarat); Ms Jean Dillon; *Evening Telegraph and Post* (Dundee); The Herald and Weekly Times Ltd; Rev. Professor J.D. McCaughey; Judge J.H. Moore; National Library of Australia; Ormond College; Ms Pip Porter; Miss Patricia Reynolds; Peter Wilkie; Ms Brenda Willcox; J.R. Willoughby